discovering
TRUTH

KEYS TO HAPPIER LIVING

Acknowledgements

Many thanks to those whose help and support made this project possible, especially Carl and Reuben, whose painstaking attention to detail were invaluable.

All verses used in this book are from the *Authorized Version* (King James Version) of the Bible.

Compiled and edited by Keith Phillips.

ISBN # 3-905332-01-9

PREFACE

We all want to be better people, and *Jesus* makes that possible. "If anyone is in Christ," the Bible tells us, "he is a new creation; old things have passed away; behold, all things have become new."[1] Of course that doesn't mean that you were instantly and forever freed from every bad habit and personal weakness the moment you received Jesus as your Savior. Like every other Christian alive today, you're a work in progress. "For it is God who works in you both to will and to do for His good pleasure."[2]

God doesn't expect you to attain sinless perfection. If He did, you'd be doomed to a life of failure and frustration. Personal perfection is not His goal at all! What He wants most is for you to grow in love—love for Him and love for others—that you might be more like Jesus.

To that end, He has given you a Bible-ful of insight and counsel on how to overcome every temptation that you could possibly face in life and develop good habits instead. The apostle Peter called these "exceedingly great and precious promises," that through these you may partake of the divine nature.[3] God's Word, combined with the miracle-working power of the Holy Spirit and a sincere desire to make positive changes, can turn any weak point you may have into a strong one!

His Word is also like a light that shines on your path to help you stay on track and avoid the pitfalls.[4]

However, finding God's counsel on a particular subject can sometimes be a problem itself, and concordances and conventional study helps only go so far. *Keys to Happier Living* presents over fifty vital topics from the perspective of God's Word, in a simple outline form. Its easy-to-follow format also makes it a quick reference tool for busy parents, teachers, and mentors.

---

[1] See 2 Corinthians 5:17.
[2] Philippians 2:13.
[3] See 2 Peter 1:4.
[4] See Matthew 7:14; Psalm 119:105.

Explanation of Technical Aspects

All quotations are from the *Authorized Version* (King James Version) of the Bible. Due to limited space, only the Bible verses most pertinent to each topic have been included. Verses of secondary importance are noted by Biblical reference only ("See also such-and-such"). Occasional parenthetical notes have been added in brackets [ ] to explain archaic words and to clarify the meaning of verses not shown in their full context.

Happy studying!

TABLE OF CONTENTS

AGGRESSIVENESS. 7

ANGER AND TEMPER 12

APPRECIATION 17

BEAUTY. 24

BITTERNESS 30

BULLYING...37

CHOICE AND DECISION MAKING 43

COMPARING YOURSELF TO OTHERS 49

COMPETITIVENESS 57

CONDEMNATION AND REMORSE...62

CONSCIENCE, KEEPING A GOOD 68

COVETOUSNESS 77

CRITICISM 86

CURSING AND FOUL LANGUAGE 94

DOUBTS..98

EMPATHY 115

ENCOURAGEMENT 122

EVIL ASSOCIATIONS, BAD COMPANY...................................129

FAIR PLAY/CHEATING..137

FASCINATION FOR EVIL 144

FEAR OF FAILURE..152

FEELING LEFT OUT 159

FLATTERY 165

FRIENDSHIP 170

FRUSTRATION 175

GENTLENESS..179

GOSSIP AND TATTLING 182

GREED..189

HABITS, OVERCOMING BAD 194

HAPPINESS AND JOY 201

HASTE; RASHNESS 211

HELP, ASKING FOR...218

INSECURITY...223

JEALOUSY AND ENVY 229

KINDNESS AND COURTESY 240

LAZINESS AND SLOTHFULNESS....................................248

LONELINESS..253

NERVOUSNESS AND FEARFULNESS 259

NIGHTMARES AND BAD DREAMS 265

PEER PRESSURE 272

POSITIVENESS/NEGATIVE THINKING...........................280

PROMISES, KEEPING 293

QUIETNESS 300

RELAXATION AND FREETIME.....................................305

REPUTATION...311

REVENGE, SEEKING..318

SAMPLE; EXAMPLE...324

SECRETS: WHEN TO KEEP, AND WHEN NOT TO......................329

SELFISHNESS AND SELF-CENTEREDNESS 342

SHYNESS AND TIMIDITY 356

SORROW..364

TOLERANCE OF OTHERS 375

WISDOM 384

WORRY 394

AGGRESSIVENESS

Definition: Aggressiveness has two contrasting definitions. The primary, being negative, means being inclined to act in a hostile manner; the secondary, but more positive meaning, refers to being bold, assertive or enterprising in getting things done. The first definition is the one explored in this section.

1. Pushy aggressiveness toward others is a worldly, carnal trait.

- **Romans 10:1-3** [Paul explained that the Jews were pushy in their service for God, but lacked really knowing the Lord:] Brethren, my heart's desire and prayer to God for Israel is, that they might be saved. [2] For I bear them record that they have a zeal of God, but not according to knowledge. [3] For they being ignorant of God's righteousness, and going about to establish their own righteousness, have not submitted themselves unto the righteousness of God.
- **Philippians 3:6-7** [Paul knew the Jew's faults, because earlier, as Saul the Pharisee, his attitude was:] Concerning zeal, persecuting the Church; touching the righteousness which is in the law, blameless. [7] But what things were gain to me, those I counted loss for Christ.
- **John 18:36a** Jesus answered, My Kingdom is not of this world: if My Kingdom were of this world, then would My servants fight. [See Matthew 26:52-54.]
- **2 Timothy 2:24** And the servant of the Lord must not strive; but be gentle unto all men, apt to teach, patient.
- **Matthew 5:38-41** Ye have heard that it hath been said, An eye for an eye, and a tooth for a tooth: [39] But I say unto you, That ye resist not evil: but whosoever shall smite thee on thy right cheek, turn to him the other also. [40] And if any man will sue thee at the law, and take away thy coat, let him have thy cloke also. [41] And whosoever shall compel thee to go a mile, go with him twain.
- **Mark 10:42-44** [Worldly leaders are often pushy and domineering, but we are taught to lead with meekness and love.] But Jesus called them to Him, and saith unto them, Ye know that they which are accounted to rule over the Gentiles exercise lordship over them;

and their great ones exercise authority upon them. [43] But so shall it not be among you: but whosoever will be great among you, shall be your minister: [44] And whosoever of you will be the chiefest, shall be servant of all.

- **Romans 13:13,14** Let us walk honestly, as in the day; not in rioting and drunkenness, not in chambering and wantonness, not in strife and envying. [14] But put ye on the Lord Jesus Christ, and make not provision for the flesh, to fulfil the lusts thereof.

- **1 Corinthians 3:3** For ye are yet carnal: for whereas there is among you envying, and strife, and divisions, are ye not carnal, and walk as men?

- **2 Corinthians 10:3** [Even though we are carnal people, we are learning to see things in the Spirit.] For though we walk in the flesh, we do not war after the flesh. [See also Colossians 1:29.]

2. Aggressiveness is often a symptom of a me-first sort of pride and selfishness.

- **Proverbs 13:10a** Only by pride cometh contention.
- **Galatians 5:26** Let us not be desirous of vain glory [conceit], provoking one another, envying one another.
- **Philippians 2:3,4** Let nothing be done through strife or vainglory [selfish ambition or conceit]; but in lowliness of mind let each esteem other better than themselves. [4] Look not every man on his own things, but every man also on the things of others.
- **James 4:1** From whence come wars and fightings among you? Come they not hence, even of your lusts that war in your members?

3. Aggressiveness between Christians undermines unity and hinders our sample.

- **Proverbs 18:19** [Once disunity is created through offenses, it takes great effort to patch it up.] A brother offended is harder to be won than a strong city: and their contentions are like the bars of a castle.
- **Matthew 12:25** And Jesus knew their thoughts, and said unto them, Every kingdom divided against itself is brought to desolation; and every city or house divided against itself shall not stand.
- **Galatians 5:15-17** But if ye bite and devour one another, take heed that ye be not consumed one of another. [16] This I say then, Walk in the Spirit, and ye shall not fulfil the lust of the flesh. [17] For the flesh lusteth against the Spirit, and the Spirit against the flesh: and these are contrary the one to the other: so that ye cannot do the things that ye would.
- **Philippians 1:15-17** [Paul referred to the insincere, ungodly, selfish aggressiveness used by some Christians, contrasted with the loving support felt from others:] Some indeed preach Christ even of envy and strife; and some also of good will: [16] The one preach Christ of contention … [17] But the other of love, knowing that I am set for the defence of the Gospel.
- **Philippians 2:14,15** Do all things without murmurings and disputings: [15] That ye may be blameless and harmless, the sons of God, without rebuke, in the midst of a crooked and perverse nation, among whom ye shine as lights in the world.

4. Worldly aggressiveness is completely contradictory to the ways of the Spirit.

- **Galatians 5:22,23** But the fruit of the Spirit is love, joy, peace, longsuffering, gentleness, goodness, faith, [23] Meekness, temperance: against such there is no law.
- **James 3:14-18** But if ye have bitter envying and strife in your hearts, glory not, and lie not against the truth. [15] This wisdom

descendeth not from above, but is earthly, sensual, devilish. [16] For where envying and strife is, there is confusion and every evil work. [17] But the wisdom that is from above is first pure, then peaceable, gentle, and easy to be intreated, full of mercy and good fruits, without partiality, and without hypocrisy. [18] And the fruit of righteousness is sown in peace of them that make peace.

5. If aggressiveness is the problem, more love and a spirit of meekness are the cure.

- **Proverbs 10:12** Hatred stirreth up strifes: but love covereth all sins. [See also Proverbs 3:30.]
- **Proverbs 25:15** [Meekness accomplishes much more than force.] By long forbearing is a prince persuaded, and a soft tongue breaketh the bone.
- **Romans 14:19** Let us therefore follow after the things which make for peace, and things wherewith one may edify another.
- **1 Corinthians 2:3-5** [Paul, who had been overly aggressive as a Jew, learned to be meek, realizing how weak he was, yet relying on the power of God.] And I was with you in weakness, and in fear, and in much trembling. [4] And my speech and my preaching was not with enticing words of man's wisdom, but in demonstration of the Spirit and of power: [5] That your faith should not stand in the wisdom of men, but in the power of God. [See also 2 Corinthians 11:29,30; 13:9.]
- **1 Corinthians 13:4,5** Charity [Love] suffereth long, and is kind; charity envieth not; charity vaunteth not itself, is not puffed up, [5] Doth not behave itself unseemly, seeketh not her own, is not easily provoked, thinketh no evil.
- **1 Corinthians 10:24** [Be aggressive in helping others, not yourself.] Let no man seek his own, but every man another's wealth.
- **2 Corinthians 1:24** [The Apostles were not domineering.] Not for that we have dominion over your faith, but are helpers of your joy: for by faith ye stand.

- **Ephesians 4:2** With all lowliness and meekness, with longsuffering, forbearing one another in love.
- **1 Peter 3:4** But let it be the hidden man of the heart, in that which is not corruptible, even the ornament of a meek and quiet spirit, which is in the sight of God of great price.
- **1 Peter 5:5** Likewise, ye younger, submit yourselves unto the elder. Yea, <u>all</u> of you be subject one to another, and be clothed with humility: for God resisteth the proud, and giveth grace to the humble.

ANGER AND TEMPER

Definition: A strong feeling of displeasure and usually of opposition toward someone or something, often brought about by real or imagined injury; rage; fury; wrath. Anger is a broad term that applies to various levels of emotion that may or may not be shown. Temper, as used here refers to "the tendency to be easily angered."

1. God's Word warns us <u>not</u> to yield to anger and wrath.

- **James 1:19,20** Wherefore, my beloved brethren, let every man be swift to hear, slow to speak, slow to wrath: [20] For the wrath of man worketh not the righteousness of God.
- **Psalm 37:8** Cease from anger, and forsake wrath: fret not thyself in any wise to do evil.
- **Ecclesiastes 7:9** Be not hasty in thy spirit to be angry: for anger resteth in the bosom of fools.

2. Anger creates a breach in our spiritual defenses.

- **Proverbs 16:32** He that is slow to anger is better than the mighty; and he that ruleth his spirit than he that taketh a city. [See also Proverbs 14:29.]
- **Proverbs 25:28** He that hath no rule over his own spirit is like a city that is broken down, and without walls.

3. Anger often results from pride and selfishness.

- **Proverbs 21:24** Proud and haughty scorner is his name, who dealeth in proud wrath.
- **James 4:1** From whence come wars and fightings among you? Come they not hence, even of your lusts that war in your members?

4. If we give place to ungodly anger, we will be the ones to suffer.

- **Proverbs 19:19a** A man of great wrath shall suffer punishment.

- **Proverbs 25:8** Go not forth hastily to strive, lest thou know not what to do in the end thereof, when thy neighbour hath put thee to shame.
- **Matthew 5:22a** But I say unto you, That whosoever is angry with his brother without a cause shall be in danger of the Judgment.
- **Romans 12:19** Dearly beloved, avenge not yourselves, but rather give place unto wrath: for it is written, Vengeance is Mine; I will repay, saith the Lord.

5. A wise man <u>controls</u> his temper because he knows it leads to mistakes and even greater problems.

- **Numbers 20:7,8,10-12; Psalm 106:32,33** [Moses' outburst of anger caused him to lose the blessing and privilege of leading his people into the Promised Land:] The Lord spake unto Moses, saying, [8] Take the rod ... and <u>speak</u> ye unto the rock before their eyes [the rebellious congregation]; and it shall give forth his water... [10] Moses ... said unto them, Hear now, ye rebels; must we fetch you water out of this rock? [11] And Moses lifted up his hand, and with his rod he <u>smote</u> the rock twice: and the water came out abundantly, and the congregation drank, and their beasts also. [12] And the Lord spake unto Moses and Aaron, Because ye believed Me not, to sanctify Me in the eyes of the children of Israel, therefore ye shall not bring this congregation into the land which I have given them. [Psalm 106:32,33] They angered him [Moses] also at the waters of strife, so that it went ill with Moses for their sakes: [33] Because they provoked his spirit, so that he spake unadvisedly with his lips.
- **Proverbs 29:11** A fool uttereth all his mind: but a wise man keepeth it in till afterwards.
- **Proverbs 14:17a** He that is soon angry dealeth foolishly.
- **Proverbs 14:29** He that is slow to wrath is of great understanding: but he that is hasty of spirit exalteth folly.
- **Proverbs 19:11** The discretion [good judgement] of a man deferreth his anger; and it is his glory to pass over a transgression.

- **Proverbs 29:22** An angry man stirreth up strife, and a furious man aboundeth in transgression.
- **Ecclesiastes 5:2,6a** Be not rash with thy mouth, and let not thine heart be hasty to utter any thing before God: for God is in Heaven, and thou upon earth: therefore let thy words be few. [6a] Suffer not thy mouth to cause thy flesh to sin.

6. An even wiser man or woman helps others to control their tempers.

- **Proverbs 15:1a** A soft answer turneth away wrath but grievous [harsh] words stir up anger. [See also Proverbs 29:8b.]
- **Proverbs 15:18b** He that is slow to anger appeaseth [pacifies] strife.
- **Genesis 13:7-9** [Abraham wisely appeased strife which arose between his and his nephew Lot's herdsmen.] And there was a strife between the herdmen of Abram's cattle and the herdmen of Lot's cattle: [8] And Abram said unto Lot, Let there be no strife, I pray thee, between me and thee, and between my herdmen and thy herdmen; for we be brethren. [9] Is not the whole land before thee? Separate thyself, I pray thee, from me: if thou wilt take the left hand, then I will go to the right; or if thou depart to the right hand, then I will go to the left.
- **1 Samuel 25:1-35** [Abigail wisely pacified the anger of Israel's king-to-be, David, as he sought to kill her husband:] [32] David said to Abigail, Blessed be the Lord God of Israel, which sent thee this day to meet me: [33] And blessed be thy advice, and blessed be thou, which hast kept me this day from coming to shed blood, and from avenging myself with mine own hand.

7. We are to forsake anger and pray for the Lord to replace anger with love, patience, meekness and forgiveness.

- **1 Corinthians 13:5** [Love] doth not behave itself unseemly, seeketh not her own, is not easily provoked, thinketh no evil;

- **Ephesians 4:31,32** Let all bitterness, and wrath, and anger, and clamour, and evil speaking, be put away from you, with all malice: [32] And be ye kind one to another, tenderhearted, forgiving one another, even as God for Christ's sake hath forgiven you.
- **Colossians 3:8,12-15** But now ye also put off all these; anger, wrath, malice, blasphemy, filthy communication out of your mouth. [12] Put on therefore, as the elect of God, holy and beloved, bowels of mercies, kindness, humbleness of mind, meekness, longsuffering; [13] Forbearing one another, and forgiving one another, if any man have a quarrel against any: even as Christ forgave you, so also do ye. [14] And above all these things put on charity, which is the bond of perfectness. [15] And let the peace of God rule in your hearts, to the which also ye are called in one body; and be ye thankful.
- **Ephesians 4:26b** Let not the sun go down upon your wrath.
  [See also James 3:17,18.]

8. Though the "wrath of man" is to be shunned, there is a time for "righteous indignation" or godly anger, a time to speak out against evil, wrongdoing and injustice. But we must be sure it is God's anger, not our own.

- **Proverbs 25:23** The north wind driveth away rain: so doth an angry countenance a backbiting tongue.
- **Ephesians 4:26a** Be ye angry, and sin not.
- **Judges 14:19; 15:14,15; 16:28-30** [The Lord anointed Samson several times to be angry and used this anger to defeat the enemies of His people.] And the Spirit of the Lord came upon him, and he went down to Ashkelon, and slew thirty men of them, and took their spoil. ... [15:14,15] The Philistines shouted against him: and the Spirit of the Lord came mightily upon him, and the cords that were upon his arms became as flax that was burnt with fire, and his bands loosed from off his hands. [15] And he found a new jawbone of an ass, and put forth his hand, and took it, and slew a thousand

men therewith. [16:28-30] And Samson called unto the Lord, and said, O Lord God, remember me, I pray Thee, and strengthen me, I pray Thee, only this once, O God, that I may be at once avenged of the Philistines for my two eyes. [29] And Samson took hold of the two middle pillars upon which the house stood. ... [30] And he bowed himself with all his might; and the house fell upon the lords, and upon all the people that were therein. So the dead which he slew at his death were more than they which he slew in his life.

- **Mark 3:5** [Jesus Himself was frequently stirred up with godly anger, such as the time His hypocritical religious enemies were watching to see if He would break the Laws of Moses by healing the man with the shrivelled hand on their holy day, the Sabbath:] And when He had looked round about on them with anger, being grieved for the hardness of their hearts, He saith unto the man, Stretch forth thine hand. And he stretched it out: and his hand was restored whole as the other. [See verses 1-4.]

- **John 2:14-16** [The crowning example of Jesus' anger was when He found certain religionists robbing and exploiting the poor in the name of God:] And [Jesus] found in the temple those that sold oxen and sheep and doves, and the changers of money sitting: [15] And when He had made a scourge [whip] of small cords, He drove them all out of the temple, and the sheep, and the oxen; and poured out the changers' money, and overthrew the tables; [16] And said unto them that sold doves, Take these things hence; make not My Father's house an house of merchandise.

APPRECIATION

Definition: Recognition of the quality, worth, or significance of people and things.

1. In the Bible, the Lord often expressed His appreciation by giving people credit, praising them for their good qualities, or for making the right decisions.

- **Job 1:8** And the Lord said unto Satan, Hast thou considered My servant Job, that there is none like him in the earth, a perfect and an upright man, one that feareth God, and escheweth evil?
- **Acts 13:22b** And [the Lord] said, I have found David the son of Jesse, a man after Mine own heart, which shall fulfil all My will.
- **John 1:47** Jesus saw Nathanael coming to Him, and saith of him, Behold an Israelite indeed, in whom is no guile [deceit]!
- **Luke 7:9** [Referring to the faith of the centurion whose servant Jesus healed:] When Jesus heard these things, He marvelled at him, and turned Him about, and said unto the people that followed Him, I say unto you, I have not found so great faith, no, not in Israel.
- **Luke 16:8a** [Jesus even praised the unjust steward for his wisdom:] And the Lord commended the unjust steward, because he had done wisely.
- **Matthew 15:22-28** [Jesus praised the Canaanite woman who did not get offended at His hard saying:] And, behold, a woman of Canaan came out of the same coasts, and cried unto Him, saying, Have mercy on me, O Lord, Thou Son of David; my daughter is grievously vexed with a devil. 23 But He answered her not a word. And His disciples came and besought Him, saying, Send her away; for she crieth after us. 24 But He answered and said, I am not sent but unto the lost sheep of the house of Israel. 25 Then came she and worshipped Him, saying, Lord, help me. 26 But He answered and said, It is not meet to take the children's bread, and to cast it to dogs. 27 And she said, truth, Lord: yet the dogs eat of the crumbs

which fall from their masters' table. [28] Then Jesus answered and said unto her, O woman, great is thy faith: be it unto thee even as thou wilt. And her daughter was made whole from that very hour.

2. The Lord also commends us when we invest our talents wisely to help others and further His Kingdom.

- **Matthew 25:21** [In the Parable of the Talents, Jesus narrated:] His lord said unto him, Well done, thou good and faithful servant: thou hast been faithful over a few things, I will make thee ruler over many things: enter thou into the joy of thy lord.
- **Luke 12:37** [Jesus said:] Blessed are those servants, whom the lord when he cometh shall find watching: verily I say unto you, that he shall gird himself, and make them to sit down to meat, and will come forth and serve them.
- **Hebrews 6:10** For God is not unrighteous to forget your work and labour of love, which ye have shewed toward His name, in that ye have ministered to the saints, and do minister.

3. The Lord also wants us to show appreciation to others.

- **Proverbs 31:30b** A woman that feareth the Lord, she shall be praised.
- **Song of Solomon 6:9** My dove, my undefiled is but one; she is the only one of her mother, she is the choice one of her that bare her. The daughters saw her, and blessed her; yea, the queens and the concubines, and they praised her.
- **1 Samuel 15:6** [King Saul remembered to show appreciation to foreign tribes for having shown kindness to his forefathers.] And Saul said unto the Kenites, Go, depart, get you down from among the Amalekites, lest I destroy you with them: for ye shewed kindness to all the children of Israel, when they came up out of Egypt. So the Kenites departed from among the Amalekites.

- **1 Samuel 25:32-33** And David said to Abigail, Blessed be the Lord God of Israel, which sent thee this day to meet me: [33] And blessed be thy advice, and blessed be thou, which hast kept me this day from coming to shed blood, and from avenging myself with mine own hand.

- **2 Samuel 10:2a** Then said David, I will shew kindness unto Hanun … as his father shewed kindness unto me. And David sent to comfort him by the hand of his servants for his father.

- **1 King 2:7** But shew kindness unto the sons of Barzillai the Gileadite, and let them be of those that eat at thy table: for so they came to me when I fled because of Absalom thy brother.

- **Romans 13:7** Render therefore to all their dues: tribute to whom tribute is due; custom to whom custom; fear to whom fear; honour to whom honour.

- **1 Thessalonians 5:18** In every thing give thanks: for this is the will of God in Christ Jesus concerning you.

- **Philippians 4:8** [Everyone has some good qualities, so let's recognize them:] Finally, brethren, whatsoever things are true, whatsoever things are honest, whatsoever things are just, whatsoever things are pure, whatsoever things are lovely, whatsoever things are of good report; if there be any virtue, and if there be any praise, think on these things.

4. The Apostle Paul's letters to the brethren were good samples of showing appreciation to others.

- **Romans 1:8** First, I thank my God through Jesus Christ for you all, that your faith is spoken of throughout the whole world.

- **Romans 16:1-2** I commend unto you Phebe our sister, which is a servant of the church which is at Cenchrea: [2] That ye receive her in the Lord, as becometh saints, and that ye assist her in whatsoever business she hath need of you: for she hath been a succourer of many, and of myself also.

- **1 Corinthians 16:15-18** [Paul made mention of the family of Stephanus and his companions, who were faithful in their missionary work.]
- **2 Corinthians 8:1-5** [Paul honored the church at Macedonia for their extreme generosity and devotion to Paul's leadership.] [See also Philippians 4:14-16.]
- **2 Corinthians 8:16-23** [Paul commended the faithfulness of Titus and his travelling companion, who administered to the material needs of the Church.]
- **Colossians 1:3-4** We give thanks to God and the Father of our Lord Jesus Christ, praying always for you, [4] Since we heard of your faith in Christ Jesus, and of the love which ye have to all the saints.
- **1 Thessalonians 1 [all]** [Paul wrote to the brethren in Thessalonica:] [3] Remembering without ceasing your work of faith, and labour of love, and patience of hope in our Lord Jesus Christ, in the sight of God and our Father. ... [7] Ye were ensamples to all that believe in Macedonia and Achaia.
- **2 Thessalonians 1:3,4** We are bound to thank God always for you, brethren, as it is meet, because that your faith groweth exceedingly, and the charity of every one of you all toward each other aboundeth; [4] So that we ourselves glory in you in the churches of God for your patience and faith in all your persecutions and tribulations that ye endure:

5. Other examples in the Bible of showing appreciation:

- **Genesis 41:39-41** [Pharaoh showed his appreciation to Joseph for interpreting his dream and for Joseph's wise counsel:] And Pharaoh said unto Joseph, Forasmuch as God hath shewed thee all this, there is none so discreet and wise as thou art: [40] Thou shalt be over my house, and according unto thy word shall all my people be ruled: only in the throne will I be greater than thou. [41] And Pharaoh said unto Joseph, See, I have set thee over all the land of Egypt. [See also Genesis 41:1-43.]

- **Exodus 2:11-21** [Reuel, the priest of Midian, scolded his daughters for not showing appreciation to Moses, who had helped them draw water:] [20] And he said unto his daughters, And where is he? Why is it that ye have left the man? Call him, that he may eat bread.

- **Ruth 3:10** [Boaz expressed his appreciation to Ruth for her unselfish devotion:] [10] And he said, Blessed be thou of the Lord, my daughter: for thou hast shewed more kindness in the latter end than at the beginning, inasmuch as thou followedst not young men, whether poor or rich. [See all of chapter 3.]

- **Nehemiah 7:2** I gave my brother Hanani, and Hananiah the ruler of the palace, charge over Jerusalem: for he was a faithful man, and feared God above many.

- **Esther 6:11b** [King Ahasuerus showed his appreciation to Mordecai for unveiling the plot against the king's life by having Mordecai dressed in royal apparel and paraded through the city:] Thus shall it be done to the man whom the king delighteth to honour. [See also Esther 6:1-11.]

- **1 King 13:1-7** [King Jeroboam of Judah was appreciative of the young prophet who had asked the Lord to restore the repentant king's hand:] [4] And it came to pass, when king Jeroboam heard the saying of the man of God, which had cried against the altar in Bethel, that he put forth his hand from the altar, saying, Lay hold on him. And his hand, which he put forth against him, dried up, so that he could not pull it in again to him. ... [6] And the king answered and said unto the man of God, Intreat now the face of the Lord thy God, and pray for me, that my hand may be restored me again. And the man of God besought the Lord, and the king's hand was restored him again, and became as it was before. [7] And the king said unto the man of God, Come home with me, and refresh thyself, and I will give thee a reward.

- **2 Kings 5:15** [After Naaman was cleansed of leprosy, he showed his appreciation to the prophet Elisha by offering him a reward:] And he returned to the man of God, he and all his company, and said, Behold, now I know that there is no God in all the earth, but in

Israel: now therefore, I pray thee, take a blessing of thy servant. [See also 2 Kings 5:1-19.]

[See also Revelation chapters 2 and 3 for a wonderful example of how the Lord faithfully shows appreciation for good qualities, even when convicting us about our errors.]

6. We should never fail to show our appreciation to the Lord by praising Him for all He has done for us.

- **Deuteronomy 8:10,11** [Moses exhorted:] When thou hast eaten and art full, then thou shalt bless the Lord thy God for the good land which He hath given thee. [11] Beware that thou forget not the Lord thy God, in not keeping His commandments, and His judgements, and His statutes, which I command thee this day.
- **Psalm 103:2** Bless the Lord, O my soul, and forget not all His benefits. [See also Psalm 105:5.]
- **Psalm 107:8** Oh that men would praise the Lord for His goodness, and for His wonderful works to the children of men!
- **Psalm 116:12-14** What shall I render unto the Lord for all His benefits toward me? [13] I will take the cup of salvation, and call upon the name of the Lord. [14] I will pay my vows unto the Lord now in the presence of all His people.
- **Luke 1:46-48** And Mary said, My soul doth magnify the Lord, [47] And my spirit hath rejoiced in God my Saviour. [48] For He hath regarded the low estate of His handmaiden: for, behold, from henceforth all generations shall call me blessed. [See also verses 49-55.]
- **Luke 17:15-19** [After Jesus healed the ten lepers, only one expressed appreciation:] And one of them, when he saw that he was healed, turned back, and with a loud voice glorified God, [16] And fell down on his face at His feet, giving Him thanks: and he was a Samaritan, [17] And Jesus answering said, Were there not ten cleansed? But where are the nine? [18] There are not found that returned to give glory to God, save this stranger. [19] And He said unto him, Arise, go thy way: thy faith hath made thee whole.

• **Hebrews 13:15** By Him therefore let us offer the sacrifice of praise to God continually, that is, the fruit of our lips giving thanks to His name.

BEAUTY

Definition: Those qualities that delight or give pleasure to the eye, ear, mind or heart; loveliness; elegance; a particular grace or charm.

1. Real beauty is on the inside.

- **1 Samuel 16:7b** For the Lord seeth not as man seeth; for man looketh on the outward appearance, but the Lord looketh on the heart.
- **Psalm 45:13a** The king's daughter is all glorious within.
- **Isaiah 28:5** [True beauty, the beauty that God bestows upon His children by His Spirit, is eternal.] In that day shall the Lord of hosts be for a crown of glory, and for a diadem [crown] of beauty, unto the residue of His people.
- **1 Peter 3:3,4** [The key to true beauty:] Whose adorning let it not be that outward adorning of plaiting the hair, and of wearing of gold, or of putting on of apparel; ⁴ But let it be the hidden man of the heart, in that which is not corruptible, even the ornament of a meek and quiet spirit, which is in the sight of God of great price.

2. it has been said "Eyes are the windows of the soul," and it is through your eyes that the beauty of your spirit, the real you, shines through.

- **Matthew 6:22** The light of the body is the eye: if therefore thine eye be single, thy whole body shall be full of light. [See also Luke 11:36.]
- **Matthew 5:14-16** [Our eyes should radiate happiness and the joy of the Lord.] Ye are the light of the world. A city that is set on an hill cannot be hid. ¹⁵ Neither do men light a candle, and put it under a bushel, but on a candlestick; and it giveth light unto all that are in the house. ¹⁶ Let your light so shine before men, that they may see your good works, and glorify your Father which is in Heaven.

- **Proverbs 15:13a** [The joy of the Lord is the best "makeup,"] A merry <u>heart</u> maketh a cheerful countenance.

3. Spiritual beauty, or beauty of character, is far better to seek after than mere physical beauty.

- **Psalm 149:4** For the Lord taketh pleasure in His people: He will beautify the meek with salvation.
- **Proverbs 31:30** Favour is deceitful, and beauty is vain: but a woman that feareth the Lord, she shall be praised.
- **Proverbs 11:16a** A <u>gracious</u> woman retaineth honour.
- **Proverbs 11:22** [Beauty without godly behaviour couldn't be less appealing.] As a jewel of gold in a swine's snout, so is a fair woman which is without discretion.
- **Isaiah 53:2a** He hath no form nor comeliness; and when we shall see Him, there is no beauty that we should desire Him.
- **Isaiah 61:3,10** [God is the giver of true beauty.] To appoint unto them that mourn in Zion, to give unto them beauty for ashes, the oil of joy for mourning, the garment of praise for the spirit of heaviness; that they might be called trees of righteousness, the planting of the Lord, that He might be glorified. ... [10] I will greatly rejoice in the Lord, my soul shall be joyful in my God; for He hath clothed me with the garments of salvation, He hath covered me with the robe of righteousness, as a bridegroom decketh himself with ornaments, and as a bride adorneth herself with her jewels.

4. As we draw closer to the Lord, our outward appearance will also be transformed and become more beautiful.

- **Exodus 34:29** [When Moses went up on the mountain to see the Lord, he returned even visibly changed so that the people were amazed.] And it came to pass, when Moses came down from Mount Sinai with the two tables of testimony in Moses' hand, when he came down from the mount, that Moses wist not that the skin of his face shone while He talked with him.

- **Job 29:14** I put on <u>righteousness</u>, and it clothed me: my <u>judgment</u> was as a robe and a diadem [crown].
- **Psalm 96:6,9** Honour and majesty are before Him: strength and beauty are in His sanctuary. ... [9]O worship the Lord in the beauty of holiness: fear before Him, all the earth.
- **Proverbs 1:9** For they [instruction and teaching] shall be an ornament of grace unto thy head, and chains about thy neck.
- **Proverbs 4:9** She [wisdom] shall give to thine head an ornament of grace: a crown of glory shall she deliver to thee.
- **Ecclesiastes 8:1b** A man's <u>wisdom</u> maketh his face to shine, and the boldness of his face shall be changed.
- **Isaiah 52:7** [Our beauty is enhanced whenever we share God's love with others.] How beautiful upon the mountains are the feet of him that bringeth good tidings, that publisheth peace; that bringeth good tidings of good, that publisheth salvation; that saith unto Zion, Thy God reigneth! [See also Daniel 12:3.]
- **Acts 6:15** [Stephen, one of the first martyrs of the Early Church, was transformed by the Lord as he witnessed.] And all that sat in the council, looking stedfastly on him, saw his face as it had been the face of an angel.
- **2 Corinthians 3:18** But we all, with open face beholding as in a glass the glory of the Lord, are changed into the same image from glory to glory, even as by the Spirit of the Lord.

5. Physical beauty is temporal.

- **Jeremiah 4:30b** In vain shalt thou make thyself fair.
- **Job 15:31** Let not him that is deceived trust in vanity: for vanity shall be his recompence.
- **Psalm 39:11** When Thou with rebukes dost correct man for iniquity, Thou makest his beauty to consume away like a moth: surely every man is vanity.

- **Psalm 49:14** [Death and God's judgments take away the "beauty" of the wicked.] Like sheep they are laid in the grave; death shall feed on them; and the upright shall have dominion over them in the morning; and their beauty shall consume in the grave from their dwelling.
- **1 John 2:15-17** Love not the world, neither the things that are in the world. If any man love the world, the love of the Father is not in him. [16] For all that is in the world, the lust of the flesh, and the lust of the eyes, and the pride of life, is not of the Father, but is of the world. [17] And the world passeth away, and the lust thereof: but he that doeth the will of God abideth for ever.

6. Physical beauty can be misused to lead others astray.

- **2 Samuel 14:25; 15:5,6** [David's son, Absalom, used his charm to steal the loyalty of David's people from him, as he intended to overthrow his father's government.] But in all Israel there was none to be so much praised as Absalom for his beauty: from the sole of his foot even to the crown of his head there was no blemish in him. ... [15:5] And it was so, that when any man came nigh to him to do him obeisance, he put forth his hand, and took him, and kissed him. [6] And on this manner did Absalom to all Israel that came to the king for judgment: so Absalom stole the hearts of the men of Israel.
- **Proverbs 6:23-25** For the commandment is a lamp; and the law is light; and reproofs of instruction are the way of life: [24] To keep thee from the evil woman, from the flattery of the tongue of a strange woman. [25] Lust not after her beauty in thine heart; neither let her take thee with her eyelids.
- **Proverbs 7:10,12-14** And, behold, there met him a woman with the attire of an harlot, and subtil of heart. ... [12] Now is she without, now in the streets, and lieth in wait at every corner. [13] So she caught him, and kissed him, and with an impudent face said unto him, [14] I have peace offerings with me; this day have I payed my vows.

- **Ezekiel 16:15** But thou didst trust in thine own beauty, and playedst the harlot because of thy renown, and pouredst out thy fornications on every one that passed by; his it was. [See also Isaiah 3:16.]
- **Revelation 17:1b-4,18; chapter 18** [God's greatest endtime wrath is poured out on Babylon, the whorish, deceitful, world materialistic System, that deceived the nations with her fleshly beauty and materialism.] Come hither; I will shew unto thee the judgment of the great whore that sitteth upon many waters: [2] With whom the kings of the earth have committed fornication, and the inhabitants of the earth have been made drunk with the wine of her fornication. [3] So he carried me away in the spirit into the wilderness: and I saw a woman. ...[4] And the woman was arrayed in purple and scarlet colour, and decked with gold and precious stones and pearls, having a golden cup in her hand full of abominations and filthiness of her fornication. ...[18] And the woman which thou sawest is that great city, which reigneth over the kings of the earth. ... [18:3] For all nations have drunk of the wine of the wrath of her fornication, and the kings of the earth have committed fornication with her, and the merchants of the earth are waxed rich through the abundance of her delicacies. ...[7] How much she hath glorified herself, and lived deliciously, so much torment and sorrow give her: for she saith in her heart, I sit a queen, and am no widow, and shall see no sorrow.

7. Lord help us to reflect His beauty.

- **Psalm 42:11** [God paints true beauty on our faces.] Why art thou cast down, O my soul? And why art thou disquieted within me? Hope thou in God: for I shall yet praise Him, who is the health of my countenance, and my God.
- **Psalm 90:17a** And let the beauty of the Lord our God be upon us. [See also Psalm 27:4; 50:2.]
- **Isaiah 61:10** I will greatly rejoice in the Lord, my soul shall be joyful in my God; for He hath clothed me with the garments of salvation, He hath covered me with the robe of righteousness, as a

bridegroom decketh himself with ornaments, and as a bride adorneth herself with her jewels.

- **Ezekiel 16:14** And thy renown went forth among the heathen for thy beauty: for it was perfect through My comeliness, which I had put upon thee, saith the Lord God.
- **Zechariah 9:17a** For how great is His goodness, and how great is His beauty! [See also Psalm 50:2; Isaiah 33:17.]
- **Ephesians 5:27** That He [God] might present it to Himself a glorious Church, not having spot, or wrinkle, or any such thing; but that it should be holy and without blemish.

BITTERNESS

Definition: Holding on to or showing feelings of intense [strong] animosity [hatred, anger], resentment or vindictiveness [wanting to get back at someone]. Other words that describe bitterness are: merciless, unforgiving, holding a grudge. Bitterness is also described as feelings resulting from something that is difficult to accept.

1. God's Word warns us against the dangers of bitterness.

- **Proverbs 18:19** [When we allow ourselves to become bitter against others, we create walls difficult to overcome, which isolates us from others.] A brother offended is harder to be won than a strong city: and their contentions are like the bars of a castle.
- **Acts 8:22,23** [Bitterness is a sin to be repented of.] Repent therefore of this thy wickedness, and pray God if perhaps the thought of thine heart may be forgiven thee. [23] For I perceive that thou art in the gall [poison] of bitterness, and in the bond of iniquity.
- **Colossians 3:19** Husbands, love your wives, and be not bitter against them.
- **Hebrews 12:15** [Be on guard against it, because even a little root of bitterness can do much harm to you and others.] Looking diligently lest any man fail of the grace of God; lest any root of bitterness springing up trouble you, and thereby many be defiled [contaminated]. [See also Deuteronomy 29:18.]
- **James 3:14** If ye have bitter envying and strife in your hearts, glory not [don't brag about it.], and lie not against the truth.

2. Do not carry or keep bitterness, but replace it with love, kindness and forgiveness.

- **Leviticus 19:18** Thou shalt not avenge, nor bear [carry or keep] any grudge [bitterness] against the children of thy people, but thou shalt love thy neighbour as thyself: I am the Lord.

- **Proverbs 17:9** [Love can overcome bitterness, but watch out about opening up old hurts felt from others. Better to forgive and forget.] He that covereth a transgression seeketh love; but he that repeateth [harps about] a matter separateth very [true] friends. [See also Proverbs10:12.]
- **Matthew 6:14,15** For if ye forgive men their trespasses, your Heavenly Father will also forgive you: [15] But if ye forgive not men their trespasses, neither will your Father forgive your trespasses.
- **Matthew 18:23-35** [In His parable of the unmerciful servant, Jesus made it clear that we will suffer if we refuse to sincerely forgive our brethren, when we know Jesus has had mercy on our sins.] [35] So likewise shall My Heavenly Father do also unto you, if ye from your hearts forgive not every one his brother their trespasses.
- **Romans 2:1-6** [Hypocritical, judgmental self-righteousness can cause us to harbor bitterness, while feeling justified for doing so, yet it ends up bringing God's punishments upon ourselves.] Therefore thou art inexcusable, O man, whosoever thou art that judgest: for wherein thou judgest another, thou condemnest thyself; for thou that judgest doest the same things. [2] But we are sure that the judgment of God is according to truth against them which commit such things. [3] And thinkest thou this, O man, that judgest them which do such things, and doest the same, that thou shalt escape the judgment of God? [4] Or despisest thou the riches of His goodness and forbearance and longsuffering; not knowing that the goodness of God leadeth thee to repentance? [5] But after thy hardness and impenitent heart treasurest up unto thyself wrath [you are saving up terrible punishment for yourselves] against the Day of Wrath and revelation of the righteous judgment of God; [6] Who will render to every man according to his deeds.
- **Ephesians 4:31,32** Let all bitterness, and wrath, and anger, and clamour [shouting or crying], and evil speaking, be put away from you, with all malice [desire to do harm]: [32] And be ye kind one to another, tenderhearted, forgiving one another, even as God for Christ's sake hath forgiven you.

• **1 Peter 4:8** [Even if someone has mistreated or wronged you, God's love is love enough to forgive.] And above all things have fervent love among yourselves: for love shall cover the multitude of sins.

3. If you allow bitterness a place in your heart, it will eventually come out of your mouth in murmuring and complaining.

• **Job 6:2,3** [Job complained to his friends:] Oh that my grief were throughly weighed, and my calamity laid in the balances together! [3] For now it would be heavier than the sand of the sea: therefore my words are swallowed up [have been rash]. [See also Job 7:11.]
• **Job 10:1** [Job also said:] My soul is weary of my life; I will leave my complaint upon myself; I will speak in the bitterness of my soul. [See also Job 16:6-16.]
• **Job 23:1-4** [Job's self-righteousness caused him to become bitter against God, thinking he knew better.] Then Job answered and said, [2] Even to day is my complaint bitter: my stroke is heavier than my groaning. [3] Oh that I knew where I might find Him! That I might come even to His seat! [4] I would order my cause before Him, and fill my mouth with arguments.
• **Matthew 12:34b** Out of the abundance of the heart the mouth speaketh. [See also Matthew 15:11,18,19.]
• **Romans 3:14b** Whose mouth is full of cursing and bitterness.

4. The Lord, in His love, can deliver you from the sin of bitterness. Here are some examples of three who overcame it, and one who didn't:

• **Genesis 45:3-15** [If anyone had cause to be bitter, it was Joseph. His brothers had despised him; they brutally sold him into slavery and lied to their father that he had been killed by a wild animal; he spent time in prison on false charges of rape; and he was left there for two years longer because Pharaoh's forgetful chief butler forgot his promise to help get Joseph out of jail. In spite of all this, here's how Joseph reconciled with his brothers:] And Joseph said unto his brethren, I am Joseph; doth my father yet live? And his brethren could not answer him; for they were troubled at his presence. [4] And Joseph said unto his brethren, Come near to me, I pray you. And they came near. And he said, I am Joseph your brother, whom ye sold into Egypt. [5] Now therefore be not grieved, nor angry with yourselves, that ye sold me hither: for God did send me before you to preserve life. [6] For these two years hath the famine been in the land: and yet there are five years, in the which there shall neither be earing nor harvest. [7] And God sent me before you to preserve you a posterity in the earth, and to save your lives by a great deliverance. [8] So now it was not you that sent me hither, but God: and He hath made me a father to Pharaoh, and lord of all his house, and a ruler throughout all the land of Egypt. ... [10] And thou shalt dwell in the land of Goshen, and thou shalt be near unto me, thou, and thy children, and thy children's children, and thy flocks, and thy herds, and all that thou hast: [11] And there will I nourish thee; for yet there are five years of famine; lest thou, and thy household, and all that thou hast, come to poverty. ... [15] Moreover he kissed all his brethren, and wept upon them: and after that his brethren talked with him.

• **1 Samuel 1:10–28;2:21** [Hannah, mother of Samuel, was sorely provoked every year by Peninnah, the second wife of her husband, Elkanah. Peninnah had children and purposely tried to make Hannah feel badly because she had no children. After years of Peninnah doing this, Hannah, having become bitter, not eating well and feeling that she somehow was not blessed of the Lord, took her bitterness to the Lord in desperate prayer, openly confessing her grief, both to the Lord, and to Eli, the priest, and finally a great victory was one, first by faith, followed by the Lord's blessings.] [10] And she was in bitterness of soul, and prayed unto the Lord, and wept sore. ... [Eli, when he saw Hannah sobbing, mistakenly thought she'd been drinking and was drunk:] [15] I am a woman of a sorrowful spirit: I have drunk neither wine nor strong drink, but have poured out my soul before the Lord. ... [She explained her prayer that God give her a son.] [17] Then Eli answered and said, Go in peace: and the God of Israel grant thee thy petition that thou hast asked of Him. [18] And she said, Let thine handmaid find grace in thy sight. So the woman went her way, and did eat, and her countenance was no more sad. [By faith Hannah had given her bitterness to the Lord, and because of it, was able to return to her family, having been freed from sadness and was even able to eat normally. Later the blessings came: the Lord not only blessed her with Samuel, her first born who she gave to the Lord, but also with three other sons and two daughters!]

- **Isaiah 38:10-17** [King Hezekiah grew bitter during a nearly fatal illness. During his worst days, he felt the Lord was cutting him off. Yet his desperate prayer and tears brought eventual healing and victory.] I said in the cutting off of my days, I shall go to the gates of the grave: I am deprived of the residue of my years. [11] I said, I shall not see the Lord, even the Lord, in the land of the living: I shall behold man no more with the inhabitants of the world. [12] Mine age is departed, and is removed from me as a shepherd's tent: I have cut off like a weaver my life: He will cut me off with pining sickness: from day even to night wilt Thou make an end of me. [13] I reckoned till morning, that, as a lion, so will He break all my bones: from day even to night wilt thou make an end of me. [14] Like a crane or a swallow, so did I chatter: I did mourn as a dove: mine eyes fail with looking upward: O Lord, I am oppressed; undertake for me. [15] What shall I say? He hath both spoken unto me, and Himself hath done it: I shall go softly all my years in the bitterness of my soul. [16] O Lord, by these things men live, and in all these things is the life of my spirit: [then Hezekiah begins to speak faith:] so wilt Thou recover me, and make me to live. [17] Behold, for peace I had great bitterness: but Thou hast in love to my soul delivered it from the pit of corruption: for Thou hast cast all my sins behind Thy back.

- **2 Samuel 13:22-29** [Absalom, son of King David, bitterly hated his half-brother, Amnon, for having raped Tamar, Absalom's full sister.

This unbridled bitterness grew for two years until Absalom had Amnon killed.] And Absalom spake unto his brother Amnon neither good nor bad: for Absalom <u>hated</u> Amnon, because he had forced his sister Tamar. ... [28] Now Absalom had commanded his servants, saying, Mark ye now when Amnon's heart is merry with wine, and when I say unto you, Smite Amnon; then kill him, fear not: have not I commanded you? Be courageous, and be valiant. [29] And the servants of Absalom did unto Amnon as Absalom had commanded. Then all the king's sons arose, and every man gat him up upon his mule, and fled.

5. Bitterness stems from feelings of anger and an unforgiving attitude towards others. Here are some more solutions from the Word on how to avoid it.

- **Proverbs 27:7** [If we are truly hungry to learn from the Lord, even bitter experiences are looked upon as "blessings in disguise."] The full soul loatheth an honeycomb; but to the hungry soul every bitter thing is sweet.
- **Matthew 5:23,24** Therefore if thou bring thy gift to the altar, and there rememberest that thy brother hath ought [grievance] against thee; [24] Leave there thy gift before the altar, and go thy way; <u>first</u> be reconciled to thy brother, and <u>then</u> come and offer thy gift.
- **Mark 11:25** And when ye stand praying, forgive, if ye have ought against any: that your Father also which is in Heaven may forgive you your trespasses.
- **Romans 8:28** [Bitterness is also described as the feelings resulting from something that is difficult to accept; so it's important to always remember that the Lord has a <u>good</u> purpose in everything that He allows to happen to us.] We know that <u>all</u> things work together for <u>good</u> to them that love God, to them who are the called according to His purpose.
- **Romans 12:2** [God's Word often speaks of "renewing our minds," which implies letting go of the old; particularly any past grievances

and bitternesses.] And be not conformed to this world: but be ye transformed by the renewing of your mind, that ye may prove what is that good, and acceptable, and perfect, will of God. [See also Ephesians 4:23.]

- **Ephesians 4:26b,27** [Going to bed in anger is an avenue for the Devil to work.] Let not the sun go down upon your wrath; [27] Neither give place to the Devil.

- **Philippians 3:13** [Bitterness is also caused by holding on to bad or angry feelings about someone or something that happened, but the Lord tells us to <u>forget</u> the things that are past.] Brethren, I count not myself to have apprehended: but this one thing I do, forgetting those things which are behind, and reaching forth unto those things which are before.

- **Colossians 3:13** Forbearing one another, and forgiving one another, if any man have a quarrel against any: even as Christ forgave you, so also do ye.

BULLYING

Definition: The use of strength or power to force or pressure others by fear; persecuting or oppressing others by force or threat of force.

1. Bullying, or "oppression" as it is commonly termed in the Bible, is expressly forbidden.

- **Deuteronomy 24:14** Thou shalt not oppress an hired servant that is poor and needy, whether he be of thy brethren, or of thy strangers that are in thy land within thy gates.
- **Leviticus 25:17** Ye shall not therefore oppress one another; but thou shalt fear thy God: for I am the Lord your God.
- **Proverbs 3:30** Strive not with a man without cause, if he have done thee no harm.
- **Proverbs 3:31** Envy thou not the oppressor, and choose none of his ways.

2. Bullying is ungodly; meekness should be our sample.

- **2 Timothy 2:24,25** And the servant of the Lord must not strive; but be gentle unto all men, apt to teach, patient, [25] In meekness instructing those that oppose themselves [who are in opposition]; if God peradventure will give them repentance to the acknowledging of the truth.
- **Galatians 5:22,23** But the fruit of the Spirit is <u>love</u>, joy, <u>peace</u>, longsuffering, <u>gentleness</u>, goodness, faith, [23] Meekness, temperance: against such there is no law.
- **Ephesians 4:31** Let all bitterness, and wrath, and anger, and clamour, and evil speaking, be put away from you, with all malice.
- **Philippians 2:3a** Let nothing be done through strife or vainglory.
- **Titus 3:2** To speak evil of no man, to be no brawlers, but gentle, shewing all meekness unto all men.
- **Hebrews 12:14** Follow peace with all men, and holiness, without which no man shall see the Lord.

- **James 3:14-18** But if ye have bitter envying and strife in your hearts, glory not, and lie not against the truth. [15] This wisdom descendeth not from above, but is earthly, sensual, devilish. [16] For where envying and strife is, there is confusion and every evil work. [17] But the wisdom that is from above is first pure, then peaceable, gentle, and easy to be intreated, full of mercy and good fruits, without partiality, and without hypocrisy. [18] And the fruit of righteousness is sown in peace of them that make peace.

3. Bullies are motivated by pride, selfishness and lack of love.

- **Proverbs 13:10a** Only by pride cometh contention.
- **Proverbs 26:21** As coals are to burning coals, and wood to fire; so is a contentious man to kindle strife.
- **Matthew 18:28** But the same servant [one who'd just been forgiven his debts] went out, and found one of his fellowservants, which owed him an hundred pence: and he laid hands on him, and took him by the throat, saying, Pay me that thou owest.
- **1 Corinthians 13:4,5** Charity [Love] suffereth long, and is kind; charity envieth not; charity vaunteth not itself, is not puffed up, [5] Doth not behave itself unseemly, seeketh not her own, is not easily provoked, thinketh no evil.

4. Bullying is an offense to the Lord.

- **Psalm 73:8-20** They are corrupt, and speak wickedly concerning oppression: they speak loftily. [9] They set their mouth against the heavens, and their tongue walketh through the earth. ... [11] And they say, How doth God know? And is there knowledge in the most High? ... [20] As a dream when one awaketh; so, O Lord, when Thou awakest, Thou shalt despise their image.
- **Proverbs 14:31a** He that oppresseth the poor reproacheth his Maker.

- **Matthew 25:40** And the King shall answer and say unto them, Verily I say unto you, Inasmuch as ye have done it unto one of the least of these My brethren, ye have done it unto Me.

5. The bully's "victory" is short lived.

- **Job 20:4,5** Knowest thou not this of old, since man was placed upon earth, [5] That the triumphing of the wicked is short, and the joy of the hypocrite but for a moment?
- **Psalm 37:35,36** I have seen the wicked in great power, and spreading himself like a green bay tree. [36] Yet he passed away, and, lo, he was not: yea, I sought him, but he could not be found.

6. The bully is "asking for trouble" because the Lord is watching and sides with the oppressed.

- **Exodus 3:9** Now therefore, behold, the cry of the children of Israel is come unto Me: and I have also seen the oppression wherewith the Egyptians oppress them.
- **Psalm 10:17,18** Lord, Thou hast heard the desire of the humble: Thou wilt prepare their heart, Thou wilt cause Thine ear to hear: [18] To judge the fatherless and the oppressed, that the man of the earth may no more oppress.
- **Psalm 12:5** For the oppression of the poor, for the sighing of the needy, now will I arise, saith the Lord; I will set him in safety from him that puffeth at him.
- **Ezekiel 34:17-31** [Here's what the Lord thinks about spiritual leaders who take advantage of their sheep:] And as for you, O My flock, thus saith the Lord God; Behold, I judge between cattle and cattle, between the rams and the he goats. [18] Seemeth it a small thing unto you to have eaten up the good pasture, but ye must tread down with your feet the residue of your pastures? And to have drunk of the deep waters, but ye must foul the residue with your feet? [19] And as for My flock, they eat that which ye have

trodden with your feet; and they drink that which ye have fouled with your feet. [20] Therefore thus saith the Lord God unto them; Behold, I, even I, will judge between the fat cattle and between the lean cattle. [21] Because ye have thrust with side and with shoulder, and pushed all the diseased with your horns, till ye have scattered them abroad; [22] Therefore will I save My flock, and they shall no more be a prey; and I will judge between cattle and cattle. [23] And I will set up one shepherd over them, and he shall feed them, even My servant David; he shall feed them, and he shall be their shepherd. [24] And I the Lord will be their God, and My servant David a prince among them; I the Lord have spoken it. [25] And I will make with them a covenant of peace, and will cause the evil beasts to cease out of the land: and they shall dwell safely in the wilderness, and sleep in the woods. ... [27] They shall be safe in their land, and shall know that I am the Lord, when I have broken the bands of their yoke, and delivered them out of the hand of those that served themselves of them. [28] And they shall no more be a prey to the heathen, neither shall the beast of the land devour them; but they shall dwell safely, and none shall make them afraid. [30] Thus shall they know that I the Lord their God am with them, and that they, even the house of Israel, are My people, saith the Lord God. [31] And ye My flock, the flock of My pasture, are men, and I am your God, saith the Lord God.

- **Luke 12:45,46** But and if that servant say in his heart, My Lord delayeth His coming; and shall begin to beat the menservants and maidens, and to eat and drink, and to be drunken; [46] The Lord of that servant will come in a day when he looketh not for Him, and at an hour when he is not aware, and will cut him in sunder, and will appoint him his portion with the unbelievers.
- **1 Peter 3:12** For the eyes of the Lord are over the righteous, and His ears are open unto their prayers: but the face of the Lord is against them that do evil.

7. Sooner or later, bullies will reap what they sow.

- **Proverbs 11:17** The merciful man doeth good to his own soul: but he that is cruel troubleth his own flesh.
- **Jeremiah 17:10** I the Lord search the heart, I try the reins, even to give every man according to his ways, and according to the fruit of his doings.
- **2 Corinthians 5:10** For we must all appear before the judgment seat of Christ; that every one may receive the things done in his body, according to that he hath done, whether it be good or bad.
- **Galatians 6:7** Be not deceived; God is not mocked: for whatsoever a man soweth, that shall he also reap.

8. Consider how <u>you</u> would feel if bullied by others.

- **Exodus 23:9** Also thou shalt not oppress a stranger: for ye know the heart of a stranger, seeing ye were strangers in the land of Egypt.
- **Luke 6:31** And as ye would that men should do to you, do ye also to them likewise.

9. Join the <u>Lord's</u> side; go to the aid of the underdog.

- **Psalm 82:3** Defend the poor and fatherless: do justice to the afflicted and needy.
- **Isaiah 1:17** Learn to do well; seek judgment, relieve the oppressed, judge the fatherless, plead for the widow.
- **Isaiah 58:6** Is not this the fast that I have chosen? To loose the bands of wickedness, to undo the heavy burdens, and to let the oppressed go free, and that ye break every yoke?
- **Jeremiah 22:16** He judged the cause of the poor and needy; then it was well with him: was not this to know Me? Saith the Lord.
- **Romans 15:1** We then that are strong ought to bear the infirmities of the weak, and not to please ourselves.

- **1 Thessalonians 5:14** Now we exhort you, brethren, warn them that are unruly, comfort the feebleminded, support the weak, be patient toward all men.

CHOICE AND DECISION MAKING

Definition: The act of selecting freely after careful consideration.

1. The Lord often engineers or allows situations as tests, to see what choices we will make.

- **Exodus 32:26a** Then Moses stood in the gate of the camp, and said, Who is on the Lord's side? Let him come unto me.
- **Deuteronomy 30:19** I [Moses] call Heaven and earth to record this day against you, that I have set before you life and death, blessing and cursing: therefore choose life, that both thou and thy seed may live.
- **Joshua 24:15a** Choose you this day whom ye will serve.
- **1 Chronicles 29:17a** I know also, my God, that Thou triest the heart, and hast pleasure in uprightness.
- **1 Kings 18:21** And Elijah came unto all the people, and said, How long halt ye between two opinions? If the Lord be God, follow Him: but if Baal, then follow him.
- **Proverbs 17:3** The fining pot is for silver, and the furnace for gold: but the Lord trieth the hearts.
- **Jeremiah 12:3a** But Thou, O Lord, knowest me: Thou hast seen me, and tried mine heart toward Thee.
- **1 Thessalonians 2:4** But as we were allowed of God to be put in trust with the Gospel, even so we speak; not as pleasing men, but God, which trieth our hearts.
- **Hebrews 11:17** By faith Abraham, when he was tried, offered up Isaac: and he that had received the promises offered up his only begotten son.
- **Revelation 3:10** [If we choose to follow the Lord, He'll give us His protection.] Because thou hast kept the Word of My patience, I also will keep thee from the hour of temptation, which shall come upon all the world, to try them that dwell upon the earth.

2. For Christians, decision making is synonymous with finding the will of God.

- **Psalm 25:4,5,9** Shew me Thy ways, O Lord; teach me Thy paths. [5] Lead me in Thy truth, and teach me: for Thou art the God of my salvation; on Thee do I wait all the day. [9] The meek will He guide in judgment: and the meek will He teach His way. [See also Psalm 86:11.]
- **Psalm 27:11** Teach Me Thy way, O Lord, and lead me in a plain path, because of mine enemies.
- **Psalm 143:10** Teach me to do Thy will; for Thou art my God: Thy Spirit is good; lead me into the land of uprightness. [See also Psalm 25:4,5]

3. Carnal reasoning is a hindrance in Spirit-led decision making.

- **Proverbs 3:5,7a** Trust in the Lord with all thine heart; and lean <u>not</u> unto thine own understanding. ... [7a] Be not wise in thine own eyes.
- **Proverbs 14:12** There is a way which seemeth right unto a man, but the end thereof are the ways of death.
- **Proverbs 19:21** There are many devices in a man's heart; nevertheless the counsel of the Lord, that shall stand.
- **Isaiah 55:8,9** For My thoughts are not your thoughts, neither are your ways My ways, saith the Lord. [9] For as the heavens are higher than the earth, so are My ways higher than your ways, and My thoughts than your thoughts.
- **Jeremiah 10:23** O Lord, I know that the way of man is not in himself: it is not in man that walketh to direct his steps.
- **Romans 8:6-9a** For to be carnally minded is death; but to be spiritually minded is life and peace. [7] Because the carnal mind is enmity against God: for it is not subject to the law of God, neither indeed can be. [8] So then they that are in the flesh cannot please God. [9] But ye are not in the flesh, but in the Spirit, if so be that the Spirit of God dwell in you.

• **Galatians 6:8** For he that soweth to his flesh shall of the flesh reap corruption; but he that soweth to the Spirit shall of the Spirit reap life everlasting.

4. Mature decisions are based on spiritual considerations and goals, rather than solely upon physical circumstances and concerns or personal desires.

• **2 Corinthians 4:18** While we look not at the things which are seen, but at the things which are not seen: for the things which are seen are temporal; but the things which are not seen are eternal.

• **Colossians 3:2** Set your affection on things above, not on things on the earth.

• **Hebrews 11:24-26** By faith Moses, when he was come to years, refused to be called the son of Pharaoh's daughter; [25] Choosing rather to suffer affliction with the people of God, than to enjoy the pleasures of sin for a season; [26] Esteeming the reproach of Christ greater riches than the treasures in Egypt: for he had respect unto the recompence of the reward.

• **1 Kings 3:5,9-14** [God always blesses unselfish choices:] The Lord appeared to Solomon in a dream by night: and God said, Ask what I shall give thee. [And Solomon answered:] [9] Give therefore Thy servant an understanding heart to judge Thy people, that I may discern between good and bad: for who is able to judge this Thy so great a people? [10] And the speech pleased the Lord, that Solomon had asked this thing. [11] And God said unto him, Because thou hast asked this thing, and hast not asked for thyself long life; neither hast asked riches for thyself, nor hast asked the life of thine enemies; but hast asked for thyself understanding to discern judgment; [12] Behold, I have done according to thy words: lo, I have given thee a wise and an understanding heart; so that there was none like thee before thee, neither after thee shall any arise like unto thee. [13] And I have also given thee that which thou hast not asked, both riches, and honour: so that there shall not be any

among the kings like unto thee all thy days. [14] And if thou wilt walk
in My ways, to keep My statutes and My commandments, as thy
father David did walk, then I will lengthen thy days.

5. The Lord always chooses the best for us.

- **Psalm 25:12** What man is he that feareth the Lord? Him shall He
  teach in the way that He shall choose.
- **Psalm 32:8** I will instruct thee and teach thee in the way which
  thou shalt go: I will guide thee with Mine eye.
- **Psalm 37:4** Delight thyself also in the Lord; and He shall give thee
  the desires of thine heart.
- **Psalm 84:11b** No good thing will He withhold from them that walk
  uprightly.
- **Proverbs 10:22** The blessing of the Lord, it maketh rich, and He
  addeth no sorrow with it.
- **Jeremiah 29:11** For I know the thoughts that I think toward you,
  saith the Lord, thoughts of peace, and not of evil, to give you an
  expected end.
- **Luke 12:32** Fear not, little flock; for it is your Father's good pleasure
  to give you the Kingdom.
- **Romans 8:28** And we know that all things work together for good
  to them that love God, to them who are the called according to His
  purpose.

6. One of the main principles involved in reaching a decision: Pray for the Lord's guidance.

- **Job 5:8** I would seek unto God, and unto God would I commit my
  cause.
- **Psalm 34:5** They looked unto Him, and were lightened: and their
  faces were not ashamed.
- **Psalm 37:5** Commit thy way unto the Lord; trust also in Him; and
  He shall bring it to pass.

- **Proverbs 3:6** In all thy ways acknowledge Him, and He shall direct thy paths.
- **Proverbs 16:3** Commit thy works unto the Lord, and thy thoughts shall be established.
- **Isaiah 30:21** And thine ears shall hear a word behind thee, saying, This is the way, walk ye in it, when ye turn to the right hand, and when ye turn to the left.
- **John 16:13** Howbeit when He, the Spirit of truth, is come, He will guide you into all truth: for He shall not speak of Himself; but whatsoever He shall hear, that shall He speak: and He will shew you things to come.
- **Colossians 1:9b** Pray ... that ye might be filled with the knowledge of His will in all wisdom and spiritual understanding.
- **James 1:5** If any of you lack wisdom, let him ask of God, that giveth to all men liberally, and upbraideth not; and it shall be given him.

7. Sound decisions are based on the <u>Word</u>.

- **Psalm 119:105** Thy Word is a lamp unto my feet, and a light unto my path.
- **Psalm 119:24** Thy testimonies also are my delight and my counsellors.
- **Psalm 119:133a** Order my steps in Thy Word.
- **Numbers 22:18b** I cannot go beyond the Word of the Lord my God, to do less or more.
- **Proverbs 6:22,23** When thou goest, it [the Word] shall lead thee; when thou sleepest, it shall keep thee; and when thou awakest, it shall talk with thee. [23] For the commandment is a lamp; and the law is light; and reproofs of instruction are the way of life.
- **Matthew 7:24,25** Therefore whosoever heareth these sayings of Mine, and doeth them, I will liken him unto a wise man, which built his house upon a rock: [25] And the rain descended, and the floods came, and the winds blew, and beat upon that house; and it fell not: for it was founded upon a rock.

- **Romans 2:18** And knowest His will, and approvest the things that are more excellent, being instructed out of the law.
- **2 Timothy 3:16** All Scripture is given by inspiration of God, and is profitable for doctrine, for reproof, for correction, for instruction in righteousness.

8. Seeking godly counsel from others often leads to sounder, wiser decisions.

- **Proverbs 11:14** Where no counsel is, the people fall: but in the multitude of counsellors there is safety.
- **Proverbs 12:15** The way of a fool is right in his own eyes: but he that hearkeneth unto counsel is wise.
- **Proverbs 15:22** Without counsel purposes are disappointed: but in the multitude of counsellors they are established.
- **Proverbs 20:18** Every purpose is established by counsel: and with good advice make war.

9. The final test for our decisions should be: Is it loving?

- **Romans 13:9b,10** If there be any other commandment, it is briefly comprehended in this saying, namely, Thou shalt love thy neighbour as thyself. [10] Love worketh no ill to his neighbour: therefore love is the fulfilling of the law.
- **1 Corinthians 16:14** Let all your things be done with [love].

COMPARING YOURSELF TO OTHERS

Definition: Comparing means examining the similarities and differences of two or more things, ideas or people. When we compare ourselves with others, it can be a form of jealousy that results from not trusting in the Lord's love and fairness.

1. Comparing ourselves <u>negatively</u> with others leads to discontment, discouragement and jealously.

- **1 Samuel 18:8,9** And Saul was very wroth, and the saying displeased him; and he said, They have ascribed unto David ten thousands, and to me they have ascribed but thousands: and what can he have more but the kingdom? [9] And Saul eyed David from that day and forward.
- **Romans 9:20,21** [Comparing ourselves unfavorably can lead to feeling inferior and then to <u>murmuring</u>:] Nay but, O man, who art thou that repliest against God? Shall the thing formed say to Him that formed it, Why hast Thou made me thus? [21] Hath not the potter power over the clay, of the same lump to make one vessel unto honour, and another unto dishonour?
- **Acts 7:9** [Joseph's brothers envied him to the point of conspiring to kill him, but God blessed and protected Joseph and made his brothers come and beg before him.] And the patriarchs, moved with envy, sold Joseph into Egypt: but God was with him. [For the whole story, see Genesis, chapters 37-50.]
- **2 Corinthians 10:12** For we dare not make ourselves of the number [classify ourselves], or compare ourselves with some that commend themselves: but they measuring themselves by themselves, and comparing themselves among themselves, are <u>not wise</u>.

[See also Jealousy and Envy, #1-5, page 229.]

2. Comparing ourselves <u>favorably</u> with others can lead to pride and self-righteousness. (However, it can also be encouraging if done for the humble purpose of counting our blessings.)

- **Luke 18:9-14** And He spake this parable unto certain which trusted in themselves that they were righteous, and despised others: [10] Two men went up into the temple to pray; the one a Pharisee, and the other a publican. [11] The Pharisee stood and prayed thus with himself, God, I thank Thee, that I am not as other men are, extortioners, unjust, adulterers, or even as this publican. [12] I fast twice in the week, I give tithes of all that I possess. [13] And the publican, standing afar off, would not lift up so much as his eyes unto Heaven, but smote upon his breast, saying, God be merciful to me a sinner. [14] I tell you, this man went down to his house justified rather than the other: for every one that exalteth himself shall be abased; and he that humbleth himself shall be exalted.

- **Romans 12:3** For I say, through the grace given unto me, to every man that is among you, not to think of himself more highly than he ought to think; but to think soberly, according as God hath dealt to every man the measure of faith.

- **Romans 14:13** [Thinking of ourselves as superior compared to others can cause others, in turn, to look upon themselves negatively.] Let us not therefore judge one another any more: but judge this rather, that no man put a stumblingblock or an occasion to fall in his brother's way.

- **1 Corinthians 4:7** [Comparing fosters a spirit of competition and pride.] For who maketh thee to differ from another? And what hast thou that thou didst not receive [from God]? Now if thou didst receive it, why dost thou glory, as if thou hadst not received it?

- **1 Corinthians 13:4** [Love] suffereth long, and is kind; [love] envieth not; [love] <u>vaunteth not itself</u>, is not puffed up.

3. Comparing is often a two-way street, as born out by the story of the sisters Rachel and Leah, wives of Jacob, who each compared themselves unfavorably with the other.

- **Genesis 29:17** [Leah didn't compare favorably with Rachel in appearance:] Leah was tender [timid or weak] eyed; but Rachel was beautiful and well favoured.
- **Genesis 30:1** And when Rachel saw that she bare Jacob no children, Rachel envied her sister; and said unto Jacob, Give me children, or else I die.
- **Genesis 30:15a** [Leah was also envious of Jacob's love for Rachel:] And [Leah] said unto [Rachel], Is it a small matter that thou hast taken my husband?

4. Comparing results from carnal mindedness and spiritual immaturity.

- **Romans 8:5** For they that are after the flesh do mind the things of the flesh; but they that are after the Spirit the things of the Spirit.
- **1 Corinthians 3:1-8** And I, brethren, could not speak unto you as unto spiritual, but as unto carnal, even as unto babes in Christ. ... [3] For ye are yet carnal: for whereas there is among you envying, and strife, and divisions, are ye not carnal, and walk as men? [4] For while one saith, I am of Paul; and another, I am of Apollos; are ye not carnal? [5] Who then is Paul, and who is Apollos, but ministers by whom ye believed, even as the Lord gave to every man? [6] I have planted, Apollos watered; but God gave the increase. [7] So then neither is he that planteth any thing, neither he that watereth; but God that giveth the increase. [8] Now he that planteth and he that watereth are one: and every man shall receive his own reward according to his own labour.
- **1 Corinthians 4:5,6** [Let the Lord be the judge. He sees the hidden man of the heart.] Therefore judge nothing before the time, until the Lord come, who both will bring to light the hidden things of

darkness, and will make manifest the counsels of the hearts: and then shall every man have praise of God. [6] And these things, brethren, I have in a figure transferred to myself and to Apollos for your sakes; that ye might learn in us not to think of men above that which is written, that no one of you be puffed up for one against another. [See also 2 Corinthians 5:12.]

- **Galatians 6:12a** Many ... desire to make a fair shew in the flesh. [See also 1 Peter 4:2.]

5. Jesus' disciples fell prey to comparing amongst themselves on several occasions.

- **Matthew 18:1-4** At the same time came the disciples unto Jesus, saying, Who is the <u>greatest</u> in the Kingdom of Heaven? [2] And Jesus called a little child unto Him, and set him in the midst of them, [3] And said, Verily I say unto you, Except ye be converted, and become as little children, ye shall not enter into the Kingdom of Heaven. [4] Whosoever therefore shall humble himself as this little child, the same is greatest in the Kingdom of Heaven.

- **Matthew 20:20,21,24-28** [Jesus used a similar situation to show His disciples how their comparing was based on <u>worldly</u>, carnal values:] Then came to Him the mother of Zebedee's children with her sons, worshipping Him, and desiring a certain thing of Him. [21] And He said unto her, What wilt thou? She saith unto Him, Grant that these my two sons may sit, the one on Thy right hand, and the other on the left, in Thy Kingdom. [24] And when the ten heard it, they were moved with indignation against the two brethren. [25] But Jesus called them unto Him, and said, Ye know that the princes of the Gentiles exercise dominion over them, and they that are great exercise authority upon them. [26] But it shall not be so among you: but whosoever will be great among you, let him be your minister; [27] And whosoever will be chief among you, let him be your servant: [28] Even as the Son of Man came not to be ministered unto, but to minister, and to give His life a ransom for many.

- **Luke 9:46-48** Then there arose a reasoning among them, which of them should be greatest. [47] And Jesus, perceiving the thought of their heart … [48] said unto them, … he that is least among you all, the same shall be great.

- **John 21:20-22** Then Peter, turning about, seeth the disciple whom Jesus loved following; which also leaned on His breast at supper. … [21] Peter seeing him saith to Jesus, Lord, and what shall this man do? [22] Jesus saith unto him, If I will that he tarry [remain here] till I come, what is that to thee? Follow thou Me.

6. The tendency to compare and be jealous seems to be part of human nature, but the Lord can help us overcome it.

[See Jealousy and Envy, #3, page 230.]

7. The best antidote for comparing is thankfulness for what we are and all that we have and trusting in the Lord's love and fairness.

- **1 Corinthians 12:4-7,11,12,14-18** [Remember, we have each been fashioned to fulfil a special role and all are equally important and necessary members of the body of Christ, His Church.] Now there are diversities of gifts, but the same Spirit. [5] And there are differences of administrations, but the same Lord. [6] And there are diversities of operations, but it is the same God which worketh all in all. [7] But the manifestation of the Spirit is given to every man to profit withal. … [11] But all these worketh that one and the selfsame Spirit, dividing to every man severally as He will. [12] For as the body is one, and hath many members, and all the members of that one body, being many, are one body: so also is Christ. … [14] For the body is not one member, but many. [15] If the foot shall say, Because I am not the hand, I am not of the body; is it therefore not of the body? [16] And if the ear shall say, Because I am not the eye, I am not of the body; is it therefore not of the body? [17] If the whole body were an eye, where were the hearing? If the whole were hearing, where were the smelling? [18] But now hath God set the members every one of them in the body, as it hath pleased Him.

- **1 Corinthians 15:9,10** [Let's learn to be thankful for how God made us, in spite of our faults. The example of Paul the Apostle:] For I am the least of the apostles, that am not meet to be called an apostle, because I persecuted the Church of God. [10] But by the grace of God I am what I am: and His grace which was bestowed upon me was not in vain; but I laboured more abundantly than they all: yet not I, but the grace of God which was with me.

- **Philippians 4:11,12** Not that I speak in respect of want: for I have learned, in whatsoever state I am, therewith to be content. [12] I know both how to be abased, and I know how to abound: every where and in all things I am instructed both to be full and to be hungry, both to abound and to suffer need.

- **1 Timothy 1:12** And I thank Christ Jesus our Lord, who hath enabled me, for that He counted me faithful, putting me into the ministry.

- **1 Timothy 6:6** But godliness with contentment is great gain. [See also verse 8.]

- **Hebrews 13:5** Let your conversation [conduct, behavior, way of life] be without covetousness; and be content with such things as ye have: for He hath said, I will never leave thee, nor forsake thee.

- **Revelation 5:9,10** [We've got a lot to be thankful for.] And they sung a new song, saying, Thou art worthy to take the book, and to open the seals thereof: for Thou wast slain, and hast redeemed us to God by Thy blood out of every kindred, and tongue, and people, and nation; [10] And hast made us unto our God kings and priests: and we shall reign on the earth.

8. Pleasing Jesus is all that really matters.

- **John 5:44** How can ye believe, which receive honour one of another, and seek not the honour that cometh from God only?

- **Romans 14:12** So then every one of us shall give account of himself to God.
- **1 Corinthians 4:5** Therefore judge nothing before the time, until the Lord come, who both will bring to light the hidden things of darkness, and will make manifest the counsels of the hearts: and then shall every man have praise of God.
- **2 Corinthians 10:17,18** But he that glorieth, let him glory in the Lord. [18] For not he that commendeth himself is approved, but whom the Lord commendeth.
- **Galatians 6:4** But let every man prove his own work, and then shall he have rejoicing in himself alone, and not in another.

9. If you must compare, compare yourself to Jesus.

- **Isaiah 53:2b-4,6b,7-10** He hath no form nor comeliness; and when we shall see Him, there is no beauty that we should desire Him. [3] He is despised and rejected of men; a man of sorrows, and acquainted with grief: and we hid as it were our faces from Him; He was despised, and we esteemed Him not. [4] Surely He hath borne our griefs, and carried our sorrows: yet we did esteem Him stricken, smitten of God, and afflicted. [6b] The Lord hath laid on Him the iniquity of us all. [7] He was oppressed, and He was afflicted, yet He opened not His mouth: He is brought as a lamb to the slaughter, and as a sheep before her shearers is dumb, so He openeth not His mouth. [8] He was taken from prison and from judgment: and who shall declare His generation? For He was cut off out of the land of the living: for the transgression of my people was He stricken. [9] And He made His grave with the wicked, and with the rich in His death; because He had done no violence, neither was any deceit in His mouth. [10] Yet it pleased the Lord to bruise Him; He hath put Him to grief: when thou shalt make His soul an offering for sin, He shall see His seed, He shall prolong His days, and the pleasure of the Lord shall prosper in His hand. [See Isaiah chapter 53: all.]

- **Hebrews 4:15** For we have not an High Priest which cannot be touched with the feeling of our infirmities; but was in all points tempted like as we are, yet without sin.
- **Hebrews 12:2-4** Looking unto Jesus the Author and Finisher of our faith; who for the joy that was set before Him endured the cross, despising the shame, and is set down at the right hand of the throne of God. ³ For <u>consider Him</u> that endured such contradiction of sinners against himself, lest ye be wearied and faint in your minds. ⁴ Ye have not yet resisted unto blood, striving against sin. [See also Hebrews 3:1.]
- **1 Peter 2:21,23** For even hereunto were ye called: because Christ also suffered for us, leaving us an example that we should follow His steps. ²³ Who, when He was reviled, reviled not again; when He suffered, He threatened not; but committed Himself to Him [God] that judgeth righteously.

COMPETITIVENESS

Definition: Behavior motivated by a desire to prove oneself superior in any given contest, endeavor or field.

1. Competitiveness is considered a virtue in the world, but <u>not</u> with the Lord!

- **Luke 22:24-26** And there was also a strife among them [Jesus' disciples], which of them should be accounted the greatest. [25] And He said unto them, The kings of the Gentiles exercise lordship over them; and they that exercise authority upon them are called benefactors. [26] But ye shall not be so: but he that is greatest among you, let him be as the younger; and he that is chief, as he that doth serve. [See also Matthew 20:26-28; Mark 9:34,35; Luke 9:46.]
- **Mark 9:33b-35** [Jesus] asked them, What was it that ye disputed among yourselves by the way? [34] But they held their peace: for by the way they had disputed among themselves, who should be the greatest. [35] And He sat down, and called the twelve, and saith unto them, If any man desire to be first, the same shall be last of all, and servant of all.
- **1 Corinthians 1:26-29** [The Lord doesn't go by worldly "strengths" or abilities.] [26] For ye see your calling, brethren, how that not many wise men after the flesh, not many mighty, not many noble, are called: [27] But God hath chosen the foolish things of the world to confound the wise; and God hath chosen the weak things of the world to confound the things which are mighty; [28] And base things of the world, and things which are despised, hath God chosen, yea, and things which are not, to bring to nought things that are: [29] That no flesh should glory in His presence.
- **1 Corinthians 3:3** For ye are yet carnal: for whereas there is among you envying, and strife, and divisions, are ye not carnal, and walk as men?

    [See also Matthew 20:20-28; Luke 9:46-48.]

2. Those who compete toward worldly goals are motivated by a false sense of values.

- **Jeremiah 9:23,24** Thus saith the Lord, Let not the wise man glory in his wisdom, neither let the mighty man glory in his might, let not the rich man glory in his riches: [24] But let him that glorieth glory in this, that he understandeth and knoweth Me, that I am the Lord which exercise lovingkindness, judgment, and righteousness, in the earth: for in these things I delight, saith the Lord.
- **1 Corinthians 9:25** And every man that striveth for the mastery [runs in a race] is temperate in all things. Now they do it to obtain a corruptible [temporal worldly] crown; but we an incorruptible.
- **1 Timothy 4:8** For bodily exercise [such as competitive sports] profiteth little: but godliness is profitable unto all things, having promise of the life that now is, and of that which is to come.

3. Carnal competitiveness is self-exaltation, born of pride; the Lord won't bless it.

- **2 Chronicles 26:16a** But when he was strong, his heart was lifted up to his destruction.
- **Obadiah 1:3** The pride of thine heart hath deceived thee ... that saith in his heart, Who shall bring me down to the ground?
- **Jeremiah 17:5** Thus saith the Lord; Cursed be the man that trusteth in man, and maketh flesh his arm, and whose heart departeth from the Lord.
- **Matthew 23:12** And whosoever shall exalt himself shall be abased; and he that shall humble himself shall be exalted.

4. Worldly competitiveness is not part of the loving, Christ-like nature.

- **1 Corinthians 13:4** [Love] suffereth long, and is kind; [love] envieth not; [love] vaunteth not itself [doesn't brag], is not puffed up.

- **Romans 12:10** Be kindly affectioned one to another with brotherly love; in honour preferring one another.
- **Romans 15:1,3a** We then that are strong ought to bear the infirmities of the weak, and not to please ourselves. [3a] For even Christ pleased not Himself.
- **Galatians 5:26** Let us not be desirous of vain glory, provoking one another, envying one another.
- **Philippians 2:3,4** Let nothing be done through strife or vainglory; but in lowliness of mind let each esteem other better than themselves. [4] Look not every man on his own things, but every man also on the things of others.

5. Competitiveness can be divisive and a tool of the Devil.

- **2 Corinthians 10:12** For we dare not make ourselves of the number [classify ourselves], or compare ourselves with some that commend themselves: but they measuring themselves by themselves, and comparing themselves among themselves, are not wise.
- **James 3:14-16** But if ye have bitter envying and strife in your hearts, glory not, and lie not against the truth. [15] This wisdom descendeth not from above, but is earthly, sensual, devilish. [16] For where envying and strife is, there is confusion and every evil work.

6. Godly ambition and/or competition, with the motive of doing our best for His glory, not our own, is commendable.

- **Proverbs 27:17** Iron sharpeneth iron; so a man sharpeneth the countenance of his friend.
- **Matthew 5:16** Let your light so shine before men, that they may see your good works, and glorify your Father which is in Heaven.
- **Romans 11:13,14** [Paul spoke often of his ministry to the Gentiles in order to provoke his fellow Jews to godly jealousy:] For I speak to you Gentiles, inasmuch as I am the apostle of the Gentiles, I

magnify mine office: [14] If by any means I may provoke to emulation them which are my flesh, and might save some of them.

- **1 Corinthians 9:24-27** [Paul encourages us to run the race to win a Heavenly crown for faithfulness in serving the Lord:] Know ye not that they which run in a race run all, but one receiveth the prize? So run, that ye may obtain. [25] And every man that striveth for the mastery is temperate in all things. Now they [the worldly] do it to obtain a corruptible crown; but we an incorruptible. [26] I therefore so run, not as uncertainly; so fight I, not as one that beateth the air: [27] But I keep under my body, and bring it into subjection: lest that by any means, when I have preached to others, I myself should be a castaway.

- **2 Timothy 2:5** [Anyone seeking to excel in the Lord's work needs to go about it the right way:] And if a man also strive for masteries, yet is he not crowned, except he strive lawfully.

- **2 Corinthians 9:2b** [Paul mentioned to the Achaians that he bragged about them to others because of their willingness to help the work, saying:] Your zeal hath provoked [stirred up] very many.

- **Hebrews 10:24** And let us consider one another to provoke [stir one another up] unto love and to good works.

7. Christians are to strive toward <u>spiritual</u> goals.

- **Philippians 1:27b** Stand fast in one spirit, with one mind <u>striving together</u> for the faith of the Gospel.

- **Philippians 2:14,16** Do all things without … disputings. … [16] Holding forth the Word of life; that I may rejoice in the day of Christ, that I have not run in vain, neither laboured in vain.

- **Philippians 3:14** I press toward the mark for the prize of the high calling of God in Christ Jesus. [See also Luke 16:16.]

- **2 Timothy 4:7,8** I have fought a good fight, I have finished my course, I have kept the faith: [8] Henceforth there is laid up for me a crown of righteousness, which the Lord, the Righteous Judge, shall give me at that day: and not to me only, but unto all them also that love His appearing.

- **Hebrews 12:1,2a** Wherefore seeing we also are compassed about with so great a cloud of witnesses, let us lay aside every weight, and the sin which doth so easily beset us, and let us run with patience the race that is set before us, [2a] Looking unto Jesus the Author and Finisher of our faith.
- **Revelation 3:21** To him that overcometh will I grant to sit with Me in My throne, even as I also overcame, and am set down with My Father in His throne. [See also Revelation 12:11.]

8. Our competition is primarily confined to the spiritual realm, contending with our opponents the Devil and the world, over whom we shall prevail.

- **Ephesians 6:12** For we wrestle not against flesh and blood, but against principalities, against powers, against the rulers of the darkness of this world, against spiritual wickedness in high places.
- **2 Corinthians 10:3,4** For though we walk in the flesh, we do not war after the flesh: [4] (For the weapons of our warfare are not carnal, but mighty through God to the pulling down of strong holds.)
- **1 Timothy 6:12** Fight the good fight of faith, lay hold on eternal life, whereunto thou art also called, and hast professed a good profession before many witnesses.
- **1 Peter 5:8,9a** Be sober, be vigilant; because your adversary the Devil, as a roaring lion, walketh about, seeking whom he may devour: [9a] Whom resist stedfast in the faith.
- **Romans 8:37** In all these things we are more than conquerors through Him that loved us.
- **1 John 5:4,5** For whatsoever is born of God overcometh the world: and this is the victory that overcometh the world, even our faith. [5] Who is he that overcometh the world, but he that believeth that Jesus is the Son of God?

CONDEMNATION AND REMORSE

Definitions: Condemnation is a pronouncement of guilt; a strong expression of disapproval; doom. Remorse is the keen pain or anguish resulting from a sense of guilt; painful memory of wrongdoing. In terms of Christian faith, condemnation and remorse often result from not accepting or believing that we have been forgiven for mistakes and sins, even though confessed.

1. The difference between conviction and condemnation: the Devil tries to make us feel condemned so that we will become discouraged and give up; the Lord convicts us that we might repent, change and go on for Him.

- **Genesis 4:6,7** [In the story of Cain and Abel, Cain became extremely angry with envy, but the Lord cautioned him, yet encouraged him that if he'd repent, God would accept him, but that sin was trying to rule over him:] And the Lord said unto Cain, Why art thou wroth? And why is thy countenance fallen? [7] If thou doest well, shalt thou not be accepted? And if thou doest not well, sin lieth at the door. And unto thee shall be his desire, and thou shalt rule over him. [Sin desires to overcome you, but you can overcome it.]

- **Psalm 37:32,33** The wicked watcheth the righteous, and seeketh to slay him. [33] The Lord will <u>not</u> leave him in his hand, nor <u>condemn</u> him when he is judged.

- **Psalm 109:31** For [God] shall stand at the right hand of the poor, to save him from those that condemn his soul.

- **Psalm 130:3,4** If Thou, Lord, shouldest mark iniquities, O Lord, who shall stand? [4] But there is forgiveness with Thee, that Thou mayest be feared.

- **Ezekiel 18:21-23** But if the wicked will turn from all his sins that he hath committed, and keep all My statutes, and do that which is lawful and right, he shall surely live, he shall not die. [22] All his transgressions that he hath committed, they shall not be mentioned unto him: in his righteousness that he hath done he shall live.

[23] Have I any pleasure at all that the wicked should die? Saith the Lord God: and not that he should return from his ways, and live? [See also Ezekiel 33:10,11.]

- **1 Corinthians 11:31,32** For if we would judge ourselves, we should not be judged. [32] But when we are judged, we are chastened of the Lord, that we should <u>not</u> be condemned with the world.
- **2 Corinthians 7:10** [Being convicted of sin leads to repentance. But self-pity, remorse, and wounded pride discourage and weaken you:] godly sorrow worketh repentance to salvation not to be repented of [regretted]: but the sorrow of the world worketh death.
- **Revelation 12:10** And I heard a loud voice saying in Heaven, Now is come salvation, and strength, and the Kingdom of our God, and the power of His Christ: for the <u>accuser of our brethren</u> [the Devil] is cast down, which accused them before our God day and night.

2. To overcome condemnation and remorse, first begin with a clear conscience by confessing your sins.

- **2 Samuel 24:10** And David's heart smote him after that he had numbered the people [which God had told him not to do]. And David said unto the Lord, I have sinned greatly in that I have done: and now, I beseech Thee, O Lord, take away the iniquity of Thy servant; for I have done very foolishly.
- **Job 34:31,32** Surely it is meet to be said unto God, I have borne chastisement, I will not offend any more: [32] That which I see not teach Thou me: if I have done iniquity, I will do no more.
- **Psalm 32:3-5** When I kept silence, my bones waxed old through my roaring all the day long. [4] For day and night Thy hand was heavy upon me: my moisture is turned into the drought of summer. Selah. [5] I acknowledged my sin unto Thee, and mine iniquity have I not hid. I said, I will confess my transgressions unto the Lord; and Thou forgavest the iniquity of my sin. Selah.

- **Psalm 34:18** The Lord is nigh unto them that are of a broken heart; and saveth such as be of a contrite [humbly sorry, penitent] spirit. [See also Pslam 51:17.]

- **Psalm 38:4,6,9,18** For mine iniquities are gone over mine head: as an heavy burden they are too heavy for me. [6] I am troubled; I am bowed down greatly; I go mourning all the day long. [9] Lord, all my desire is before Thee; and my groaning is not hid from Thee. [18] For I will declare mine iniquity; I will be sorry for my sin.

- **Psalm 51:3,10** For I acknowledge my transgressions: and my sin is ever before me. [10] Create in me a clean heart, O God; and renew a right spirit within me.

- **Psalm 73:21-23** Thus my heart was grieved, and I was pricked in my reins [conscience stricken]. [22] So foolish was I, and ignorant: I was as a beast before Thee. [23] Nevertheless I am continually with Thee: Thou hast holden me by my right hand.

- **Proverbs 28:13** He that covereth his sins shall not prosper: but whoso confesseth and forsaketh them shall have mercy.

- **Isaiah 55:6,7** Seek ye the Lord while He may be found, call ye upon Him while He is near: [7] Let the wicked forsake his way, and the unrighteous man his thoughts: and let him return unto the Lord, and He will have mercy upon him; and to our God, for He will abundantly pardon.

- **Jeremiah 3:12b,13a** I am merciful, saith the Lord, and I will not keep anger for ever. [13] Only acknowledge thine iniquity, that thou hast transgressed against the Lord thy God.

- **Jeremiah 4:14** O Jerusalem, wash thine heart from wickedness, that thou mayest be saved. How long shall thy vain thoughts lodge within thee? [See also Jeremiah 18:8.]

- **2 Corinthians 7:11** For behold this selfsame thing, that ye sorrowed after a godly sort, what carefulness it wrought in you, yea, what clearing of yourselves, yea, what indignation, yea, what fear, yea, what vehement desire, yea, what zeal, yea, what revenge! In all things ye have approved yourselves to be clear in this matter. [See verses 8-11; 2 Chronicles 7:14.]

3. Believe and accept that the blood of Jesus cleanses us from every sin, by faith.

• **John 3:17,18a** For God sent not His Son into the world to condemn the world; but that the world through Him might be saved. [18a] He that believeth on Him is not condemned.

• **John 5:24** Verily, verily, I say unto you, He that heareth My Word, and believeth on Him that sent Me, hath everlasting life, and shall not come into condemnation; but is passed from death unto life.

• **1 John 1:7b,9** The blood of Jesus Christ His Son cleanseth us from all sin. [9] If we confess our sins, He is faithful and just to forgive us our sins, and to cleanse us from all unrighteousness.

4. Once we've confessed and repented, God doesn't remember our sins; neither should we!

• **Psalm 103:9-13** He will not always chide: neither will He keep His anger for ever. [10] He hath not dealt with us after our sins; nor rewarded us according to our iniquities. [11] For as the Heaven is high above the earth, so great is His mercy toward them that fear Him. [12] As far as the east is from the west, so far hath He removed our transgressions from us. [13] Like as a father pitieth his children, so the Lord pitieth them that fear Him.

Isaiah 44:22 I have blotted out, as a thick cloud, thy transgressions, and, as a cloud, thy sins: return unto Me; for I have redeemed thee.

• **Jeremiah 31:34** I will forgive their iniquity, and I will remember their sin no more. [See also Hebrews 8:12; 10:17.]

• **Romans 8:1** There is therefore now no condemnation to them which are in Christ Jesus, who walk not after the flesh, but after the Spirit. [See also Romans 5:1.]

• **1 John 3:19-21** And hereby we know that we are of the truth, and shall assure our hearts before Him. [20] For if our heart condemn us, God is greater than our heart, and knoweth all things. [21] Beloved, if our heart condemn us not, then have we confidence toward God.

5. We must not continue to condemn ourselves, even if we feel that others may have not yet "forgiven and forgotten."

- **Isaiah 50:9a** Behold, the Lord God will help me; who is he that shall condemn me?
- **Romans 8:33,34** Who shall lay any thing to the charge of God's elect? It is God that justifieth. [34] Who is he that condemneth? It is Christ that died, yea rather, that is risen again, who is even at the right hand of God, who also maketh intercession for us.
- **Romans 14:4** Who art thou that judgest another man's servant? To his own master he standeth or falleth. Yea, he shall be holden up: for God is able to make him stand.

6. Remorse and condemnation bear no good fruit! We should acknowledge our sin, accept God's forgiveness, and get on with living for His honour and glory.

- **Psalm 51:12,13** Restore unto me the joy of Thy salvation; and uphold me with Thy free spirit. [13] Then will I teach transgressors Thy ways; and sinners shall be converted unto Thee.
- **John 8:11b** [Jesus said to the adulteress:] Neither do I condemn thee: go, and sin no more.
- **2 Corinthians 2:7b,8** [We should likewise forgive others, so that they don't fall into condemnation and remorse.] Ye ought rather to forgive him, and comfort him, lest perhaps such a one should be swallowed up with overmuch sorrow. Wherefore I beseech you that ye would confirm your love toward him.
- **Philippians 3:13b,14** Forgetting those things which are behind, and reaching forth unto those things which are before, [14] I press toward the mark for the prize of the high calling of God in Christ Jesus.
- **Hebrews 12:11-13** Now no chastening for the present seemeth to be joyous, but grievous; nevertheless afterward it yieldeth the peaceable fruit of righteousness unto them which are exercised thereby. [12] Wherefore lift up the hands which hang down, and the

feeble knees; [13] And make straight paths for your feet, lest that which is lame be turned out of the way; but let it rather be healed.

CONSCIENCE, KEEPING A GOOD

Definition: Conscience is the knowledge of right and wrong, and a feeling that one should do what is right.

1. Conscience is the guiding voice of God in man.

- **Proverbs 20:27** The spirit of man is the candle of the Lord, searching all the inward parts of the belly. [See also Job 32:8.]
- **Isaiah 30:21** And thine ears shall hear a word behind thee, saying, This is the way, walk ye in it, when ye turn to the right hand, and when ye turn to the left.
- **John 1:9** [Jesus' Spirit touches every man:] That was the true Light, which <u>lighteth every man</u> that cometh into the world. [See also John 14:6.]
- **Romans 2:14,15** [Even those who don't personally know Jesus have a godly conscience, which the Lord has given to every man.] For when the Gentiles, which have not the law, do by nature the things contained in the law, these, having not the law, are a law unto themselves: ¹⁵ Which shew the work of the law written in their hearts, their conscience also bearing witness, and their thoughts the mean while accusing or else excusing one another.

2. We must choose whether or not to obey our conscience.

- **Job 27:6b** My heart shall not reproach me so long as I live.
- **Acts 24:16** And herein do I exercise myself, to have always a conscience void of offence toward God, and toward men.
- **2 Corinthians 1:12** For our rejoicing is this, the testimony of our conscience, that in simplicity and godly sincerity, not with fleshly wisdom, but by the grace of God, we have had our conversation in the world, and more abundantly to you-ward.
- **1 Timothy 3:9** Holding the mystery of the faith in a pure conscience.

3. A guilty conscience convicts us of sin.

- **Job 15:20a,21a,24a** The wicked man travaileth with pain all his days, [21a] A dreadful sound is in his ears: [24a] Trouble and anguish shall make him afraid; they shall prevail against him.
- **Psalm 40:12b** [King David prayed:] Mine iniquities have taken hold upon me, so that I am not able to look up; they are more than the hairs of mine head: therefore my heart faileth me.
- **Psalm 73:21** Thus my heart was grieved, and I was pricked in my reins.
- **Isaiah 59:12** For our transgressions are multiplied before Thee, and our sins testify against us: for our transgressions are with us; and as for our iniquities, we know them.
- **Romans 1:18,19** [God convicts all men about wrongdoing.] For the wrath of God is revealed from Heaven against all ungodliness and unrighteousness of men, who hold the truth in unrighteousness; [19] Because that which may be known of God is manifest in them; for God hath shewed it unto them.

4. Truth resisted loses its power over the mind. If we refuse to heed our conscience, we eventually become dull to it.

- **Jeremiah 6:15a** Were they ashamed when they had committed abomination? Nay, they were not at all ashamed, neither could they blush.
- **Matthew 6:22,23** The light of the body is the eye: if therefore thine eye be single, thy whole body shall be full of light. [23] But if thine eye be evil, thy whole body shall be full of darkness. If therefore the light that is in thee be darkness, how great is that darkness! [See also Luke 11:34,35.]
- **Romans 1:21** Because that, when they knew God, they glorified Him not as God, neither were thankful; but became vain in their imaginations, and their foolish heart was darkened.

- **Ephesians 4:17-19** This I say therefore, and testify in the Lord, that ye henceforth walk not as other Gentiles walk, in the vanity of their mind, [18] Having the understanding darkened, being alienated from the life of God through the ignorance that is in them, because of the blindness of their heart: [19] Who being past feeling have given themselves over unto lasciviousness, to work all uncleanness with greediness.

- **2 Thessalonians 2:10-12** And with all deceivableness of unrighteousness in them that perish; because they received not the love of the truth, that they might be saved. [11] And for this cause God shall send them strong delusion, that they should believe a lie: [12] That they all might be damned who believed not the truth, but had pleasure in unrighteousness.

- **1 Timothy 4:2** Speaking lies in hypocrisy; having their conscience seared with a hot iron.

- **Titus 1:15** Unto the pure all things are pure: but unto them that are defiled and unbelieving is nothing pure; but even their mind and conscience is defiled.

- **2 Thessalonians 2:7** [In the Last Days, the convicting Holy Spirit will no longer restrain man's lawlessness and rebellion, and all Hell will break loose on earth:] For the mystery of iniquity [the spirit of the Antichrist] doth already work: only He [the Holy Spirit] who now letteth will let, until He be taken out of the way.

5. Biblical examples of guilty consciences:

- **Genesis 3:6b-11** [After partaking of the forbidden fruit, Adam and Eve had a guilty conscience:] She took of the fruit thereof, and did eat, and gave also unto her husband with her; and he did eat. [7] And the eyes of them both were opened, and they knew that they were naked; and they sewed fig leaves together, and made themselves aprons. [8] And they heard the voice of the Lord God walking in the garden in the cool of the day: and Adam and his wife hid themselves from the presence of the Lord God amongst the trees of the garden. [9] And the Lord God called unto Adam, and said unto him, Where art thou? [10] And he said, I heard Thy voice in the garden, and I was afraid, because I was naked; and I hid myself. [11] And He said, Who told thee that thou wast naked? Hast thou eaten of the tree, whereof I commanded thee that thou shouldest not eat?

- **Genesis 42:21** [Joseph's brothers:] And they said one to another, We are verily guilty concerning our brother, in that we saw the anguish of his soul, when he besought us, and we would not hear; therefore is this distress come upon us.

- **Exodus 9:27** [Pharaoh of Egypt:] And Pharaoh sent, and called for Moses and Aaron, and said unto them, I have sinned this time: the Lord is righteous, and I and my people are wicked.

- **1 Samuel 24:5-6** [King David was convicted for secretly cutting King Saul's robe:] And it came to pass afterward, that David's heart smote him, because he had cut off Saul's skirt. [6] And he said unto his men, The Lord forbid that I should do this thing unto my master, the Lord's anointed, to stretch forth mine hand against him, seeing he is the anointed of the Lord.

- **2 Samuel 24:10** [King David:] And David's heart smote him after that he had numbered the people. And David said unto the Lord, I have sinned greatly in that I have done: and now, I beseech Thee, O Lord, take away the iniquity of Thy servant; for I have done very foolishly.

- **Ezra 9:6** [Ezra, the priest and scribe said:] O my God, I am ashamed and blush to lift up my face to Thee, my God: for our iniquities are increased over our head, and our trespass is grown up unto the Heavens.

- **Daniel 5:6** [King Belshazzar of Babylon:] Then the king's countenance was changed, and his thoughts troubled him [when he saw God's judgement message, the "handwriting on the wall"], so that the joints of his loins were loosed, and his knees smote one against another.

- **Matthew 26:75** [Peter the Apostle:] And Peter remembered the word of Jesus, which said unto him, Before the cock crow, thou shalt deny Me thrice. And he went out, and wept bitterly. [See also Mark 14:72 and Luke 22:61,62.]

- **Matthew 27:3-5** [Judas Iscariot:] Then Judas, which had betrayed Him, when he saw that He was condemned, repented himself, and brought again the thirty pieces of silver to the chief priests and elders, ⁴ Saying, I have sinned in that I have betrayed the innocent blood. And they said, What is that to us? See thou to that. ⁵ And he cast down the pieces of silver in the temple, and departed, and went and hanged himself.

- **John 8:9** [The scribes and Pharisees, who had accused the harlot and were about to stone her to death:] And they which heard it [Jesus' defense of the woman], being convicted by their own conscience, went out one by one, beginning at the eldest, even unto the last: and Jesus was left alone, and the woman standing in the midst.

- **Acts 2:37** [The crowd to whom Peter witnessed about Jesus:] Now when they heard this, they were pricked in their heart, and said unto Peter and to the rest of the apostles, Men and brethren, what shall we do?

- **Acts 9:5** [Saul of Tarsus, who had persecuted the Christians, and who later became Paul, the Apostle:] And he said, Who art Thou, Lord? And the Lord said, I am Jesus whom thou persecutest: it is hard for thee to kick against the pricks [of his convicted conscience]. (See also Acts 26:14.)

6. Salvation through grace clears the conscience of condemnation over past sins.

- **Romans 8:1** There is therefore now no condemnation to them which are in Christ Jesus, who walk not after the flesh, but after the Spirit.

- **Hebrews 9:14** How much more shall the blood of Christ, who through the eternal Spirit offered Himself without spot to God, purge your conscience from dead works to serve the living God?
- **Hebrews 10:22** Let us draw near with a true heart in full assurance of faith, having our hearts sprinkled from an evil conscience, and our bodies washed with pure water.
- **1 John 3:19-21** And hereby we know that we are of the truth, and shall assure our hearts before Him. [20] For if our heart condemn us, God is greater than our heart, and knoweth all things. [21] Beloved, if our heart condemn us not, then have we confidence toward God.

    [See also Condemnation and Remorse, #3 and #4, page 65.]

7. To go against our conscience is a violation of our faith, which is a sin.

- **Romans 14:22a,23b** Hast thou faith? Have it to thyself before God. [23b] For whatsoever is not of faith is sin.
- **Romans 7:22,23** For I delight in the law of God after the inward man: [23] But I see another law in my members, warring against the law of my mind, and bringing me into captivity to the law of sin which is in my members.
- **1 Corinthians 8:7b** [Paul spoke of those coming from pagan religions who had eaten food sacrificed to idols, during their worship of those idols, who after becoming Christians were at times tempted to continue in such practices.] For some with conscience of the idol unto this hour eat it as a thing offered unto an idol; and their conscience being weak is defiled.
- **1 Timothy 1:19** Holding [onto] faith, and a good conscience; which some having put away concerning faith have made shipwreck.

8. A clear conscience towards God gives us conviction, enabling us to rise above circumstances and the opinions of man.

- **Proverbs 28:1** The wicked flee when no man pursueth: but the righteous are bold as a lion.
- **Acts 4:19,20** [Peter and John were faithful to obey their conscience and convictions.] But Peter and John answered and said unto them, Whether it be right in the sight of God to hearken unto you more than unto God, judge ye. [20] For we cannot but speak the things which we have seen and heard. [See also Acts 5:29.]
- **Acts 23:1** And Paul, earnestly beholding the council, said, Men and brethren, I have lived in all good conscience before God until this day.
- **Romans 9:1** I say the truth in Christ, I lie not, my conscience also bearing me witness in the Holy Ghost.
- **Romans 14:22b** Happy is he that condemneth not himself in that thing which he alloweth.
- **1 Timothy 1:5** Now the end of the commandment is charity out of a pure heart, and of a good conscience, and of faith unfeigned [sincere].
- **Hebrews 13:18** Pray for us: for we trust we have a good conscience, in all things willing to live honestly.

9. However, even if our conscience permits us something, we should nevertheless be mindful of others' faith.

- **Romans 14:1-7** Him that is weak in the faith receive ye, but not to doubtful disputations. [2] For one believeth that he may eat all things: another, who is weak, eateth herbs. [3] Let not him that eateth despise him that eateth not; and let not him which eateth not judge him that eateth: for God hath received him. [4] Who art thou that judgest another man's servant? To his own master he standeth or falleth. Yea, he shall be holden up: for God is able to make him stand. [5] One man esteemeth one day above another: another esteemeth every day alike. Let every man be fully persuaded in his own mind. [6] He that regardeth the day, regardeth it unto the Lord; and he that regardeth not the day, to the Lord he doth not regard it. He that eateth, eateth to the Lord, for he giveth God thanks; and he that eateth not, to the Lord he eateth not, and giveth God thanks. [7] For none of us liveth to himself, and no man dieth to himself.

• **Romans 14:14-20** I know, and am persuaded by the Lord Jesus, that there is nothing unclean of itself: but to him that esteemeth any thing to be unclean, to him it is unclean. [15] But if thy brother be grieved with thy meat, now walkest thou not charitably. Destroy not him with thy meat, for whom Christ died. [16] Let not then your good be evil spoken of: [17] For the Kingdom of God is not meat and drink; but righteousness, and peace, and joy in the Holy Ghost. [18] For he that in these things serveth Christ is acceptable to God, and approved of men. [19] Let us therefore follow after the things which make for peace, and things wherewith one may edify another. [20] For meat destroy not the work of God. All things indeed are pure; but it is evil for that man who eateth with offence.

• **1 Corinthians 8:9-13** But take heed lest by any means this liberty of yours become a stumblingblock to them that are weak. [10] For if any man see thee which hast knowledge sit at meat in the idol's temple, shall not the conscience of him which is weak be emboldened to eat those things which are offered to idols; [11] And through thy knowledge shall the weak brother perish, for whom Christ died? [12] But when ye sin so against the brethren, and wound their weak conscience, ye sin against Christ. [13] Wherefore, if meat make my brother to offend, I will eat no flesh while the world standeth, lest I make my brother to offend. [See also 1 Corinthians 10:28-32.]

10. Keeping a good conscience is also an important part of our Christian example.

• **Romans 13:5** [We need to obey the laws of the land, not just to avoid punishment, but to obey what we know is right.] Wherefore ye must needs be subject, not only for wrath, but also for conscience sake.

- **2 Corinthians 4:2** But have renounced the hidden things of dishonesty, not walking in craftiness, nor handling the Word of God deceitfully; but by manifestation of the truth commending ourselves to every man's conscience in the sight of God.
- **Hebrews 13:18** Pray for us: for we trust we have a good conscience, in all things willing to live honestly.
- **1 Peter 3:16** Having a good conscience; that, whereas they speak evil of you, as of evildoers, they may be ashamed that falsely accuse your good conversation in Christ.

COVETOUSNESS

Definitions: Being excessively desirous of the possessions of another; an extreme desire to acquire or possess. Possessiveness, which is quite similar, is an attitude toward ownership or possession which is overprotective, selfish or hoarding. The word "covetousness" is used in this study.

1. Covetousness is directly contrary to Jesus' law of love, which is based on sharing and unselfishness.

- **Matthew 10:8b** Freely ye have received, freely give.
- **Acts 20:33-35** I have coveted no man's silver, or gold, or apparel. [34] Yea, ye yourselves know, that these hands have ministered unto my necessities, and to them that were with me. [35] I have shewed you all things, how that so labouring ye ought to support the weak, and to remember the words of the Lord Jesus, how He said, It is <u>more blessed to give</u> than to receive.
- **Romans 13:8,9** Owe no man any thing, but to love one another: for he that loveth another hath fulfilled the law. [9] For this … Thou shalt not steal, … Thou shalt not covet; and if there be any other commandment, it is briefly comprehended [summed up] in this saying, namely, Thou shalt love thy neighbour as thyself.
- **1 Corinthians 10:24,33** Let no man seek his own, but every man another's wealth. [33] Even as I please all men in all things, not seeking mine own profit, but the profit of many, that they may be saved.
- **1 Corinthians 13:5** [Love] seeketh not her own.
- **2 Corinthians 8:9** For ye know the grace of our Lord Jesus Christ, that, though He was rich, yet for your sakes He became poor, that ye through His poverty might be rich.
- **2 Corinthians 9:7** Every man according as he purposeth in his heart, so let him give; not grudgingly, or of necessity: for God loveth a cheerful giver.

- **1 John 3:16** Hereby perceive we the love of God, because He laid down His life for us: and we ought to lay down our lives for the brethren.

2. Being thankful for what God gives us helps us avoid covetousness.

- **1 Chronicles 29:12** Both riches and honour come of Thee, and Thou reignest over all; and in Thine hand is power and might; and in Thine hand it is to make great, and to give strength unto all. [See also Deuteronomy 8:18.]
- **Psalm 128:1,2** Blessed is every one that feareth the Lord; that walketh in His ways. [2] For thou shalt eat the labour of thine hands: happy shalt thou be, and it shall be well with thee.
- **Proverbs 10:22** The blessing of the Lord, it maketh rich, and He addeth no sorrow with it.
- **Proverbs 22:4** By humility and the fear of the Lord are riches, and honour, and life.
- **Ecclesiastes 5:19** Every man also to whom God hath given riches and wealth, and hath given him power to eat thereof, and to take his portion, and to rejoice in his labour; this is the gift of God. [See also Ecclesiastes 3:13.]
- **1 Timothy 6:17** Charge them that are rich in this world, that they be not highminded, nor trust in uncertain riches, but in the living God, who giveth us richly all things to enjoy.
- **James 1:17** Every good gift and every perfect gift is from above, and cometh down from the Father of lights, with whom is no variableness, neither shadow of turning.

3. Covetousness is a lack of faith in God's loving provision of our physical needs.

- **Matthew 6:25-33** [Jesus said:] Take no thought for your life, what ye shall eat, or what ye shall drink; nor yet for your body, what ye shall put on. Is not the life more than meat, and the body than raiment? [26] Behold the fowls of the air: for they sow not, neither do they reap, nor gather into barns; yet your Heavenly Father feedeth them. Are ye not much better than they? [27] Which of you by taking thought can add one cubit unto his stature? [28] And why take ye thought for raiment? Consider the lilies of the field, how they grow; they toil not, neither do they spin: [29] And yet I say unto you, That even Solomon in all his glory was not arrayed like one of these. [30] Wherefore, if God so clothe the grass of the field, which to day is, and to morrow is cast into the oven, shall He not much more clothe you, O ye of little faith? [31] Therefore take no thought, saying, What shall we eat? Or, What shall we drink? Or, Wherewithal shall we be clothed? [32] (For after all these things do the Gentiles seek:) for your Heavenly Father knoweth that ye have need of all these things. [33] But seek ye first the Kingdom of God, and His righteousness; and all these things shall be added unto you.

- **Philippians 4:19** But my God shall supply all your need according to His riches in glory by Christ Jesus. [See also Psalm 84:11b.]
- **Hebrews 13:5** Let your conversation be without covetousness; and be content with such things as ye have: for He hath said, I will never leave thee, nor forsake thee.

4. God forbade covetousness in one of the Ten Commandments.

- **Exodus 20:17** Thou shalt not covet thy neighbour's house, thou shalt not covet thy neighbour's wife, nor his manservant, nor his maidservant, nor his ox, nor his ass, nor any thing that is thy neighbour's.

    [See also Romans 7:7.]

5. Covetousness hinders our relationship with the Lord and our spiritual growth.

- **Matthew 13:22** He also that received seed among the thorns is he that heareth the Word; and the care of this world, and the deceitfulness of riches, choke the Word, and he becometh unfruitful.
- **Mark 8:36,37** For what shall it profit a man, if he shall gain the whole world, and lose his own soul? [37] Or what shall a man give in exchange for his soul?
- **Luke 12:15** And He said unto them, Take heed, and beware of covetousness: for a man's life consisteth not in the abundance of the things which he possesseth.
- **1 Timothy 6:6-10** But godliness with contentment is great gain. [7] For we brought nothing into this world, and it is certain we can carry nothing out. [8] And having food and raiment let us be therewith content. [9] But they that will be rich fall into temptation and a snare, and into many foolish and hurtful lusts, which drown men in destruction and perdition. [10] For the love of money is the root of all evil: which while some coveted after, they have erred from the faith, and pierced themselves through with many sorrows.
- **2 Timothy 2:4** No man that warreth entangleth himself with the affairs of this life; that he may please Him who hath chosen him to be a soldier.
- **1 John 2:15-17** Love not the world, neither the things that are in the world. If any man love the world, the love of the Father is not in him. [16] For all that is in the world, the lust of the flesh, and the lust of the eyes, and the pride of life, is not of the Father, but is of the world. [17] And the world passeth away, and the lust thereof: but he that doeth the will of God abideth for ever.
- **1 John 3:17** But whoso hath this world's good, and seeth his brother have need, and shutteth up his bowels of compassion from him, how dwelleth the love of God in him?

6. Examples of how covetousness opens the door to other sins, as well:

- **Psalm 10:3** [Pride:] For the <u>wicked</u> boasteth of his heart's desire, and blesseth the covetous, whom the Lord <u>abhorreth</u>.
- **Isaiah 56:11b** [Selfishness and self-centeredness:] They all look to their own way, every one for his gain, from his quarter.
- **Ezekiel 33:31** [Compromise and disobedience:] And they come unto thee [the prophet] as the people cometh, and they sit before thee as My people, and they hear thy words, but they will not do them: for with their mouth they shew much love, but their heart goeth after their covetousness.
- **Micah 2:2** [Stealing and violence:] And they covet fields, and take them by <u>violence</u>; and houses, and take them away: so they oppress a man and his house, even a man and his heritage.
- **Micah 3:11** [Hypocrisy and deceit:] The heads thereof judge for reward, and the priests thereof teach for hire, and the prophets thereof divine for money: yet will they lean upon the Lord, and say, Is not the Lord among us? None evil can come upon us.

7. Here are a few examples of how God dealt very sternly with the sin of covetousness:

- **Joshua 7:20-21,24-26** [Covetousness on the part of one man, Achan, was responsible for Israel losing a vital battle. Achan and his family paid for this with their lives:] And Achan answered Joshua, and said, Indeed I have sinned against the Lord God of Israel, and thus and thus have I done: [21] When I saw among the spoils a goodly Babylonish garment, and two hundred shekels of silver, and a wedge of gold of fifty shekels weight, then I coveted them, and took them; and, behold, they are hid in the earth in the midst of my tent, and the silver under it. ... [24] And Joshua, and all Israel with him, took Achan the son of Zerah, and the silver, and the garment, and the wedge of gold, and his sons, and his daughters, and his oxen,

and his asses, and his sheep, and his tent, and all that he had: and
they brought them unto the valley of Achor. [25] And Joshua said,
Why hast thou troubled us? The Lord shall trouble thee this day.
And all Israel stoned him with stones, and burned them with fire,
after they had stoned them with stones. [26] And they raised over him
a great heap of stones unto this day. So the Lord turned from the
fierceness of His anger [against Israel]. [See Joshua 7:10-26.]

- **1 Samuel 15:9,26** [Covetousness had a part in King Saul's
disobedience which eventually lost him his kingdom:] But Saul and
the people spared [wicked King] Agag, and the best of the sheep,
and of the oxen, and of the fatlings, and the lambs, and all that was
good, and would not utterly destroy them [which the Lord had
explicitly commanded them to do]: but every thing that was vile
and refuse, that they destroyed utterly. [26] And Samuel said unto
Saul, … for thou hast rejected the Word of the Lord, and the Lord
hath rejected thee from being king over Israel. [See verses 1-28.]

- **2 Kings 5:20,26,27** [As a result of his covetousness, Gehazi was
smitten with leprosy:] But Gehazi, the servant of Elisha the man of
God, said, Behold, my master hath spared Naaman this Syrian, in
not receiving at his hands that which he brought: but, as the Lord
liveth, I will run after him, and take somewhat of him. … [26] And
[Elisha] said unto him, … Is it a time to receive money, and to
receive garments, and oliveyards, and vineyards, and sheep, and
oxen, and menservants, and maidservants? [27] The leprosy therefore
of Naaman shall cleave unto thee, and unto thy seed for ever. And
he went out from his presence a leper as white as snow. [See verses
15-27.]

8. Overcome covetousness by making a conscious effort to help others with their needs.

- **Psalm 37:26** [A godly man] is ever merciful, and lendeth; and his
seed is blessed.

- **Psalm 112:5a,9** A good man sheweth favour, and lendeth. ... [9] He hath dispersed, he hath given to the poor; his righteousness endureth for ever; his horn shall be exalted with honour.
- **Proverbs 3:27,28** Withhold not good from them to whom it is due, when it is in the power of thine hand to do it. [28] Say not to thy neighbour, Go, and come again, and to morrow I will give; when thou hast it by thee.
- **Proverbs 11:24,25** There is that scattereth, and yet increaseth; and there is that withholdeth more than is meet, but it tendeth to poverty. [25] The liberal soul shall be made fat: and he that watereth shall be watered also himself.
- **Proverbs 13:7** There is that maketh himself rich, yet hath nothing: there is that maketh himself poor, yet hath great riches.
- **Proverbs 19:17** He that hath pity upon the poor lendeth unto the Lord; and that which he hath given will He pay him again.
- **Matthew 5:42** Give to him that asketh thee, and from him that would borrow of thee turn not thou away.
- **Luke 6:38** Give, and it shall be given unto you; good measure, pressed down, and shaken together, and running over, shall men give into your bosom. For with the same measure that ye mete withal it shall be measured to you again.
- **1 Corinthians 10:33** Even as I please all men in all things, not seeking mine own profit, but the profit of many, that they may be saved.
- **Acts 20:35** I have shewed you all things, how that so labouring ye ought to support the weak, and to remember the words of the Lord Jesus, how He said, It is more blessed to give than to receive.

9. Overcome covetousness by keeping your heart and mind fixed on spiritual values.

- **Psalm 119:14,36** [Covet the treasures of God's Word:] I have rejoiced in the way of Thy testimonies, as much as in all riches. [36] Incline my heart unto Thy testimonies, and not to covetousness.

- **Psalm 119:162** I rejoice at Thy Word, as one that findeth great spoil.
- **Proverbs 22:1** A good name is rather to be chosen than great riches, and loving favour rather than silver and gold.
- **Jeremiah 9:23,24** [Strive for a closer relationship with the Lord:] Thus saith the Lord, Let not the wise man glory in his wisdom, neither let the mighty man glory in his might, let not the rich man glory in his riches: [24] But let him that glorieth glory in this, that he understandeth and knoweth Me, that I am the Lord which exercise lovingkindness, judgment, and righteousness, in the earth: for in these things I delight, saith the Lord.
- **1 Corinthians 12:31** But covet earnestly the best [spiritual] gifts: and yet shew I unto you a more excellent way. [After this verse Paul continues with 1 Corinthians 13, the "Love Chapter"; see also 1Corinthians 14:39.]
- **Colossians 3:2** [Ask the Lord to help you to be heavenly minded:] Set your affection on things above, not on things on the earth.

10. Leaders cannot afford to be covetous. Covetousness and materialism have been the downfall of many religious organizations.

- **Exodus 18:21** Moreover thou shalt provide out of all the people able men, such as fear God, men of truth, hating covetousness; and place such over them, to be rulers of thousands, and rulers of hundreds, rulers of fifties, and rulers of tens:
- **Proverbs 28:16** The prince that wanteth [lacks] understanding is also a great oppressor: but he that hateth covetousness shall prolong his days.
- **Isaiah 1:23-26** Thy princes are rebellious, and companions of thieves: every one loveth gifts, and followeth after rewards: they judge not the fatherless, neither doth the cause of the widow come unto them. … [25] And I will turn My hand upon thee, and purely purge away thy dross, and take away all thy tin: [26] And I will restore

thy judges as at the first, and thy counsellors as at the beginning: afterward thou shalt be called, The city of righteousness, the faithful city.

- **Isaiah 56:11,12** Yea, they are greedy dogs which can never have enough, and they are shepherds that cannot understand: they all look to their own way, every one for his gain, from his quarter. [12] Come ye, say they, I will fetch wine, and we will fill ourselves with strong drink; and to morrow shall be as this day, and much more abundant.

- **Jeremiah 6:13,15** For from the least of them even unto the greatest of them every one is given to covetousness; and from the prophet even unto the priest every one dealeth falsely. [15] Were they ashamed when they had committed abomination? Nay, they were not at all ashamed, neither could they blush: therefore they shall fall among them that fall: at the time that I visit them they shall be cast down, saith the Lord.

- **Matthew 6:24** No man can serve two masters: for either he will hate the one, and love the other; or else he will hold to the one, and despise the other. Ye cannot serve God and mammon [wealth].

- **1 Timothy 3:2,3** A bishop then must be blameless, the husband of one wife, vigilant, sober, of good behaviour, given to hospitality, apt to teach; [3] Not given to wine, no striker, not greedy of filthy lucre; but patient, not a brawler, not covetous.

- **1 Peter 5:2** Feed the flock of God which is among you, taking the oversight thereof, not by constraint, but willingly; not for filthy lucre, but of a ready mind. [See also Titus 1:11.]

- **2 Peter 2:1-3** But there were false prophets also among the people, even as there shall be false teachers among you, who privily shall bring in damnable heresies, even denying the Lord that bought them, and bring upon themselves swift destruction. [2] And many shall follow their pernicious ways; by reason of whom the way of truth shall be evil spoken of. [3] And through covetousness shall they with feigned [deceptive] words make merchandise of you.

CRITICISM

Definition: The act of examining or judging the value or merits of something; judging with severity; fault finding.

1. There's a big difference between constructive criticism and being critical.

- **Proverbs 10:11** The mouth of a righteous man is a well of life: but violence covereth the mouth of the wicked.
- **Proverbs 11:9a** An hypocrite with his mouth destroyeth his neighbour.
- **Proverbs 12:18** There is that speaketh like the piercings of a sword: but the tongue of the wise is health.
- **Proverbs 15:4** A wholesome tongue is a tree of life: but perverseness therein is a breach in the spirit.
- **Proverbs 18:21** Death and life are in the power of the tongue: and they that love it shall eat the fruit thereof.
- **John 7:24** Judge not according to the appearance, but judge righteous judgment.
- **Jeremiah 1:9-10** [Although Jeremiah's iconoclastic message was very harsh and critical of the disobedient Kingdom of Judah, the ultimate purpose was to clear away the evil so that it could be replaced with the good.] Then the Lord put forth His hand, and touched my mouth. And the Lord said unto me, Behold, I have put My words in thy mouth. [10] See, I have this day set thee over the nations and over the kingdoms, to root out, and to pull down, and to destroy, and to throw down, to build, and to plant.

2. When tempted to criticise others, first consider your own faults.

- **Psalm 130:3** If Thou, Lord, shouldest mark iniquities, O Lord, who shall stand?
- **Matthew 7:1-5** Judge not, that ye be not judged. [2] For with what judgment ye judge, ye shall be judged: and with what measure ye

mete, it shall be measured to you again. [3] And why beholdest thou the mote that is in thy brother's eye, but considerest not the beam that is in thine own eye? [4] Or how wilt thou say to thy brother, Let me pull out the mote out of thine eye; and, behold, a beam is in thine own eye? [5] Thou hypocrite, first cast out the beam out of thine own eye; and then shalt thou see clearly to cast out the mote out of thy brother's eye.

- **John 8:7** So when they continued asking Him, He lifted up Himself, and said unto them, He that is without sin among you, let him first cast a stone at her.
- **Romans 14:10** But why dost thou judge thy brother? Or why dost thou set at nought thy brother? For we shall all stand before the judgment seat of Christ.
- **Galatians 6:1** Brethren, if a man be overtaken in a fault, ye which are spiritual, restore such an one in the spirit of meekness; considering thyself, lest thou also be tempted.

3. A critical spirit is born of self-righteousness.

- **Matthew 23:24,28** Ye blind guides, which strain at a gnat, and swallow a camel. [28] Even so ye also outwardly appear righteous unto men, but within ye are full of hypocrisy and iniquity.
- **Luke 13:13-15** [The spiritually proud pharisees, blinded by self-righteousness, criticized Jesus even for doing good.] And He laid His hands on her: and immediately she was made straight, and glorified God. [14] And the ruler of the synagogue answered with indignation, because that Jesus had healed on the sabbath day, and said unto the people, There are six days in which men ought to work: in them therefore come and be healed, and not on the sabbath day. [15] The Lord then answered him, and said, Thou hypocrite, doth not each one of you on the sabbath loose his ox or his ass from the stall, and lead him away to watering?
- **Romans 2:1,3** [Beware of the double standard!] Therefore thou art inexcusable, O man, whosoever thou art that judgest: for wherein

thou judgest another, thou condemnest thyself; for thou that judgest doest the same things. [3] And thinkest thou this, O man, that judgest them which do such things, and doest the same, that thou shalt escape the judgment of God?

- **James 4:11,12** Speak not evil one of another, brethren. He that speaketh evil of his brother, and judgeth his brother, speaketh evil of the law, and judgeth the law: but if thou judge the law, thou art not a doer of the law, but a judge. [12] There is one lawgiver, who is able to save and to destroy: who art thou that judgest another?

- **3 John 1:9,10** I wrote unto the church: but Diotrephes, who loveth to have the preeminence among them, receiveth us not. [10] Wherefore, if I come, I will remember his deeds which he doeth, <u>prating against us with malicious words</u>: and not content therewith, neither doth he himself receive the brethren, and forbiddeth them that would, and casteth them out of the church.

4. Criticalness sows strife, disunity and discord amongst brethren.

- **Proverbs 6:16,19** These six things doth the Lord hate: yea, seven are an abomination unto Him. ... [19] A false witness that speaketh lies, and he that soweth discord among brethren. [See also verse 14.]

- **Proverbs 16:28** A froward [perverse] man soweth strife: and a whisperer separateth chief friends.

- **Proverbs 22:10** Cast out the scorner, and contention shall go out; yea, strife and reproach shall cease.

5. Criticalness views things carnally and is more likely to be wrong than right.

- **1 Samuel 16:7b** The Lord seeth not as man seeth; for man looketh on the outward appearance, but the Lord looketh on the heart. [See also Isaiah 55:8,9.]

- **Isaiah 11:3,4** And shall make Him of quick understanding in the fear of the Lord: and He shall not judge after the sight of his eyes, neither reprove after the hearing of His ears: [4] But with righteousness shall He judge the poor, and reprove with equity for the meek of the earth: and He shall smite the earth with the rod of his mouth, and with the breath of his lips shall He slay the wicked.
- **John 7:24** Judge not according to the appearance, but judge righteous judgment.
- **John 8:15,16** [Even Jesus only judged with God's help and understanding.] Ye judge after the flesh; I judge no man. [16] And yet if I judge, My judgment is true: for I am not alone, but I and the Father that sent Me.

6. Fault-finders lose friendships, as well as favor with God.

- **Proverbs 17:9** He that covereth a transgression seeketh love; but he that repeateth a matter separateth very friends.
- **1 Timothy 6:4,5b** [Paul exhorted the brethren to avoid fellowshipping with faultfinders.] He is proud, knowing nothing, but doting about questions and strifes of words, whereof cometh envy, strife, railings, evil surmisings [suspicions], [5b] From such withdraw thyself.
- **James 2:13** [If we unmercifully criticize others, we forfeit God's mercy on ourselves!] For he shall have judgment without mercy, that hath shewed no mercy; and mercy rejoiceth against judgment. [See also Matthew 6:14,15; Luke 6:37.]

7. We should "watch and pray," not watch and criticize.

- **Isaiah 29:20,21** For the terrible one is brought to nought, and the scorner is consumed, and all that <u>watch for iniquity</u> are cut off: [21] That make a man an offender for a word, and lay a snare for him that reproveth in the gate [the defendant in court], and turn aside the just for a thing of nought.

- **Romans 15:30** Now I beseech you, brethren, for the Lord Jesus Christ's sake, and for the love of the Spirit, that ye strive together with me in your prayers to God for me.
- **Ephesians 6:18** Praying always with all prayer and supplication in the Spirit, and watching thereunto with all perseverance and supplication for all saints.
- **1 Thessalonians 1:2** We give thanks to God always for you all, making mention of you in our prayers.
- **James 5:16** Confess your faults one to another, and pray one for another, that ye may be healed [spiritually as well as physically]. The effectual fervent prayer of a righteous man availeth much.

8. Before voicing criticism, put yourself in the other person's shoes.

- **Matthew 7:12** Therefore all things whatsoever ye would that men should do to you, do ye even so to them: for this is the law and the prophets.
- **Romans 14:4** [Watch out about being judgemental. You may not know the whole story.] Who art thou that judgest another man's servant? To his own master he standeth or falleth. Yea, he shall be holden up: for God is able to make him stand.
- **Romans 14:13** Let us not therefore judge one another any more: but judge this rather, that no man put a stumblingblock or an occasion to fall in his brother's way.

9. Those with a tendency to criticize need to learn to hold their tongues.

- **Proverbs 10:19** In the multitude of words there wanteth not sin: but he that refraineth his lips is wise.
- **Proverbs 29:11** A fool uttereth all his mind: but a wise man keepeth it in till afterwards.

- **Ecclesiastes 5:2,6a** Be not rash with thy mouth, and let not thine heart be hasty to utter any thing before God: for God is in Heaven, and thou upon earth: therefore let thy words be few. [6a] Suffer not thy mouth to cause thy flesh to sin.
- **Acts 19:36** Seeing then that these things cannot be spoken against, ye ought to be quiet, and to do nothing rashly.
- **1 Thessalonians 4:8-11** [Criticizing others can lead to criticizing God!] He therefore that despiseth, despiseth not man, but God, who hath also given unto us His Holy Spirit. [9] But as touching brotherly love ye need not that I write unto you: for ye yourselves are taught of God to love one another. [11] And that ye study to be quiet, and to do your own business, and to work with your own hands, as we commanded you.
- **James 1:19,20** Wherefore, my beloved brethren, let every man be swift to hear, slow to speak, slow to wrath: [20] For the wrath of man worketh not the righteousness of God.

10. God's blessings are upon those who don't fall into being critical or negative.

- **Psalm 15:1,3** Lord, who shall abide in Thy tabernacle? Who shall dwell in Thy holy hill? [3] He that backbiteth not with his tongue, nor doeth evil to his neighbour, nor taketh up a reproach against his neighbour.
- **Psalm 34:12-14** What man is he that desireth life, and loveth many days, that he may see good? [13] Keep thy tongue from evil, and thy lips from speaking guile. [14] Depart from evil, and do good; seek peace, and pursue it.
- **1 Corinthians 4:5** Therefore judge nothing before the time, until the Lord come, who both will bring to light the hidden things of darkness, and will make manifest the counsels of the hearts: and then shall every man have praise of God.

11. Jesus came not to criticize others, but to save them.

- **John 3:17** For God sent not His Son into the world to condemn the world; but that the world through Him might be saved.
- **John 8:10-11** [Jesus did not criticize the adulteress as would have the critical Pharisees:] When Jesus had lifted up himself, and saw none but the woman, He said unto her, Woman, where are those thine accusers? Hath no man condemned thee? [11] She said, No man, Lord. And Jesus said unto her, Neither do I condemn thee: go, and sin no more.
- **Mark 9:38-40** [Jesus encouraged His disciples to be less critical and more inclusive:] And John answered Him, saying, Master, we saw one casting out devils in Thy name, and he followeth not us: and we forbad him, because he followeth not us. [9] But Jesus said, Forbid him not: for there is no man which shall do a miracle in My name, that can lightly speak evil of Me. [40] For he that is not against us is on our part.
- **Luke 9:54-55** [Jesus was not pleased when His over-zealous disciples condemned some unreceptive Samaritans:] And when His disciples James and John saw this, they said, Lord, wilt Thou that we command fire to come down from Heaven, and consume them, even as Elias did? [55] But He turned, and rebuked them, and said, Ye know not what manner of spirit ye are of.

12. The "cure" for a critical spirit is to learn to walk in love.

- **1 Corinthians 16:14** Let all your things be done with charity [love].
- **Philippians 1:9** And this I pray, that your love may abound yet more and more in knowledge and in all judgment.
- **1 Peter 3:8** Finally, be ye all of one mind, having compassion one of another, love as brethren, be pitiful, be courteous.
- **1 Peter 4:8** And above all things have fervent charity [love] among yourselves: for charity shall cover the multitude of sins.

13. <u>Constructive</u> criticism, a form of wise judgment, can help to uphold a good moral standard.

- **Exodus 18:21,22** [The judges of old were appointed to offer constructive criticism and judgment.] Moreover thou shalt provide out of all the people able men, such as fear God, men of truth, hating covetousness; and place such over them, to be rulers of thousands, and rulers of hundreds, rulers of fifties, and rulers of tens: ²² And <u>let them judge</u> the people at all seasons: and it shall be, that every great matter they shall bring unto thee, but every small matter they shall judge: so shall it be easier for thyself, and they shall bear the burden with thee.

- **Leviticus 19:15** Ye shall do no unrighteousness in judgment: thou shalt not respect the person of the poor, nor honour the person of the mighty: but in righteousness shalt thou judge thy neighbour.

- **Deuteronomy 1:16** And I charged your judges at that time, saying, Hear the causes between your brethren, and judge righteously between every man and his brother, and the stranger that is with him.

- **1 Kings 3:9** Give therefore Thy servant an understanding heart to judge Thy people, that I may discern between good and bad: for who is able to judge this Thy so great a people?

- **2 Chronicles 19:6b** Take heed what ye do: for ye judge not for man, but for the Lord, who is with you in the judgment.

- **1 Corinthians 6:2,3** [If we're going to eventually judge angels in the next life, shouldn't we be able to prayerfully offer constructive judgment or criticism now?] Do ye not know that the saints shall judge the world? And if the world shall be judged by you, are ye unworthy to judge the smallest matters? ³ Know ye not that we shall judge angels? How much more things that pertain to this life?

CURSING AND FOUL LANGUAGE

Definition: In this instance, swearing or cursing is the use of blasphemous, profane or vulgar language.

1. Cursing is ungodly and immoral, coming from an evil heart.

- **Matthew 12:34b,35** How can ye, being evil, speak good things? For out of the abundance of the heart the mouth speaketh. [35] A good man out of the good treasure of the heart bringeth forth good things: and an evil man out of the evil treasure bringeth forth evil things.
- **Psalm 10:7** [The psalmist David described the wicked:] His mouth is full of cursing and deceit and fraud: under his tongue is mischief and vanity.
- **Proverbs 15:28b** The mouth of the wicked poureth out evil things.
- **Romans 3:12-14** They are all gone out of the way, they are together become unprofitable; there is none that doeth good, no, not one. [13] Their throat is an open sepulchre; with their tongues they have used deceit; the poison of asps is under their lips: [14] Whose mouth is full of cursing and bitterness.

2. Cursing will defile and corrupt you and others.

- **Psalm 109:17** As he loved cursing, so let it come unto him: as he delighted not in blessing, so let it be far from him.
- **Proverbs 10:14b** The mouth of the foolish is near destruction.
- **Proverbs 12:13a** The wicked is snared by the transgression of his lips. [See also Proverbs 13:3b.]
- **Proverbs 18:7** A fool's mouth is his destruction, and his lips are the snare of his soul.
- **Ecclesiastes 10:12b** The lips of a fool will swallow up himself.
- **Matthew 12:36,37** But I say unto you, That every idle word that men shall speak, they shall give account thereof in the day of

judgment. [37] For by thy words thou shalt be justified, and by thy words thou shalt be condemned.

- **Matthew 15:18** But those things which proceed out of the mouth come forth from the heart; and they defile the man.
- **1 Corinthians 15:33** Be not deceived: evil communications corrupt good manners.
- **2 Timothy 2:16** But shun profane [irreverent] and vain babblings: for they will increase unto more ungodliness.
- **James 3:6,9** And the tongue is a fire, a world of iniquity: so is the tongue among our members, that it defileth the whole body, and setteth on fire the course of nature; and it is set on fire of Hell. [9] Therewith bless we God, even the Father; and therewith curse we men, which are made after the similitude of God. [See also Psalm 109:17,18.]

3. Cursing is a chink in your armor, an inroad for Satan.

- **Proverbs 15:4** A wholesome tongue is a tree of life: but perverseness therein is a breach in the spirit.
- **Matthew 26:74** [Peter, in his third denial of Christ, resorted to cursing:] Then began he to curse and to swear, saying, I know not the Man. And immediately the cock crew.

4. Take a positive stand against cursing, both in your own life and in your associations with others.

- **Psalm 17:3b** I am purposed that my mouth shall not transgress.
- **Psalm 50:23** Whoso offereth praise glorifieth Me: and to him that ordereth his conversation aright will I shew the salvation of God.
- **Psalm 141:3** Set a watch, O Lord, before my mouth; keep the door of my lips.
- **Proverbs 4:24** Put away from thee a froward mouth, and perverse lips put far from thee.

- **Proverbs 8:13** The fear of the Lord is to hate evil: pride, and arrogancy, and the evil way, and the froward mouth, do I hate.
- **Ephesians 4:29** Let no corrupt communication proceed out of your mouth, but that which is good to the use of edifying, that it may minister grace unto the hearers.
- **Ephesians 5:4** Neither filthiness, nor foolish talking, nor jesting, which are not convenient: but rather giving of thanks.
- **Ephesians 5:11** And have no fellowship with the unfruitful works of darkness, but rather reprove them. [12] For it is a shame even to speak of those things which are done of them in secret.
- **Colossians 3:8** But now ye also put off all these; anger, wrath, malice, blasphemy, filthy communication out of your mouth.

5. Cursing is often a result of pride or attempts to appear "cool."

- **Psalm 12:4** Who have said, With our tongue will we prevail; our lips are our own: who is lord over us?
- **Psalm 59:12** For the sin of their mouth and the words of their lips let them even be taken in their pride: and for cursing and lying which they speak.
- **1 Samuel 17:43** [Goliath was a classic example of the ungodly cursing the righteous:] And the Philistine said unto David, Am I a dog, that thou comest to me with staves? And the Philistine cursed David by his gods.

6. Cursing is often the result of anger or impatience.

- **Proverbs 29:20** Seest thou a man that is hasty in his words? There is more hope of a fool than of him.
- **Ecclesiastes 5:2** Be not rash with thy mouth, and let not thine heart be hasty to utter any thing before God: for God is in Heaven, and thou upon earth: therefore let thy words be few.
- **James 1:19,20** Wherefore, my beloved brethren, let every man be swift to hear, slow to speak, slow to wrath: [20] For the wrath of man worketh not the righteousness of God.

Don't even <u>think</u> of uttering a curse.

Ecclesiastes 10:20 Curse not the king, no not in thy thought; and curse not the rich in thy bedchamber: for a bird of the air shall carry the voice, and that which hath wings shall tell the matter.

Proverbs 30:32 If thou hast done foolishly in lifting up thyself, or if thou hast thought evil, lay thine hand upon thy mouth [before you speak it].

Don't let others' cursing provoke you to retaliate or resort to foul language.

Job 2:7,9,10 [When the Lord allowed Satan to afflict Job's wealth, family and health, Job refused to curse God:] So went Satan forth from the presence of the Lord, and smote Job with sore boils from the sole of his foot unto his crown. [9] Then said his wife unto him, Dost thou still retain thine integrity [godliness]? Curse God, and die. [10] But he said unto her, Thou speakest as one of the foolish women speaketh. What? Shall we receive good at the hand of God, and shall we not receive evil? In all this did not Job sin with his lips.

Psalm 39:1 I said, I will take heed to my ways, that I sin not with my tongue: I will keep my mouth with a bridle, while the wicked is before me.

Ecclesiastes 7:21a,22 Also take no heed unto all words that are spoken. [22] For oftentimes also thine own heart knoweth that thou thyself likewise hast cursed others.

James 3:10 Out of the same mouth proceedeth blessing and cursing. My brethren, these things ought not so to be.

1 Peter 3:9,10 Not rendering evil for evil, or railing for railing [insult for insult]: but contrariwise blessing; knowing that ye are thereunto called, that ye should inherit a blessing. [10] For he that will love life, and see good days, let him refrain his tongue from evil, and his lips that they speak no guile.

DOUBTS

Definition: To call to question or to mistrust; the inclination to disbelieve; to be in a state of uncertainty or indecision in regards to truth; to waver in opinion.

1. It's the Devil's business to tempt us to doubt God's Word and to try to get us to believe his word.

- **Genesis 3:1-6** Now the serpent was more subtil than any beast of the field which the Lord God had made. And he said unto the woman, Yea, hath God said, Ye shall not eat of every tree of the garden? [2] And the woman said unto the serpent, We may eat of the fruit of the trees of the garden: [3] But of the fruit of the tree which is in the midst of the garden, God hath said, Ye shall not eat of it, neither shall ye touch it, lest ye die. [4] And the serpent said unto the woman, Ye shall not surely die: [5] For God doth know that in the day ye eat thereof, then your eyes shall be opened, and ye shall be as gods, knowing good and evil. [6] And when the woman saw that the tree was good for food, and that it was pleasant to the eyes, and a tree to be desired to make one wise, she took of the fruit thereof, and did eat, and gave also unto her husband with her; and he did eat.
- **2 Corinthians 11:3** [The Enemy likes to undermine simple, childlike faith.] But I fear, lest by any means, as the serpent beguiled Eve through his subtilty, so your minds should be corrupted from the simplicity that is in Christ.
- **2 Corinthians 2:11** [When the Devil can persuade us to believe his lies, he gains the upper hand:] Lest Satan should get an advantage of us: for we are not ignorant of his devices. [See also Romans 6:16.]
- **John 8:44b** [The Devil is the father of lies.] He was a murderer from the beginning, and abode not in the truth, because there is no truth in him. When he speaketh a lie, he speaketh of his own: for he is a liar, and the father of it. [See also Acts 13:10; Revelation 12:9.]

- **1 John 4:1** [Beware of voices that breed doubt and fear in your mind. Test them with the Word, prayer and godly counsel.] Beloved, believe not every spirit, but try the spirits whether they are of God: because many false prophets are gone out into the world.

2. It's not a sin to be tempted with doubts, but it is a sin to entertain doubts and yield to them.

- **Romans 14:23b** For whatsoever is not of faith is sin.
- **1 Corinthians 10:13** There hath no temptation taken you but such as is common to man: but God is faithful, who will not suffer you to be tempted above that ye are able; but will with the temptation also make a way to escape, that ye may be able to bear it.
- **Hebrews 3:12** Take heed, brethren, lest there be in any of you an evil heart of unbelief, in departing from the living God.
- **James 1:12-15** Blessed is the man that endureth temptation: for when he is tried, he shall receive the crown of life, which the Lord hath promised to them that love Him. [13] Let no man say when he is tempted, I am tempted of God: for God cannot be tempted with evil, neither tempteth He any man: [14] But every man is tempted, when he is drawn away of his own lust, and enticed. [15] Then when lust hath conceived, it bringeth forth sin: and sin, when it is finished, bringeth forth death.

3. The Devil's lies, or others' doubts, don't change the facts of God's truth.

- **Numbers 23:19** God is not a man, that He should lie; neither the son of man, that He should repent: hath He said, and shall He not do it? Or hath He spoken, and shall He not make it good?
- **Isaiah 55:11** So shall My Word be that goeth forth out of My mouth: it shall not return unto Me void, but it shall accomplish that which I please, and it shall prosper in the thing whereto I sent it.
- **Malachi 3:6a** For I am the Lord, I change not.

- **Matthew 24:35** Heaven and earth shall pass away, but My Words shall not pass away.
- **Romans 3:3** For what if some did not believe? Shall their unbelief make the faith of God without effect?
- **2 Timothy 2:13** If we believe not, yet He abideth faithful: He cannot deny Himself.

4. Common causes of doubts and doubting:

- **Proverbs 29:18** [Loss of connection with the Word:] Where there is no vision, the people perish: but he that keepeth the law, happy is he.
- **Malachi 3:14a** [Weariness in well-doing:] Ye have said, It is vain to serve God: and what profit is it that we have kept His ordinance?
- **Matthew 14:30,31** [Looking at circumstances instead of the Lord:] But when he [Peter] saw the wind boisterous, he was afraid; and beginning to sink, he cried, saying, Lord, save me. [31] And immediately Jesus stretched forth His hand, and caught him, and said unto him, O thou of little faith, wherefore didst thou doubt?
- **Luke 12:29,30** [Over-concern about physical needs:] And seek not ye what ye shall eat, or what ye shall drink, neither be ye of doubtful mind. [30] For all these things do the nations of the world seek after: and your Father knoweth that ye have need of these things.
- **John 5:44** [Failure to keep the Lord in first place:] How can ye believe, which receive honour one of another, and seek not the honour that cometh from God only?
- **Hebrews 10:35,36** [Impatience:] Cast not away therefore your confidence [faith], which hath great recompence of reward. [36] For ye have need of patience, that, after ye have done the will of God, ye might receive the promise. [See also Psalm 31:22a.]
- **Psalm 78:11,19,20** [Forgetting all the wonderful things that the Lord has done:] And [they] forgat His works, and His wonders that He had shewed them. [19] Yea, they spake against God; they said, Can

God furnish a table in the wilderness? [20] Behold, He [through Moses] smote the rock, that the waters gushed out, and the streams overflowed; can He give bread also? Can He provide flesh for His people?

5. Doubt is voiced in murmuring. Those who voice doubt are spreading Satan's propaganda.

• **Numbers 13:31-33; 14:1,2** [The men of Israel who brought back a doubtful exaggerated and negative report concerning the land which God promised to them, caused the people to murmur against Moses.] But the men that went up with him said, We be not able to go up against the people; for they are stronger than we. [32] And they brought up an evil report of the land which they had searched unto the children of Israel, saying, The land, through which we have gone to search it, is a land that eateth up the inhabitants thereof; and all the people that we saw in it are men of a great stature. [33] And there we saw the giants, the sons of Anak, which come of the giants: and we were in our own sight as grasshoppers, and so we were in their sight. [14:1,2] And all the congregation lifted up their voice, and cried; and the people wept that night. [2] And all the children of Israel murmured against Moses and against Aaron: and the whole congregation said unto them, Would God that we had died in the land of Egypt! Or would God we had died in this wilderness!

• **Psalm 106:24,25** Yea, they [the Children of Israel] despised the pleasant land, they believed not His Word: [25] But murmured in their tents, and hearkened not unto the voice of the Lord. [See also Numbers 14:36; Deuteronomy 1:28.]

• **Ephesians 4:29** Let no corrupt communication proceed out of your mouth, but that which is good to the use of edifying, that it may minister grace unto the hearers.

6. Some of the other consequences of doubts:

- **Hebrews 11:6** [Doubts cause us to disappoint and displease God:] But without faith it is impossible to please Him: for he that cometh to God must believe that He is, and that He is a rewarder of them that diligently seek Him.

- **Isaiah 7:9b** [Doubts cause the Lord to withhold His blessings:] If ye will not believe, surely ye shall not be established.

- **Matthew 13:58** [Doubts limit what the Lord can do in our behalf:] And He did not many mighty works there because of their unbelief.

- **Mark 4:40** [Doubts open the door to fears:] And He said unto them, Why are ye so fearful? How is it that ye have no faith?

- **Mark 11:22,23** [Doubts hinder His ability to work through us:] And Jesus answering saith unto them, Have faith in God. [23] For verily I say unto you, That whosoever shall say unto this mountain, Be thou removed, and be thou cast into the sea; and shall not doubt in his heart, but shall believe that those things which he saith shall come to pass; he shall have whatsoever he saith.

- **Romans 14:22b** [Doubts rob us of happiness:] Happy is he that condemneth not himself in the thing which he alloweth.

- **Hebrews 3:18,19** [Doubts rob us of the Lord's peace and rest:] And to whom sware He that they should not enter into His rest, but to them that believed not? [19] So we see that they could not enter in because of unbelief.

- **Hebrews 4:2** [Doubts cause the Word to lose its miracle-working power in our lives:] For unto us was the Gospel preached, as well as unto them: but the Word preached did not profit them, not being mixed with faith in them that heard it. [See also Deuteronomy 32:20.]

- **James 1:6,7** [Doubts cause the Lord to withhold answers to our prayers:] But let him ask in faith, nothing wavering. For he that wavereth is like a wave of the sea driven with the wind and tossed. [7] For let not that man think that he shall receive any thing of the Lord.

. If we don't receive the truth, we are left to doubts and elusions.

Matthew 13:15 For this people's heart is waxed gross, and their ears are dull of hearing, and their eyes they have <u>closed</u>; lest at any time they should see with their eyes, and hear with their ears, and should understand with their heart, and should be converted, and I should heal them.

2 Corinthians 4:3,4 But if our Gospel be hid, it is hid to them that are lost: 4 In whom the god of this world hath blinded the minds of them which believe not, lest the light of the glorious Gospel of Christ, who is the image of God, should shine unto them.

Luke 8:12 Those by the way side are they that hear [the Word]; then cometh the Devil, and taketh away the Word out of their hearts, lest they should believe and be saved.

1 Timothy 1:18b,19 War a good warfare, 19 Holding faith, and a good conscience; which some having put away concerning faith have made shipwreck.

2 Timothy 4:3,4 [Watch out when you can't take the truth, and seek for teachings which make you comfortable.] For the time will come when they will not endure sound doctrine; but after their own lusts shall they heap to themselves teachers, having itching ears; 4 And they shall turn away their ears from the truth, and shall be turned unto fables.

2 Thessalonians 2:12 That they all might be damned [judged] who believed not the truth, but had pleasure in unrighteousness.

1 Peter 2:7,8 Unto you therefore which believe He is precious: but unto them which be disobedient, the stone which the builders disallowed, the same is made the head of the corner, 8 And a stone of stumbling, and a rock of offence, even to them which stumble at the Word, being disobedient: whereunto also they were appointed.

8. It is the <u>Lord</u> who overcomes our doubts in response to our sincere concern and prayers.

- **Psalm 51:10-13** [David prayed:] Create in me a clean heart, O God; and renew a right spirit within me. [11] Cast me not away from Thy presence; and take not Thy Holy Spirit from me. [12] Restore unto me the joy of Thy salvation; and uphold me with Thy free spirit. [13] Then will I teach transgressors Thy ways; and sinners shall be converted unto Thee.

- **Psalm 138:8** The Lord will perfect that which concerneth me: Thy mercy, O Lord, endureth for ever: forsake not the works of Thine Own hands.

- **Mark 9:23,24,28b,29** Jesus said unto him, If thou canst believe, all things are possible to him that believeth. [24] And straightway the father of the [demon-possessed] child cried out, and said with tears, Lord, I believe; <u>help Thou mine unbelief</u>. [After Jesus rebuked the foul spirit and the child was healed:] [28b] His disciples asked Him privately, Why could not we cast him out? [29] And He said unto them, This kind can come forth by nothing, but by prayer and fasting.

- **Luke 17:5** And the apostles said unto the Lord, Increase our faith.

- **Hebrews 12:2** Looking unto Jesus the Author and Finisher of our faith; who for the joy that was set before Him endured the cross, despising the shame, and is set down at the right hand of the throne of God.

- **1 Peter 1:22,23** Seeing ye have purified your souls in obeying the truth through the Spirit unto unfeigned love of the brethren, see that ye love one another with a pure heart fervently: [23] Being born again, not of corruptible seed, but of incorruptible, by the Word of God, which liveth and abideth for ever.

9. Resist the Devil and yield your mind to the Lord.

- **Isaiah 55:7** Let the wicked forsake his way, and the unrighteous man his thoughts: and let him return unto the Lord, and He will have mercy upon him; and to our God, for He will abundantly pardon.

- **Jeremiah 4:14** O Jerusalem, wash thine heart from wickedness, that thou mayest be saved. How long shall thy vain thoughts lodge within thee?
- **Matthew 15:19** For out of the heart proceed evil thoughts, murders, adulteries, fornications, thefts, false witness, blasphemies: [See also Jeremiah 17:9.]
- **2 Corinthians 10:5** Casting down imaginations, and every high thing that exalteth itself against the knowledge of God, and bringing into captivity every thought to the obedience of Christ.
- **Ephesians 4:27** [Don't entertain doubts or they will grow:] Neither give place to the Devil.
- **Ephesians 6:13,16,17** Wherefore take unto you the whole armour of God, that ye may be able to withstand in the evil day, and having done all, to stand. [16] Above all, taking the shield of faith, wherewith ye shall be able to quench all the fiery darts of the wicked. [17] And take the helmet of salvation, and the sword of the Spirit, which is the Word of God.
- **1 Peter 1:13a** Wherefore gird up the loins of your mind, be sober. [See also Luke 12:35.]

10. Carnal mindedness leads to doubt. We can't understand the Lord's ways with our carnal minds.

- **Proverbs 3:5** Trust in the Lord with all thine heart; and lean not unto thine own understanding.
- **Isaiah 55:8,9** For My thoughts are not your thoughts, neither are your ways My ways, saith the Lord. [9] For as the Heavens are higher than the earth, so are My ways higher than your ways, and My thoughts than your thoughts.
- **Matthew 16:16,17** [Peter's belief that Jesus was the Son of God was through the Spirit, not carnal reasoning.] And Simon Peter answered and said, Thou art the Christ, the Son of the living God. [17] And Jesus

answered and said unto him, Blessed art thou, Simon Barjona: for flesh and blood hath not revealed it unto thee, but My Father which is in Heaven.

- **Mark 2:5-8** [Carnal reasoning got the learned scribes nowhere, except to cause them to doubt in Jesus.] When Jesus saw their faith [those who brought the sick man to Jesus], He said unto the sick of the palsy, Son, thy sins be forgiven thee. [6] But there were certain of the scribes sitting there, and reasoning in their hearts, [7] Why doth this Man thus speak blasphemies? Who can forgive sins but God only? [8] And immediately when Jesus perceived in His Spirit that they so reasoned within themselves, He said unto them, Why reason ye these things in your hearts?

- **John 3:3,4,7,9,10,12** [Even the learned rabbi, Nicodemus, could not understand the simple spiritual truths of Jesus, until he stopped his carnal analyzing.] Jesus answered and said unto him, Verily, verily, I say unto thee, Except a man be born again, he cannot see the Kingdom of God. [4] Nicodemus saith unto Him, How can a man be born when he is old? Can he enter the second time into his mother's womb, and be born? [7] [Jesus said:] Marvel not that I said unto thee, Ye must be born again. [9] Nicodemus answered and said unto Him, How can these things be? [10] Jesus answered and said unto him, Art thou a master of Israel, and knowest not these things? [12] If I have told you earthly things, and ye believe not, how shall ye believe, if I tell you of heavenly things?

- **John 6:53,60,61,66-69** [Carnal reasoning, when tested by the Lord through His radical message, hurt the faith of some disciples, yet it was simple abiding faith that kept the true disciples through it all.] Then Jesus said unto them, Verily, verily, I say unto you, Except ye eat the flesh of the Son of man, and drink His blood, ye have no life in you. [60] Many therefore of His disciples, when they had heard this, said, This is an hard saying; who can hear it? [61] When Jesus knew in Himself that His disciples murmured at it, He said unto them, Doth this offend you? [66] From that time many of His disciples went back, and walked no more with Him. [67] Then said Jesus unto the twelve,

Will ye also go away? [68] Then Simon Peter answered Him, Lord, to whom shall we go? Thou hast the Words of Eternal Life. [69] And we believe and are sure that Thou art that Christ, the Son of the living God.

- **John 14:26** [The Holy Ghost will help you overcome doubts and come to greater understanding.] But the Comforter, which is the Holy Ghost, whom the Father will send in My Name, He shall teach you all things, and bring all things to your remembrance, whatsoever I have said unto you.

- **Romans 8:7-9** Because the carnal mind is enmity [full of hatred] against God: for it is not subject to the law of God, neither indeed can be. [8] So then they that are in the flesh cannot please God. [9] But ye are not in the flesh, but in the Spirit, if so be that the Spirit of God dwell in you. Now if any man have not the Spirit of Christ, he is none of His.

- **1 Corinthians 1:21** [Worldly wisdom doesn't help us receive the things of the Spirit.] For after that in the wisdom of God the world by wisdom knew not God, it pleased God by the foolishness of preaching to save them that believe.

- **1 Corinthians 2:11-16** [Only God can reveal His spiritual truths to you.] For what man knoweth the things of a man, save the spirit of man which is in him? Even so the things of God knoweth no man, but the Spirit of God. [12] Now we have received, not the spirit of the world, but the Spirit which is of God; that we might know the things that are freely given to us of God. [13] Which things also we speak, not in the words which man's wisdom teacheth, but which the Holy Ghost teacheth; comparing spiritual things with spiritual. [14] But the natural man receiveth not the things of the Spirit of God: for they are foolishness unto him: neither can he know them, because they are spiritually discerned. [15] But he that is spiritual judgeth all things, yet he himself is judged of no man. [16] For who hath known the mind of the Lord, that he may instruct Him? But we have the mind of Christ.

- **Ephesians 4:17,18** This I say therefore, and testify in the Lord, that ye henceforth walk not as other Gentiles walk, in the vanity of their mind, [18] Having the understanding darkened, being alienated from the life of God through the ignorance that is in them, because of the blindness of their heart.
- **Galatians 1:11,12** [Saul of Tarsus, after his conversion to the faith, became the Apostle Paul, who testified that his learning and enlightenment was not from carnal man.] But I certify you, brethren, that the Gospel which was preached of me is not after man. [12] For I neither received it of man, neither was I taught it, but by the revelation of Jesus Christ.

11. Only weak or doubting faith seeks miracles and signs.

- **Matthew 16:1** The Pharisees also with the Sadducees came, and tempting desired Him that He would shew them a sign from Heaven. [See also 1 Corinthians 1:22.]
- **Matthew 16:4a** A wicked and adulterous generation seeketh after a sign.
- **Luke 16:31** [When the rich man, who was in Hell, begged Abraham to allow Lazarus to go back (in order to) warn his brothers, Abraham explains:] If they hear not Moses and the prophets [the Word], neither will they be persuaded, though one rose from the dead.
- **Luke 23:8-9** And when Herod saw Jesus, he was exceeding glad: for he was desirous to see Him of a long season, because he had heard many things of Him; and he hoped to have seen some miracle done by Him. [9] Then he questioned with Him in many words; but He [Jesus] answered him nothing.
- **John 4:48** Then said Jesus unto him, Except ye see signs and wonders, ye will not believe.
- **John 20:29** Jesus saith unto him, Thomas, because thou hast seen Me, thou hast believed: blessed are they that have not seen, and yet have believed.

• **1 Corinthians 1:22,23** For the Jews require a sign, and the Greeks seek after wisdom: [23] But we preach Christ crucified, unto the Jews a stumblingblock, and unto the Greeks foolishness.

12. The sure cure for doubts is the <u>Word</u>.

• **Romans 10:17** So then faith cometh by hearing, and hearing by the Word of God.
• **John 20:30,31** And many other signs truly did Jesus in the presence of His disciples, which are not written in this Book: [31] But these are written, that ye might believe that Jesus is the Christ, the Son of God; and that believing ye might have life through His name.
• **Romans 15:4** For whatsoever things were written aforetime were written for our learning, that we through patience and comfort of the Scriptures might have hope.
• **1 Timothy 4:6b** [Feed your faith and your doubts will starve to death.] Nourished up in the words of faith and of good doctrine, whereunto thou hast attained.
• **Hebrews 4:12** For the Word of God is quick, and powerful, and sharper than any twoedged sword, piercing even to the dividing asunder of soul and spirit, and of the joints and marrow, and is a discerner of the thoughts and intents of the heart.
• **2 Peter 1:16,19** For we have not followed cunningly devised fables, when we made known unto you the power and coming of our Lord Jesus Christ, but were eyewitnesses of His majesty. [19] We have also a more sure Word of prophecy; whereunto ye do well that ye take heed, as unto a light that shineth in a dark place, until the day dawn, and the day star arise in your hearts.

13. One of our best defenses against doubts is to stay positive by keeping our eyes on Jesus and His goodness.

• **Psalm 27:13** I had fainted, unless I had believed to see the goodness of the Lord in the land of the living.

- **Psalm 94:19** In the multitude of my thoughts within me Thy comforts delight my soul.
- **Psalm 119:165** Great peace have they which love Thy law: and nothing shall offend them.
- **Isaiah 26:3** Thou wilt keep him in perfect peace, whose mind is stayed on Thee: because he trusteth in Thee.
- **Philippians 4:8** [Fill your mind and heart with His truth and there will be no room for the lies of the Devil:] Finally, brethren, whatsoever things are true, whatsoever things are honest, whatsoever things are just, whatsoever things are pure, whatsoever things are lovely, whatsoever things are of good report; if there be any virtue, and if there be any praise, think on these things.

14. Encouraging testimonies from others also strengthens our faith.

- **2 Kings 5:1-4** [Hearing the little Hebrew maid's testimony of faith inspired Naaman, commander of the Syrian army:] Now Naaman, captain of the host of the king of Syria, was a great man with his master, and honourable, because by him the Lord had given deliverance unto Syria: he was also a mighty man in valour, but he was a leper. ² And the Syrians had gone out by companies, and had brought away captive out of the land of Israel a little maid; and she waited on Naaman's wife. ³ And she said unto her mistress, Would God my lord were with the prophet that is in Samaria! For he would recover him of his leprosy. ⁴ And one went in, and told his lord, saying, Thus and thus said the maid that is of the land of Israel. [Naaman went, and after following Elisha's instructions, was not only healed of his leprosy, but became a believer. For the full story, read the whole chapter.]
- **John 4:28-30,39** [The woman at the well:] The woman then left her waterpot, and went her way into the city, and saith to the men, ²⁹ Come, see a Man, which told me all things that ever I did: is not this the Christ? ³⁰ Then they went out of the city, and came unto

Him. ... [39] And many of the Samaritans of that city believed on Him for the saying of the woman, which testified, He told me all that ever I did.

- **John 17:20** Neither pray I for these [His original twelve disciples] alone, but for them also which shall believe on Me through their word.

15. Sometimes the only thing we can do is hold on and keep trusting that God knows best!

- **Psalm 31:24** Be of good courage, and He shall strengthen your heart, all ye that hope in the Lord.
- **1 Corinthians 16:13** Watch ye, stand fast in the faith, quit you [be courageous] like men, be strong.
- **Colossians 1:23a** If ye continue in the faith grounded and settled, and be not moved away from the hope of the Gospel, which ye have heard...
- **Colossians 2:6,7** As ye have therefore received Christ Jesus the Lord, so walk ye in Him: [7] Rooted and built up in Him, and stablished in the faith, as ye have been taught, abounding therein with thanksgiving.
- **Hebrews 10:23** Let us hold fast the profession of our faith without wavering; (for He is faithful that promised.)
- **Hebrews 11:27b** By faith he [Moses] ... endured, as seeing Him who is invisible.

16. Some of the greatest men in the Bible were tempted with bouts of doubts, but they fought through to victory, and their examples inspire us to do likewise!

- **Genesis 15:7,8** [Abraham at first doubted God's promise to him that he would inherit the land of Canaan. But he obeyed anyway, and went on to become the father of faith.] And He said unto him, I am the Lord that brought thee out of Ur of the Chaldees, to give thee this land to inherit it. [8] And he said, Lord God, whereby shall I know that I shall inherit it? [See also Galatians 3:6-9.]

- **Genesis 18:12-14; Hebrews 11:11** [Sarah, Abraham's wife, doubted God's incredible claim that she would give birth many years past the age of childbearing, but she went on to believe, and gave birth to Isaac.] Therefore Sarah laughed within herself, saying, After I am waxed old shall I have pleasure, my lord being old also? [13] And the Lord said unto Abraham, Wherefore did Sarah laugh, saying, Shall I of a surety bear a child, which am old? [14] Is any thing too hard for the Lord? At the time appointed I will return unto thee, according to the time of life, and Sarah shall have a son. [Hebrews 11:11] Through faith also Sara herself received strength to conceive seed, and was delivered of a child when she was past age, because she judged him faithful who had promised.

- **Exodus 3:11,12** And Moses said unto God, Who am I, that I should go unto Pharaoh, and that I should bring forth the children of Israel out of Egypt? [12] And He said, Certainly I will be with thee; and this shall be a token unto thee, that I have sent thee: When thou hast brought forth the people out of Egypt, ye shall serve God upon this mountain.

- **Exodus 4:10-12** [Still, Moses felt insecure about leading the people; but he did, and God blessed him for it.] And Moses said unto the Lord, O my Lord, I am not eloquent, neither heretofore, nor since Thou hast spoken unto Thy servant: but I am slow of speech, and of a slow tongue. [11] And the Lord said unto him, Who hath made man's mouth? Or who maketh the dumb, or deaf, or the seeing, or the blind? Have not I the Lord? [12] Now therefore go, and I will be with thy mouth, and teach thee what thou shalt say. [Moses still doubted, as shown by verses 13-16, so God let his brother Aaron be Moses' spokesman.]

- **Psalm 31:22** [King David had his times of doubts and despair also, but the Lord always saw him through:] For I said in my haste, I am cut off from before Thine eyes: nevertheless Thou heardest the voice of my supplications when I cried unto Thee.

- **Matthew 11:2,3** [John the Baptist, who baptized Jesus and originally proclaimed and acknowledged His divinity, later began to question whether Jesus was the actual Messiah or not. Yet he went on to become the first martyr of the Early Church.] Now when <u>John</u> had heard in the prison the works of Christ, he sent two of his disciples, ³And said unto Him, Art Thou He that should come, or do we look for another?

- **Matthew 16:21-23** [Peter misguidedly rebuked and attempted to counsel Jesus, thinking he was encouraging His faith. However, Jesus was not pleased that Peter doubted the prophetic words He had just spoken:] From that time forth began Jesus to shew unto His disciples, how that He must go unto Jerusalem, and suffer many things of the elders and chief priests and scribes, and be killed, and be raised again the third day. ²²Then Peter took Him, and began to rebuke Him, saying, Be it far from Thee, Lord: this shall not be unto Thee. ²³But He turned, and said unto Peter, Get thee behind Me, Satan: thou art an offence unto Me: for thou savourest not the things that be of God, but those that be of men.

- **John 20:27,28** [<u>Thomas</u>, who is widely remembered for his doubting nature, is said to have gone on to reach India with the Gospel, where he later was martyred.] Then saith He [Jesus] to Thomas, Reach hither thy finger, and behold My hands; and reach hither thy hand, and thrust it into My side: and be not faithless, but believing. ²⁸And Thomas answered and said unto Him, My Lord and my God. [See also Matthew 28:17.]

17. We are called to simply believe in the unseen by faith.

- **2 Chronicles 20:20b** <u>Believe</u> in the Lord your God, so shall ye be established; believe His prophets, so shall ye prosper.
- **Matthew 9:29b** According to your <u>faith</u> be it unto you.
- **Romans 1:17** For therein is the righteousness of God revealed from faith to faith: as it is written, The just shall live by <u>faith</u>.

- **Romans 12:3b** According as God hath dealt to every man the measure of faith.
- **Romans 5:1** Therefore being justified by <u>faith</u>, we have peace with God through our Lord Jesus Christ.
- **2 Corinthians 4:18** While we look not at the things which are seen, but at the things which are not seen: for the things which are seen are temporal; but the things which are not seen are eternal.
- **2 Corinthians 5:7** For we walk by <u>faith</u>, not by sight.
- **1 John 5:4** For whatsoever is born of God overcometh the world: and this is the victory that overcometh the world, even our <u>faith</u>.

EMPATHY

Definition: Identifying oneself with another person's feelings, experiences, and emotions, particularly in regards to misfortune; compassion, sympathy, understanding.

1. We should put ourselves in the place of others, and consider how we would feel if positions were reversed.

- **Job 2:11,13** [Realizing that Job had been overcome by calamity and his grief was too great for words, his friends thoughtfully kept him company several days without engaging in conversation.] Now when Job's three friends heard of all this evil that was come upon him, they ... made an appointment together to come to mourn with him and to comfort him. [13] So they sat down with him upon the ground seven days and seven nights, and none spake a word unto him: for they saw that his grief was very great.

- **Jonah 4:10,11** [The Lord chastened the prophet Jonah for his lack of empathy towards the people of Nineveh. God had sent Jonah to Nineveh to prophesy its immediate destruction, yet relented after the people turned from their wickedness upon hearing Jonah's prophecy. This angered Jonah, who protested that God had mercy on them, when he'd foretold their destruction.] Then said the Lord ... [11] And should not I spare Nineveh, that great city, wherein are more than sixscore thousand persons that cannot discern between their right hand and their left hand; and also much cattle?

- **Matthew 7:12** Therefore all things whatsoever ye would that men should do to you, do ye even so to them: for this is the law and the prophets. [See also Luke 6:31.]

- **Matthew 22:39b** Thou shalt love thy neighbour as thyself.

- **Romans 12:15** Rejoice with them that do rejoice, and weep with them that weep.

- **1 Corinthians 12:25b,26** Members [of the body of believers] should have the same care one for another. [26] And whether one member suffer, all the members suffer with it; or one member be honoured, all the members rejoice with it. [See also verses 20-27.]

- **Philippians 2:2-4** Fulfil ye my joy, that ye be likeminded, having the same love, being of one accord, of one mind. [3] Let nothing be done through strife or vainglory; but in lowliness of mind let each esteem other better than themselves. [4] Look not every man on his own things, but every man also on the things of others.

- **Hebrews 13:3** Remember them that are in bonds, as bound with them; and them which suffer adversity, as being yourselves also in the body [as if you yourselves were suffering].

- **1 Peter 3:8** Finally, be ye all of one mind, having compassion one of another, love as brethren, be pitiful, be courteous.

2. The difference between pity and compassion: While pity feels sorry, compassion does something about it!

- **Luke 10:33,34** But a certain Samaritan, as he journeyed, came [upon a man who'd been robbed, wounded and abandoned by the roadside] where he was: and when he saw him, he had compassion on him, [34] And went to him, and bound up his wounds, pouring in oil and wine, and set him on his own beast, and brought him to an inn, and took care of him. [See also verses 30-37.]

- **James 2:15-17** If a brother or sister be naked, and destitute of daily food, [16] And one of you say unto them, Depart in peace, be ye warmed and filled; notwithstanding ye give them not those things which are needful to the body; what doth it profit? [17] Even so faith, if it hath not works, is dead, being alone.

- **1 John 3:16-18** Hereby perceive we the love of God, because He laid down His life for us: and we ought to lay down our lives for the brethren. [17] But whoso hath this world's good, and seeth his brother have need, and shutteth up his bowels of compassion from him, how dwelleth the love of God in him? [18] My little children, let us not love in word, neither in tongue; but in deed and in truth.

3. The Lord will punish those who deal unlovingly and without compassion.

- **Matthew 18:23,24,27,28,32-34** Therefore is the Kingdom of Heaven likened unto a certain king, which would take account of his servants. [24] And when he had begun to reckon, one was brought unto him, which owed him ten thousand talents. [27] Then the lord of that servant was moved with compassion, and loosed him, and forgave him the debt. [28] But the same servant went out, and found one of his fellowservants, which owed him an hundred pence: and he laid hands on him, and took him by the throat, saying, Pay me that thou owest. [32] Then his lord, after that he had called him, said unto him, O thou wicked servant, I forgave thee all that debt, because thou desiredst me: [33] Shouldest not thou also have had compassion on thy fellowservant, even as I had pity on thee? [34] And his lord was wroth, and delivered him to the tormentors, till he should pay all that was due unto him.

- **Matthew 25:41-45** Then [on the Judgement Day] shall He say also unto them on the left hand, Depart from Me, ye cursed, into everlasting fire, prepared for the Devil and his angels: [42] For I was an hungred, and ye gave Me no meat: I was thirsty, and ye gave Me no drink: [43] I was a stranger, and ye took Me not in: naked, and ye clothed Me not: sick, and in prison, and ye visited Me not. [44] Then shall they also answer Him, saying, Lord, when saw we Thee an hungred, or athirst, or a stranger, or naked, or sick, or in prison, and did not minister unto Thee? [45] Then shall He answer them, saying, Verily I say unto you, Inasmuch as ye did it not to one of the least of these, ye did it not to Me.

4. Examples of people moved with compassion:

- **Exodus 2:5,6** [God touched the heart of Pharaoh's daughter to adopt baby Moses as her own son:] And the daughter of Pharaoh came down to wash herself at the river; and her maidens walked along by the river's side; and when she saw the ark among the flags, she sent her maid to fetch it. [6] And when she had opened it, she saw the child: and, behold, the babe wept. And she had compassion on him, and said, This is one of the Hebrews' children. [See also verses 5-10.]

- **2 Chronicles 28:15** [After conquering the army of Judah under wicked King Ahaz' rule, the Israelites, convicted by the words of a prophet of the Lord, had compassion upon their captives:] And the men which were expressed by name rose up, and took the captives, and with the spoil clothed all that were naked among them, and arrayed them, and shod them, and gave them to eat and to drink, and anointed them, and carried all the feeble of them upon asses, and brought them to Jericho, the city of palm trees, to their brethren: then they returned to Samaria.
- **2 Kings 5:1-14** [The little Hebrew maid compassionately compelled leprous Naaman, the commander of the Syrian army, to travel to Samaria to seek healing from the prophet Elisha.]

5. God empathizes with us; He is compassionate and understands our limitations and needs.

- **Psalm 103:13,14** Like as a father pitieth his children, so the Lord pitieth them that fear Him. [14] For He knoweth our frame; He remembereth that we are dust.
- **Psalm 139:1-4** O Lord, Thou hast searched me, and known me. [2] Thou knowest my downsitting and mine uprising, Thou understandest my thought afar off. [3] Thou compassest my path and my lying down, and art acquainted with all my ways. [4] For there is not a word in my tongue, but, lo, O Lord, Thou knowest it altogether.
- **Isaiah 49:15,16** Can a woman forget her sucking child, that she should not have compassion on the son of her womb? Yea, they may forget, yet will I not forget thee. [16] Behold, I have graven thee upon the palms of My hands; thy walls are continually before Me.

- **Isaiah 63:9** In all their affliction He [Jesus the Savior] was afflicted, and the angel of His presence saved them: in His love and in His pity He redeemed them; and He bare them, and carried them all the days of old.
- **Matthew 6:32b** For your Heavenly Father knoweth that ye have need of all these things.
- **Hebrews 4:15** For we have not an high priest which cannot be touched with the feeling of our infirmities; but was in all points tempted like as we are, yet without sin.

6. The Lord even has pity and compassion on the wicked or those who go astray, if they will only turn to Him.

- **Psalm 107:17-20,43** Fools because of their transgression, and because of their iniquities, are afflicted. [18] Their soul abhorreth all manner of meat; and they draw near unto the gates of death. [19] Then they cry unto the Lord in their trouble, and He saveth them out of their distresses. [20] He sent His Word, and healed them, and delivered them from their destructions. [43] Whoso is wise, and will observe these things, even they shall understand the lovingkindness of the Lord.
- **Jeremiah 31:20** [God's mercy was shown to the once backslidden tribe of Ephraim suffering under Babylonian captivity:] Is Ephraim My dear son? Is he a pleasant child? For since I spake against him, I do earnestly remember him still: Therefore My bowels are troubled for him; I will surely have mercy upon him, saith the Lord.
- **Matt 18:11-13** For the Son of Man is come to save that which was lost. [12] How think ye? If a man have an hundred sheep, and one of them be gone astray, doth he not leave the ninety and nine, and goeth into the mountains, and seeketh that which is gone astray? [13] And if so be that he find it, verily I say unto you, he rejoiceth more of that sheep, than of the ninety and nine which went not astray.
- **Matt 23:37** O Jerusalem, Jerusalem, thou that killest the prophets, and stonest them which are sent unto thee, how often would I have

gathered thy children together, even as a hen gathereth her chickens under her wings, and ye would not!

- **Luke 15:20** And [the prodigal son] arose, and came to his father. But when he was yet a great way off, his father saw him, and had compassion, and ran, and fell on his neck, and kissed him. [See also verses 11-32.]
- **Luke 19:41-42** And when He was come near, He beheld the city, and wept over it, [42] Saying, If thou hadst known, even thou, at least in this thy day, the things which belong unto thy peace! But now they are hid from thine eyes.

7. Jesus teaches us to empathize with others by His Own loving example.

- **Isaiah 53:4a** Surely He hath borne our griefs, and carried our sorrows: yet we did esteem Him stricken, smitten of God, and afflicted.
- **Matthew 9:36** But when He saw the multitudes, He was moved with compassion on them, because they fainted, and were scattered abroad, as sheep having no shepherd.
- **Matthew 8:16,17** When the even was come, they brought unto Him many that were possessed with devils: and He cast out the spirits with his word, and healed all that were sick: [17] That it might be fulfilled which was spoken by Esaias the prophet, saying, Himself took our infirmities, and bare our sicknesses.
- **Matthew 14:14** And Jesus went forth, and saw a great multitude, and was moved with compassion toward them, and He healed their sick.
- **Mark 1:41** [Jesus healed the leper:] And Jesus, moved with compassion, put forth His hand, and touched him, and saith unto him, I will; be thou clean.
- **Mark 8:2** I have compassion on the multitude, because they have now been with Me three days, and have nothing to eat.

- **John 11:33-35** [Jesus was summoned by Martha and Mary to raise up Lazarus, their dead brother.] When Jesus therefore saw [Mary] weeping, and the Jews also weeping which came with her, He groaned in the Spirit, and was troubled, [34] And said, Where have ye laid him? They said unto Him, Lord, come and see. [35] Jesus wept. [Then Jesus prayed, and Lazarus, who had been dead four days, miraculously arose from the dead.]

- **2 Corinthians 8:9** For ye know the grace of our Lord Jesus Christ, that, though He was rich, yet for your sakes He became poor, that ye through His poverty might be rich.

ENCOURAGEMENT

Definition: That which inspires courage, confidence, hope, renewed strength of heart and soul; moral support.

1. The positive effects of encouragement:

- **Proverbs 12:25** Heaviness in the heart of man maketh it stoop: but a good word maketh it glad.
- **Proverbs 15:23b** A word spoken in due season, how good is it!
- **Proverbs 16:24** Pleasant words are as an honeycomb, sweet to the soul, and health to the bones.
- **Proverbs 27:9** Ointment and perfume rejoice the heart: so doth the sweetness of a man's friend by hearty counsel.
- **2 Chronicles 15:8a** When [King] Asa heard these words, and the prophecy of Oded the prophet, he took courage.
- **1 John 1:4** And these things write we unto you, that your joy may be full. [See also John 15:11.]

2. Encourage others by just being there when others need you.

- **Ecclesiastes 4:9,10** Two are better than one; because they have a good reward for their labour. [10] For if they fall, the one will lift up his fellow: but woe to him that is alone when he falleth; for he hath not another to help him up.
- **Proverbs 18:24b** There is a friend that sticketh closer than a brother.
- **Proverbs 17:17** A friend loveth at all times, and a brother is born for adversity.

3. Share words of comfort, love and appreciation with those who are feeling low.

- **Job 4:4** [Eliphaz told Job:] Thy words have upholden him that was falling, and thou hast strengthened the feeble knees.

- **Isaiah 35:3,4a** Strengthen ye the weak hands, and confirm the feeble knees. [4] Say to them that are of a fearful heart, Be strong, fear not.
- **1 Thessalonians 4:18** Wherefore comfort one another with these words. [See also 1 Thessalonians 5:11.]

4. Forgive and reassure those who've made mistakes.

- **2 Corinthians 2:7,8** So that contrariwise ye ought rather to forgive him [who'd committed a serious wrong, but was sorry for it], and comfort him, lest perhaps such a one should be swallowed up with overmuch sorrow. [8] Wherefore I beseech you that ye would confirm your love toward him.
- **Lamentations 3:31-32** For the Lord will not cast off for ever: [32] But though He cause grief, yet will He have compassion according to the multitude of His mercies.
- **Galatians 6:1** Brethren, if a man be overtaken in a fault, ye which are spiritual, restore such an one in the spirit of meekness; considering thyself, lest thou also be tempted.

5. Assist those who are burdened with troubles or a heavy load.

- **Romans 15:1,2** We then that are strong ought to bear the infirmities of the weak, and not to please ourselves. [2] Let every one of us please his neighbour for his good to edification.
- **Galatians 6:2** Bear ye one another's burdens, and so fulfil the law of Christ.
- **1 Thessalonians 5:14b** Comfort the feebleminded, support the weak, be patient toward all men.

6. Remembering times when God gave us victories over our discouragement motivates us to want to encourage others.

- **2 Corinthians 1:4-7** Who comforteth us in all our tribulation, that we may be able to comfort them which are in any trouble, by the comfort wherewith we ourselves are comforted of God. [5] For as the sufferings of Christ abound in us, so our consolation also aboundeth by Christ. [6] And whether we be afflicted, it is for your consolation and salvation, which is effectual in the enduring of the same sufferings which we also suffer: or whether we be comforted, it is for your consolation and salvation. [7] And our hope of you is stedfast, knowing, that as ye are partakers of the sufferings, so shall ye be also of the consolation.

7. Talk about Jesus and what He's done for you, and can do for others!

- **2 Chronicles 32:6-8,21** [Hezekiah, king of Judah, encouraged his people to trust in the Lord when an evil king laid siege to their country:] And he set captains of war over the people, and gathered them together to him in the street of the gate of the city, and spake comfortably to them, saying, [7] Be strong and courageous, be not afraid nor dismayed for the king of Assyria, nor for all the multitude that is with him: for there be more with us than with him: [8] With him is an arm of flesh; but with us is the Lord our God to help us, and to fight our battles. And the people rested themselves upon the words of Hezekiah king of Judah. ... [21] And the Lord sent an angel, which cut off all the mighty men of valour, and the leaders and captains in the camp of the king of Assyria.
- **Psalm 66:16** Come and hear, all ye that fear God, and I will declare what He hath done for my soul.
- **Psalm 78:2-7** I will open my mouth in a parable: I will utter dark sayings of old: [3] Which we have heard and known, and our fathers have told us. [4] We will not hide them from their children, shewing to the generation to come the praises of the Lord, and His strength, and His wonderful works that He hath done. [5] For He established a testimony in Jacob, and appointed a law in Israel, which He commanded our fathers, that they should make them known to their children: [6] That the generation to come might know them,

even the children which should be born; who should arise and declare them to their children: [7] That they might set their hope in God, and not forget the works of God, but keep His commandments. [See also Psalm 145:1,4,7,11.]

- **Psalm 34:2** My soul shall make her boast in the Lord: the humble shall hear thereof, and be glad.
- **Psalm 69:30-32** I will praise the name of God with a song, and will magnify Him with thanksgiving. … [32] The humble shall see this, and be glad.
- **Psalm 119:74** They that fear Thee will be glad when they see me; because I have hoped in Thy Word.
- **Isaiah 63:7** I will mention the lovingkindnesss of the Lord, and the praises of the Lord, according to all that the Lord hath bestowed on us, and the great goodness toward the house of Israel, which He hath bestowed on them according to His mercies, and according to the multitude of His lovingkindnesss.
- **1 Peter 3:15** But sanctify the Lord God in your hearts: and be ready always to give an answer to every man that asketh you a reason of the hope that is in you with meekness and fear.

8. Encourage yourself by thinking positive thoughts.

[See Positiveness/Negative Thinking, #5 and #11, page 283.]

9. United prayer and fellowship is a source of renewed encouragement.

- **Psalm 133:1** Behold, how good and how pleasant it is for brethren to dwell together in unity!
- **Acts 4:23-33** [Returning from severe persecution, Peter and John prayed a courageous prayer together with the other disciples:] [31] And when they had prayed, the place was shaken where they were assembled together; and they were all filled with the Holy Ghost, and they spake the word of God with boldness. … [33] And

with great power gave the apostles witness of the resurrection of
the Lord Jesus: and great grace was upon them all.

- **Romans 1:11,12** For I long to see you ... [12] That I may be comforted
together with you by the mutual faith both of you and me.
- **Colossians 2:2a** [Paul wanted the Colossians to know how much he
battled in spirit for them] that their hearts might be comforted,
being knit together in love. ...

10. The Lord and His Word is our greatest source of encouragement.

- **Isaiah 41:13** For I the Lord thy God will hold thy right hand, saying
unto thee, Fear not; I will help thee.
- **Matthew 14:27** But straightway Jesus spake unto them, saying, Be
of good cheer; it is I; be not afraid.
- **Psalm 31:24** Be of good courage, and He shall strengthen your
heart, all ye that hope in the Lord.
- **Psalm 46:1** God is our refuge and strength, a very present help in
trouble.
- **Psalm 145:14** The Lord upholdeth all that fall, and raiseth up all
those that be bowed down.
- **John 6:63** It is the Spirit that quickeneth; the flesh profiteth nothing:
the Words that I speak unto you, they are Spirit, and they are Life.
- **Luke 24:32** And they said one to another, Did not our heart burn
within us, while He talked with us by the way, and while He opened
to us the Scriptures?
- **Colossians 3:16** Let the Word of Christ dwell in you richly in all
wisdom; teaching and admonishing one another in psalms and
hymns and spiritual songs, singing with grace in your hearts to the
Lord.
- **1 Thessalonians 4:16-18** [Hearing about the return of Jesus is a
great encouragement:] For the Lord Himself shall descend from
Heaven with a shout, with the voice of the archangel, and with the

trump of God. ... [18] Wherefore comfort one another with these Words.

11. Encouragement is a two-way street: When we encourage others, we ourselves are encouraged.

- **1 Samuel 30:1-19** [When King David's small militia suffered loss of their home town to an enemy attack and his own disheartened troops considered stoning him to death, he prayed and "encouraged himself in the Lord." And when he told his men that God had promised to recover their families and homes, they took courage and went into battle with him, recovering all in magnanimous victory. As David encouraged his men, the Lord also encouraged him, leading them together into triumph.]
- **Isaiah 58:10** And if thou draw out thy soul to the hungry, and satisfy the afflicted soul; then shall thy light rise in obscurity, and thy darkness be as the noonday:
- **Proverbs 11:25** The liberal [generous] soul shall be made fat: and he that watereth shall be watered also himself.
- **Luke 6:38** Give, and it shall be given unto you; good measure, pressed down, and shaken together, and running over, shall men give into your bosom. For with the same measure that ye mete withal it shall be measured to you again. [See also Acts 20:35.]
- **2 Corinthians 9:6b** But this I say, He which soweth sparingly shall reap also sparingly; and he which soweth bountifully shall reap also bountifully.

12. The ability to encourage others is a gift from God, which He gives to you for the asking.

- **Isaiah 50:4** The Lord God hath given me the tongue of the learned, that I should know how to speak a word in season to him that is weary: He wakeneth morning by morning, He wakeneth mine ear to hear as the learned.

- **1 Peter 4:11** If any man speak, let him speak as the oracles of God; if any man minister, let him do it as of the ability which God giveth: that God in all things may be glorified through Jesus Christ, to whom be praise and dominion for ever and ever. Amen.

- **1 Corinthians 14:3,12,31** [The Lord sometimes uses the gift of prophecy to encourage His children.] But he that prophesieth speaketh unto men to edification, and exhortation, and comfort. ... [12] Even so ye, forasmuch as ye are zealous of spiritual gifts, seek that ye may excel to the edifying of the Church. ... [31] For ye may all prophesy one by one, that all may learn, and all may be comforted.

- **Hebrews 3:13** But exhort [encourage] one another daily, while it is called To day; lest any of you be hardened through the deceitfulness of sin.

EVIL ASSOCIATIONS, BAD COMPANY

Definition: Friendships or partnerships which have negative effects upon our attitudes, actions, or physical or spiritual well-being.

1. We are influenced, for better or for worse, by those with whom we associate.

- **Proverbs 13:20** He that walketh with wise men shall be wise: but a companion of fools shall be destroyed.
- **1 Corinthians 15:33** Be not deceived: evil communications [companions] corrupt good manners.
- **Galatians 5:7-9** [The influence of bad company can be disastrous.] Ye did run well; who did hinder you that ye should not obey the truth? [8] This persuasion cometh not of Him that calleth you. [9] A little leaven leaveneth the whole lump.

2. We should associate with those by whom we will be influenced for the good.

- **Psalm 119:63** I am a companion of all them that fear Thee, and of them that keep Thy precepts.
- **Proverbs 2:20** Walk in the way of good men, and keep the paths of the righteous.
- **Proverbs 15:31** The ear that heareth the reproof of life abideth among the wise.

3. God's Word likens bad associations to "snares" or traps set by the Devil.

- **Exodus 23:33** [As the children of Israel entered the Promised Land, God was specific in commanding them not to associate with the heathen living there:] They shall not dwell in thy land, lest they make thee sin against Me: for if thou serve their gods, it will surely be a <u>snare</u> unto thee. [See also Numbers 33:52.]

- **Exodus 34:12** Take heed to thyself, lest thou make a covenant with the inhabitants of the land whither thou goest, lest it be for a snare in the midst of thee.
- **Deuteronomy 12:30** Take heed to thyself that thou be not snared by following [unbelievers], after that they be destroyed from before thee; and that thou inquire not after their gods, saying, How did these nations serve their gods? Even so will I do likewise.
- **Psalm 106:34-43** [Here is what resulted when God's people didn't keep themselves separate from their worldly neighbors, whom the Lord forbade them to live with:] They did not destroy the nations, concerning whom the Lord commanded them: [35] But were mingled among the heathen, and learned their works. [36] And they served their idols: which were a snare unto them. [37] Yea, they sacrificed their sons and their daughters unto devils. ... [39] Thus were they defiled with their own works. ... [40] Therefore was the wrath of the Lord kindled against His people, insomuch that He abhorred His own inheritance. [41] And He gave them into the hand of the heathen and they that hated them ruled over them. [42] Their enemies also oppressed them, and they were brought into subjection under their hand. [43] Many times did He deliver them; but they provoked Him with their counsel, and were brought low for their iniquity.
- **Proverbs 22:5** Thorns and snares are in the way of the froward [false, perverse]: he that doth keep his soul shall be far from them.

4. Bad associations can cause us to compromise our convictions.

- **Proverbs 12:26** The righteous is more excellent than his neighbou but the way of the wicked seduceth them.
- **Proverbs 16:29** A violent man enticeth his neighbour, and leadeth him into the way that is not good.
- **Proverbs 19:27** [Overexposure to worldly counsel and the media, such as music, movies and TV, can lead you astray.] Cease, my son to hear the instruction that causeth to err from the words of knowledge.

- **Proverbs 22:24,25** Make no friendship with an angry man; and with a furious man thou shalt not go: [25] Lest thou learn his ways, and get a snare to thy soul.
- **Ecclesiastes 9:18b** One sinner destroyeth much good.
- **1 Corinthians 5:6b** Know ye not that a little leaven leaveneth the whole lump?

5. The Enemy tempts us by making the way of the ungodly appear desirable—but consider their end!

- **Proverbs 24:1** Be not thou envious against evil men, neither desire to be with them.
- **Psalm 37:1b,2** [Remember, the "good things" that the ungodly seem to be enjoying now are only temporary:] Neither be thou envious against the workers of iniquity. [2] For they shall soon be cut down like the grass, and wither as the green herb.
- **Psalm 73:3,17,18** For I was envious at the foolish, when I saw the prosperity of the wicked … [17] Until I went into the sanctuary of God; then understood I their end. [18] Surely Thou didst set them in slippery places: Thou castedst them down into destruction.
- **Psalm 141:4** Incline not my heart to any evil thing, to practice wicked works with men that work iniquity: and let me not eat of their dainties.
- **Proverbs 23:6,7** Eat thou not the bread of him that hath an evil eye, neither desire thou his dainty meats. [7] For as he thinketh in his heart, so is he: Eat and drink, saith he to thee; but his heart is not with thee.

6. We need conviction to separate ourselves from ungodly, unfruitful associations.

- **Psalm 1:1** Blessed is the man that walketh not in the counsel of the ungodly, nor standeth in the way of sinners, nor sitteth in the seat of the scornful. [See also Genesis 49:6a.]

- **Psalm 26:4,5** I have not sat with vain persons, neither will I go in with dissemblers. [5] I have hated the congregation of evil doers; and will not sit with the wicked.

- **Psalm 84:10** For a day in Thy courts is better than a thousand. I had rather be a doorkeeper in the house of my God, than to dwell in the tents of wickedness.

- **Psalm 101:4,7** A froward [stubbornly contrary, disobedient] heart shall depart from me: I will not know a wicked person. ... [7] He that worketh deceit shall not dwell within my house: he that telleth lies shall not tarry in my sight.

- **Psalm 119:115** Depart from me, ye evildoers: for I will keep the commandments of my God.

- **Psalm 139:19-22** Surely Thou wilt slay the wicked, O God: depart from me therefore, ye bloody men. [20] For they speak against Thee wickedly, and Thine enemies take Thy name in vain. [21] Do not I hate them, O Lord, that hate Thee? And am not I grieved with those that rise up against Thee? [22] I hate them with perfect hatred: I count them mine enemies.

- **Proverbs 1:10,15** My son, if sinners entice thee, consent thou not. ... [15] My son, walk not thou in the way with them; refrain thy foot from their path.

- **Proverbs 9:6** Forsake the foolish, and live; and go in the way of understanding.

- **2 Corinthians 6:14,17** Be ye not unequally yoked together with unbelievers: for what fellowship hath righteousness with unrighteousness? And what communion hath light with darkness? ... [17] Wherefore come out from among them, and be ye separate, saith the Lord, and touch not the unclean thing; and I will receive you.

- **Ephesians 5:11** And have no fellowship with the unfruitful works of darkness, but rather reprove them.

- **Revelation 18:4** And I heard another voice from Heaven, saying, Come out of her [Babylon], My people, that ye be not partakers of her sins, and that ye receive not of her plagues. [See also Jeremiah 51:6.]

7. If we continue to keep bad company, we will be punished with them.

- **Genesis 13:12,13; 2 Peter 2:7,8** [Lot chose to live a life of ease in the wicked city of Sodom and suffered the consequences; he lost his wife and troubled his own soul:] Abram dwelled in the land of Canaan, and Lot dwelled in the cities of the plain, and pitched his tent toward Sodom. [13] But the men of Sodom were wicked and sinners before the Lord exceedingly. [Although God delivered Lot out of Sodom, he suffered from having lived with them for many years:] [2 Peter 2:7,8] And [God] delivered just Lot, vexed with the filthy conversation of the wicked: [8](For that righteous man dwelling among them, in <u>seeing and hearing</u>, <u>vexed</u> his righteous soul from day to day with their unlawful deeds;) (See Genesis chapter 19.)
- **Numbers 16:26** [Moses warned his brethren not to associate with those who sowed dissension in the ranks of the Children of Israel.] And he spake unto the congregation, saying, Depart, I pray you, from the tents of these wicked men, and touch nothing of theirs, lest ye be consumed in all their sins. [The Lord later destroyed them. See verses 31-35.]
- **2 Chronicles 19:2b** Shouldest thou help the ungodly, and love them that hate the Lord? Therefore is wrath upon thee from before the Lord.
- **Ezra 9:14** Should we again break Thy commandments, and join in affinity with the people of these abominations? Wouldest not Thou be angry with us till Thou hadst consumed us, so that there should be no remnant nor escaping?
- **Proverbs 21:16** The man that wandereth out of the way of understanding shall remain in the congregation of the dead. [See also Proverbs 27:8.]
- **Proverbs 28:19b** He that followeth after vain persons shall have poverty enough.
- **Ephesians 5:6-8** Let no man deceive you with vain words: for because of these things cometh the wrath of God upon the children

of disobedience. [7] Be not ye therefore partakers with them. [8] For ye were sometimes darkness, but now are ye light in the Lord: walk as children of light:

- **2 John 1:10,11** If there come any unto you, and bring not this doctrine, receive him not into your house, neither bid him God speed: [11] For he that biddeth him God speed is partaker of his evil deeds.

8. We should not even associate with other Christians who persist in being wilfully disobedient.

- **Romans 16:17** Now I beseech you, brethren, mark them which cause divisions and offences contrary to the doctrine which ye have learned; and avoid them. [See also Matthew 18:15-17.]
- **1 Corinthians 5:11** But now I have written unto you not to keep company, if any man that is called a brother be a fornicator, or covetous, or an idolater, or a railer, or a drunkard, or an extortioner; with such an one no not to eat.
- **2 Thessalonians 3:6** Now we command you, brethren, in the name of our Lord Jesus Christ, that ye withdraw yourselves from every brother that walketh disorderly, and not after the tradition which he received of us.
- **2 Thessalonians 3:14,15** And if any man obey not our word by this epistle, note that man, and have no company with him, that he may be ashamed. [15] Yet count him not as an enemy, but admonish [gently warn or reprove] him as a brother.
- **1 Timothy 6:3-5** If any man teach otherwise, and consent not to wholesome words, even the words of our Lord Jesus Christ, and to the doctrine which is according to godliness; [4] He is proud, knowing nothing, but doting about questions and strifes of words, whereof cometh envy, strife, railings, evil surmisings, [5] Perverse disputings of men of corrupt minds, and destitute of the truth, supposing that gain is godliness: from such withdraw thyself.

2 Timothy 3:5 [In the Last Days, some men will be] having a form of godliness, but denying the power thereof: from such turn away.

Titus 3:10 A man that is an heretick [one who sows dissension, or holds to false beliefs] after the first and second admonition reject.

2 Peter 2:18-22 For when they speak great swelling words of vanity, they allure through the lusts of the flesh, through much wantonness, those that were clean escaped from them who live in error. [19] While they promise them liberty, they themselves are the servants of corruption: for of whom a man is overcome, of the same is he brought in bondage. [20] For if after they have escaped the pollutions of the world through the knowledge of the Lord and Saviour Jesus Christ, they are again entangled therein, and overcome, the latter end is worse with them than the beginning. [21] For it had been better for them not to have known the way of righteousness, than, after they have known it, to turn from the holy commandment delivered unto them. [22] But it is happened unto them according to the true proverb, The dog is turned to his own vomit again; and the sow that was washed to her wallowing in the mire.

). Pray for the Lord's help, wisdom and discernment to escape the snare of bad associations.

• **Genesis 49:6** [The patriarch, Jacob, even prayed that he wouldn't listen to the bad counsel of his own errant sons, Simeon and Levi:] O my soul, come not thou into their secret; unto their assembly, mine honour, be not thou united: for in their anger they slew a man, and in their selfwill they digged down a wall.

• **Psalm 56:13** For Thou hast delivered my soul from death: wilt not Thou deliver my feet from falling, that I may walk before God in the light of the living?

• **Psalm 141:4** [King David prayed:] Incline not my heart to any evil thing, to practise wicked works with men that work iniquity: and let me not eat of their dainties.

- **Psalm 119:51** The proud have had me greatly in derision: yet have I not declined from Thy law.
- **Proverbs 2:11,12** Discretion shall preserve thee, understanding shall keep thee: [12] To deliver thee from the way of the evil man, from the man that speaketh froward things.
- **Proverbs 9:6** Forsake the foolish, and live; and go in the way of understanding.
- **Proverbs 14:7** Go from the presence of a foolish man, when thou perceivest not in him the lips of knowledge.
- **Matthew 6:13** And lead us not into temptation, but deliver us from evil: For Thine is the Kingdom, and the power, and the glory, for ever. Amen.

FAIR PLAY/CHEATING

Definition: Fair play is conformity to godly rules. Cheating is obtaining advantage by unfair or fraudulent means; dishonest behavior; deception; trickery.

1. Fair play is a fundamental characteristic of the righteous that sets them apart from the wicked.

- **Psalm 15:1-2** Lord, who shall abide in Thy tabernacle? Who shall dwell in Thy holy hill? [2] He that walketh uprightly, and worketh righteousness, and speaketh the truth in his heart.
- **Psalm 36:1,3** The transgression of the wicked saith within my heart, that there is no fear of God before his eyes. … [3] The words of his mouth are iniquity and deceit: he hath left off to be wise, and to do good.
- **Proverbs 12:5** The thoughts of the righteous are right [fair]: but the counsels of the wicked are deceit.
- **Psalm 26:9-11** Gather not my soul with sinners, nor my life with bloody men: [10] In whose hands is mischief, and their right hand is full of bribes. [11] But as for me, I will walk in mine integrity: redeem me, and be merciful unto me.
- **Proverbs 20:7** The just man walketh in his integrity [honesty and principle]: his children are blessed after him. [See also Psalm 26:1.]
- **Isaiah 33:15,16** [A wonderful promise to those who treat others fairly:] He that walketh righteously, and speaketh uprightly; he that despiseth the gain of oppressions, that shaketh his hands from holding of bribes, that stoppeth his ears from hearing of blood, and shutteth his eyes from seeing evil; [16] He shall dwell on high: his place of defence shall be the munitions of rocks: bread shall be given him; his waters shall be sure.

2. The Lord commands His people not to cheat, deceive or take unfair advantage of others.

- **Proverbs 21:3** To do justice and judgment is more acceptable to the Lord than sacrifice.
- **Micah 6:8** He hath shewed thee, O man, what is good; and what doth the Lord require of thee, but to do justly, and to love mercy, and to walk humbly with thy God?
- **Luke 3:12-14** Then came also publicans to be baptized, and said unto Him, Master, what shall we do? [13] And He said unto them, Exact no more than that which is appointed you. [14] And the soldiers likewise demanded of Him, saying, And what shall we do? And He said unto them, Do violence to no man, neither accuse any falsely; and be content with your wages.
- **Colossians 4:1** Masters, give unto your servants that which is just and equal; knowing that ye also have a Master in Heaven.
- **1 Corinthians 5:8** Therefore let us keep the feast, not with old leaven, neither with the leaven of malice and wickedness; but with the unleavened bread of sincerity and truth.

3. Fair play or judgment is a basic requirement for leaders in God's work.

- **Deuteronomy 16:18,20** Judges and officers shalt thou make thee in all thy gates, which the Lord thy God giveth thee, throughout thy tribes: and they shall judge the people with just judgment. ... [20] That which is altogether just shalt thou follow, that thou mayest live, and inherit the land which the Lord thy God giveth thee.
- **2 Samuel 23:3** The God of Israel said, the Rock of Israel spake to me, He that ruleth over men must be just, ruling in the fear of God.
- **Acts 6:3** Wherefore, brethren, look ye out among you seven men of honest report, full of the Holy Ghost and wisdom, whom we may appoint over this business.

- **Acts 20:33,34** [Paul had this testimony:] I have coveted no man's silver, or gold, or apparel. [34] Yea, ye yourselves know, that these hands have ministered unto my necessities, and to them that were with me.
- **Titus 1:7b** For a bishop must be blameless, as the steward of God.
- **1 Peter 5:2** Feed the flock of God which is among you, taking the oversight thereof, not by constraint, but willingly; not for filthy lucre [for dishonest gain], but of a ready mind.

4. Cheating often leads to a vicious cycle of more cheating, being cheated, and mutual mistrust—as illustrated in the life of Jacob, the deceiver.

- **Genesis 25:29-33** [First Jacob took advantage of Esau in order to seize his brother's birthright:] And Jacob sod pottage [cooked stew]: and Esau came from the field, and he was faint: [30] And Esau said to Jacob, Feed me, I pray thee, with that same red pottage; for I am faint. ... [31] And Jacob said, Sell me this day thy birthright. [32] And Esau said, Behold, I am at the point to die: and what profit shall this birthright do to me? [33] And Jacob said, Swear to me this day; and he sware unto him: and he sold his birthright unto Jacob.

Genesis 27:6-17 [Then Jacob's mother, Rebekah, also conspired with Jacob to steal the blessing that his father, who by then was blind, intended for Esau:] [11] And Jacob said to Rebekah his mother, Behold, Esau my brother is a hairy man, and I am a smooth man: [12] My father peradventure will feel me, and I shall seem to him as a deceiver; and I shall bring a curse upon me, and not a blessing. [13] And his mother said unto him, Upon me be thy curse, my son: only obey my voice, and go fetch me them. [14] And he went, and fetched, and brought them to his mother: and his mother made savoury meat, such as his father loved. [15] And Rebekah took goodly raiment of her eldest son Esau, which were with her in the house, and put them upon Jacob her younger son: [16] And she put the skins of the kids of the goats upon his hands, and upon the smooth of his neck: [17] And she gave the savoury meat and the bread, which she had prepared, into the hand of her son Jacob.

- **Genesis 29:21-27** [After Jacob had served Laban for seven years in order to marry Rachel, Laban's daughter, Jacob was cheated, just as he had cheated his brother. Laban gave him Leah, the oldest daughter rather than Rachel:] [25] And he said to Laban, What is this thou hast done unto me? Did not I serve with thee for Rachel? Wherefore then hast thou beguiled me?

- **Genesis 30:31-43** [Years later Jacob turned around and cheated Laban, by breeding strong herds of cattle and goats for himself, only leaving the weaker ones for Laban:] [41] And it came to pass, whensoever the stronger cattle did conceive, that Jacob laid the rods before the eyes of the cattle in the gutters, that they might conceive among the rods. [42] But when the cattle were feeble, he put them not in: so the feebler were Laban's, and the stronger Jacob's. [43] And [Jacob] increased exceedingly, and had much cattle, and maidservants, and menservants, and camels, and asses.

- **Genesis 31:32-35** [Jacob's wife, Rachel, cheated her father Laban by stealing his household idols, unbeknownst to her husband. Jacob said to Laban:] With whomsoever thou [Laban] findest thy gods, let him not live: before our brethren discern thou what is thine with me, and take it to thee. For Jacob knew not that Rachel had stolen them. [34] Now Rachel had taken the images, and put them in the camel's furniture, and sat upon them. And Laban searched all the tent, but found them not. [35] And she said to her father, Let it not displease my lord that I cannot rise up before thee; for the custom of women is upon me [menstruation]. And he searched, but found not the images.

- **Genesis 32:24-29** [It was only after Jacob had an encounter with an angel that his name (and character) was changed from Jacob, which meant "deceiver," to Israel; then he began to live a more honest life:] And Jacob was left alone; and there wrestled [an angel] with him until the breaking of the day. ... [27] And [the angel] said unto him, What is thy name? And he said, Jacob. [28] And he said, Thy name shall be called no more Jacob, but Israel: for as a prince hast thou power with God and with men, and hast prevailed.

5. In the Bible, the Lord often uses balances [scales] to illustrate the concepts of honesty and fair play.

- **Proverbs 11:1** A false balance is abomination to the Lord: but a just weight is His delight.
- **Leviticus 19:35,36** Ye shall do no unrighteousness in judgment, in meteyard, in weight, or in measure. [36] Just balances, just weights, a just ephah [dry measure] and a just hin [liquid measure], shall ye have: I am the Lord your God, which brought you out of the land of Egypt.
- **Deuteronomy 25:13,15** Thou shalt not have in thy bag divers weights, a great and a small. ... [15] But thou shalt have a perfect and just weight, a perfect and just measure shalt thou have: that thy days may be lengthened in the land which the Lord thy God giveth thee.
- **Proverbs 16:2,11** All the ways of a man are clean in his own eyes; but the Lord weigheth the spirits. ... [11] A just weight and balance are the Lord's: all the weights of the bag are His work.
- **Proverbs 20:10** Divers weights, and divers measures, both of them are alike abomination to the Lord. [See also Hosea 12:7;Amos 8:5.]

6. Sooner or later, cheating is always uncovered.

- **Numbers 32:23b** Be sure your sin will find you out.
- **Proverbs 10:9** He that walketh uprightly walketh surely: but he that perverteth his ways shall be known.
- **Proverbs 15:3** The eyes of the Lord are in every place, beholding the evil and the good.
- **Proverbs 20:17** Bread of deceit is sweet to a man; but afterwards his mouth shall be filled with gravel.

- **Jeremiah 7:9-11** Will ye steal ... and swear falsely ... [10] And come and stand before Me in this house, which is called by My name, and say, We are delivered to do all these abominations? [11] Is this house, which is called by My name, become a den of robbers in your eyes? Behold, even <u>I have seen it</u>, saith the Lord. [See also Jeremiah 9:4-9; Ezekiel 22:29-31.]

- **Luke 12:2** For there is nothing covered, that shall not be revealed; neither hid, that shall not be known.

- **1 Corinthians 4:5b** The Lord ... will bring to light the hidden things of darkness, and will make manifest the counsels of the hearts: and then shall every man have praise of God.

7. The Lord will judge and reward us according to our works, whether we have cheated and dealt falsely or whether we have dealt fairly and righteously.

- **Psalm 24:3-5** Who shall ascend into the hill of the Lord? Or who shall stand in His holy place? [4] He that hath clean hands, and a pure heart; who hath not lifted up his soul unto vanity, nor sworn deceitfully. [5] He shall receive the blessing from the Lord, and righteousness from the God of his salvation.

- **Psalm 125:4,5a** Do good, O Lord, unto those that be good, and to them that are upright in their hearts. [5a] As for such as turn aside unto their crooked ways, the Lord shall lead them forth with the workers of iniquity.

- **Proverbs 11:18** The wicked worketh a deceitful work: but to him that soweth righteousness shall be a sure reward.

- **Proverbs 24:12** If thou sayest, Behold, we knew it not; doth not He that pondereth the heart consider it? And He that keepeth thy soul, doth not He know it? And shall not He render to every man according to his works?

- **Jeremiah 17:10** I the Lord search the heart, I try the reins, even to give every man according to his ways, and according to the fruit of his doings.

- **Jeremiah 32:19** Great in counsel, and mighty in work: for Thine eyes are open upon all the ways of the sons of men: to give every one according to his ways, and according to the fruit of his doings.
- **Matthew 16:27** For the Son of man shall come in the glory of His Father with His angels; and then He shall reward every man according to his works.
- **Revelation 20:12** And I saw the dead, small and great, stand before God; and the books were opened: and another book was opened, which is the Book of Life: and the dead were judged out of those things which were written in the books, according to their works.
- **Revelation 22:11-12,14-15** He that is unjust, let him be unjust still: and he which is filthy, let him be filthy still: and he that is righteous, let him be righteous still: and he that is holy, let him be holy still. [12] And, behold, I come quickly; and My reward is with Me, to give every man according as his work shall be. ... [14] Blessed are they that do His commandments, that they may have right to the tree of life, and may enter in through the gates into the city. [15] For without are dogs, and sorcerers, and whoremongers, and murderers, and idolaters, and whosoever loveth and maketh a lie.

FASCINATION FOR EVIL

Definition: To fascinate is to grip so as to take away the power to move, act, or think for oneself; to attract and hold by charming qualities.

1. Because the Lord abhors evil, those who are drawn to it alienate themselves from Him.

- **Genesis 6:5,6** And God saw that the wickedness of man was great in the earth, and that every imagination of the thoughts of his heart was only evil continually. [6] And it repented the Lord that He had made man on the earth, and it grieved Him at His heart.
- **Psalm 66:18** If I regard iniquity in my heart, the Lord will not hear me.
- **Proverbs 1:28,29** Then shall they call upon Me, but I will not answer; they shall seek Me early, but they shall not find Me: [29] For that they hated knowledge, and did not choose the fear of the Lord.
- **Proverbs 6:16,18** These six things doth the Lord hate: yea, seven are an abomination unto Him: … [18] An heart that deviseth wicked imaginations, feet that be swift in running to mischief.
- **Proverbs 15:26a** The thoughts of the wicked are an abomination unto the Lord.
- **Isaiah 59:2** But your iniquities have separated between you and your God, and your sins have hid His face from you, that He will not hear.
- **Micah 3:4** Then shall they cry unto the Lord, but He will not hear them: He will even hide His face from them at that time, as they have behaved themselves ill in their doings.
- **1 Corinthians 10:5,6** But with many of them God was not well pleased: for they were overthrown in the wilderness. [6] Now these things were our examples, to the intent we should not lust after evil things, as they also lusted.

2. It is not a sin to be tempted with evil; it becomes a sin when we choose to entertain it.

- **Romans 7:19-23** [The enemy is always trying to tempt us; but we don't have to give in.] For the good that I would I do not: but the evil which I would not, that I do. [22] For I delight in the law of God after the inward man: [23] But I see another law in my members, warring against the law of my mind, and bringing me into captivity to the law of sin which is in my members.
- **1 Thessalonians 3:5** For this cause … I sent to know your faith, lest by some means the Tempter have tempted you, and our labour be in vain.
- **James 1:13,14** Let no man say when he is tempted, I am tempted of God: for God cannot be tempted with evil, neither tempteth He any man: [14] But every man is tempted, when he is drawn away of his own lust, and enticed.

3. We can't be thinking the Lord's thoughts while enticed by Satan's thoughts.

- **Matthew 6:24a** No man can serve two masters: for either he will hate the one, and love the other; or else he will hold to the one, and despise the other.
- **Luke 11:34** The light of the body is the eye: therefore when thine eye is single, thy whole body also is full of light; but when thine eye is evil, thy body also is full of darkness.
- **Romans 6:16** Know ye not, that to whom ye yield yourselves servants to obey, his servants ye are to whom ye obey; whether of sin unto death, or of obedience unto righteousness?
- **1 Corinthians 10:21** Ye cannot drink the cup of the Lord, and the cup of devils: ye cannot be partakers of the Lord's table, and of the table of devils.
- **2 Corinthians 6:14b** What fellowship hath righteousness with unrighteousness? And what communion hath light with darkness?

4. The Lord will judge those who entertain a fascination for evil instead of choosing His ways.

- **Deuteronomy 30:19** I call Heaven and earth to record this day against you, that I have set before you life and death, blessing and cursing: therefore choose life, that both thou and thy seed may live.
- **1 Kings 18:21a** And Elijah came unto all the people, and said, How long halt ye between two opinions? If the Lord be God, follow Him: but if Baal, then follow him. [See also Amos 5:15.]
- **Proverbs 1:29-31** For that they hated [godly] knowledge, and did not choose the fear of the Lord: [30] They would none of My counsel: they despised all My reproof. [31] Therefore shall they eat of the fruit of their own way, and be filled with their own devices.
- **Isaiah 65:12** Therefore will I number you to the sword, and ye shall all bow down to the slaughter: because when I called, ye did not answer; when I spake, ye did not hear; but did evil before Mine eyes, and did choose that wherein I delighted not.
- **Isaiah 66:4** I also will choose their delusions, and will bring their fears upon them; because when I called, none did answer; when I spake, they did not hear: but they did evil before Mine eyes, and chose that in which I delighted not.

5. Those who entertain the Devil's thoughts will eventually act upon them.

- **Proverbs 23:7a** For as he thinketh in his heart, so is he.
- **Matthew 12:34b,35** [As the saying goes: "The thought is the father of the deed."] For out of the abundance of the heart the mouth speaketh. [35] A good man out of the good treasure of the heart bringeth forth good things: and an evil man out of the evil treasure bringeth forth evil things.
- **Romans 1:21,28** Because that, when they knew God, they glorified Him not as God, neither were thankful; but became vain in their imaginations, and their foolish heart was darkened. [28] And even as

they did not like to retain God in their knowledge, God gave them over to a reprobate mind, to do those things which are not convenient.

• **James 1:15** Then when lust hath conceived, it bringeth forth sin: and sin, when it is finished, bringeth forth death.

6. Although it may seem innocent enough at the start, toying with the Devil is a deadly game!

• **Genesis 3:1a** [The only one smarter than the Devil is God, and without His help we're no match for the old Serpent:] Now the serpent was more subtil than any beast of the field which the Lord God had made.

• **Proverbs 26:24,25** [We need discernment to see when others are trying to deceive us to get into mischief:] He that hateth, dissembleth [disguises it] with his lips, and layeth up deceit within him; 25 When he speaketh fair, believe him not: for there are seven abominations in his heart. [See also Proverbs 12:20; Jeremiah 9:4-8]

• **Matthew 7:13** Enter ye in at the strait gate: for wide is the gate, and broad is the way, that leadeth to destruction, and many there be which go in thereat.

• **Luke 22:31** And the Lord said, Simon, Simon, behold, Satan hath desired to have you, that he may sift you as wheat.

• **2 Corinthians 11:3** But I fear, lest by any means, as the serpent beguiled Eve through his subtilty, so your minds should be corrupted from the simplicity that is in Christ.

• **1 Peter 5:8,9** Be sober, be vigilant; because your adversary the Devil, as a roaring lion, walketh about, seeking whom he may devour: 9 Whom resist stedfast in the faith, knowing that the same afflictions are accomplished in your brethren that are in the world.

7. Don't entertain evil for an instant!

- **Proverbs 3:31** Envy thou not the oppressor, and choose none of his ways.
- **Proverbs 4:14-16** Enter not into the path of the wicked, and go not in the way of evil men. [15] Avoid it, pass not by it, turn from it, and pass away. [16] For they sleep not, except they have done mischief; and their sleep is taken away, unless they cause some to fall.
- **Proverbs 4:23** Keep thy heart with all diligence; for out of it are the issues of life.
- **Matthew 26:41** Watch and pray, that ye enter not into temptation: the spirit indeed is willing, but the flesh is weak.
- **Luke 8:13** [If you stray from the Word for long, you're open prey for the Enemy to attack:] They on the rock are they, which, when they hear, receive the word with joy; and these have no root, which for a while believe, and in time of temptation fall away.
- **2 Corinthians 10:5** [Cast] down imaginations, and every high thing that exalteth itself against the knowledge of God, and bringing into captivity every thought to the obedience of Christ.
- **Ephesians 4:26,27** … Sin not … [27] Neither give place to the Devil.

8. Don't allow the Devil a point of entry; avoid situations which lead to temptation.

- **Deuteronomy 7:25,26** The graven images of their gods shall ye burn with fire: thou shalt not desire the silver or gold that is on them, nor take it unto thee, lest thou be snared therein: for it is an abomination to the Lord thy God. [26] Neither shalt thou bring an abomination into thine house, lest thou be a cursed thing like it: but thou shalt utterly detest it, and thou shalt utterly abhor it; for it is a cursed thing.
- **Psalm 101:3** I will set no wicked thing before mine eyes: I hate the work of them that turn aside; it shall not cleave to me.

- **Psalm 119:37** [David prayed desperately:] Turn away mine eyes from beholding vanity; and quicken Thou me in Thy way.
- **Proverbs 4:25-27** Let thine eyes look right on, and let thine eyelids look straight before thee. [26] Ponder the path of thy feet, and let all thy ways be established. [27] Turn not to the right hand nor to the left: remove thy foot from evil.
- **1 Peter 3:11** Let him eschew [turn away from] evil, and do good; let him seek peace, and ensue [pursue] it.

9. Have no fellowship with those who promote evil.

- **Ephesians 5:6,7,11** Let no man deceive you with vain words: for because of these things cometh the wrath of God upon the children of disobedience. [7] Be not ye therefore partakers with them. [11] And have no fellowship with the unfruitful works of darkness, but rather reprove them.
- **Exodus 23:2a** Thou shalt not follow a multitude to do evil.
- **Psalm 1:1** Blessed is the man that walketh not in the counsel of the ungodly, nor standeth in the way of sinners, nor sitteth in the seat of the scornful.
- **Proverbs 1:10** My son, if sinners entice thee, consent thou not.
- **Proverbs 4:14,15** Enter not into the path of the wicked, and go not in the way of evil men. [15] Avoid it, pass not by it, turn from it, and pass away.
- **Proverbs 24:1,2** Be not thou envious against evil men, neither desire to be with them. [2] For their heart studieth destruction, and their lips talk of mischief.
- **2 Corinthians 6:14-18** Be ye not unequally yoked together with unbelievers: for what fellowship hath righteousness with unrighteousness? And what communion hath light with darkness? [15] And what concord hath Christ with Belial? Or what part hath he that believeth with an infidel? [16] And what agreement hath the temple of God with idols? For ye are the temple of the living God; as God hath said, I will dwell in them, and walk in them; and I will

be their God, and they shall be My people. ¹⁷ Wherefore come out from among them, and be ye separate, saith the Lord, and touch not the unclean thing; and I will receive you, ¹⁸ And will be a Father unto you, and ye shall be My sons and daughters, saith the Lord Almighty.

- **Ephesians 5:11** And have no fellowship with the unfruitful works of darkness, but rather reprove them.
- **2 Peter 3:17** Ye therefore, beloved, seeing ye know these things before, beware lest ye also, being led away with the error of the wicked, fall from your own stedfastness.
- **Revelation 18:4** And I heard another voice from Heaven, saying, Come out of her [Babylon], My people, that ye be not partakers of her sins, and that ye receive not of her plagues. [See also Evil Associations/Bad Company, page 114.]

10. Pray for a godly hatred for all the Devil's dirt!

- **Psalm 97:10a** Ye that love the Lord, hate evil.
- **Psalm 119:104** Through Thy precepts I get understanding: therefore I hate every false way.
- **Proverbs 8:13** The fear of the Lord is to hate evil: pride, and arrogancy, and the evil way, and the froward mouth, do I hate.
- **Amos 5:15a** Hate the evil, and love the good, and establish judgment in the gate.
- **Romans 12:9b** Abhor that which is evil; cleave to that which is good.

11. The Lord can keep you from evil, when you cooperate with Him and do your part.

- **Job 5:19** He shall deliver thee in six troubles: yea, in seven there shall no evil touch thee.
- **Matthew 6:13a** [Keep close to God in prayer, as Jesus did:] And lead us not into temptation, but deliver us from evil.

- **1 Corinthians 10:13** There hath no temptation taken you but such as is common to man: but God is faithful, who will not suffer you to be tempted above that ye are able; but will with the temptation also make a way to escape, that ye may be able to bear it.
- **Ephesians 6:13** Wherefore take unto you the whole armour of God, that ye may be able to withstand in the evil day, and having done all, to stand.
- **2 Peter 2:9a** The Lord knoweth how to deliver the godly out of temptations.
- **Revelation 3:10** [Hang onto the Word:] Because thou hast kept the word of My patience, I also will keep thee from the hour of temptation, which shall come upon all the world, to try them that dwell upon the earth.

FEAR OF FAILURE

Definition: A worrisome concern about a possibly unsuccessful performance or endeavor. Fear of failure is often born of pride; it's fear of what others will think, fear of embarrassment, fear of being ashamed.

1. Fear of failure comes from a lack of faith, which actually causes failure; for only faith succeeds.

- **Number 13:27,28,30-33; 14:1-3,34** [Ten of the twelve returning spies brought back a fearful report that the giants in the Promised Land would make it impossible to conquer. This caused the people to fear—thus resulting in a 40-year setback in claiming the land:] And they [the 10 fearful spies] told him [Moses], and said, We came unto the land whither thou sentest us, and surely it floweth with milk and honey; and this is the fruit of it. [28] Nevertheless the people be strong that dwell in the land, and the cities are walled, and very great: and moreover we saw the children of Anak there. [30] And Caleb stilled the people before Moses, and said, Let us go up at once, and possess it; for we are well able to overcome it. [31] But the men that went up with him said, We be not able to go up against the people; for they are stronger than we, [32] And they brought up an evil report of the land which they had searched unto the children of Israel, saying, The land, through which we have gone to search it, is a land that eateth up the inhabitants thereof; and all the people that we saw in it are men of a great stature. [33] And there we saw the giants, the sons of Anak, which come of the giants: and we were in our own sight as grasshoppers, and so we were in their sight. [14:1-3,34] And all the congregation lifted up their voice, and cried; and the people wept that night. [2] And all the children of Israel murmured against Moses and against Aaron: and the whole congregation said unto them, Would God that we had died in the land of Egypt! Or would God we had died in this wilderness! [3] And wherefore hath the Lord brought us unto this land, to fall by the sword, that our wives and our children should be a prey? Were it not better for us to return into Egypt? [34] [God said:] After the number of the days in which ye searched the land, even forty days, each day for a year, shall ye bear your iniquities, even forty years, and ye shall know My breach of promise.

- **Job 3:25** For the thing which I greatly feared is come upon me, and that which I was afraid of is come unto me.
- **Isaiah 7:9b** If ye will not believe, surely ye shall not be established.
- **Matthew 13:58** And He [Jesus] did not many mighty works there because of their unbelief.
- **Matthew 17:16,19,20** And I brought him to Thy disciples, and they could not cure him. ... [19] Then came the disciples to Jesus apart, and said, Why could not we cast him [the evil spirit] out? [20] And Jesus said unto them, Because of your unbelief: for verily I say unto you, If ye have faith as a grain of mustard seed, ye shall say unto this mountain, Remove hence to yonder place; and it shall remove; and nothing shall be impossible unto you.
- **Philippians 4:6,7** Be careful [anxious or worried] for nothing; but in every thing by prayer and supplication with thanksgiving let your requests be made known unto God. [7] And the peace of God, which passeth all understanding, shall keep your hearts and minds through Christ Jesus.
- **James 1:6,7** But let him ask in faith, nothing wavering. For he that wavereth is like a wave of the sea driven with the wind and tossed. [7] For let not that man think that he shall receive any thing of the Lord.

2. If we're trusting in the Lord, we have nothing to fear, for Jesus never fails.

- **Number 23:19** God is not a man, that He should lie; neither the Son of man, that He should repent: hath He said, and shall He not do it? Or hath He spoken, and shall He not make it good?
- **Job 42:2a** I know that Thou canst do everything.

- **Psalm 37:5** Commit thy way unto the Lord; trust also in Him; and He shall bring it to pass.
- **Psalm 55:22** Cast thy burden upon the Lord, and He shall sustain thee: He shall never suffer the righteous to be moved.
- **Jeremiah 32:27** Behold, I am the Lord, the God of all flesh: is there any thing too hard for Me?
- **Matthew 9:28b** Jesus saith unto them, Believe ye that I am able to do this?
- **Matthew 19:26** But Jesus beheld them, and said unto them, With men this is impossible; but with God all things are possible.
- **2 Corinthians 1:20** For all the promises of God in Him are yea, and in Him Amen, unto the glory of God by us.
- **Philippians 4:13** I can do all things through Christ which strengtheneth me.
- **1 Peter 5:7** Casting all your care upon Him; for He careth for you.

3. If we try to do things in our own strength by carnal means, we have everything to fear because we will fail.

- **1 Samuel 2:9b** For by strength shall no man prevail.
- **Psalm 33:16,17** There is no king saved by the multitude of an host: a mighty man is not delivered by much strength. [17] An horse is a vain thing for safety: neither shall he deliver any by his great strength.
- **Psalm 127:1a** Except the Lord build the house, they labour in vain that build it.
- **Jeremiah 17:5** Thus saith the Lord; Cursed be the man that trusteth in man, and maketh flesh his arm, and whose heart departeth from the Lord.
- **John 15:5** I am the vine, ye are the branches: He that abideth in Me, and I in him, the same bringeth forth much fruit: for without Me ye can do nothing.
- **1 Corinthians 10:12** Wherefore let him that thinketh he standeth take heed lest he fall.

4. When we feel week and incapable, God can more powerfully work through us.

- **Isaiah 40:29** He giveth power to the faint; and to them that have no might He increaseth strength.
- **2 Corinthians 1:8b,9** We were pressed out of measure, above strength, insomuch that we despaired even of life: ⁹ But we had the sentence of death in ourselves, that we should not trust in ourselves, but in God which raiseth the dead.
- **2 Corinthians 4:7** But we have this treasure in earthen vessels, that the excellency of the power may be of God, and not of us.
- **2 Corinthians 12:9,10b** And He said unto me, My grace is sufficient for thee: for My strength is made perfect in weakness. Most gladly therefore will I rather glory in my infirmities, that the power of Christ may rest upon me. ... ^{10b} For when I am weak, then am I strong.
- **Hebrews 11:34** [God's men of faith] quenched the violence of fire, escaped the edge of the sword, out of weakness were made strong, waxed valiant in fight, turned to flight the armies of the aliens.

5. However, if we fear failure in accomplishing what God calls us to do, we are not really doubting ourselves, but the Lord and His Word.

- **Romans 9:20,21a** Nay but, O man, who art thou that repliest against God? Shall the thing formed say to Him that formed it, Why hast Thou made me thus? ^{21a} Hath not the potter power over the clay?
- **Numbers 11:21-23** And Moses said, The people, among whom I am, are six hundred thousand footmen; and Thou hast said, I will give them flesh, that they may eat a whole month. ²² Shall the flocks and the herds be slain for them, to suffice them? Or shall all the fish of the sea be gathered together for them, to suffice them? ²³ And the

Lord said unto Moses, Is the Lord's hand waxed short? Thou shalt see now whether My Word shall come to pass unto thee or not.

- **1 Samuel 27:1a** [Even though God had promised him the throne, David feared failure.] And David said in his heart, I shall now perish one day by the hand of Saul. ... [See 1 Samuel 16:13.]

- **Luke 1:13,18-20** But the angel said unto him, Fear not, Zacharias: for thy prayer is heard; and thy wife Elisabeth shall bear thee a son, and thou shalt call his name John. ... [18] And Zacharias said unto the angel, Whereby shall I know this? For I am an old man, and my wife well stricken in years. [19] And the angel answering said unto him, I am Gabriel, that stand in the presence of God; and am sent to speak unto thee, and to shew thee these glad tidings. [20] And, behold, thou shalt be dumb, and not able to speak, until the day that these things shall be performed, because thou believest not my words, which shall be fulfilled in their season.

6. If we are believing and obeying His Word, we cannot fail!

- **Joshua 1:8** This Book of the Law shall not depart out of thy mouth; but thou shalt meditate therein day and night, that thou mayest observe to do according to all that is written therein: for then thou shalt make thy way prosperous, and then thou shalt have good success.

- **Deuteronomy 29:9** Keep therefore the words of this covenant, and do them, that ye may prosper in all that ye do.

- **2 Chronicles 20:20b** Believe in the Lord your God, so shall ye be established; believe His prophets, so shall ye prosper.

- **Psalm 1:2,3** But his delight is in the law of the Lord; and in His law doth he meditate day and night. [3] And he shall be like a tree planted by the rivers of water, that bringeth forth his fruit in his season; his leaf also shall not wither; and whatsoever he doeth shall prosper.

- **Matthew 7:24,25** Therefore whosoever heareth these sayings of Mine, and doeth them, I will liken him unto a wise man, which built his house upon a rock: [25] And the rain descended, and the floods

came, and the winds blew, and beat upon that house; and it fell
not: for it was founded upon a rock.
- **James 1:25** But whoso looketh into the perfect law of liberty, and
continueth therein, he being not a forgetful hearer, but a doer of
the work, this man shall be blessed in his deed.

7. Keep your eyes on Jesus and His promises!
- **Psalm 27:13** I had fainted, unless I had believed to see the
goodness of the Lord in the land of the living.
- **Matthew 14:25-31** [As long as Peter kept his eyes on Jesus, he
walked upon the sea:] And in the fourth watch of the night Jesus
went unto them, walking on the sea. [26] And when the disciples saw
Him walking on the sea, they were troubled, saying, It is a spirit;
and they cried out for fear. [27] But straightway Jesus spake unto
them, saying, Be of good cheer; it is I; be not afraid. [28] And Peter
answered Him and said, Lord, if it be Thou, bid me come unto Thee
on the water. [29] And He said, Come. And when Peter was come
down out of the ship, he walked on the water, to go to Jesus. [30] But
when he saw the wind boisterous, he was afraid; and beginning to
sink, he cried, saying, Lord, save me. [31] And immediately Jesus
stretched forth His hand, and caught him, and said unto him, O
thou of little faith, wherefore didst thou doubt?
- **Philippians 3:13,14** Brethren, I count not myself to have
apprehended: but this one thing I do, forgetting those things which
are behind, and reaching forth unto those things which are before,
[14] I press toward the mark for the prize of the high calling of God in
Christ Jesus.
- **2 Timothy 1:12b** I am not ashamed: for I know whom I have
believed, and am persuaded that He is able to keep that which I
have committed unto Him against that day.
- **Hebrews 12:2a,3b** Looking unto Jesus the author and finisher of
our faith; who for the joy that was set before Him endured the

cross, despising the shame, and is set down at the right hand of the throne of God. ... [3b] Lest ye be wearied and faint in your minds.

8. As long as we desire and obey the Lord's will above all, He'll see to it that we don't fail.

- **2 Chronicles 16:9a** For the eyes of the Lord run to and fro throughout the whole earth, to shew Himself strong in the behalf of them whose heart is perfect [loyal, fully committed] toward Him.
- **2 Chronicles 31:21** And in every work that he [King Hezekiah] began in the service of the house of God, and in the law, and in the commandments, to seek his God, he did it with all his heart, and prospered.
- **Psalm 37:23,24** The steps of a good man are ordered by the Lord: and He delighteth in his way. [24] Though he fall, he shall not be utterly cast down: for the Lord upholdeth him with His hand.
- **Psalm 68:28** Thy God hath commanded thy strength: strengthen, O God, that which Thou hast wrought for us.
- **Psalm 94:17,18** Unless the Lord had been my help, my soul had almost dwelt in silence. [18] When I said, My foot slippeth; Thy mercy, O Lord, held me up.
- **Ecclesiastes 8:12b** Surely I know that it shall be well with them that fear God, which fear before Him.
- **2 Corinthians 3:4,5** And such trust have we through Christ to God-ward: [5] Not that we are sufficient of ourselves to think any thing as of ourselves; but our sufficiency is of God.
- **Philippians 1:6** Being confident of this very thing, that He which hath begun a good work in you will perform it until the Day of Jesus Christ.

FEELING LEFT OUT

Definition: Related to feelings of loneliness, isolation, or rejection; feeling left out is an awareness, either real or imagined, of being excluded from the company or activities of others.

1. Jesus sometimes felt left out, too. So He knows how it feels.

- **Matthew 26:55,56b** In that same hour said Jesus to the multitudes, Are ye come out as against a thief with swords and staves for to take Me? I sat daily with you teaching in the temple, and ye laid no hold on Me. [56b] Then all the disciples forsook Him, and fled.
- **Luke 23:49** [Jesus saw His friends and disciples standing <u>afar off</u>, as He died on the cross.] And all His acquaintance, and the women that followed Him from Galilee, stood afar off, beholding these things. (See also Mark 15:40,41.)
- **John 16:32** Behold, the hour cometh, yea, is now come, that ye shall be scattered, every man to his own, and shall leave Me alone: and yet I am not alone, because the Father is with Me.

2. Feeling left out can drive us closer to the Lord and help us appreciate His love and fellowship.

- **Job 19:13-21** [Job experienced horrendous trials during his affliction, when he did lose many of his friends, yet the Enemy no doubt aggravated things by making him think he'd lost them <u>all</u>, when in actuality he hadn't.] He [the Lord] hath put my brethren far from me, and mine acquaintance are verily estranged from me. [14] My kinsfolk have failed, and my familiar friends have forgotten me. [15] They that dwell in mine house, and my maids, count me for a stranger: I am an alien in their sight. [16] I called my servant, and he gave me no answer; I intreated him with my mouth. [17] My breath is strange to my wife, though I intreated for the children's sake of mine own body. … [19] All my inward friends abhorred me: and they whom I loved are turned against me. [This wasn't completely true, as he still had very dear, close friends, who were trying to understand his grief and help him.] [20] My bone cleaveth to my skin and to my flesh, and I am escaped with the skin of my teeth. [21] Have pity upon me, have pity upon me, O ye my friends; for the hand of God hath touched me. [But in his misery, Job turned to God and began to have renewed faith.] … For I know that my Redeemer liveth, and that He shall stand at the Latter Day upon the earth: [26] And though after my skin worms destroy this body, yet in my flesh shall I see God.

- **Psalm 38:10,11,15** [David, lonely and afflicted, feeling separated from his loved ones, drew close to God.] My heart panteth, my strength faileth me: as for the light of mine eyes, it also is gone from me. [11] My lovers and my friends stand aloof from my sore; and my kinsmen stand afar off. … [15] In Thee, O Lord, do I hope: Thou wilt hear, O Lord my God.

- **Proverbs 18:24b** There is a friend [including Jesus, our Best Friend] that sticketh closer than a brother.

- **Matthew 28:20b** Lo, I am with you alway, even unto the end of the world. [See also Isaiah 44:21b.]

- **John 14:18** [The Lord is our ever-present Comforter.] I will not leave you comfortless: I will come to you.

- **Romans 8:38,39** For I am persuaded, that neither death, nor life, nor angels, nor principalities, nor powers, nor things present, nor things to come, [39] Nor height, nor depth, nor any other creature, shall be able to separate us from the love of God, which is in Christ Jesus our Lord.

- **2 Timothy 4:16a,17a** At my first answer no man stood with me, but all men forsook me: … [17a] Notwithstanding the <u>Lord</u> stood with me, and strengthened me.

- **Hebrews 13:5b** For He hath said, I will never leave thee, nor forsake thee.

3. Feeling left out can sometimes help us learn compassion for others who have the same trial.

- **2 Corinthians 1:4** [God] comforteth us in all our tribulation, that we may be able to comfort them which are in any trouble, by the comfort wherewith we ourselves are comforted of God.
- **Exodus 23:9b** For ye know the heart of a stranger, seeing ye were strangers in the land of Egypt.
- **Luke 6:31** And as ye would that men should do to you, do ye also to them likewise.

4. Feelings of being left out are often exaggerated by the Enemy.

- **Psalm 22:6,7a** [At times David felt like all had left him, but that wasn't really the case. He said:] But I am a worm, and no man; a reproach of men, and despised of the people. [7a] All they that see me laugh me to scorn.
- **Psalm 31:12; 88:18; 102:7** [Again David said, when in the middle of heavy trials:] I am forgotten as a dead man out of mind: I am like a broken vessel. [88:18] Lover and friend hast thou put far from me, and mine acquaintance into darkness. [102:7] I watch, and am as a sparrow alone upon the house top.
- **Psalm 142:4,5** [No matter how badly David felt, each time he turned to the Lord for refuge.] I looked on my right hand, and beheld, but there was no man that would know me: refuge failed me; no man cared for my soul. [5] I cried unto Thee, O Lord: I said, Thou art my refuge and my portion in the land of the living.

5. Sometimes it's simply a matter of needing to communicate our feelings to the others involved.

- **Proverbs 27:19** As in water face answereth to face, so the heart of man to man. [See also Psalm 33:15.]
- **James 4:2b** [Don't be afraid to ask for help.] Ye have not, because ye ask not.

- **Hebrews 13:16a** But to do good and to communicate forget not.
- **1 John 1:7** But if we walk in the light, as He is in the light, we have fellowship one with another, and the blood of Jesus Christ His Son cleanseth us from all sin.

6. Sometimes we may alienate ourselves from others by our own mistakes and sins.

- **Psalm 31:10-12,14** [David felt isolated in his sins and his distress, but ended up turning more to the Lord for help and comfort.] For my life is spent with grief, and my years with sighing: my strength faileth because of mine iniquity, and my bones are consumed. [11] I was a reproach among all mine enemies, but especially among my neighbours, and a fear to mine acquaintance: they that did see me without fled from me. … [14] But I trusted in Thee, O Lord: I said, Thou art my God.
- **Proverbs 18:19** [When we've offended someone, it can take real effort to win back their friendship.] A brother offended is harder to be won than a strong city: and their contentions are like the bars of a castle.
- **Matthew 5:23,24** [Jesus taught the importance of reconciliation among brethren.] Therefore if thou bring thy gift to the altar, and there rememberest that thy brother hath ought against thee; [24] Leave there thy gift before the altar, and go thy way; first be reconciled to thy brother, and then come and offer thy gift.

7. If you're feeling left out, get out of yourself and think of others. Or if you see someone who is feeling left out, go out of your way to spend time with them.

- **Romans 12:15** Rejoice with them that do rejoice, and weep with them that weep.

- **1 Corinthians 9:22** To the weak became I as weak, that I might gain the weak: I am made all things to all men, that I might by all means save some.
- **1 Corinthians 10:33** [This verse refers to pleasing others in a way that pleases God, rather than manpleasing, which is pleasing others in order to please yourself.] I please all men in all things, not seeking mine own profit, but the profit of many, that they may be saved.
- **1 Corinthians 12:25,26** [Lord help us to see the need and give special love and attention to those who need it.] That there should be no schism in the body; but that the members should have the same care one for another. [26] And whether one member suffer, all the members suffer with it; or one member be honoured, all the members rejoice with it.
- **Philippians 2:4** Look not every man on his own things, but every man also on the things of others.

8. Seek to be a friend and you'll find friends everywhere.

- **Proverbs 11:25** The liberal [generous, outgoing] soul shall be made fat: and he that watereth shall be watered also himself.
- **Proverbs 18:24a** A man that hath [or <u>would</u> have] friends must shew himself friendly.
- **Luke 6:38** Give, and it shall be given unto you; good measure, pressed down, and shaken together, and running over, shall men give into your bosom. For with the same measure that ye mete withal it shall be measured to you again.

9. If you feel left out by the worldly system and worldly people, you're in good company.

- **Isaiah 53:3** [Jesus was not called of God to be "popular."] He is despised and rejected of men; a Man of sorrows, and acquainted with grief: and we hid as it were our faces from Him; He was despised, and we esteemed Him not. [See also John 1:11.]

- **Matthew 21:42a** Jesus saith unto them, Did ye never read in the Scriptures, The stone which the builders rejected, the same is become the head of the corner.
- **John 5:43** I am come in My Father's name, and ye receive Me not: if another shall come in his own name, him ye will receive.
- **Luke 6:22,23,26** Blessed are ye, when men shall hate you, and when they shall separate you from their company, and shall reproach you, and cast out your name as evil, for the Son of Man's sake. [23] Rejoice ye in that day, and leap for joy: for, behold, your reward is great in Heaven: for in the like manner did their fathers unto the prophets. ... [26] [Watch out about trying to become too popular!] Woe unto you, when all men shall speak well of you! For so did their fathers to the false prophets.

FLATTERY

Definition: Excessive or insincere praise; praising another to promote one's own interests.

1. Jesus gave no place to those who tempted Him with flattery.

- **Luke 20:20-23** And they watched Him [Jesus], and sent forth spies, which should feign [pretend to be] themselves just men, that they might take hold of His Words, that so they might deliver Him unto the power and authority of the governor. [21] And they asked Him, saying, Master, we know that Thou sayest and teachest rightly, neither acceptest Thou the person of any, but teachest the way of God truly: [22] Is it lawful for us to give tribute unto Caesar, or no? [23] But He perceived their craftiness, and said unto them, Why tempt ye Me?
- **Matthew 7:21** [Jesus said:] Not every one that saith unto Me, Lord, Lord, shall enter into the Kingdom of Heaven; but he that doeth the will of My Father which is in Heaven.
- **Mark 7:6** [Jesus] answered and said unto them, Well hath Esaias prophesied of you hypocrites, as it is written, This people honoureth Me with their lips, but their heart is far from Me. [See also Isaiah 29:13; Ezekiel 33:31.]
- **John 5:41,42,44** [Jesus said:] I receive not honour from men. [42] But I know you, that ye have not the love of God in you. ... [44] How can ye believe, which receive honour one of another, and seek not the honour that cometh from God only?

2. The insincerity of flattery:

- **Psalm 12:2** They speak vanity every one with his neighbour: with flattering lips and with a double heart do they speak.
- **Psalm 5:9** For there is no faithfulness in their mouth; their inward part is very wickedness; their throat is an open sepulchre; they flatter with their tongue.

- **Psalm 62:4** They only consult to cast him down from his excellency: they delight in lies: they bless with their mouth, but they curse inwardly.
- **Psalm 78:36-37** They did flatter Him with their mouth, and they lied unto Him with their tongues. [37] For their heart was not right with Him, neither were they stedfast in His covenant.

3. Flattery is motivated by self-interest.

- **Proverbs 19:4,6** Wealth maketh many friends; but the poor is separated from his neighbour. [6] Many will intreat the favour of the prince: and every man is a friend to him that giveth gifts. [See also Proverbs 14:20.]
- **Isaiah 5:21,23** Woe unto them … which justify the wicked for reward, and take away the righteousness of the righteous from him!
- **Ezekiel 33:31b** With their mouth they shew much love, but their heart goeth after their covetousness.
- **Romans 16:17,18** Mark them which cause divisions and offences contrary to the doctrine which ye have learned; and avoid them. [18] For they that are such serve not our Lord Jesus Christ, but their own belly; and by good words and fair speeches deceive the hearts of the simple.
- **Jude 1:16** These are murmurers, complainers, walking after their own lusts; and their mouth speaketh great swelling words, having men's persons in admiration because of advantage.

4. Examples of flattery:

- **2 Samuel 15:2-6** [Absalom, the son of King David, used flattery on the people to win political favor and to undermine his father's influence. Later on he tried to steal the kingdom from David.] And Absalom rose up early, and stood beside the way of the gate: and it was so, that when any man that had a controversy came to the king for judgment, then Absalom called unto him, and said, Of what city art thou? And he said, Thy servant is of one of the tribes of

Israel. [3] And Absalom said unto him, See, thy matters are good and right; but there is no man deputed of the king to hear thee. [4] Absalom said moreover, Oh that I were made judge in the land, that every man which hath any suit or cause might come unto me, and I would do him justice! [5] And it was so, that when any man came nigh to him to do him obeisance, he put forth his hand, and took him, and kissed him. [6] And on this manner did Absalom to all Israel that came to the king for judgment: so Absalom stole the hearts of the men of Israel.

- **2 Kings 22:11-38** [False prophets spoke flattering prophecies to King Ahab, but were exposed by Micaiah, the true prophet, who prophesied Ahab's death. Micaiah risked his life and was imprisoned for speaking the truth, but the Lord's Word was fulfilled.]
- **Proverbs 7** [This chapter is an allegory in which the wicked, greedy materialists of the world are depicted as an harlot:] [2] Keep my commandments, and live; and my law as the apple of thine eye … [5] That they may keep thee from the strange woman, from the stranger which flattereth with her words. … [21] With her much fair speech she caused him to yield, with the flattering of her lips she forced him. [22] He goeth after her straightway, as an ox goeth to the slaughter, or as a fool to the correction of the stocks.
- **Daniel 11:21b** [The Antichrist will use flattery to deceive:] He shall come in peaceably, and obtain the kingdom by flatteries. [See also Daniel 11:34.]

5. Although flattery gives the impression of "building up" the other person, it actually works against them.

- **Proverbs 26:28b** A flattering mouth worketh ruin.
- **Proverbs 29:5** A man that flattereth his neighbour spreadeth a net for his feet.

6. People will appreciate loving honesty more than shallow flattery.

- **Psalm 141:5a** Let the righteous smite me; it shall be a kindness: and let him reprove me; it shall be an excellent oil, which shall not break my head.
- **Proverbs 25:12** As an earring of gold, and an ornament of fine gold, so is a wise reprover upon an obedient ear.
- **Proverbs 27:5,6** Open rebuke is better than secret love. [6] Faithful are the wounds of a friend; but the kisses of an enemy are deceitful.
- **Proverbs 28:23** He that rebuketh a man shall find more favour afterwards than he that flattereth with the tongue. [See also Matthew 18:15.]

7. The Lord does not bless those who use flattery.

- **Job 32:21,22** [Elihu said:] Let me not, I pray you, accept any man's person, neither let me give flattering titles unto man. [22] For I know not to give flattering titles; in so doing my Maker would soon take me away.
- **Proverbs 24:24** He that saith unto the wicked, Thou are righteous; him shall the people curse, nations shall abhor him.
- **Psalm 12:3** The Lord shall cut off all flattering lips, and the tongue that speaketh proud things.

8. The Word clearly warns us of the dangers of accepting flattery.

- **Proverbs 6:23,24** For the commandment is a lamp; and the law is light; and reproofs of instruction are the way of life: [24] To keep thee from the evil woman, from the flattery of the tongue of a strange woman. [See Proverbs chapter 7.]
- **Proverbs 20:19** He that goeth about as a talebearer revealeth secrets: therefore meddle not with him that flattereth with his lips.
- **Luke 6:26** Woe unto you, when all men shall speak well of you! For so did their fathers to the false prophets.

9. For the Lord's blessing and for the sake of our sample and ministry, we must not be guilty of flattery.

- **Psalm 15:1,2** Lord, who shall abide in Thy tabernacle? Who shall dwell in Thy holy hill? [2] He that walketh uprightly, and worketh righteousness, and speaketh the truth in his heart.
- **Galatians 1:10** For do I now persuade men, or God? Or do I seek to please men? For if I yet pleased men, I should not be the servant of Christ.
- **1 Thessalonians 2:3-6a** For our exhortation was not of deceit, nor of uncleanness, nor in guile: [4] But as we were allowed of God to be put in trust with the Gospel, even so we speak; not as pleasing men, but God, which trieth our hearts. [5] For neither at any time used we flattering words, as ye know, nor a cloke of covetousness; God is witness: [6a] Nor of men sought we glory.

10. The Word gives us wisdom to discern and escape the snare of flattery.

- **Proverbs 2:10,11,16** When wisdom entereth into thine heart, and knowledge is pleasant unto thy soul; [11] Discretion shall preserve thee, understanding shall keep thee: [16] To deliver thee from the strange woman, even from the stranger which flattereth with her words.
- **Proverbs 7:1-5** My son, keep my words, and lay up my commandments with thee. [2] Keep my commandments, and live; and my law as the apple of thine eye. [3] Bind them upon thy fingers, write them upon the table of thine heart. [4] Say unto wisdom, Thou art my sister; and call understanding thy kinswoman: [5] That they may keep thee from the strange woman, from the stranger which flattereth with her words. [See also Proverbs 6:23,24.]

FRIENDSHIP

Definition: The attachment of one person to another marked by mutual affection and trust; intimacy.

1. Seeking the right kind of friendship is encouraging, strengthening and bears good fruit.

- **Psalm 119:63** I am a companion of all them that fear Thee, and of them that keep Thy precepts.
- **Proverbs 2:20b** Walk in the way of good men, and keep the paths of the righteous.
- **Proverbs 13:20** He that walketh with wise men shall be wise: but a companion of fools shall be destroyed.
- **Proverbs 27:9** Ointment and perfume rejoice the heart: so doth the sweetness of a man's friend by hearty counsel.

2. Jesus is the best foundation upon which true friendships can be built.

- **Ephesians 2:19-22** Now therefore ye are no more strangers and foreigners, but fellowcitizens with the saints, and of the household of God; [20] And are built upon the foundation of the apostles and prophets, Jesus Christ Himself being the chief corner stone; [21] In whom all the building fitly framed together groweth unto an holy temple in the Lord: [22] In whom ye also are builded together for an habitation of God through the Spirit.
- **Colossians 1:17** [If Jesus is the glue, your friendship will hold through anything.] And He is before all things, and by Him all things consist [are held together].
- **1 John 1:7** But if we walk in the light, as He is in the light, we have fellowship one with another, and the blood of Jesus Christ His Son cleanseth us from all sin.

3. Some of the qualities of true and lasting friendships are:

- **Job 6:14a** [Compassion—showing understanding and pity in especially trying times:] To him that is afflicted pity should be shewed from his friend.

- **Proverbs 17:9** [Forgiveness—letting it pass when wronged and not drawing undue attention to others' mistakes:] He that covereth a transgression seeketh love; but he that repeateth a matter separateth very friends. [See also 1 Peter 4:8.]

- **Proverbs 17:17** [Supportiveness—being a strength in difficult times:] A friend loveth at all times, and a brother is born for adversity.

- **Proverbs 18:24a** [Initiative—making the first move to be outgoing and friendly:] A man that hath [wants to have] friends must shew himself friendly.

- **Proverbs 25:17** [Discretion—knowing when to part company, lest we "wear out our welcome":] Withdraw thy foot from thy neighbour's house; lest he be weary of thee, and so hate thee.

- **Proverbs 27:6a** [Loving counsel and correction:] Faithful are the wounds of a friend.

- **Proverbs 27:10a** [Loyalty:] Thine own friend, and thy father's friend, forsake not.

- **Proverbs 27:14** [Consideration:] He that blesseth his friend with a loud voice, rising early in the morning, it shall be counted a curse to him.

- **Proverbs 27:17** [Encouragement:] Iron sharpeneth iron; so a man sharpeneth the countenance of his friend.

- **Ecclesiastes 4:9,10** [Teamwork:] Two are better than one; because they have a good reward for their labour. [10] For if they fall, the one will lift up his fellow: but woe to him that is alone when he falleth; for he hath not another to help him up.

- **Amos 3:3** [Unity—discovering and dwelling on points in common:] Can two walk together, except they be agreed?

- **John 3:29** [True understanding—appreciating one another's victories:] He that hath the bride is the bridegroom: but the friend of the bridegroom, which standeth and heareth him, rejoiceth greatly because of the bridegroom's voice: this my joy therefore is fulfilled.

- **John 15:13** [Self-sacrifice:] Greater love hath no man than this, that a man lay down his life for his friends.
- **John 15:15** [Communication—being open and honest:] Henceforth I call you not servants; for the servant knoweth not what his lord doeth: but I have called you friends; for all things that I have heard of My Father I have made known unto you.
- **Romans 15:1,2** [Unselfishness—putting the needs of others before our own:] We then that are strong ought to bear the infirmities of the weak, and not to please ourselves. [2] Let every one of us please his neighbour for his good to edification.
- **Philippians 2:4** [Mutual concern:] Look not every man on his own things, but every man also on the things of others.
- **Colossians 3:16** [Mutual edification and inspiration:] Let the Word of Christ dwell in you richly in all wisdom; teaching and admonishing one another in psalms and hymns and spiritual songs, singing with grace in your hearts to the Lord.
- **Hebrews 10:24** [Positive peer pressure—being a good influence on one another:] And let us consider one another to provoke unto love and to good works.
- **1 Peter 4:8** [Love—the mortar that holds the building blocks in place:] And above all things have fervent charity [love] among yourselves: for charity shall cover the multitude of sins.

4. Choose your friendships wisely!

- **Proverbs 22:24,25** Make no friendship with an angry man; and with a furious man thou shalt not go: [25] Lest thou learn his ways, and get a snare to thy soul.
- **James 4:4** [True friendship does not mean fraternizing with the world.] Know ye not that the friendship of the world is enmity with God? Whosoever therefore will be a friend of the world is the enemy of God.

5. Being faithful to lift up <u>Jesus</u> will help attract the right kind of friends.

- **John 12:32** And I, if I be lifted up from the earth, will draw all men unto Me.
- **Psalm 119:74** They that fear Thee will be glad when they see me; because I have hoped in Thy Word.
- **Psalm 34:2,3** My soul shall make her boast in the Lord: the humble shall hear thereof, and be glad. ³ O magnify the Lord with me, and let us exalt His name together.
- **Proverbs 22:11** He that loveth pureness of heart, for the grace of his lips the king shall be his friend. [See Proverbs 16:7.]

6. The Bible testified of those special friendships which glorified the Lord and helped to further His Kingdom.

- **Ruth 1:16,17** [Ruth's undying loyalty to Naomi, her mother-in-law:] And Ruth said, Intreat me not to leave thee, or to return from following after thee: for whither thou goest, I will go; and where thou lodgest, I will lodge: thy people shall be my people, and thy God my God: ¹⁷ Where thou diest, will I die, and there will I be buried: the Lord do so to me, and more also, if ought but death part thee and me.
- **1 Samuel 18:1** [David and Jonathan discovered a loving friendship which was built upon deep and lasting love:] And it came to pass, when he had made an end of speaking unto Saul, that the soul of Jonathan was knit with the soul of David, and Jonathan loved him as his own soul. [See also 2 Samuel 1:26.]
- **2 Kings 2:2** [Elisha and Elijah stuck together:] And Elijah said unto Elisha, Tarry here, I pray thee; for the Lord hath sent me to Bethel. And Elisha said unto him, As the Lord liveth, and as thy soul liveth, I will not leave thee. So they went down to Bethel.

7. There are times when some friendships fall short—but Jesus' friendship never fails.

- **Job 16:20** [Sometimes friendship falls short, but Jesus never fails.] My friends scorn me: but mine eye poureth out tears unto God.

- **Job 19:14,19** My kinsfolk have failed, and my familiar friends have forgotten me. ... [19] All my inward friends abhorred me: and they whom I loved are turned against me.

- **Psalm 38:11** My lovers and my friends stand aloof from my sore; and my kinsmen stand afar off.

- **Psalm 41:9** Yea, mine own familiar friend, in whom I trusted, which did eat of my bread, hath lifted up his heel against me.

- **Psalm 55:12-14** [Sometimes friendship turns sour, especially when our friend's loyalty to the Lord has grown weak.] For it was not an enemy that reproached me; then I could have borne it: neither was it he that hated me that did magnify himself against me; then I would have hid myself from him: [13] But it was thou, a man mine equal, my guide, and mine acquaintance. [14] We took sweet counsel together, and walked unto the house of God in company. [See also Psalm 88:18.]

- **Psalm 27:10** When my father and my mother [or friends] forsake me, then the Lord will take me up.

- **James 2:23** Abraham believed God, and it was imputed unto him for righteousness: and he was called the friend of God.

- **John 15:14,15b,16a** Ye are My friends, if ye do whatsoever I command you. [15b] ... I have called you friends; for all things that I have heard of My Father I have made known unto you. [16a] Ye have not chosen Me, but I have chosen you.

FRUSTRATION

Definition: A feeling of disappointment or defeat at being unable to accomplish one's purpose.

1. Frustration is an indication of a lack of faith and trust in the Lord.

- **Psalm 119:165** Great peace have they which love Thy law: and nothing shall offend them.
- **Isaiah 26:3** Thou wilt keep him in perfect peace, whose mind is stayed on Thee: because he trusteth in Thee.
- **Romans 8:25** But if we hope for that we see not, then do we with patience wait for it.
- **Philippians 4:6,7** Be careful [anxious; troubled with cares] for nothing; but in every thing by prayer and supplication with thanksgiving let your requests be made known unto God. [7] And the peace of God, which passeth all understanding, shall keep your hearts and minds through Christ Jesus.
- **Hebrews 10:35,36** Cast not away therefore your confidence, which hath great recompence of reward. [36] For ye have need of patience, that, after ye have done the will of God, ye might receive the promise.

2. Sometimes the Lord allows our plans to be frustrated because it's simply not His time or His will.

- **Numbers 22:18b** I cannot go beyond the Word of the Lord my God, to do less or more.
- **Proverbs 13:12** [God's delays are not always denials.] Hope deferred maketh the heart sick: but when the desire cometh, it is a tree of life.
- **Proverbs 21:30** [If the Lord doesn't want something done, no matter how "good" your ideas and plans are, they won't work!]

There is no wisdom nor understanding nor counsel against the Lord.

- **Ecclesiastes 3:1** To every thing there is a season, and a time to every purpose under the Heaven.
- **2 Corinthians 13:8** For we can do nothing against the truth, but for the truth.
- **James 4:13-15** Go to now, ye that say, To day or to morrow we will go into such a city, and continue there a year, and buy and sell, and get gain: [14] Whereas ye know not what shall be on the morrow. For what is your life? It is even a vapour, that appeareth for a little time, and then vanisheth away. [15] For that ye ought to say, If the Lord will, we shall live, and do this, or that.
- **Psalm 37:4,5** [If you put the Lord first and trust Him, He'll help things to work out.] Delight thyself also in the Lord; and He shall give thee the desires of thine heart. [5] Commit thy way unto the Lord; trust also in Him; and He shall bring it to pass.

3. Frustration can result from trying to do things in our own strength.

- **Psalm 20:7,8** Some trust in chariots, and some in horses: but we will remember the name of the Lord our God. [8] They are brought down and fallen: but we are risen, and stand upright.
- **Psalm 44:6** I will not trust in my bow, neither shall my sword save me.
- **Psalm 127:1a** Except the Lord build the house, they labour in vain that build it.
- **Jeremiah 17:5** Thus saith the Lord; Cursed be the man that trusteth in man, and maketh flesh his arm, and whose heart departeth from the Lord.
- **Zechariah 4:6b** Not by might, nor by power, but by My Spirit, saith the Lord of hosts. [See also Psalm 118:8.]

- **John 15:5** I am the vine, ye are the branches: He that abideth in Me, and I in him, the same bringeth forth much fruit: for without Me ye can do nothing. [See also John 9:33.]

4. Sometimes frustration results from attempting a task that is beyond our training and experience or is not our "calling."

- **Psalm 131:1** Lord, my heart is not haughty, nor mine eyes lofty: neither do I exercise myself in great matters, or in things too high for me.
- **Proverbs 15:22** [Taking good counsel before any endeavor is a good way to avoid potential frustrations.] Without counsel purposes are disappointed: but in the multitude of counsellors they are established.
- **Jeremiah 45:5a** Seekest thou great things for thyself? Seek them not.
- **Luke 14:28-30** For which of you, intending to build a tower, sitteth not down first, and counteth the cost, whether he have sufficient to finish it? [29] Lest haply, after he hath laid the foundation, and is not able to finish it, all that behold it begin to mock him, [30] Saying, This man began to build, and was not able to finish.
- **Romans 12:16b** Mind not high things, but condescend to men of low estate. Be not wise in your own conceits.
- **1 Corinthians 7:20** Let every man abide in the same calling wherein he was called. [See also Proverbs 27:8.]

5. Regardless of the source of frustration, pray to be more <u>patient</u>, trusting, and dependent upon the Lord.

- **Psalm 55:22** Cast thy burden upon the Lord, and He shall sustain thee: He shall never suffer the righteous to be moved.
- **Psalm 145:18-19** The Lord is nigh unto all them that call upon Him, to all that call upon Him in truth. [19] He will <u>fulfil the desire</u> of them that fear Him: He also will hear their cry, and will save them.

- **Luke 8:15b** Bring forth fruit with patience.
- **Romans 5:3-5a** And not only so, but we glory in tribulations also: knowing that tribulation worketh patience; [4] And patience, experience; and experience, hope: [5a] And hope maketh not ashamed [disappointed].
- **Galatians 6:9** And let us not be weary in well doing: for in due season we shall reap, if we faint not.
- **2 Peter 1:5,6** And beside this, giving all diligence, add to your faith … [6] temperance; and to temperance patience; and to patience godliness.

6. Let the Lord do it through you—in His way and in His time.

- **Isaiah 30:15a** For thus saith the Lord God, the Holy One of Israel; In returning and rest shall ye be saved; in quietness and in confidence shall be your strength.
- **Matthew 6:10b** Thy will be done in earth, as it is in Heaven.
- **Matthew 19:26** But Jesus beheld them, and said unto them, With men this is impossible; but with God all things are possible.
- **2 Corinthians 3:4,5** And such trust have we through Christ to God-ward: [5] Not that we are sufficient of ourselves to think any thing as of ourselves; but our sufficiency is of God.
- **Matthew 26:39b** [Jesus had to yield His will to God, too.] O My Father, if it be possible, let this cup pass from Me: nevertheless not as I will, but as Thou wilt.
- **John 5:30** I can of Mine own self do nothing: as I hear, I judge: and My judgment is just; because I seek not Mine own will, but the will of the Father which hath sent Me.

GENTLENESS

Definition: Kindness, consideration, tenderness, friendliness; not severe, violent or loud.

1. Jesus is often characterized in both the Old and New Testaments by His gentleness.

- **Isaiah 40:11** He shall feed His flock like a shepherd: He shall gather the lambs with His arm, and carry them in His bosom, and shall gently lead those that are with young.
- **Isaiah 42:3** A bruised reed shall He not break, and the smoking flax shall He not quench: He shall bring forth judgment unto truth.
- **Isaiah 53:7** [Jesus gently laid down His life for us as a sacrificial lamb:] He was oppressed, and He was afflicted, yet He opened not His mouth: He is brought as a lamb to the slaughter, and as a sheep before her shearers is dumb, so He openeth not His mouth.
- **Matthew 11:29** Take My yoke upon you, and learn of Me; for I am meek and lowly in heart: and ye shall find rest unto your souls.
- **Luke 13:14b** How oft I would have gathered thy children together, as a hen doth gather her brood under her wings, and ye would not!
- **Romans 2:4** Or despisest thou the riches of His goodness and forbearance and longsuffering; not knowing that the goodness of God leadeth thee to repentance?
- **2 Corinthians 10:1a** Now I Paul myself beseech you by the meekness and gentleness of Christ.
- **James 5:11b** The Lord is very pitiful [compassionate], and of tender mercy.

2. Gentleness is a fruit of the Holy Spirit.

- **Galatians 5:22,23** But the fruit of the Spirit is love, joy, peace, longsuffering, <u>gentleness</u>, goodness, faith, [23] Meekness, temperance: against such there is no law.

- **James 3:17,18** But the wisdom that is from Above is first pure, then peaceable, <u>gentle</u>, and easy to be intreated, full of mercy and good fruits, without partiality, and without hypocrisy. [18] And the fruit of righteousness is sown in peace of them that make peace.

3. Contrary to modern worldly concepts, gentleness is a strength rather than a sign of weakness.

- **Psalm 18:35b** Thy gentleness hath made me great. [See also 2 Samuel 22:36.]
- **Proverbs 16:32** He that is slow to anger is better than the mighty; and he that ruleth his spirit than he that taketh a city.
- **Ecclesiastes 7:8b** The patient in spirit is better than the proud in spirit.
- **Isaiah 30:15b** In quietness and in confidence shall be your strength.
- **Zechariah 4:6b** Not by might, nor by power, but by My Spirit, saith the Lord of hosts.
- **Philemon 1:8,9a** Wherefore, though I might be much bold in Christ to enjoin [order, command] thee that which is convenient, [9] Yet for love's sake I rather beseech [appeal to] thee.
- **James 1:19,20** Wherefore, my beloved brethren, let every man be swift to hear, slow to speak, slow to wrath: [20] For the wrath of man worketh not the righteousness of God.

4. A gentle spirit is a requirement of true Christians.

- **Romans 12:10** Be kindly affectioned one to another with brotherly love; in honour preferring one another.
- **Philippians 4:5a** Let your moderation [gentleness] be known unto all men.
- **2 Timothy 2:24,25** And the servant of the Lord must not strive; but be gentle unto all men, apt to teach, patient, [25] In meekness instructing those that oppose themselves; if God peradventure will give them repentance to the acknowledging of the truth.

- **Colossians 3:12** Put on therefore, as the elect of God, holy and beloved, bowels of mercies, kindness, humbleness of mind, meekness, longsuffering.

- **Titus 3:2,3** [Gentleness is a part of the sample that our lives have been changed by the power of God.] Speak evil of no man, to be no brawlers, but gentle, shewing all meekness unto all men. [3] For we ourselves also were sometimes foolish, disobedient, deceived, serving divers lusts and pleasures, living in malice and envy, hateful, and hating one another.

- **1 Thessalonians 2:7-8** [The Apostle Paul was a good example of a gentle shepherd.] But we were gentle among you, even as a nurse cherisheth her children: [8] So being affectionately desirous of you, we were willing to have imparted unto you, not the Gospel of God only, but also our own souls, because ye were dear unto us.

- **1 Peter 3:8-9** Finally, be ye all of one mind, having compassion one of another, love as brethren, be pitiful [tenderhearted], be courteous: [9] Not rendering evil for evil, or railing for railing: but contrariwise blessing; knowing that ye are thereunto called, that ye should inherit a blessing.

GOSSIP AND TATTLING

Definition: Idle talk or rumor, especially about other people, and usually in a critical or condescending vein; the telling of secrets; repeating or discussing scandal.

1. The Bible clearly forbids gossip.

- **Leviticus 19:16a** Thou shalt not go up and down as a talebearer among thy people.
- **Psalm 15:1,3** Lord, who shall abide in Thy tabernacle? Who shall dwell in Thy holy hill? … [3] He that backbiteth <u>not</u> with his tongue, nor doeth evil to his neighbour, nor taketh up a reproach against his neighbour.
- **Proverbs 26:20** Where no wood is, there the fire goeth out: so where there is no talebearer, the strife ceaseth.
- **Ephesians 4:31** Let all bitterness, and wrath, and anger, and clamour, and evil speaking, be put away from you, with all malice.
- **Titus 3:2** [Exhort others] to speak evil of no man, to be no brawlers, but gentle, shewing all meekness unto all men.
- **James 4:11a** Speak not evil one of another, brethren.
- **1 Peter 2:1** Wherefore [lay] aside all malice, and all guile, and hypocrisies, and envies, and all evil speakings.

2. Gossip is unloving and destructive.

- **Genesis 37:2b,4** Joseph, being seventeen years old, was feeding the flock with his brethren; and the lad was with [his half-brothers] the sons of Bilhah, and with the sons of Zilpah, his father's wives: and Joseph brought unto his father their evil report [a bad report about them]. … [4] And when his brethren saw that their father loved him more than all his brethren, they hated him, and could not speak peaceably unto him.

- **1 Samuel 24:9** [Some of King Saul's men spread rumors that David wanted to kill him.] And David said to Saul, Wherefore hearest thou men's words, saying, Behold, David seeketh thy hurt?
- **Psalm 38:12b** They that seek my hurt speak mischievous things, and imagine deceits all the day long.
- **Psalm 41:7** All that hate me whisper together against me: against me do they devise my hurt.
- **Proverbs 11:9a** An hypocrite with his mouth destroyeth his neighbour.
- **Proverbs 11:13** A talebearer revealeth secrets: but he that is of a faithful spirit concealeth the matter.
- **Proverbs 16:27** An ungodly man diggeth up evil: and in his lips there is as a burning fire. [See also James 3:5,6.]
- **Proverbs 18:8** The words of a talebearer are as wounds, and they go down into the innermost parts of the belly.
- **Proverbs 26:20** Where no wood is, there the fire goeth out: so where there is no talebearer, the strife ceaseth.
- **Jeremiah 9:4** [Israel was so divided by disobedient slanderers, no one could trust anyone.] Take ye heed every one of his neighbour, and trust ye not in any brother: for every brother will utterly supplant, and every neighbour will walk with slanders.
- **Ezekiel 22:9** [Gossip helped bring about Israel's downfall, which the Lord sent His prophets to expose.] In thee are men that carry tales to shed blood.
- **2 Corinthians 12:20** For I fear, lest, when I come, I shall not find you such as I would, and that I shall be found unto you such as ye would not: lest there be debates, envyings, wraths, strifes, backbitings, whisperings, swellings, tumults.
- **James 3:5,6** Even so the tongue is a little member, and boasteth great things. Behold, how great a matter a little fire kindleth! [6] And the tongue is a fire, a world of iniquity: so is the tongue among our members, that it defileth the whole body, and setteth on fire the course of nature; and it is set on fire of Hell.

• **James 3:10** Out of the same mouth proceedeth blessing and cursing. My brethren, these things ought not so to be.

3. Gossip can undermine and destroy friendship.

• **1 Samuel 24:9** [Young David chided King Saul for listening to gossips who said he was seeking to harm Saul:] And David said to Saul, Wherefore hearest thou men's words, saying, Behold, David seeketh thy hurt?
• **Proverbs 16:28** A froward man soweth strife: and a whisperer separateth chief friends.
• **Proverbs 17:9** He that covereth a transgression seeketh love; but he that repeateth a matter separateth very friends.

4. Gossiping undermines our spiritual defenses and victory.

• **Proverbs 15:4** A wholesome tongue is a tree of life: but perverseness therein is a breach in the spirit.
• **Matthew 15:18,19** But those things which proceed out of the mouth come forth from the heart; and they defile the man. [19] For out of the heart proceed evil thoughts ... false witness. ... [See also Romans 1:29.]
• **2 Corinthians 12:20** [Often gossips talk more freely when leaders are away, as in Paul's case with the Corinthians. "While the cat's away the mice do play!"] For I fear, lest, when I come, I shall not find you such as I would, and that I shall be found unto you such as ye would not: lest there be debates, envyings, wraths, strifes, backbitings, whisperings, swellings, tumults:
• **2 Timothy 2:16,17a** But shun profane and vain babblings: for they will increase unto more ungodliness. [17a] And their word will eat as doth a canker. ...
• **1 Peter 3:10** For he that will love life, and see good days, let him refrain his tongue from evil, and his lips that they speak no guile.

5. Gossipers must answer to God.

- **Matthew 12:36,37** But I say unto you, That every idle word that men shall speak, they shall give account thereof in the Day of Judgment. [37] For by thy words thou shalt be justified, and by thy words thou shalt be condemned.
- **Jeremiah 17:10** I the Lord search the heart, I try the reins, even to give every man according to his ways, and according to the fruit of his doings. [See also Jeremiah 32:19; Psalm 62:12; Romans 2:6.]

6. The Lord doesn't bless gossiping.

- **Psalm 15:1-3** Lord, who shall abide in Thy tabernacle? Who shall dwell in Thy holy hill? [2] He that walketh uprightly, and worketh righteousness, and speaketh the truth in his heart. [3] He that backbiteth not with his tongue, nor doeth evil to his neighbour, nor taketh up a reproach against his neighbour.
- **Psalm 101:5a** Whoso privily slandereth his neighbour, him will I [the Lord] cut off.
- **Isaiah 29:20,21** [Jerusalem's—also called Ariel—terrible condition:] For the terrible one is brought to nought, and the scorner is consumed, and all that watch for iniquity are cut off: [21] That make a man an offender for a word, and lay a snare for him that reproveth in the gate, and turn aside the just for a thing of nought.

7. Ask the Lord for the spiritual maturity not to gossip, and to avoid those who do.

Psalm 50:20,21 [Rather than get sucked into idle gossip, get militant against it.] Thou sittest and speakest against thy brother; thou slanderest thine own mother's son. [21] These things hast thou done, and I kept silence; thou thoughtest that I was altogether such an one as thyself: but I will reprove thee, and set them in order before thine eyes. [See also Ephesians 5:11.]

- **Proverbs 11:13** A talebearer revealeth secrets: but he that is of a faithful spirit concealeth the matter.
- **Proverbs 10:12** Hatred stirreth up strifes: but love covereth all sins.
- **Proverbs 20:19** He that goeth about as a talebearer revealeth secrets: therefore meddle not [don't keep company] with him that flattereth with his lips.
- **Ephesians 4:22,23** [Gossiping is a fleshly, carnal tendency, which we can avoid by walking in the Spirit.] That ye put off concerning the former conversation the old man, which is corrupt according to the deceitful lusts; [23] And be renewed in the spirit of your mind.
- **1 Timothy 6:3,5** If any man … consent not to wholesome words … [5] from such withdraw thyself.

8. It takes maturity to know the difference between reporting a serious wrong and gossiping or tattling; these simple "tests" may help:

- **Habakkuk 1:3a** [What are your motives?] Why dost thou shew Me iniquity, and cause Me to behold grievance?
- **John 8:7b** [Are you just as guilty?] He that is without sin among you, let him first cast a stone at her.
- **Philippians 2:3** [Are you perhaps trying to exalt yourself by putting another down?] Let nothing be done through strife or vainglory; but in lowliness of mind let each esteem other better than themselves.
- **Colossians 3:13,14** [Are you being understanding and forgiving?] Forbearing one another, and forgiving one another, if any man have a quarrel against any: even as Christ forgave you, so also do ye. [14] And above all these things put on charity [love], which is the bond of perfectness. [See also Ephesians 4:32.]
- **1 Peter 3:9** [Are you perhaps trying to get back at the other person?] Not rendering evil for evil, or railing for railing: but contrariwise blessing; knowing that ye are thereunto called, that ye should inherit a blessing.

9. Remember, the Lord sees and understands the situation better than we do, so it's sometimes best to hold off and trust Him to handle things.

- **Job 34:21** For His eyes are upon the ways of man, and He seeth all his goings.
- **Proverbs 5:21** For the ways of man are before the eyes of the Lord, and He pondereth all his goings.
- **Proverbs 15:3** The eyes of the Lord are in every place, beholding the evil and the good.
- **Romans 2:2** But we are sure that the judgment of God is according to truth against them which commit such things.
- **Romans 14:10,12** But why dost thou judge thy brother? Or why dost thou set at nought thy brother? For we shall all stand before the Judgment Seat of Christ. ... [12] So then every one of us shall give account of himself to God.
- **1 Corinthians 4:5** Therefore judge nothing before the time, until the Lord come, who both will bring to light the hidden things of darkness, and will make manifest the counsels of the hearts: and then shall every man have praise of God.
- **Hebrews 4:13** Neither is there any creature that is not manifest in His sight: but all things are naked and opened unto the eyes of Him with whom we have to do.
- **1 Peter 4:19** Wherefore let them that suffer according to the will of God commit the keeping of their souls to Him in well doing, as unto a faithful Creator.

10. Idleness can easily lead to gossiping, so keep busy for the Lord and stay positive.

Proverbs 14:23 In all labour there is profit: but the talk of the lips tendeth only to penury [poverty].

- **2 Thessalonians 3:11** For we hear that there are some which walk among you disorderly, working not at all, but are busybodies. [See also 1 Peter 4:15.]
- **1 Timothy 5:13** And withal they learn to be idle, wandering about from house to house; and not only idle, but tattlers also and busybodies, speaking things which they ought not.
- **Ephesians 4:29** Let no corrupt communication proceed out of your mouth, but that which is good to the use of edifying, that it may minister grace unto the hearers.
- **Philippians 4:8** Finally, brethren, whatsoever things are true, whatsoever things are honest, whatsoever things are just, whatsoever things are pure, whatsoever things are lovely, whatsoever things are of good report; if there be any virtue, and if there be any praise, think on [and talk about] these things.

GREED

Definition: Desire for possessing more than one needs, especially money or property.

1. Although the objective of greed is gratification, the result is always greater unhappiness.

- **Proverbs 15:27a** He that is greedy of gain troubleth his own house.
- **Proverbs 27:20** Hell and destruction are never full; so the eyes of man are never satisfied. [See also Ecclesiastes 4:8b.]
- **Ecclesiastes 5:10** He that loveth silver shall not be satisfied with silver; nor he that loveth abundance with increase: this is also vanity.
- **Ecclesiastes 5:12** The sleep of a labouring man is sweet, whether he eat little or much: but the abundance of the rich will not suffer him to sleep.
- **1 Timothy 6:9,10** But they that will [desire to] be rich fall into temptation and a snare, and into many foolish and hurtful lusts, which drown men in destruction and perdition [damnation, spiritual death]. [10] For the love of money is the root of all evil: which while some coveted after, they have erred from the faith, and pierced themselves through with many sorrows.

2. Greed is a characteristic of the ungodly and leads to more ungodliness.

- **Psalm 73:12** Behold, these are the ungodly, who prosper in the world; they increase in riches.
- **Proverbs 28:22** He that hasteth to be rich hath an evil eye, and considereth not that poverty shall come upon him.
- **Jeremiah 5:27,28** As a cage is full of birds, so are their houses full of deceit: therefore they are become great, and waxen rich. [28] They are waxen fat, they shine: yea, they overpass the deeds of the

wicked: they judge not the cause, the cause of the fatherless, yet they prosper; and the right of the needy do they not judge.

• **Hosea 12:7** [A picture of the greedy materialist:] He is a merchant, the balances of deceit are in his hand: he loveth to oppress.

3. Greed leads to spiritual poverty and ruin.

• **Mark 8:36,37** For what shall it profit a man, if he shall gain the whole world, and lose his own soul? [37] Or what shall a man give in exchange for his soul?

• **Luke 12:16-21** And He [Jesus] spake a parable unto them, saying, The ground of a certain rich man brought forth plentifully: [17] And he thought within himself, saying, What shall I do, because I have no room where to bestow my fruits? [18] And he said, This will I do: I will pull down my barns, and build greater; and there will I bestow all my fruits and my goods. [19] And I will say to my soul, Soul, thou hast much goods laid up for many years; take thine ease, eat, drink, and be merry. [20] But God said unto him, Thou fool, this night thy soul shall be required of thee: then whose shall those things be, which thou hast provided? [21] So is he that layeth up treasure for himself, and is not rich toward God.

• **Proverbs 11:24b** There is that withholdeth more than is meet, but i tendeth to poverty.

• **Ecclesiastes 5:13** There is a sore evil which I have seen under the sun, namely, riches kept for the owners thereof to their hurt.

• **Habakkuk 2:9,10** Woe to him that coveteth an evil covetousness tc his house, that he may set his nest on high, that he may be delivered from the power of evil! [10] Thou hast consulted shame to thy house by cutting off many people, and hast sinned against thy soul.

• **Luke 1:53** He hath filled the hungry with good things; and the rich He hath sent empty away.

• **Luke 16:25** [Abraham spoke to the greedy rich man, who disregarded the poor:] But Abraham said, Son, remember that thou

in thy lifetime receivedst thy good things, and likewise Lazarus evil
things: but now he is comforted, and thou art tormented.
- **James 5:3** Your gold and silver is cankered; and the rust of them
shall be a witness against you, and shall eat your flesh as it were
fire. Ye have heaped treasure together for the last days.
- **Revelation 3:17** Because thou sayest, I am rich, and increased with
goods, and have need of nothing; and knowest not that thou art
wretched, and miserable, and poor, and blind, and naked.

4. Greed is futile!

- **Job 20:15** He hath swallowed down riches, and he shall vomit
them up again: God shall cast them out of His belly.
- **Psalm 39:6** Surely every man walketh in a vain shew: surely they
are disquieted in vain: he heapeth up riches, and knoweth not who
shall gather them.
- **Proverbs 10:2a** Treasures of wickedness profit nothing.
- **Proverbs 21:6** The getting of treasures by a lying tongue is a vanity
tossed to and fro of them that seek death.
- **Proverbs 23:4-5** Labour not to be rich: cease from thine own
wisdom. [5] Wilt thou set thine eyes upon that which is not? For riches
certainly make themselves wings; they fly away as an eagle toward
heaven. [See also John 6:27.]
- **Haggai 1:6** Ye have sown much, and bring in little; ye eat, but ye
have not enough; ye drink, but ye are not filled with drink; ye
clothe you, but there is none warm; and he that earneth wages
earneth wages to put it into a bag with holes. [See also Ecclesiastes
5:14a.]
- **Revelation 18:14,17a** And the fruits that thy soul lusted after are
departed from thee, and all things which were dainty and goodly
are departed from thee, and thou shalt find them no more at all.
[17a] For in one hour so great riches is come to nought.

5. Greed has no place in the Lord's work, especially in leadership.

- **1 Samuel 8:3** [Like Eli's sons, Samuel's two sons were total disappointments.] And his sons walked not in his ways, but turned aside after lucre [material gain, profit], and took bribes, and perverted judgment.
- **1 Timothy 3:3** [Concerning the office leaders within the church, Paul wrote that they should be] not given to wine, no striker, <u>not greedy of filthy lucre</u>; but patient, not a brawler, <u>not covetous</u>.
- **1 Timothy 6:5** [Those who reject God's Word are full of] perverse disputings of men of corrupt minds, and destitute of the truth, <u>supposing that gain is godliness</u>: from such withdraw thyself. [See verses 3-6.]
- **Titus 1:7** For a bishop [overseer] must be blameless, as the steward of God; not selfwilled, not soon angry, not given to wine, no striker, <u>not given to filthy lucre</u>. [See also 1 Timothy 3:8.]
- **1 Peter 5:2** Feed the flock of God which is among you, taking the oversight thereof, not by constraint, but willingly; <u>not for filthy lucre</u>, but of a ready mind.
- **2 Peter 2:3a** [Peter described false prophets and religionists, greedy for gain:] And through covetousness shall they with feigned [pretended] words make merchandise of you.

6. The road to happiness is paved with contentment—not greedy gain.

- **Psalm 37:16** A little that a righteous man hath is better than the riches of many wicked.
- **Proverbs 16:8** Better is a little with righteousness than great revenues without right. [See also 17:1; Ecclesiastes 4:6.]
- **Proverbs 30:8,9** Remove far from me vanity and lies: give me neither poverty nor riches; feed me with food convenient for me. [9] Lest I be full, and deny Thee, and say, Who is the Lord? Or lest I be poor, and steal, and take the name of my God in vain.

- **Philippians 4:11,12** Not that I speak in respect of want: for I have learned, in whatsoever state I am, therewith to be content. [12] I know both how to be abased, and I know how to abound: every where and in all things I am instructed both to be full and to be hungry, both to abound and to suffer need.
- **1 Timothy 6:6-8** But godliness with contentment is great gain. [7] For we brought nothing into this world, and it is certain we can carry nothing out. [8] And having food and raiment let us be therewith content.
- **Hebrews 13:5** Let your conversation be without covetousness; and be content with such things as ye have: for He hath said, I will never leave thee, nor forsake thee.

7. Go the way of unselfishness!

[See Covetousness, #8, page 82, and Selfishness and Self-centeredness, #8 through #13, page 348.]

HABITS, OVERCOMING BAD

Definition: A habit is a recurrent, often unconscious pattern of behavior that is acquired through frequent repetition; an established state of mind or character; customary manner or practice. Habits, of course, can be either good or bad, helpful or harmful.

1. Some common causes of bad habits:

- **Psalm 55:19b** [Being comfortable and familiar with our situation:] Because they have no changes, therefore they fear not God.
- **Ecclesiastes 8:11** [Not nipping problems in the bud:] Because sentence against an evil work is not executed speedily, therefore the heart of the sons of men is fully set in them to do evil.
- **Jeremiah 22:21b** [Because we logically think, "Well, I have <u>always</u> behaved this way."] This hath been thy manner from thy youth.
- **Jeremiah 13:23** [Thinking "But this is the way God made me."] Can the Ethiopian change his skin, or the leopard his spots? Then may ye also do good, that are accustomed to do evil.
- **Luke 5:39** [It is the carnal nature of man to be resistant to change:] No man also having drunk old wine straightway desireth new: for he saith, The old is better.
- **James 1:14,15** [Repeatedly yielding to temptation ends up in a destructive bad habit.] But every man is tempted, when he is drawn away of his own lust, and enticed. [15] Then when lust hath conceived, it bringeth forth sin: and sin, when it is finished, bringeth forth death. [See also Romans 6:12;7:23.]

2. In order to continue to grow spiritually, we need to strive to replace old bad habits with positive new ones.

- **Psalm 19:13a** [King David prayed that his sins wouldn't become hard-to-break habits:] Keep back Thy servant also from pre-sumptuous [proud] sins; let them not have dominion over me. [See also Psalm 119:133.]

- **1 Corinthians 5:6,7a** Know ye not that a little leaven leaveneth the whole lump? [7a] Purge out therefore the old leaven, that ye may be a new lump.
- **Ephesians 4:22-24** [It takes a spiritual renewing:] That ye put off concerning the former conversation the old man, which is corrupt according to the deceitful lusts; [23] And be renewed in the spirit of your mind; [24] And that ye put on the new man, which after God is created in righteousness and true holiness. [See also Colossians 3:7,8.]
- **2 Timothy 2:21** If a man therefore purge himself from these, he shall be a vessel unto honour, sanctified, and meet for the master's use, and prepared unto every good work.
- **1 Peter 1:22** Seeing ye have purified your souls in obeying the truth through the Spirit unto unfeigned love of the brethren, see that ye love one another with a pure heart fervently.

3. The Lord can help us change and overcome <u>anything</u>; all He needs is our yieldedness and cooperation.

- **1 Samuel 10:6,9** [God changed young King Saul into a new man by the power of the Holy Spirit. The prophet Samuel told him:] And the Spirit of the Lord will come upon thee, and thou shalt prophesy with them, and shalt be turned into another man. … [9] And it was so, that when he had turned his back to go from Samuel, God gave him another heart: and all those signs came to pass that day.
- **Psalm 138:8** The Lord will perfect that which concerneth me: Thy mercy, O Lord, endureth for ever: forsake not the works of Thine own hands.
- **Jeremiah 18:3-6** Then I went down to the potter's house, and, behold, he wrought a work on the wheels. [4] And the vessel that he made of clay was marred in the hand of the potter: so he made it again another vessel, as seemed good to the potter to make it. [5] Then the Word of the Lord came to me, saying, [6] O house of Israel, cannot I do with you as this potter? Saith the Lord. Behold, as the

clay is in the potter's hand, so are ye in Mine hand, O house of Israel.

- **Jeremiah 32:27** Behold, I am the Lord, the God of all flesh: is there any thing too hard for Me?
- **Ezekiel 36:26,27** A new heart also will I give you, and a new spirit will I put within you: and I will take away the stony heart out of your flesh, and I will give you an heart of flesh. [27] And I will put My Spirit within you, and cause you to walk in My statutes, and ye shall keep My judgments, and do them.
- **Mark 10:27** And Jesus looking upon them saith, With men it is impossible, but not with God: for with God all things are possible.
- **John 8:36** If the Son therefore shall make you free, ye shall be free indeed.
- **1 John 4:4** Ye are of God, little children, and have overcome them: because greater is He that is in you, than he that is in the world.

4. We need to shun bad habits not only for our own sake, but also for the sake of others; it's a part of love.

- **Romans 14:21** It is good neither to eat flesh, nor to drink wine, nor any thing whereby thy brother stumbleth, or is offended, or is made weak.
- **Galatians 5:13,14** For, brethren, ye have been called unto liberty; only use not liberty for an occasion to the flesh, but by love serve one another. [14] For all the law is fulfilled in one word, even in this; Thou shalt love thy neighbour as thyself.
- **1 John 2:10** He that loveth his brother abideth in the light, and there is none occasion of stumbling in him.

5. We need to get militant against bad habits for God's work's sake.

- **Hebrews 12:1** Wherefore seeing we also are compassed about with so great a cloud of witnesses, let us lay aside every weight, and the

sin which doth so easily beset us, and let us run with patience the race that is set before us.
- **Philippians 3:13,14** Brethren, I count not myself to have apprehended: but this one thing I do, forgetting those things which are behind, and reaching forth unto those things which are before, [14] I press toward the mark for the prize of the high calling of God in Christ Jesus.

6. Some of the more serious "bad habits" may have evil spirits at the root.

- **2 Corinthians 2:11** Lest Satan should get an advantage of us: for we are not ignorant of his devices.
- **2 Corinthians 11:3** But I fear, lest by any means, as the serpent beguiled Eve through his subtilty, so your minds should be corrupted from the simplicity that is in Christ.
- **Ephesians 6:10-12** Finally, my brethren, be strong in the Lord, and in the power of His might. [11] Put on the whole armour of God, that ye may be able to stand against the <u>wiles of the Devil</u>. [12] For we wrestle not against flesh and blood, but against principalities, against powers, against the rulers of the darkness of this world, against spiritual wickedness in high places.
- **1 Peter 5:8,9a** Be sober, be vigilant; because your adversary the Devil, as a roaring lion, walketh about, seeking whom he may devour. [9a] Whom resist stedfast in the faith.

7. We need to pray for a "can do" attitude toward overcoming our bad habits.

- **Philippians 4:13** I can do all things through Christ which strengtheneth me.
- **Romans 4:20,21** He [Abraham] staggered not at the promise of God through unbelief; but was strong in faith, giving glory to God; [21] And

being fully persuaded that, what He had promised, He was able also to perform.

- **2 Corinthians 3:18** [Keep your eyes on Jesus and the "new creature" He is making of you:] But we all, with open face beholding as in a glass the glory of the Lord, are changed into the same image from glory to glory, even as by the Spirit of the Lord.
- **2 Corinthians 5:17** Therefore if any man be in Christ, he is a new creature: old things are passed away; behold, all things are become new.

8. Especially when we are beginning to form new positive habits, we need to ask the Lord to remind us when we are falling back into our old ways, so that we can learn to catch and correct ourselves.

- **Psalm 32:8,9** I will instruct thee and teach thee in the way which thou shalt go: I will guide thee with Mine eye. [9] Be ye not as the horse, or as the mule, which have no understanding: whose mouth must be held in with bit and bridle, lest they come near unto thee.
- **Psalm 143:8,10** Cause me to hear Thy lovingkindness in the morning; for in Thee do I trust: cause me to know the way wherein I should walk; for I lift up my soul unto Thee. ... [10] Teach me to do Thy will; for Thou art my God: Thy Spirit is good; lead me into the land of uprightness.
- **Isaiah 30:21** And thine ears shall hear a word behind thee, saying, This is the way, walk ye in it, when ye turn to the right hand, and when ye turn to the left.
- **Isaiah 42:16** And I will bring the blind by a way that they knew not; I will lead them in paths that they have not known: I will make darkness light before them, and crooked things straight. These things will I do unto them, and not forsake them.
- **John 16:13a** Howbeit when He, the Spirit of truth, is come, He will guide you into all truth.

9. We need the prayers and safeguarding of others to keep from falling into bad habits.

- **Ecclesiastes 4:9,10** Two are better than one; because they have a good reward for their labour. [10] For if they fall, the one will lift up his fellow: but woe to him that is alone when he falleth; for he hath not another to help him up.
- **Matthew 18:19,20** Again I say unto you, That if two of you shall agree on earth as touching any thing that they shall ask, it shall be done for them of My Father which is in Heaven. [20] For where two or three are gathered together in My name, there am I in the midst of them.
- **Hebrews 3:13** But exhort one another daily, while it is called To day; lest any of you be hardened through the deceitfulness of sin.
- **Hebrews 10:24,25** And let us consider one another to provoke [stir up] unto love and to good works: [25] Not forsaking the assembling of ourselves together, as the manner of some is; but exhorting one another: and so much the more, as ye see the day approaching.
- **James 5:16** Confess your faults one to another, and pray one for another, that ye may be healed. The effectual fervent prayer of a righteous man availeth much.

10. Once we've determined to change, we need to be on guard and rebuke every temptation to fall back into our old habits.

- **Galatians 5:1** Stand fast therefore in the liberty wherewith Christ hath made us free, and be not entangled again with the yoke of bondage. [See also 1 Corinthians 16:13.]
- **Ephesians 4:27** Neither give place to the Devil.
- **1 Thessalonians 5:17** Pray without ceasing.
- **James 4:7** Submit yourselves therefore to God. Resist the Devil, and he will flee from you.

11. With conscious effort and the Lord's help, positive new habits will come more naturally.

- **Job 17:9** [Holding on to the Lord brings strength:] The righteous also shall hold on his way, and he that hath clean hands shall be stronger and stronger.
- **Psalm 84:7** They go from strength to strength, every one of them in Zion appeareth before God.
- **Proverbs 4:18** But the path of the just is as the shining light, that shineth more and more unto the perfect day.
- **John 8:31,32** [Living in the Word helps you break free from your old man:] Then said Jesus to those Jews which believed on Him, If ye continue in My Word, then are ye My disciples indeed; [32] And ye shall know the truth, and the truth shall make you free.
- **Galatians 6:9** [Don't give up:] And let us not be weary in well doing: for in due season we shall reap, if we faint not. [See also Hebrews 6:15; 10:35,36.]
- **1 Timothy 4:15** Meditate upon these things; give thyself wholly to them; that thy profiting may appear to all.

HAPPINESS AND JOY

Definitions: Happiness is a state of well-being and contentment. Joy is a feeling of great pleasure or happiness that comes from success, good fortune, or a sense of well-being; gladness.

1. True happiness is a gift from God.

- **Psalm 4:7** Thou hast put gladness in my heart, more than in the time that their corn and their wine increased.
- **Ecclesiastes 2:26a** For God giveth to a man that is good in His sight wisdom, and knowledge, and joy.
- **Ecclesiastes 8:15** Then I commended mirth, because a man hath no better thing under the sun, than to eat, and to drink, and to be merry: for that shall abide with him of his labour the days of his life, which God giveth him under the sun.
- **Acts 13:52** And the disciples were filled with joy, and with the Holy Ghost.
- **Romans 14:17** For the Kingdom of God is not meat and drink; but righteousness, and peace, and joy in the Holy Ghost.
- **Romans 15:13** Now the God of hope fill you with all joy and peace in believing, that ye may abound in hope, through the power of the Holy Ghost.
- **Galatians 5:22** But the fruit of the Spirit is love, joy, peace, longsuffering, gentleness, goodness, faith,

2. True happiness comes from living close to the Lord and His Word.

- **1 Chronicles 16:27** Glory and honour are in His presence; strength and gladness are in His place.
- **Psalm 16:8,9,11** I have set the Lord always before me: because He is at my right hand, I shall not be moved. [9] Therefore my heart is glad, and my glory rejoiceth: my flesh also shall rest in hope. ...

[11] Thou wilt shew me the path of life: in Thy presence is fulness of joy; at Thy right hand there are pleasures for evermore.
- **Psalm 19:8a** The statutes of the Lord [the Word] are right, rejoicing the heart.
- **Psalm 43:4** Then will I go unto the altar of God, unto God my exceeding joy: yea, upon the harp will I praise Thee, O God my God.
- **Psalm 89:15,16** Blessed is the people that know the joyful sound: they shall walk, O Lord, in the light of Thy countenance. [16] In Thy name shall they rejoice all the day: and in Thy righteousness shall they be exalted.
- **Psalm 104:34** My meditation of Him shall be sweet: I will be glad in the Lord.
- **Psalm 118:24** This is the day which the Lord hath made; we will rejoice and be glad in it.
- **Psalm 119:111** Thy testimonies have I taken as an heritage for ever: for they are the rejoicing of my heart.
- **Psalm 119:162** I rejoice at Thy Word, as one that findeth great spoil.
- **Psalm 146:5** Happy is he that hath the God of Jacob for his help, whose hope is in the Lord his God.
- **Jeremiah 15:16a** Thy Words were found, and I did eat them; and Thy Word was unto me the joy and rejoicing of mine heart.
- **Acts 2:28** Thou hast made known to me the ways of life; Thou shalt make me full of joy with Thy countenance.

3. True happiness is the fruit of obedience to the Lord.

- **Psalm 40:8** I delight to do Thy will, O my God: yea, Thy law is within my heart.
- **Psalm 45:7** Thou lovest righteousness, and hatest wickedness: therefore God, Thy God, hath anointed Thee with the oil of gladness above Thy fellows.
- **Psalm 92:4** For Thou, Lord, hast made me glad through Thy work: I will triumph in the works of Thy hands.

- **Psalm 97:11** Light is sown for the righteous, and gladness for the upright in heart.
- **Psalm 128:1,2** Blessed is every one that feareth the Lord; that walketh in His ways. [2] For thou shalt eat the labour of thine hands: happy shalt thou be, and it shall be well with thee.
- **Matthew 25:21** [Jesus explained in the parable:] His lord said unto him, Well done, thou good and faithful servant: thou hast been faithful over a few things, I will make thee ruler over many things: enter thou into the joy of thy lord.
- **Luke 11:27,28** And it came to pass, as He [Jesus] spake these things, a certain woman of the company lifted up her voice, and said unto Him, Blessed is the womb that bare Thee, and the paps which Thou hast sucked. [28] But He said, Yea rather, blessed are they that hear the Word of God, and keep it.
- **John 13:17** If ye know these things [about obeying the Lord in love], happy are ye if ye do them.
- **John 15:10,11** If ye keep My commandments, ye shall abide in My love; even as I have kept My Father's commandments, and abide in His love. [11] These things have I spoken unto you, that My joy might remain in you, and that your joy might be full.
- **Acts 2:46** [It is a joy to be one of the Lord's disciples.] And they [the members of the Early Church], continuing daily with one accord in the temple, and breaking bread from house to house, did eat their meat with gladness and singleness of heart.
- **1 John 5:3** For this is the love of God, that we keep His commandments: and His commandments are not grievous.

4. Happiness and joy are manifestations of our faith and trust in the Lord.

- **Psalm 5:11** But let all those that put their trust in Thee rejoice: let them ever shout for joy, because Thou defendest them: let them also that love Thy name be joyful in Thee.

- **Psalm 13:5** But I have trusted in Thy mercy; my heart shall rejoice in Thy salvation.
- **Psalm 28:7** The Lord is my strength and my shield; my heart trusted in Him, and I am helped: therefore my heart greatly rejoiceth; and with my song will I praise Him. [See also Psalm 33:21.]
- **Proverbs 16:20b** Whoso trusteth in the Lord, happy is he.
- **Acts 16:34** [After Paul's and Silas' bonds were miraculously loosed, the keeper to the prison became a believer:] And when he had brought them into his house, he set meat before them, and rejoiced, believing in God with all his house.
- **1 Peter 1:8** Whom having not seen, ye love; in whom, though now ye see Him not, yet believing, ye rejoice with joy unspeakable and full of glory.

5. Happiness and joy come from being concerned about others and wishing them happiness.

- **Proverbs 14:21b** He that hath mercy on the poor, happy is he.
- **John 3:29** He that hath the bride is the bridegroom: but the friend of the bridegroom, which standeth and heareth him, rejoiceth greatly because of the bridegroom's voice: This My joy therefore is fulfilled.
- **Romans 12:15** Rejoice with them that do rejoice, and weep with them that weep.
- **1 Corinthians 12:26** And whether one member suffer, all the members suffer with it; or one member be honoured, all the members rejoice with it.
- **Philippians 2:2** [Paul wrote:] Fulfil ye my joy, that ye be likeminded, having the same love, being of one accord, of one mind.
- **1 Thessalonians 2:19,20** For what is our hope, or joy, or crown of rejoicing? Are not even ye in the presence of our Lord Jesus Christ at His coming? [20] For ye are our glory and joy. [See also 2 Corinthians 1:14.]

• **3 John 4** [John wrote:] I have no greater joy than to hear that my children walk in truth.

6. When we count our many blessings, our joy overflows in song and praise.

• **Psalm 65:13b** They shout for joy, they also sing.
• **Psalm 95:2** Let us come before His presence with thanksgiving, and make a joyful noise unto Him with psalms.
• **Psalm 100:1,2,4** Make a joyful noise unto the Lord, all ye lands. [2] Serve the Lord with gladness: come before His presence with singing. ... [4] Enter into His gates with thanksgiving, and into His courts with praise: be thankful unto Him, and bless His name.
• **Psalm 144:15** Happy is that people, that is in such a case: yea, happy is that people, whose God is the Lord.
• **Isaiah 51:3b** Joy and gladness shall be found therein, thanksgiving, and the voice of melody.
• **Jeremiah 33:11** The voice of joy, and the voice of gladness, the voice of the bridegroom, and the voice of the bride, the voice of them that shall say, Praise the Lord of hosts: for the Lord is good; for His mercy endureth for ever: and of them that shall bring the sacrifice of praise into the house of the Lord.
• **Luke 10:20b** Rejoice, because your names are written in Heaven.
• **1 Timothy 6:6** But godliness with contentment is great gain.

7. The Lord wants us to be happy.

• **Deuteronomy 12:18b** Thou shalt rejoice before the Lord thy God in all that thou puttest thine hands unto.
• **Nehemiah 8:10b** The joy of the Lord is your strength.
• **John 16:24** Hitherto have ye asked nothing in My name: Ask, and ye shall receive, that your joy may be full.
• **Philippians 4:4** Rejoice in the Lord alway: and again I say, Rejoice.

8. Our trials and sorrows are followed by greater victory, greater joy.

- **Job 5:17** Behold, happy is the man whom God correcteth: therefore despise not thou the chastening of the Almighty.
- **Job 42:10,12** [Job, the man who was once called "the greatest of all the men of the East," lost everything, but then ...] The Lord gave Job twice as much as he had before. [12] So the Lord blessed the latter end of Job more than his beginning.
- **Psalm 30:5** For His anger endureth but a moment; in His favour is life: weeping may endure for a night, but joy cometh in the morning.
- **Psalm 126:5,6** They that sow in tears shall reap in joy. [6] He that goeth forth and weepeth, bearing precious seed, shall doubtless come again with rejoicing, bringing his sheaves with him.
- **Matthew 5:4** Blessed are they that mourn: for they shall be comforted.
- **John 16:20-22** [Jesus told His disciples:] Verily, verily, I say unto you, That ye shall weep and lament, but the world shall rejoice: and ye shall be sorrowful, but your sorrow shall be turned into joy. [21] A woman when she is in travail hath sorrow, because her hour is come: but as soon as she is delivered of the child, she remembereth no more the anguish, for joy that a man is born into the world. [22] And ye now therefore have sorrow: but I will see you again, and your heart shall rejoice, and your joy no man taketh from you.
- **John 16:33** These things I have spoken unto you, that in Me ye might have peace. In the world ye shall have tribulation: but be of good cheer; I have overcome the world.
- **Hebrews 10:34** [Paul explained that losses are not such a problem for God's people, as they look forward to heavenly gains.] For ye had compassion of me in my bonds, and took joyfully the spoiling of your goods, knowing in yourselves that ye have in Heaven a better and an enduring substance.

- **Hebrews 12:2b** [Jesus endured suffering by looking ahead to His heavenly reward and happy return to live with the Father.] Jesus the author and finisher of our faith; who for the joy that was set before Him endured the cross, despising the shame, and is set down at the right hand of the throne of God.
- **Hebrews 12:11** Now no chastening for the present seemeth to be joyous, but grievous: nevertheless afterward it yieldeth the peaceable fruit of righteousness unto them which are exercised thereby.

9. The Lord can give us inward spiritual happiness in times of difficulty and suffering.

- **Isaiah 29:19** The meek also shall increase their joy in the Lord, and the poor among men shall rejoice in the Holy One of Israel.
- **Isaiah 61:3** To appoint unto them that mourn in Zion, to give unto them beauty for ashes, the oil of joy for mourning, the garment of praise for the spirit of heaviness; that they might be called trees of righteousness, the planting of the Lord, that He might be glorified.
- **Habakkuk 3:17,18** Although the fig tree shall not blossom, neither shall fruit be in the vines; the labour of the olive shall fail, and the fields shall yield no meat; the flock shall be cut off from the fold, and there shall be no herd in the stalls: [18] Yet I will rejoice in the Lord, I will joy in the God of my salvation.
- **Romans 5:1,2** Therefore being justified by faith, we have peace with God through our Lord Jesus Christ: [2] By whom also we have access by faith into this grace wherein we stand, and rejoice in hope of the glory of God.
- **2 Corinthians 6:4,10** In all things approving ourselves as the ministers of God, ... [10] As sorrowful, yet alway rejoicing; as poor, yet making many rich; as having nothing, and yet possessing all things.
- **2 Corinthians 7:4b** [Paul wrote:] I am filled with comfort, I am exceeding joyful in all our tribulation.

- **Colossians 1:10,11** Walk worthy of the Lord unto all pleasing, ... [11] Strengthened with all might, according to His glorious power, unto all patience and longsuffering with joyfulness.

- **Philippians 4:11,12** Not that I speak in respect of want: for I have learned, in whatsoever state I am, therewith to be content. [12] I know both how to be abased, and I know how to abound: every where and in all things I am instructed both to be full and to be hungry, both to abound and to suffer need.

- **James 1:2,3** My brethren, count it all joy when ye fall into divers temptations; [3] Knowing this, that the trying of your faith worketh patience.

- **James 5:11** [Even when we are just holding on and smiling by faith, the Lord counts it as happiness.] Behold, we count them happy which endure. Ye have heard of the patience of Job, and have seen the end of the Lord; that the Lord is very pitiful, and of tender mercy. [See also James 1:12.]

- **1 Peter 3:14a** But and if ye suffer for righteousness' sake, happy are ye.

- **1 Peter 4:12-14** Beloved, think it not strange concerning the fiery trial which is to try you, as though some strange thing happened unto you: [13] But rejoice, inasmuch as ye are partakers of Christ's sufferings; that, when His glory shall be revealed, ye may be glad also with exceeding joy. [14] If ye be reproached for the name of Christ, happy are ye; for the Spirit of glory and of God resteth upon you: on their part He is evil spoken of, but on your part He is glorified.

- **Acts 5:40,41** And to him [Gamaliel] they agreed: and when they had called the apostles, and beaten them, they commanded that they should not speak in the name of Jesus, and let them go. [41] And they departed from the presence of the council, rejoicing that they were counted worthy to suffer shame for His name. [See also 1 Thessalonians 1:6.]

10. Our happy, joyful spirits testify of the Lord's goodness to us. It's part of our witness.

- **Psalm 40:2,3** He brought me up also out of an horrible pit, out of the miry clay, and set my feet upon a rock, and established my goings. [3] And He hath put a new song in my mouth, even praise unto our God: many shall see it, and fear, and shall trust in the Lord.
- **Psalm 40:16** Let all those that seek Thee rejoice and be glad in Thee; let such as love Thy salvation say continually, The Lord be magnified.
- **Psalm 69:30,32** I will praise the name of God with a song, and will magnify Him with thanksgiving. ... [32] The humble shall see this, and be glad: and your heart shall live that seek God.
- **Psalm 107:1-2** O give thanks unto the Lord, for He is good: for His mercy endureth for ever. [2] Let the redeemed of the Lord say so, whom He hath redeemed from the hand of the enemy.
- **Proverbs 15:13,15** A merry heart maketh a cheerful countenance: but by sorrow of the heart the spirit is broken. ... [15] All the days of the afflicted are evil: but he that is of a merry heart hath a continual feast.
- **Nehemiah 12:43** Also that day they offered great sacrifices, and rejoiced: for God had made them rejoice with great joy: the wives also and the children rejoiced: so that the joy of Jerusalem was heard even afar off.
- **Psalm 51:12,13** [King David prayed:] Restore unto me the joy of Thy salvation; and uphold me with Thy free Spirit. [13] Then will I teach transgressors Thy ways; and sinners shall be converted unto Thee.
- **Isaiah 61:10** [Our happiness is like an adornment which is admired by others.] I will greatly rejoice in the Lord, my soul shall be joyful in my God; for He hath clothed me with the garments of salvation, He hath covered me with the robe of righteousness, as a bridegroom decketh himself with ornaments, and as a bride adorneth herself with her jewels.

- **Acts 3:8-10** [When the Lord, through Peter and John, healed the lame man on the steps of the temple, it was the man's own joyous reaction that attracted a huge crowd, resulting in the salvation of over five thousand souls:] And he leaping up stood, and walked, and entered with them into the temple, walking, and leaping, and praising God. [9] And all the people saw him walking and praising God: [10] And they knew that it was he which sat for alms at the Beautiful gate of the temple: and they were filled with wonder and amazement at that which had happened unto him.
- **James 5:13b** Is any merry? Let him sing psalms.

HASTE; RASHNESS

Definition: Haste is quickness; hurry; an overeagerness to act; rashness. Rashness is unwise haste; recklessness; a response without due deliberation (prayerfulness and forethought) or caution.

1. Haste is often the Devil's trap to get us moving too quickly and catch us in an unprayerful, unguarded moment.

- **Proverbs 14:29b** He that is hasty of spirit exalteth folly.
- **Proverbs 19:2b** He that hasteth with his feet sinneth.
- **Proverbs 25:28** [Being hasty causes you to run out from under the Lord's protection, making you the Devil's next target.] He that hath no rule over his own spirit is like a city that is broken down, and without walls.
- **Acts 19:36a** Ye ought to be quiet, and to do nothing rashly.

2. Haste also causes us to say and do unloving things which we later regret.

- **Psalm 116:11** I said in my haste, All men are liars.
- **Proverbs 18:13** He that answereth a matter before he heareth it, it is folly and shame unto him.
- **Proverbs 25:8** Go not forth hastily to strive, lest thou know not what to do in the end thereof, when thy neighbour hath put thee to shame.
- **Proverbs 29:20** Seest thou a man that is hasty in his words? There is more hope of a fool than of him.
- **Ecclesiastes 5:2** Be not rash with thy mouth, and let not thine heart be hasty to utter any thing before God: for God is in Heaven, and thou upon earth: therefore let thy words be few.
- **Luke 9:54,55** [Jesus' disciples were hasty in judging a village who didn't readily welcome Jesus.] And when His disciples James and John saw this, they said, Lord, wilt Thou that we command fire to come down from Heaven, and consume them, even as Elias did?

[55] But He turned, and rebuked them, and said, Ye know not what manner of spirit ye are of.

3. "The hurrier I go, the behinder I get!"

- **Proverbs 21:5** The thoughts of the diligent tend only to plenteousness; but of every one that is hasty only to want.
- **Luke 14:28-30** [Look before you leap; count the cost.] For which of you, intending to build a tower, sitteth not down first, and counteth the cost, whether he have sufficient to finish it? [29] Lest haply, after he hath laid the foundation, and is not able to finish it, all that behold it begin to mock him, [30] Saying, This man began to build, and was not able to finish.

4. Haste is sometimes the result of angry impatience, which is a lack of faith.

- **Numbers 20:10-12** [The Lord told Moses to speak to the rock, but Moses, being upset, hastily struck the rock instead. As a result, the Lord didn't allow Moses and Aaron to go into the Promised Land.] And Moses and Aaron gathered the congregation together before the rock, and he said unto them, Hear now, ye rebels; must we fetch you water out of this rock? [11] And Moses lifted up his hand, and with his rod he smote the rock twice: and the water came out abundantly, and the congregation drank, and their beasts also. [12] And the Lord spake unto Moses and Aaron, Because ye believed Me not, to sanctify Me in the eyes of the children of Israel, therefore ye shall not bring this congregation into the land which I have given them.
- **Job 13:5** O that ye would altogether hold your peace! And it should be your wisdom.
- **Proverbs 14:29** He that is slow to wrath is of great understanding: but he that is hasty of spirit exalteth folly.

- **Ecclesiastes 7:9** Be not hasty in thy spirit to be angry: for anger resteth in the bosom of fools.
- **James 1:19,20** Wherefore, my beloved brethren, let every man be swift to hear, slow to speak, slow to wrath: [20] For the wrath of man worketh not the righteousness of God.

5. Follow the Lord and let <u>Him</u> lead instead of acting impulsively or in haste.

- **Psalm 23:1-3** The Lord is my shepherd; I shall not want. [2] He maketh me to lie down in green pastures: He leadeth me beside the still waters. [3] He restoreth my soul: He leadeth me in the paths of righteousness for His name's sake.
- **Hosea 6:3a** Then shall we know, if we follow on to know the Lord.
- **John 8:12** Then spake Jesus again unto them, saying, I am the light of the world: he that followeth Me shall not walk in darkness, but shall have the light of life.
- **John 10:14,27** I am the Good Shepherd, and know My sheep, and am known of Mine. … [27] My sheep hear My voice, and I know them, and they follow Me.
- **John 12:26a** If any man serve Me, let him follow Me; and where I am, there shall also My servant be.
- **Revelation 14:4b** [Those who love Him most follow closest.] These are they which follow the Lamb whithersoever He goeth.

6. Counsel with others to avoid making rash decisions.

- **Proverbs 11:14** Where no counsel is, the people fall: but in the multitude of counsellors there is safety.
- **Proverbs 15:22** Without counsel purposes are disappointed: but in the multitude of counsellors they are established.

7. Don't panic or act rashly when under stress. Have faith and patience, and trust the Lord.

- **Ecclesiastes 7:8b** The patient in spirit is better than the proud in spirit.
- **Isaiah 30:15a** For thus saith the Lord God, the Holy One of Israel; In returning and rest shall ye be saved; in quietness and in confidence shall be your strength.
- **Zechariah 4:6b** Not by might, nor by power, but by My Spirit, saith the Lord of hosts.
- **Luke 21:19** In your patience possess ye your souls.
- **Romans 12:12** [You should be] rejoicing in hope; patient in tribulation; continuing instant in prayer.
- **Hebrews 6:12** Be not slothful, but followers of them who through faith and patience inherit the promises.
- **Hebrews 10:35,36** Cast not away therefore your confidence, which hath great recompence of reward. [36] For ye have need of patience, that, after ye have done the will of God, ye might receive the promise.

8. Be prayerful, not impulsive or rash.

- **Numbers 9:8** And Moses said unto them, Stand still, and I will hear what the Lord will command concerning you.
- **1 Samuel 9:27** [Samuel asked Saul to be still first, before telling him the words which God had given Samuel for him.] And as they were going down to the end of the city, Samuel said to Saul, Bid the servant pass on before us, (and he passed on,) but stand thou still a while, that I may shew thee the Word of God.
- **Psalm 46:10a** Be still, and know that I am God.
- **Isaiah 28:16b** He that believeth shall not make haste.
- **1 Corinthians 14:33a** [If you're confused, stop and pray!] For God is not the author of confusion.
- **1 Thessalonians 5:17** Pray without ceasing.

9. Some examples in the Bible of hastiness and rashness:

- **Exodus 2:11-14** [Moses, acting in haste, made a serious mistake, causing him to be a terrible sample to his brethren and forcing him to flee Egypt for his life:] And it came to pass in those days, when Moses was grown, that he went out unto his brethren, and looked on their burdens: and he spied an Egyptian smiting an Hebrew, one of his brethren. [12] And he looked this way and that way, and when he saw that there was no man, he slew the Egyptian, and hid him in the sand. [13] And when he went out the second day, behold, two men of the Hebrews strove together: and he said to him that did the wrong, Wherefore smitest thou thy fellow? [14] And he said, Who made thee a prince and a judge over us? Intendest thou to kill me, as thou killedst the Egyptian? And Moses feared, and said, Surely this thing is known.

- **2 Kings 5:11,12** [Naaman, the commander of the Syrian army, was told to wash in the Jordan River to be healed of his leprosy. He was highly offended and impulsively turned to go back home:] But Naaman was wroth, and went away, and said, Behold, I thought, He [Elisha] will surely come out to me, and stand, and call on the name of the Lord his God, and strike his hand over the place, and recover the leper. [12] Are not Abana and Pharpar, rivers of Damascus, better than all the waters of Israel? May I not wash in them, and be clean? So he turned and went away in a rage. [Then his servants helped him to come to his senses and yield, whereupon he washed in the Jordan and was both healed and accepted the Lord!]

- **2 Chronicles 35:20-24** [King Josiah hastily went into battle against a foreign king who was not threatening Judah, and who had a message from God that said that Josiah should not fight him:] [21] But [the foreign king] sent ambassadors to him [King Josiah], saying, What have I to do with thee, thou king of Judah? I come not against thee this day, but against the house [the city of Carchemish] wherewith I have war: for God commanded me to make haste: forbear thee from meddling with God, who is with me, that He destroy thee not. [22] Nevertheless Josiah would not turn his face from him, but disguised himself, that he might fight with him, and hearkened not unto the words of Necho from the mouth of God, and came to fight in the valley of Megiddo. [23] And the archers shot at King Josiah; and the king said to his servants, Have me away; for I am sore wounded. ... [24] And he died.

- **Psalm 31:22** [One of those hasty outbursts, prompted by the Enemy, in which David despaired for his life:] For I said in my haste, I am cut off from before Thine eyes: nevertheless Thou heardest the voice of my supplications when I cried unto Thee. [See also 1 Samuel 27:1.]

- **Matthew 16:21-23** [Watch out! Acting, or speaking on impulse can sometimes be prompted by the Devil.] From that time forth began Jesus to shew unto His disciples, how that He must go unto Jerusalem, and suffer many things of the elders and chief priests and scribes, and be killed, and be raised again the third day. [22] Then Peter took Him, and began to rebuke Him, saying, Be it far from Thee, Lord: this shall not be unto Thee. [23] But He turned, and said unto Peter, Get thee behind Me, Satan: thou art an offence unto Me: for thou savourest not the things that be of God, but those that be of men.

- **Acts 21:4,10-14** [Paul rashly insisted on going to Jerusalem, even though prophecies told him not to.] And finding disciples, we tarried there seven days: who said to Paul through the Spirit, that he should not go up to Jerusalem. ... [14] And as we tarried there many days, there came down from Judaea a certain prophet, named Agabus. [11] And when he was come unto us, he took Paul's girdle, and bound his own hands and feet, and said, Thus saith the Holy Ghost, So shall the Jews at Jerusalem bind the man that owneth this girdle, and shall deliver him into the hands of the Gentiles. [12] And when we heard these things, both we, and they of that place, besought him not to go up to Jerusalem. [13] Then Paul answered, What mean ye to weep and to break mine heart? For I am ready not to be bound only, but also to die at Jerusalem for the name of the Lord Jesus. [14] And when he would not be persuaded, we ceased, saying, The will of the Lord be done.

10. Some examples of the right kind of hastiness:

- **1 Samuel 21:8b** [Sometimes things need to be done without delay.] The king's business required haste.
- **Psalm 119:59-60** [Don't delay to obey!] I thought on my ways, and turned my feet unto Thy testimonies. [60] I made haste, and delayed not to keep Thy commandments.
- **Luke 19:5-6** [When the Lord says to jump, jump!] And when Jesus came to the place, He looked up, and saw him, and said unto him, Zacchaeus, make haste, and come down; for to day I must abide at thy house. [6] And he made haste, and came down, and received Him joyfully.
- **Acts 22:17-18** [Paul, giving his testimony, explained where the Lord told him to move hastily:] And it came to pass, that, when I was come again to Jerusalem, even while I prayed in the temple, I was in a trance; [18] And saw Him saying unto me, Make haste, and get thee quickly out of Jerusalem: for they will not receive thy testimony concerning Me.
- **Psalm 141:1** [David desperately prayed that the Lord would answer speedily.] Lord, I cry unto Thee: make haste unto me; give ear unto my voice, when I cry unto Thee.

HELP, ASKING FOR

1. God designed us to need the help of others.

- **Genesis 2:18** And the Lord God said, It is not good that the man should be alone; I will make him an help meet for him.
- **1 Corinthians 12:12,21,25** For as the body is one, and hath many members, and all the members of that one body, being many, are one body: so also is Christ. ... [21] And the eye cannot say unto the hand, I have no need of thee: nor again the head to the feet, I have no need of you. ... [25] That there should be no schism in the body; but that the members should have the same care one for another.

2. God wants to provide the help we need.

- **2 Chronicles 32:8b** With us is the Lord our God to help us, and to fight our battles.
- **Psalm 20:1,2** The Lord hear thee in the day of trouble; the name of the God of Jacob defend thee; [2] Send thee help from the sanctuary, and strengthen thee out of Zion.
- **Psalm 28:7a** The Lord is my strength and my shield; my heart trusted in Him, and I am helped.
- **Psalm 33:20** Our soul waiteth for the Lord: He is our help and our shield.
- **Psalm 42:5** Why art thou cast down, O my soul? And why art thou disquieted in me? Hope thou in God: for I shall yet praise Him for the help of His countenance.
- **Psalm 46:1** God is our refuge and strength, a very present help in trouble.
- **Psalm 63:7** Because Thou hast been My help, therefore in the shadow of Thy wings will I rejoice.
- **Psalm 94:17** Unless the Lord had been my help, my soul had almost dwelt in silence.

- **Psalm 115:11** Ye that fear the Lord, trust in the Lord: He is their help and their shield.
- **Psalm 121:1,2** I will lift up mine eyes unto the hills, from whence cometh my help. [2] My help cometh from the Lord, which made Heaven and earth.
- **Psalm 146:5** Happy is he that hath the God of Jacob for his help, whose hope is in the Lord his God.
- **Isaiah 41:10** Fear thou not; for I am with thee: be not dismayed; for I am thy God: I will strengthen thee; yea, I will help thee; yea, I will uphold thee with the right hand of My righteousness.
- **Isaiah 65:24** And it shall come to pass, that before they call, I will answer; and while they are yet speaking, I will hear.
- **Philippians 4:19** But my God shall supply all your need according to His riches in glory by Christ Jesus.

3. But we must ask for His help.

- **Psalm 22:19** But be not Thou far from me, O Lord: O my strength, haste Thee to help me.
- **Psalm 60:11** Give us help from trouble: for vain is the help of man.
- **Psalm 40:17** But I am poor and needy; yet the Lord thinketh upon me: Thou art my help and my deliverer; make no tarrying, O my God.
- **Psalm 119:173** Let thine hand help me; for I have chosen Thy precepts.
- **Matthew 7:7,8** Ask, and it shall be given you; seek, and ye shall find; knock, and it shall be opened unto you: [8] For every one that asketh receiveth; and he that seeketh findeth; and to him that knocketh it shall be opened.
- **Matthew 21:22** And all things, whatsoever ye shall ask in prayer, believing, ye shall receive.
- **John 14:14** If ye shall ask any thing in My name, I will do it.
- **John 16:24** Hitherto have ye asked nothing in My name: ask, and ye shall receive, that your joy may be full.

- **Hebrews 4:16** Let us therefore come boldly unto the throne of grace, that we may obtain mercy, and find grace to help in time of need.
- **James 4:2b** Ye have not, because ye ask not.
- **1 John 5:14,15** And this is the confidence that we have in Him, that, if we <u>ask</u> any thing according to His will, He heareth us: [15] And if we know that He hear us, whatsoever we ask, we know that we have the petitions that we desired of Him.

4. We need the help of <u>others</u> as well.

- **1 Samuel 23:16** [These two close friends were a great strength one to another.] And Jonathan Saul's son arose, and went to David into the wood, and strengthened his hand in God.
- **1 Chronicles 19:10-12** [Joab and his brother, Abishai, were a strength in battle, one to another.] Now when Joab saw that the battle was set against him before and behind, he chose out of all the choice of Israel, and put them in array against the Syrians. [11] And the rest of the people he delivered unto the hand of Abishai his brother, and they set themselves in array against the children of Ammon. [12] And he said, If the Syrians be too strong for me, then thou shalt help me: but if the children of Ammon be too strong for thee, then I will help thee.
- **Ecclesiastes 4:9,10,12** Two are better than one; because they have a good reward for their labour. [10] For if they fall, the one will lift up his fellow: but woe to him that is alone when he falleth; for he hath not another to help him up. ... [12] And if one prevail against him, two shall withstand him; and a threefold cord is not quickly broken.
- **Ezra 1:3,4** [King Cyrus, who allowed and helped the Jews to rebuild their temple, encouraged those who didn't actually do the work to at least help the work financially.] Who is there among you of all his people? His God be with him, and let him go up to Jerusalem, which is in Judah, and build the house of the Lord God of Israel, (He is the God,) which is in Jerusalem. [4] And whosoever remaineth in

any place where he sojourneth, let the men of his place help him with silver, and with gold, and with goods, and with beasts, beside the freewill offering for the house of God that is in Jerusalem.

• **Proverbs 15:22** Without counsel purposes are disappointed: but in the multitude of counsellors they are established. [See also Proverbs 11:14.]

• **Proverbs 27:17** Iron sharpeneth iron; so a man sharpeneth the countenance of his friend.

• **Mark 6:7** [Jesus sent out His disciples two by two, to be a strength to one another.] And He called unto Him the twelve, and began to send them forth by two and two; and gave them power over unclean spirits.

5. Even Moses, with all of his talents, training, anointing and divine calling, needed the help of others.

• **Exodus 4:10,14b,16** And Moses said unto the Lord, O my Lord, I am not eloquent, neither heretofore, nor since thou hast spoken unto Thy servant: but I am slow of speech, and of a slow tongue. ... [14b] And He said, Is not Aaron the Levite thy brother? I know that he can speak well. And also, behold, he cometh forth to meet thee: and when he seeth thee, he will be glad in his heart. ... [16] And he shall be thy spokesman unto the people: and he shall be, even he shall be to thee instead of a mouth, and thou shalt be to him instead of God. [See also verses 10-16.]

• **Exodus 17:12** But Moses' hands were heavy; and they took a stone, and put it under him, and he sat thereon; and Aaron and Hur stayed up his hands, the one on the one side, and the other on the other side; and his hands were steady until the going down of the sun.

• **Exodus 18:18,21,22** [Jethro counseled Moses to delegate some of his responsibilities:] Thou wilt surely wear away, both thou, and this people that is with thee: for this thing is too heavy for thee; thou art not able to perform it thyself alone. ... [21] Moreover thou shalt provide out of all the people able men, such as fear God, men of truth, hating covetousness; and place such over them, to be rulers of thousands, and rulers of hundreds, rulers of fifties, and rulers of tens: [22] And let them judge the people at all seasons: and it shall be, that every great matter they shall bring unto thee, but every small matter they shall judge: so shall it be easier for thyself, and they shall bear the burden with thee. [See also verses 13-26.]

- **Exodus 24:13** And Moses rose up, and his minister [servant] Joshua: and Moses went up into the mount of God. [See also Exodus 33:11.]

6. If we are wise, we will avail ourselves of the strengths and talents of others.

- **Proverbs 1:5** A wise man will hear, and will increase learning; and a man of understanding shall attain unto wise counsels. [See also Proverbs 11:14; 15:22; 19:20.]
- **Proverbs 13:20a** He that walketh with wise men shall be wise.
- **Proverbs 20:5** Counsel in the heart of man is like deep water; but a man of understanding will draw it out.

7. As Christians motivated by the Lord's love, we can always depend upon one another for help.

- **Proverbs 17:17** A friend loveth at all times, and a brother is born for adversity.
- **Proverbs 18:24b** There is a friend that sticketh closer than a brother.
- **Galatians 5:13b** By love serve one another.
- **Galatians 6:2** Bear ye one another's burdens, and so fulfil the law of Christ.

INSECURITY

Definition: The tendency to feel fearful, anxious, unsafe; apprehension regarding present or future situations or circumstances.

1. We must learn to draw our security from the great stabilizers: Jesus and His Word.

- **Hebrews 13:8** Jesus Christ [is] the same yesterday, and to day, and for ever.
- **Matthew 7:24,25** Therefore whosoever heareth these sayings of Mine, and doeth them, I will liken him unto a wise man, which built his house upon a rock: [25] And the rain descended, and the floods came, and the winds blew, and beat upon that house; and it fell not: for it was founded upon a rock.
- **Matthew 24:35** Heaven and earth shall pass away, but My Words shall not pass away.
- **Romans 8:35,38,39** Who shall separate us from the love of Christ? Shall tribulation, or distress, or persecution, or famine, or nakedness, or peril, or sword? ... [38] For I am persuaded, that neither death, nor life, nor angels, nor principalities, nor powers, nor things present, nor things to come, [39] Nor height, nor depth, nor any other creature, shall be able to separate us from the love of God, which is in Christ Jesus our Lord.

2. We can't look to the things of this world for our security.

- **Luke 12:19,20** [The rich fool trusted in his riches, but lost his life in one night.] And I [the rich man] will say to my soul, Soul, thou hast much goods laid up for many years; take thine ease, eat, drink, and be merry. [20] But God said unto him, Thou fool, this night thy soul shall be required of thee: then whose shall those things be, which thou hast provided?

- **2 Corinthians 4:18** While we look not at the things which are seen, but at the things which are not seen: for the things which are seen are temporal; but the things which are not seen are eternal.
- **Colossians 3:2** Set your affection on things above, not on things on the earth.
- **Hebrews 13:5** Let your conversation be without covetousness; and be content with such things as ye have: for He hath said, I will never leave thee, nor forsake thee.
- **2 Peter 3:11** Seeing then that all these things shall be dissolved, what manner of persons ought ye to be in all holy conversation and godliness.
- **1 John 2:15a,17** Love not the world, neither the things that are in the world. ... [17] And the world passeth away, and the lust thereof: but he that doeth the will of God abideth for ever.

3. Insecurity often stems from over-concern for our physical situation or needs.

- **Matthew 6:25,26,28-33** Therefore I say unto you, Take no thought for your life, what ye shall eat, or what ye shall drink; nor yet for your body, what ye shall put on. Is not the life more than meat, and the body than raiment? [26] Behold the fowls of the air: for they sow not, neither do they reap, nor gather into barns; yet your Heavenly Father feedeth them. Are ye not much better than they? ... [28] And why take ye thought for raiment? Consider the lilies of the field, how they grow; they toil not, neither do they spin: [29] And yet I say unto you, That even Solomon in all his glory was not arrayed like one of these. [30] Wherefore, if God so clothe the grass of the field, which to day is, and to morrow is cast into the oven, shall He not much more clothe you, O ye of little faith? [31] Therefore take no thought, saying, What shall we eat? Or, What shall we drink? or, Wherewithal shall we be clothed? [32] (For after all these things do the Gentiles seek:) for your Heavenly Father knoweth that ye have need of all these things. [33] But seek ye first the Kingdom of God, and His righteousness; and all these things shall be added unto you.

- **Matthew 10:29-31** Are not two sparrows sold for a farthing? And one of them shall not fall on the ground without your Father. [30] But the very hairs of your head are all numbered. [31] Fear ye not therefore, ye are of more value than many sparrows.
- **Luke 12:32** Fear not, little flock; for it is your Father's good pleasure to give you the Kingdom.
- **1 Peter 5:7** Casting all your care upon Him; for He careth for you.

4. Though human security and assurance may fall short, the Lord never fails.

[See Loneliness, #2, page 254.]

5. Anywhere with Jesus, we can feel safe, secure and loved.

- **Genesis 28:15a** And, behold, I am with thee, and will keep thee in all places whither thou goest.
- **Joshua 1:9** Have not I commanded thee? Be strong and of a good courage; be not afraid, neither be thou dismayed: for the Lord thy God is with thee whithersoever thou goest.

Psalm 125:1 They that trust in the Lord shall be as Mount Zion, which cannot be removed, but abideth for ever.

Psalm 139:7-10 Whither shall I go from Thy Spirit? Or whither shall I flee from Thy presence? [8] If I ascend up into Heaven, Thou art there: if I make my bed in Hell, behold, Thou art there. [9] If I take the wings of the morning, and dwell in the uttermost parts of the sea; [10] Even there shall Thy hand lead me, and Thy right hand shall hold me.

Isaiah 41:10 Fear thou not; for I am with thee: be not dismayed; for I am thy God: I will strengthen thee; yea, I will help thee; yea, I will uphold thee with the right hand of My righteousness.

- **Isaiah 43:2** When thou passest through the waters, I will be with thee; and through the rivers, they shall not overflow thee: when thou walkest through the fire, thou shalt not be burned; neither shall the flame kindle upon thee.

  [See also Loneliness, #1, page 253.]

6. In Jesus we have unfailing confidence and assurance!

- **Psalm 27:13** I had fainted, unless I had believed to see the goodness of the Lord in the land of the living.
- **Proverbs 3:26** For the Lord shall be thy confidence, and shall keep thy foot from being taken.
- **Proverbs 14:26a** In the fear of the Lord is strong confidence.
- **Isaiah 32:17** [Assurance comes from knowing we're in the Lord's will and doing our best to please Him.] And the work of righteousness shall be peace; and the effect of righteousness quietness and assurance for ever.
- **Romans 15:13** Now the God of hope fill you with all joy and peace in believing, that ye may abound in hope, through the power of the Holy Ghost.
- **Philippians 1:6** Being confident of this very thing, that He which hath begun a good work in you will perform it until the Day of Jesus Christ.
- **2 Timothy 1:12b** For I know whom I have believed, and am persuaded that He is able to keep that which I have committed unto Him against that day.
- **Hebrews 6:19a** Which hope we have as an anchor of the soul, both sure and stedfast.

7. In Jesus' arms we have perfect security.

- **Deuteronomy 33:27a** The eternal God is thy refuge, and underneath are the everlasting arms.
- **Psalm 37:23,24** [Even when <u>we</u> fail, His loving care for us never fails.] The steps of a good man are ordered by the Lord: and he

delighteth in His way. [24] Though he fall, he shall not be utterly cast down: for the Lord upholdeth him with His hand.

- **Isaiah 40:11a** He shall feed His flock like a shepherd: He shall gather the lambs with His arm, and carry them in His bosom.
- **Isaiah 41:13** For I the Lord thy God will hold thy right hand, saying unto thee, Fear not; I will help thee.
- **Matthew 14:31** [When Jesus and Peter walked on the water, Peter eventually fell when he became doubtful and afraid, but Jesus was there to help him.] And immediately Jesus stretched forth His hand, and caught him, and said unto him, O thou of little faith, wherefore didst thou doubt?
- **John 10:28** And I give unto them eternal life; and they shall never perish, neither shall any man pluck them out of My hand.

8. We can be channels of the Lord's comfort and reassurance to one another.

- **Isaiah 40:1** Comfort ye, comfort ye My people, saith your God.
- **Colossians 2:2a** That their hearts might be comforted, being knit together in love, and unto all riches of the full assurance of understanding.
- **1 Thessalonians 1:5a** For our Gospel came not unto you in word only, but also in power, and in the Holy Ghost, and in much assurance.
- **1 Thessalonians 4:18** Wherefore comfort one another with these Words.

9. When tempted with feelings of insecurity, we need to keep our eyes Heaven-ward.

- **Psalm 31:24** Be of good courage, and He shall strengthen your heart, all ye that hope in the Lord.
- **Psalm 61:2** From the end of the earth will I cry unto Thee, when my heart is overwhelmed: lead me to the Rock that is higher than I.

- **John 14:1-3** Let not your heart be troubled: ye believe in God, believe also in Me. [2] In My Father's house are many mansions: if it were not so, I would have told you. I go to prepare a place for you. [3] And if I go and prepare a place for you, I will come again, and receive you unto Myself; that where I am, there ye may be also.

- **2 Corinthians 4:18** While we look not at the things which are seen, but at the things which are not seen: for the things which are seen are temporal; but the things which are not seen are eternal.

- **Hebrews 12:28** Wherefore we receiving a kingdom which cannot be moved [Heaven], let us have grace, whereby we may serve God acceptably with reverence and godly fear.

- **Luke 21:28** And when these things [the Endtime signs of the times] begin to come to pass, then look up, and lift up your heads; for your redemption draweth nigh.

JEALOUSY AND ENVY

Definitions: Jealousy is the uneasiness felt due to suspicion, resentment or fear of rivalry, especially in regards to love or affection. Envy is the feeling of resentment, discontentment or jealousy of another's position or success.

1. Jealousy and envy have their roots in pride, vanity and selfishness.

- **Ecclesiastes 4:4** Again, I considered all travail, and every right work, that for this a man is envied of his neighbour. This is also vanity and vexation of spirit.
- **Galatians 5:26** Let us not be desirous of <u>vain glory</u>, provoking one another, envying one another.
- **1 Timothy 6:4** He is proud, knowing nothing, but doting about questions and strifes of words, whereof cometh envy, strife, railings, evil surmisings.

2. Jealousy and envy is a spirit of complaint and murmuring.

- **Genesis 37:4** And when [Joseph's] brethren saw that their father loved him more than all his brethren, they hated him, and could not speak peaceably unto him.
- **Numbers 16:3** [Rebellious Korah and his followers envied Moses' leadership position and spoke against him, falsely accusing him:] And they gathered themselves together against Moses and against Aaron, and said unto them, Ye take too much upon you, seeing all the congregation are holy, every one of them, and the Lord is among them: wherefore then lift ye up yourselves above the congregation of the Lord? [See Psalm 106:16-18.]
- **1 Samuel 18:7-9** And the women answered one another as they played, and said, Saul hath slain his thousands, and David his ten thousands. [8] And Saul was very wroth, and the saying displeased him; and he said, They have ascribed unto David ten thousands, and to me they have ascribed but thousands: and what can he

have more but the kingdom? [9] And Saul eyed David from that day and forward. [See also verses 27,28; 20:30,31.]

- **Matthew 20:8-12** So when even was come, the lord of the vineyard saith unto his steward, Call the labourers, and give them their hire, beginning from the last unto the first. [9] And when they came that were hired about the eleventh hour, they received every man a penny. [10] But when the first came, they supposed that they should have received more; and they likewise received every man a penny. [11] And when they had received it, they murmured against the goodman of the house, [12] Saying, These last have wrought but one hour, and thou hast made them equal unto us, which have borne the burden and heat of the day.

- **Acts 13:44,45** And the next Sabbath day came almost the whole city together to hear the Word of God. [45] But when the Jews saw the multitudes, they were filled with envy, and spake against those things which were spoken by Paul, contradicting and blaspheming.

3. Jealousy and envy are products of our carnal hearts and must be overcome by the power of God's Spirit of love.

- **Jeremiah 17:9** The heart is deceitful above all things, and desperately wicked: who can know it? [See also Matthew 15:19.]

- **Matthew 20:20-28** Then came to Him the mother of Zebedee's children with her sons, worshipping Him, and desiring a certain thing of Him. [21] And He said unto her, What wilt thou? She saith unto Him, Grant that these my two sons may sit, the one on Thy right hand, and the other on the left, in Thy Kingdom. ... [24] And when the ten heard it, they were moved with indignation against the two brethren. ... [26] [Jesus said:] But it shall not be so among you: but whosoever will be great among you, let him be your minister; [27] And whosoever will be chief among you, let him be your servant: [28] Even as the Son of Man came not to be ministered unto, but to minister, and to give His life a ransom for many.

- **Romans 13:11-14** And that, knowing the time, that now it is high time to awake out of sleep: for now is our salvation nearer than when we believed. [12] The night is far spent, the day is at hand: let us therefore cast off the works of darkness, and let us put on the armour of light. [13] Let us walk honestly, as in the day ... not in strife and envying. [14] But put ye on the Lord Jesus Christ, and make not provision for the flesh, to fulfil the lusts thereof.

- **1 Corinthians 3:3** For ye are yet carnal: for whereas there is among you envying, and strife, and divisions, are ye not carnal, and walk as men?

- **Galatians 5:14-16** For all the law is fulfilled in one word, even in this; Thou shalt love thy neighbour as thyself. [15] But if ye bite and devour one another, take heed that ye be not consumed one of another. [16] This I say then, Walk in the Spirit, and ye shall not fulfil the lust of the flesh.

- **Galatians 5:19a,21-23** Now the works of the flesh are manifest, which are these; ... [21] Envyings ... and such like. [22] But the fruit of the Spirit is love, joy, peace, longsuffering, gentleness, goodness, faith, [23] Meekness, temperance: against such there is no law.

- **Galatians 5:24-26** And they that are Christ's have crucified the flesh with the affections and lusts. [25] If we live in the Spirit, let us also walk in the Spirit. [26] Let us not be desirous of vain glory, provoking one another, envying one another.

- **Titus 3:3,4** For we ourselves also were sometimes foolish, disobedient, deceived, serving divers lusts and pleasures, living in malice and envy, hateful, and hating one another. [4] But after that the kindness and love of God our Saviour toward man appeared.

- **James 3:15-17** This wisdom descendeth not from above, but is earthly, sensual, devilish. [16] For where envying and strife is, there is confusion and every evil work. [17] But the wisdom that is from above is first pure, then peaceable, gentle, and easy to be intreated, full of mercy and good fruits, without partiality, and without hypocrisy.

- **James 4:5-7** [Carnal envying and pride are products of our sinful nature, which the Devil preys upon; we have to fight them with the

Word and prayer.] Do ye think that the Scripture saith in vain, The spirit that dwelleth in us lusteth to envy? [6] But He giveth more grace. Wherefore He saith, God resisteth the proud, but giveth grace unto the humble. [7] Submit yourselves therefore to God. Resist the Devil, and he will flee from you.

4. Jealousy and envy are devices of the Devil and only bear bad fruit.

- **Proverbs 6:34,35** For jealousy is the rage of a man: therefore he will not spare in the day of vengeance. [35] He will not regard any ransom; neither will he rest content, though thou givest many gifts.
- **Proverbs 14:30** A sound heart is the life of the flesh: but envy the rottenness of the bones.
- **Proverbs 27:4** Wrath is cruel, and anger is outrageous; but who is able to stand before envy?
- **James 3:16** For where envying and strife is, there is confusion and every evil work.

5. Jealousy is an unwillingness to share and often results in total loss of that which is not shared.

- **Genesis 37:4-11;19,20** [Joseph's brothers were jealous of his being favored by his father, and sought to kill him. But Joseph survived and prospered, while they lost their wealth in a great drought and had to beg Joseph for help. See chapters 45 and 46 regarding his brothers' plea and Joseph's forgiveness to them.]
- **Proverbs 11:24** There is that scattereth, and yet increaseth; and there is that withholdeth more than is meet, but it tendeth to poverty.
- **Mark 4:25** For he that hath, to him shall be given: and he that hath not, from him shall be taken even that which he hath. [See also Luke 8:18.]

• **Galatians 6:7b** For whatsoever a man soweth, that shall he also reap.

6. Don't be led astray by being envious of the ungodly.

• **Psalm 37:1** Fret not thyself because of evildoers, neither be thou envious against the workers of iniquity. [See also verse 7.]

• **Psalm 73:3,12,14,16-18,21,22a** For I was envious at the foolish, when I saw the prosperity of the wicked. ... [12] Behold, these are the ungodly, who prosper in the world; they increase in riches. ... [14] For all the day long have I been plagued, and chastened every morning. ... [16] When I thought to know this, it was too painful for me; [17] Until I went into the sanctuary of God; then understood I their end. [18] Surely thou didst set them in slippery places: thou castedst them down into destruction. ... [21] Thus my heart was grieved, and I was pricked in my reins. ... [22a] So foolish was I, and ignorant. [See also Job 21:7-30.]

• **Proverbs 3:31** Envy thou not the oppressor, and choose none of his ways.

• **Proverbs 23:17** Let not thine heart envy sinners: but be thou in the fear of the Lord all the day long.

• **Proverbs 24:1** Be not thou envious against evil men, neither desire to be with them.

7. Jealousy and envy provide the motivation for wrongdoing.

• **Genesis 16:5,6** And Sarai said unto Abram, My wrong be upon thee: I have given my maid [Hagar] into thy bosom; and when she saw that she had conceived, I was despised in her eyes: the Lord judge between me and thee. [6] But Abram said unto Sarai, Behold, thy maid is in thy hand; do to her as it pleaseth thee. And when Sarai dealt hardly with her, she fled from her face. [See also chapter 21:9,10.]

• **1 Samuel 18:6-9** [Saul envied David and made several attempts to murder him.]

- **Esther 5:11,13,14a** And Haman told them of the glory of his riches, and the multitude of his children, and all the things wherein the king had promoted him, and how he had advanced him above the princes and servants of the king. … ¹³ Yet all this availeth me nothing, so long as I see Mordecai the Jew sitting at the king's gate. ^{14a} Then said Zeresh his wife and all his friends unto him, Let a gallows be made fifty cubits high, and to morrow speak thou unto the king that Mordecai may be hanged thereon.

- **Daniel 6:3-5** Then this Daniel was preferred above the presidents and princes, because an excellent spirit was in him; and the king thought to set him over the whole realm. ⁴ Then the presidents and princes sought to find occasion against Daniel concerning the kingdom; but they could find none occasion nor fault; forasmuch as he was faithful, neither was there any error or fault found in him. ⁵ Then said these men, We shall not find any occasion against this Daniel, except we find it against him concerning the law of his God. [Then they conspired against him.]

- **Mark 11:18** And the scribes and chief priests heard [Jesus' preaching], and sought how they might destroy Him: for they feared Him, because all the people was astonished at His doctrine.

- **Acts 13:44,45** And the next Sabbath day came almost the whole city together to hear the Word of God. ⁴⁵ But when the Jews saw the multitudes, they were filled with envy, and spake against those things which were spoken by Paul, contradicting and blaspheming.

8. Some Biblical examples of sibling rivalry as a result of envy:

- **Genesis 4:3-5,8** And in process of time it came to pass, that Cain brought of the fruit of the ground an offering unto the Lord. ⁴ And Abel, he also brought of the firstlings of his flock and of the fat thereof. And the Lord had respect unto Abel and to his offering: ⁵ But unto Cain and to his offering He had not respect. And Cain was very wroth, and his countenance fell. … ⁸ And Cain talked with Abel his brother: and it came to pass, when they were in the field, that Cain rose up against Abel his brother, and slew him.

- **Genesis 37,44,45** [Joseph's brothers were jealous of him, and planned to kill him, but then opted to sell him into slavery, lying to their father that he had been killed by a wild beast. They all were later reconciled and forgiven in Egypt.]

- **Numbers 12:1-2,9a,10b,15a** And Miriam and Aaron spake against Moses because of the Ethiopian woman whom he had married: for he had married an Ethiopian woman. [2] And they said, Hath the Lord indeed spoken only by Moses? Hath He not spoken also by us? And the Lord heard it. ... [9a] And the anger of the Lord was kindled against them. ... [10b] And, behold, Miriam became leprous, white as snow. ... [15a] And Miriam was shut out from the camp seven days [until she was mercifully and quickly healed].

- **Luke 10:38b-40** [Martha was a little jealous of her sister, Mary, who was sitting at Jesus' feet:] A certain woman named Martha received Him into her house. [39] And she had a sister called Mary, which also sat at Jesus' feet, and heard His Word. [40] But Martha was cumbered about much serving, and came to Him, and said, Lord, dost Thou not care that my sister hath left me to serve alone? Bid her therefore that she help me.

- **Luke 15:25-30** [Upon the return of the lost prodigal son to the father's house:] Now his elder son was in the field: and as he came and drew nigh to the house, he heard musick and dancing. [26] And he called one of the servants, and asked what these things meant. [27] And he said unto him, Thy brother is come; and thy father hath killed the fatted calf, because he hath received him safe and sound. [28] And he was angry, and would not go in: therefore came his father out, and intreated him. [29] And he answering said to his father, Lo, these many years do I serve thee, neither transgressed I at any time thy commandment: and yet thou never gavest me a kid, that I might make merry with my friends: [30] But as soon as this thy son was come, which hath devoured thy living with harlots, thou hast killed for him the fatted calf.

9. The cure for jealousy and envy is to pray for more of the Lord's love, to be more like Jesus.

- **Song of Solomon 8:6** Set Me as a seal upon thine heart, as a seal upon thine arm: for love is strong as death; jealousy is cruel as the grave: the coals thereof are coals of fire, which hath a most vehement flame.
- **Romans 13:13,14** Let us walk honestly, as in the day ... not in strife and envying. [14] But put ye on the Lord Jesus Christ, and make not provision for the flesh, to fulfil the lusts thereof.
- **1 Corinthians 13:4** Charity [love] suffereth long, and is kind; charity envieth not; charity vaunteth not itself, is not puffed up.
- **1 Peter 2:1,2** Wherefore laying aside all malice, and all guile, and hypocrisies, and envies, and all evil speakings, [2] As newborn babes, desire the sincere milk of the Word, that ye may grow thereby.

10. Helpful verses to claim when battling jealousy:

- **Psalm 61:2b** When my heart is overwhelmed: lead me to the Rock that is higher than I.
- **Psalm 103:14** For He knoweth our frame; He remembereth that we are dust.
- **Isaiah 59:19b** When the Enemy shall come in like a flood, the Spirit of the Lord shall lift up a standard against him.
- **1 Corinthians 10:13** There hath no temptation taken you but such as is common to man: but God is faithful, who will not suffer you to be tempted above that ye are able; but will with the temptation also make a way to escape, that ye may be able to bear it.
- **2 Corinthians 1:10** Who delivered us from so great a death, and doth deliver: in whom we trust that He will yet deliver us.
- **2 Corinthians 9:7** Every man according as he purpose in his heart, so let him give; not grudgingly, or of necessity: for God loveth a cheerful giver.

- **Galatians 6:9** And let us not be weary in well doing: for in due season we shall reap if we faint not.
- **2 Timothy 2:3,4** Thou therefore endure hardness, as a good soldier of Jesus Christ. ⁴ No man that warreth entangleth himself with the affairs of this life; that he may please Him who hath chosen him to be a soldier.
- **2 Timothy 4:18** And the Lord shall deliver me from every evil work, and will preserve me unto His Heavenly Kingdom: to whom be glory for ever and ever. Amen.
- **1 Peter 5:10** But the God of all grace, who hath called us unto His eternal glory by Christ Jesus, after that ye have suffered a while, make you perfect, stablish, strengthen, settle you.

11. Persecution is often the result of religious envy.

- **Mark 15:9-11** [Envious religionists pushed the people to call for Jesus' death:] But Pilate answered them, saying, Will ye that I release unto you the King of the Jews? ¹⁰ For he knew that the chief priests had delivered Him for envy. ¹¹ But the chief priests moved the people, that he should rather release Barabbas [a murderer] unto them.
- **Acts 13:45** But when the Jews saw the multitudes, they were filled with envy, and spake against those things which were spoken by Paul, contradicting and blaspheming.
- **Acts 14:1,2** And it came to pass in Iconium, that they went both together into the synagogue of the Jews, and so spake, that a great multitude both of the Jews and also of the Greeks believed. ² But the unbelieving Jews stirred up the Gentiles, and made their minds evil affected against the brethren.
- **Act 17:5** [Envious Jews stirred up a Greek mob to persecute Paul and the brethren in Thessalonica, after seeing Paul's success with the people:] But the Jews which believed not, moved with envy, took unto them certain lewd fellows of the baser sort, and gathered

a company, and set all the city on an uproar, and assaulted the
house of Jason, and sought to bring them out to the people.

12. God becomes jealous when we put the love of material things, others, or even our service to Him, above our love for Him!

- **Exodus 20:3,5,6** Thou shalt have no other gods before Me. …
  [5] Thou shalt not bow down thyself to them, nor serve them: for I the
  Lord thy God am a jealous God, visiting the iniquity of the fathers
  upon the children unto the third and fourth generation of them that
  hate Me; [6] And shewing mercy unto thousands of them that love
  Me, and keep My commandments.
- **Exodus 34:14** For thou shalt worship no other god: for the Lord,
  whose name is Jealous, is a jealous God. [See also Exodus 20:5.]
- **Numbers 25:11** Phinehas, the son of Eleazar, the son of Aaron the
  priest, hath turned My wrath away from the children of Israel, while
  he was zealous for My sake among them, that I consumed not the
  children of Israel in My jealousy. [See also 1 Corinthians 10:22.]
- **Deuteronomy 4:24** For the Lord thy God is a consuming fire, even
  a jealous God. [See also 5:9; 6:14,15.]
- **Zechariah 8:2** Thus saith the Lord of hosts; I was jealous for Zion
  with great jealousy, and I was jealous for her with great fury. [See
  also 1:14.]
- **Matthew 10:37** He that loveth father or mother more than Me is
  not worthy of Me: and he that loveth son or daughter more than
  Me is not worthy of Me.
- **John 21:15** Jesus saith to Simon Peter, Simon, son of Jonas, lovest
  thou Me more than these? He saith unto Him, Yea, Lord; Thou
  knowest that I love Thee. He saith unto him, Feed My lambs.
- **2 Corinthians 11:2** [Paul had a godly jealousy for his flock, that
  they would stay faithful to the Lord and not go astray.] For I am
  jealous over you with godly jealousy: for I have espoused you to
  one Husband, that I may present you as a chaste virgin to Christ.

- **1 John 2:15** Love not the world, neither the things that are in the world. If any man love the world, the love of the Father is not in him.

- **Revelation 2:1-7** Unto the angel of the church of Ephesus write; ... [4] Nevertheless I [Jesus] have somewhat against thee, because thou hast left thy First Love. [5] Remember therefore from whence thou art fallen, and repent, and do the first works; or else I will come unto thee quickly, and will remove thy candlestick out of his place, except thou repent.

KINDNESS AND COURTESY

Definition: Kindness is a readiness to assist or show consideration for others; of a gentle, sympathetic, or benevolent nature; helpfulness, thoughtfulness. Courtesy is polite behavior; consideration in interacting with others.

1. God's kindness towards His children is boundless, steadfast and unconditional.

- **Psalm 89:33** My lovingkindness will I not utterly take from him, nor suffer My faithfulness to fail.
- **Psalm 117:2** For His merciful kindness is great toward us: and the truth of the Lord endureth for ever. Praise ye the Lord.
- **Isaiah 54:10** For the mountains shall depart, and the hills be removed; but My kindness shall not depart from thee, neither shall the covenant of My peace be removed, saith the Lord that hath mercy on thee.
- **Joel 2:13b** [God is willing to forgive and relent from sending His justified punishments:] He is gracious and merciful, slow to anger, and of great kindness, and repenteth Him of the evil.
- **Hosea 2:19** [The Lord said to His people:] And I will betroth [promise to marry] thee unto Me for ever; yea, I will betroth thee unto Me in righteousness, and in judgment, and in lovingkindness, and in mercies.
- **Ephesians 2:7** That in the ages to come He might shew the exceeding riches of His grace in His kindness toward us through Christ Jesus.

2. Just as God is kind to us, He expects us to be kind to others.

- **Proverbs 3:27** Withhold not good from them to whom it is due, when it is in the power of thine hand to do it.
- **Zechariah 7:9b** Shew mercy and compassions every man to his brother.

- **Romans 12:13** [We should strive to be] distributing to the necessity of saints; given to hospitality.
- **Ephesians 4:32** And be ye kind one to another, tenderhearted, forgiving one another, even as God for Christ's sake hath forgiven you.
- **Galatians 6:10** As we have therefore opportunity, let us do good unto all men, especially unto them who are of the household of faith.
- **Hebrews 13:2** Be not forgetful to entertain strangers: for thereby some have entertained angels unawares.
- **1 Peter 3:8,9** Finally, be ye all of one mind, having compassion one of another, love as brethren, be pitiful, be courteous: [9] Not rendering evil for evil, or railing for railing: but contrariwise blessing; knowing that ye are thereunto called, that ye should inherit a blessing.

3. Unkind speech leads to unkind actions.

- **Proverbs 11:9a** An hypocrite with his mouth destroyeth his neighbour.
- **Proverbs 12:18** There is that speaketh like the piercings of a sword: but the tongue of the wise is health.
- **Proverbs 18:21** Death and life are in the power of the tongue: and they that love it shall eat the fruit thereof.
- **Proverbs 26:18,19** As a mad man who casteth firebrands, arrows, and death, [19] So is the man that deceiveth his neighbour, and saith, Am not I in sport?

4. The virtue of kind speech:

- **Proverbs 31:26** [Said of the virtuous woman:] She openeth her mouth with wisdom; and in her tongue is the law of kindness.
- **Proverbs 16:24** Pleasant words are as an honeycomb, sweet to the soul, and health to the bones.
- **Proverbs 25:15** By long forbearing is a prince persuaded, and a soft tongue breaketh the bone.

- **1 Peter 3:9** Not rendering evil for evil, or railing for railing: but contrariwise blessing; knowing that ye are thereunto called, that ye should inherit a blessing.

5. We should be kind and courteous to <u>all</u> people, regardless of who they are.

- **Deuteronomy 10:17-19** [Taking care of needy strangers is part of Christian kindness.] For the Lord your God is God of gods, and Lord of lords, a great God, a mighty, and a terrible, which regardeth not persons, nor taketh reward: [18] He doth execute the judgment of the fatherless and widow, and loveth the stranger, in giving him food and raiment. [19] Love ye therefore the stranger: for ye were strangers in the land of Egypt. [See also Leviticus 19:34a.]

- **Luke 6:30-34** [True kindness gives without expecting to receive.] Give to every man that asketh of thee; and of him that taketh away thy goods ask them not again. [31] And as ye would that men should do to you, do ye also to them likewise. [32] For if ye love them which love you, what thank have ye? For sinners also love those that love them. [33] And if ye do good to them which do good to you, what thank have ye? For sinners also do even the same. [34] And if ye lend to them of whom ye hope to receive, what thank have ye? For sinners also lend to sinners, to receive as much again.

- **Luke 10:30-37** [Jesus told a parable of the Good Samaritan, who was of a people hated of the Jews, yet who showed kind concern for the wounded Jew he encountered while traveling. This example clearly illustrated that kindness should be shown to all men, regardless of race or creed. And Jesus asked, after having said that we should love our neighbors as ourselves:] [36] Which now of these three, thinkest thou, was neighbour unto him that fell among the thieves? [37] And he said, He that shewed mercy on him [the Good Samaritan]. Then said Jesus unto him, Go, and do thou likewise.

6. Show kindness to those who oppose us.

- **Genesis 50:20-21** [Joseph forgave and showed kindness to his brothers during a time of famine, despite the fact they had almost killed him, and had sold him as a slave to Egypt. For the whole story see Genesis chapters 37, 41-45.] But as for you, ye thought evil against me; but God meant it unto good, to bring to pass, as it is this day, to save much people alive. [21] Now therefore fear ye not: I will nourish you, and your little ones. And he comforted them, and spake kindly unto them.

- **Exodus 23:4** If thou meet thine enemy's ox or his ass going astray, thou shalt surely bring it back to him again. [See also Deuteronomy 22:1.]

- **Proverbs 25:21,22** [Show kindness to your enemies; let the Lord take care of giving them their just punishment in His time.] If thine enemy be hungry, give him bread to eat; and if he be thirsty, give him water to drink: [22] For thou shalt heap coals of fire upon his head, and the Lord shall reward thee.

- **Luke 6:35** But love ye your enemies, and do good, and lend, hoping for nothing again; and your reward shall be great, and ye shall be the children of the Highest: for He is kind unto the unthankful and to the evil. [See also Matthew 5:43-48; Proverbs 25:21,22.]

7. Being kind and courteous is part of showing love.

- **Romans 13:10** Love worketh no ill to his neighbour: therefore love is the fulfilling of the law.

- **1 Corinthians 13:4a** [Love] suffereth long, and is kind.

- **Colossians 3:13,14** Forbearing one another, and forgiving one another, if any man have a quarrel against any: even as Christ forgave you, so also do ye. [14] And above all these things put on [love], which is the bond of perfectness.

8. Kindness and courtesy considers others' feelings, weaknesses and limitations.

- **Acts 20:35** I have shewed you all things, how that so labouring ye ought to support the weak, and to remember the words of the Lord Jesus, how He said, It is more blessed to give than to receive.

- **Romans 14:13** Let us not therefore judge one another any more: but judge this rather, that no man put a stumblingblock or an occasion to fall in his brother's way.

- **Romans 14:21** It is good neither to eat flesh, nor to drink wine, nor any thing whereby thy brother stumbleth, or is offended, or is made weak. [See also 1 Corinthians 8:13.]

- **Romans 15:1,2** We then that are strong ought to bear the infirmities of the weak, and not to please ourselves. [2] Let every one of us please his neighbour for his good to edification.

- **1 Peter 4:8** And above all things have fervent love for one another, for love will cover a multitude of sins.

9. Kindness and courtesy often means unselfishly putting others' needs before our own.

- **Isaiah 58:6,7** Is not this the fast that I have chosen? To loose the bands of wickedness, to undo the heavy burdens, and to let the oppressed go free, and that ye break every yoke? [7] Is it not to deal thy bread to the hungry, and that thou bring the poor that are cast out to thy house? When thou seest the naked, that thou cover him; and that thou hide not thyself from thine own flesh [kinfolk]?

- **Romans 12:10** Be kindly affectioned one to another with brotherly love; in honour preferring one another;

- **1 Corinthians 12:25b,26** That there should be no schism in the body; but that the members should have the same care one for another. [26] And whether one member suffer, all the members suffer with it; or one member be honoured, all the members rejoice with it.

- **Philippians 2:4** Look not every man on his own things, but every man also on the things of others.

10. Being kind and courteous is part of our Christian sample.

- **John 13:35** By this shall all men know that ye are My disciples, if ye have love one to another.
- **2 Corinthians 6:4a,6** But in all things approving ourselves as the ministers of God, in much patience … [6] By pureness, by knowledge, by longsuffering, by kindness, by the Holy Ghost, by love unfeigned [unpretended, sincere].
- **2 Peter 1:5-8** And beside this, giving all diligence, add to your faith virtue; and to virtue knowledge; [6] And to knowledge temperance; and to temperance patience; and to patience godliness; [7] And to godliness brotherly kindness; and to brotherly kindness charity. [8] For if these things be in you, and abound, they make you that ye shall neither be barren nor unfruitful in the knowledge of our Lord Jesus Christ.

11. The Lord sees every deed of kindness and compassion, and will reward us accordingly, both on earth and in the Hereafter.

- **Proverbs 15:3** The eyes of the Lord are in every place, beholding the evil and the good.
- **Proverbs 19:17** He that hath pity upon the poor lendeth unto the Lord; and that which he hath given will He pay him again.
- **Isaiah 58:10** And if thou draw out thy soul to the hungry, and satisfy the afflicted soul; then shall thy light rise in obscurity, and thy darkness be as the noonday:
- **Luke 10:35** [In the story of the Good Samaritan, the Samaritan is an illustration of Jesus, and each of us the innkeeper.] And on the morrow when he [the Samaritan] departed, he took out two pence, and gave them to the host, and said unto him, Take care of him;

and whatsoever thou spendest more, when I come again, I will repay thee. [See verses 30-35]

• **Hebrews 6:10** For God is not unrighteous to forget your work and labour of love, which ye have shewed toward His name, in that ye have ministered to the saints, and do minister.

12. Often in the Bible, little deeds of kindness resulted in great blessings.

• **Genesis 18:1-5** [Abraham very graciously invited three traveling strangers to stay with him, later discovering that one was the Lord Himself, accompanied by two angels. It was during this visit that the Lord told Abraham he and his old and barren wife would have a son who would become "a great and mighty nation."]

• **Genesis 19:1-29** [Lot kindly warned two strangers to not stay out in the dangerous streets of Sodom, and then invited them to come home with him. They turned out to be angels who saved him and his two daughters from the destruction of Sodom.]

• **Exodus 2:16-21** [Moses' kindness to Jethro's seven daughters at the well resulted in him being taken into their home for the 40 years he was a fugitive from Egypt, as well as being given one of Jethro's daughters, Zipporah, to marry.]

• **Joshua 2:1-14; 6:16-25** [Rahab the harlot hid the two Hebrew men who had come to spy out the city of Jericho. When the city was later destroyed, Rahab and her family were the only ones spared.]

• **Esther 2:7** [After her parents died, Mordecai took care of his young cousin Esther, treating her as his own daughter. Later, after receiving years of good training from her uncle, Esther was chosen to be queen by King Ahasuerus of Persia, and ended up saving the lives of Mordecai and his countrymen, who were to be killed in a conspiracy against them. Finally, Mordecai was highly honored by the king:] For Mordecai the Jew was next unto King Ahasuerus, and great among the Jews, and accepted of the multitude of his brethren, seeking the wealth of his people, and speaking peace to all his seed.

- **2 Samuel 17:27-29; 1 Kings 2:7** Barzillai the Gileadite of Rogelim, [28] Brought beds, and basons, and earthen vessels, and wheat, and barley, and flour, and parched corn, and beans, and lentiles, and parched pulse, [29] And honey, and butter, and sheep, and cheese of kine, for David, and for the people that were with him, to eat: for they said, The people is hungry, and weary, and thirsty, in the wilderness. [1 Kings 2:7] [Later, David directed his son Solomon to take good care of his friend who had helped supply him and his men with food when they were in the wilderness:] But shew kindness unto the sons of Barzillai the Gileadite, and let them be of those that eat at thy table: for so they came to me when I fled because of Absalom thy brother.

- **1 King 17:8-24** [A poor widow obediently give her last bit of food to Elijah, and then God not only miraculously supplied her with flour and oil for the duration of the famine, but also revived her son who had died from sunstroke.]

- **Acts 27:42-43** [During a storm and shipwreck, Paul's life and ministry, as well as his fellow-prisoners, almost ended, except for the kindness of a Roman centurion:] And the soldiers' counsel was to kill the prisoners, lest any of them should swim out, and escape. [43] But the centurion, willing to save Paul, kept them from their purpose; and commanded that they which could swim should cast themselves first into the sea, and get to land.

- **Acts 28:2,7-8** [Publius, the governor of Malta, received Paul kindly. Then when Publius' father lay ill, Paul prayed for him and he was healed.]

LAZINESS AND SLOTHFULNESS

Definitions: The biblical term for laziness is slothfulness, which is habitual inactivity, reluctance to work or exert oneself in any way, sluggishness. Another term the Bible uses for a lazy person is a "sluggard."

1. The lazy person takes what he thinks is the easy way out, but always suffers in the end.

- **Proverbs 6:9-11** How long wilt thou sleep, O sluggard? When wilt thou arise out of thy sleep? [10] Yet a little sleep, a little slumber, a little folding of the hands to sleep: [11] So shall thy poverty come as one that travelleth, and thy want as an armed man.
- **Proverbs 10:4a** He becometh poor that dealeth with a slack hand.
- **Proverbs 12:24** The hand of the diligent shall bear rule: but the slothful shall be under tribute.
- **Proverbs 13:4** The soul of the sluggard desireth, and hath nothing: but the soul of the diligent shall be made fat.
- **Proverbs 19:15** Slothfulness casteth into a deep sleep; and an idle soul shall suffer hunger.
- **Proverbs 20:13a** Love not sleep, lest thou come to poverty.
- **Proverbs 21:25** The desire of the slothful killeth him; for his hands refuse to labour.
- **Proverbs 23:21b** Drowsiness shall clothe a man with rags.
- **Proverbs 24:30-34** I went by the field of the slothful, and by the vineyard of the man void of understanding; [31] And, lo, it was all grown over with thorns, and nettles had covered the face thereof, and the stone wall thereof was broken down. [32] Then I saw, and considered it well: I looked upon it, and received instruction. [33] Yet a little sleep, a little slumber, a little folding of the hands to sleep: [34] So shall thy poverty come as one that travelleth; and thy want as an armed man.
- **Ecclesiastes 10:18** By much slothfulness the building decayeth; and through idleness of the hands the house droppeth through [leaks].

2. The lazy person always has lots of excuses why he's not doing what he should.

- **Proverbs 22:13** The slothful man saith, There is a lion without, I shall be slain in the streets.

- **Proverbs 20:4** The sluggard will not plow by reason of the cold; therefore shall he beg in harvest, and have nothing.

- **Proverbs 26:16** [A lazy person often won't listen to other's good reasoning.] The sluggard is wiser in his own conceit than seven men that can render a reason.

- **Matthew 25:24,25** Then he which had received the one talent came and said, Lord, I knew thee that thou art an hard man, reaping where thou hast not sown, and gathering where thou hast not strawed [scattered seed]: [25] And I was afraid, and went and hid thy talent in the earth: lo, there thou hast that is thine.

- **James 2:17-20** [For those who try to excuse themselves by saying that they are justified by faith alone:] Even so faith, if it hath not works, is dead, being alone. [17] Even so faith, if it hath not works, is dead, being alone. [18] Yea, a man may say, Thou hast faith, and I have works: shew me thy faith without thy works, and I will shew thee my faith by my works. [19] Thou believest that there is one God; thou doest well: the devils also believe, and tremble. [20] But wilt thou know, O vain man, that faith without works is dead?

3. Laziness is often related to idle talk.

- **Proverbs 14:23** In all labour there is profit: but the talk of the lips tendeth only to penury [poverty].

- **Acts 17:21** (For all the Athenians and strangers which were there spent their time in nothing else, but either to tell, or to hear some new thing.)

- **1 Timothy 5:13** And withal they learn to be idle, wandering about from house to house; and not only idle, but tattlers also and busybodies, speaking things which they ought not.

4. Laziness is wastefulness.

- **Proverbs 12:27** The slothful man roasteth not that which he took in hunting: but the substance of a diligent man is precious.
- **Proverbs 18:9** He also that is slothful in his work is brother to him that is a great waster.
- **Luke 15:13,14** [Sad story of the Prodigal Son:] And not many days after the younger son gathered all together, and took his journey into a far country, and there wasted his substance with riotous living. [14] And when he had spent all, there arose a mighty famine in that land; and he began to be in want. [See verses 11-32 for the whole story.]

5. A reputation for laziness will cause others to lose confidence and to separate company.

- **Proverbs 10:26** As vinegar to the teeth, and as smoke to the eyes, so is the sluggard to them that send him.
- **Proverbs 25:19** Confidence in an unfaithful man in time of trouble is like a broken tooth, and a foot out of joint.
- **2 Thessalonians 3:10-12** For even when we were with you, this we commanded you, that if any would not work, neither should he eat. [11] For we hear that there are some which walk among you disorderly, working not at all, but are busybodies. [12] Now them that are such we command and exhort by our Lord Jesus Christ, that with quietness they work, and eat their own bread.

6. To overcome laziness, we must have goals and a vision for what we are doing.

- **Proverbs 6:6-8** Go to the ant, thou sluggard; consider her ways, and be wise: [7] Which having no guide, overseer, or ruler, [8] Provideth her meat in the summer, and gathereth her food in the harvest.
- **Proverbs 10:5** He that gathereth in summer is a wise son: but he that sleepeth in harvest is a son that causeth shame.

- **Proverbs 15:19** [As we step out by faith, the Lord increases our vision:] The way of the slothful man is as an hedge of thorns: but the way of the righteous is made plain.
- **Proverbs 31:27** She [the virtuous woman] looketh well to the ways of her household, and eateth not the bread of idleness.
- **John 4:34** Jesus saith unto them, My meat is to do the will of Him that sent Me, and to finish His work.
- **John 9:4** I must work the works of Him that sent Me, while it is day: the night cometh, when no man can work.
- **1 Corinthians 9:24** Know ye not that they which run in a race run all, but one receiveth the prize? So run, that ye may obtain.
- **Philippians 3:13-14** Brethren, I count not myself to have apprehended: but this one thing I do, forgetting those things which are behind, and reaching forth unto those things which are before, [14] I press toward the mark for the prize of the high calling of God in Christ Jesus.
- **1 Corinthians 7:29a** But this I say, brethren, the time is short.

7. To overcome laziness and lethargy, pray to be filled with the Holy Spirit and go on the attack!

- **Ecclesiastes 9:10a** Whatsoever thy hand findeth to do, do it with thy might. [See also Colossians 3:23.]
- **Romans 12:11** [Be] not slothful in business; fervent in spirit; serving the Lord.
- **1 Corinthians 9:27a** But I keep under my body, and bring it into subjection.
- **1 Corinthians 15:10** By the grace of God I am what I am: and His grace which was bestowed upon me was not in vain; but I laboured more abundantly than they all: yet not I, but the grace of God which was with me.
- **Ephesians 5:16,18** Redeeming the time, because the days are evil. …[18] And be not drunk with wine, wherein is excess; but be filled with the Spirit.

- **Hebrews 6:12** That ye be not slothful, but followers of them who through faith and patience inherit the promises.
- **2 Timothy 1:6b** Stir up the gift of God, which is in thee.

LONELINESS

Definition: Sadness resulting from a feeling of being alone; of lacking friends or companionship.

1. Once we have Jesus in our hearts, we always have His company and love.

- **Deuteronomy 31:6b** For the Lord thy God, He it is that doth go with thee; He will not fail thee, nor forsake thee.
- **Isaiah 44:21b** Thou shalt not be forgotten of Me.
- **Isaiah 54:10a** For the mountains shall depart, and the hills be removed; but My kindness shall not depart from thee.
- **Jeremiah 31:3b** I [the Lord] have loved thee with an everlasting love: therefore with lovingkindness have I drawn thee.
- **Matthew 28:20b** Lo, I [Jesus] am with you alway, even unto the end of the world. Amen.
- **John 14:18** I [Jesus] will not leave you comfortless: I will come to you.
- **John 16:32** [Jesus said:] Behold, the hour cometh, yea, is now come, that ye shall be scattered, every man to his own, and shall leave Me alone: and yet I am not alone, because the Father is with Me.
- **Romans 8:38,39** For I am persuaded, that neither death, nor life, nor angels, nor principalities, nor powers, nor things present, nor things to come, [39] Nor height, nor depth, nor any other creature, shall be able to separate us from the love of God, which is in Christ Jesus our Lord.
- **2 Timothy 4:16,17a** At my first answer no man stood with me, but all men forsook me: I pray God that it may not be laid to their charge. [17a] Notwithstanding the Lord stood with me, and strengthened me.
- **Hebrews 13:5b** I [the Lord] will never leave thee, nor forsake thee.
  [See also Insecurity, #5, page 225.]

2. Though earthly companionships may fail, the Lord never fails.

- **Psalm 27:10** When my father and my mother forsake me, then the Lord will take me up.
- **Psalm 73:25,26** Whom have I in Heaven but Thee? And there is none upon earth that I desire beside [more than] Thee. [26] My flesh and my heart faileth: but God is the strength of my heart, and my portion for ever.
- **Psalm 142:4,5** I looked on my right hand, and beheld, but there was no man that would know me: refuge failed me; no man cared for my soul. [5] I cried unto Thee, O Lord: I said, Thou art my refuge and my portion in the land of the living.
- **Proverbs 18:24b** There is a Friend that sticketh closer than a brother.
- **Isaiah 49:15,16** Can a woman forget her sucking child, that she should not have compassion on the son of her womb? Yea, they may forget, yet will I not forget thee. [16] Behold, I have graven thee upon the palms of My hands; thy walls are continually before Me.
- **Isaiah 66:13a** As one whom his mother comforteth, so will I [the Lord] comfort you.
- **John 14:18** I will not leave you comfortless: I will come to you. [See also Isaiah 51:12a; John 14:16.]
- **2 Thessalonians 2:16,17** Now our Lord Jesus Christ Himself, and God, even our Father, which hath loved us, and hath given us everlasting consolation and good hope through grace, [17] Comfort your hearts, and stablish you in every good word and work.

3. Sometimes the Lord lets us feel lonely to drive us closer to Him.

- **Psalm 38:11,15** My lovers and my friends stand aloof from my sore; and my kinsmen stand afar off. ... [15] In Thee, O Lord, do I hope: thou wilt hear, O Lord my God.
- **Psalm 63:1, 5-7** O God, Thou art my God; early will I seek Thee: my soul thirsteth for Thee, my flesh longeth for Thee in a dry and thirsty land, where no water is, ... [5] My soul shall be satisfied as with

marrow and fatness; and my mouth shall praise Thee with joyful lips: [6] When I remember Thee upon my bed, and meditate on Thee in the night watches. [7] Because thou hast been my help, therefore in the shadow of Thy wings will I rejoice.

- **Psalm 73:25,26,28a** Whom have I in Heaven but Thee? And there is none upon earth that I desire beside Thee. [26] My flesh and my heart faileth: but God is the strength of my heart, and my portion for ever. ... [28a] It is good for me to draw near to God.

- **Psalm 84:10a** For a day in Thy courts is better than a thousand.

- **Song of Solomon 3:3,4a** The watchmen that go about the city found me: to whom I said, Saw ye Him whom my soul loveth? [4] It was but a little that I passed from them, but I found Him whom my soul loveth: I held Him, and would not let Him go.

- **Isaiah 26:9a** With my soul have I desired Thee in the night; yea, with my spirit within me will I seek Thee early.

- **Matthew 22:37** Jesus said unto him, Thou shalt love the Lord thy God with all thy heart, and with all thy soul, and with all thy mind.

- **Philippians 3:8** Yea doubtless, and I count all things but loss for the excellency of the knowledge of Christ Jesus my Lord: for whom I have suffered the loss of all things, and do count them but dung, that I may win Christ.

- **Colossians 2:10a** And ye are complete in Him.

- **Colossians 3:2** Set your affection on things above, not on things on the earth.

4. Even Jesus felt and feels lonely and forsaken at times.

- **Isaiah 53:3,4,6b,12b** He is despised and rejected of men; a man of sorrows, and acquainted with grief: and we hid as it were our faces from Him; He was despised, and we esteemed Him not. [4] Surely He hath borne our griefs, and carried our sorrows: yet we did esteem Him stricken, smitten of God, and afflicted. ... [6b] The Lord hath laid on Him the iniquity of us all. ... [12b] He hath poured out His soul unto death: and He was numbered with the transgressors; and He bare the sin of many, and made intercession for the transgressors.

- **Matthew 26:56b** [He was abandoned by His closest followers that night in the garden of Gethsemane:] Then all the disciples forsook Him, and fled.

- **Matthew 27:46** [Jesus suffered the ultimate loneliness, experiencing separation from God and death, in order to save us:] And about the ninth hour Jesus cried with a loud voice, saying, Eli, Eli, lama sabachthani? That is to say, My God, My God, why hast Thou forsaken Me? [See Psalm 22.]

- **Hebrews 4:15-16** For we have not an High Priest which cannot be touched with the feeling of our infirmities; but was in all points tempted like as we are, yet without sin. [16] Let us therefore come boldly unto the throne of grace, that we may obtain mercy, and find grace to help in time of need.

5. Making an effort and taking the initiative to reach out to others and <u>be</u> a friend, is an antidote for loneliness.

- **Job 2:11** Now when Job's three friends heard of all this evil that was come upon him, they came every one from his own place; Eliphaz the Temanite, and Bildad the Shuhite, and Zophar the Naamathite: for they had made an appointment together to come to mourn with him and to comfort him.

- **Job 6:14a** To him that is afflicted pity should be shewed from his friend.

- **1 Samuel 23:16** [Fellowship with others can be strengthening.] And Jonathan Saul's son arose, and went to David into the wood, and strengthened his hand in God.

- **Proverbs 18:24a** A man that hath friends [or <u>desires</u> friends] must shew himself friendly.

- **Proverbs 27:10b** Better is a neighbour that is near than a brother far off.

- **Luke 6:31** And as ye would that men should do to you, do ye also to them likewise.
- **1 Corinthians 10:13a** [We all feel lonely at some time or other.] There hath no temptation taken you but such as is common to man.
- **Philippians 2:4** Look not every man on his own things, but every man also on the things of others.
- **1 Thessalonians 3:12a** And the Lord make you to increase and abound in love one toward another, and toward all men.

6. Winning souls with the Lord's love even helps you overcome personal loneliness.

- **Psalm 126:5,6** They that sow in tears shall reap in joy. [6] He that goeth forth and weepeth, bearing precious seed, shall doubtless come again with rejoicing, bringing his sheaves with him.
- **Matthew 5:15-16** Neither do men light a candle, and put it under a bushel, but on a candlestick; and it giveth light unto all that are in the house. [16] Let your light so shine before men, that they may see your good works, and glorify your Father which is in Heaven.
- **Luke 14:23** And the lord said unto the servant, Go out into the highways and hedges, and compel them to come in, that my house may be filled.
- **Romans 10:14,15** How then shall they call on Him in whom they have not believed? And how shall they believe in Him of whom they have not heard? And how shall they hear without a preacher? [15] And how shall they preach, except they be sent? As it is written, How beautiful are the feet of them that preach the Gospel of peace, and bring glad tidings of good things!

7. If you show a real love for others, you won't have a hard time winning friends.

- **John 12:32** And I, if I be lifted up from the earth, will draw all men unto Me.
- **2 Corinthians 9:6** But this I say, He which soweth sparingly shall reap also sparingly; and he which soweth bountifully shall reap also bountifully.
- **Colossians 3:14** And above all these things put on charity, which is the bond of perfectness.
- **1 Peter 3:8** Finally, be ye all of one mind, having compassion one of another, love as brethren, be pitiful, be courteous. [See also 1 Peter 4:8.]
- **1 Corinthians 13:8a** Charity [Love] never faileth.

NERVOUSNESS AND FEARFULNESS

Definition: The state of being easily excited or irritated, timid or fearful; instability due to uncomfortable feelings.

1. Nervousness indicates a lack of faith and trust in the Lord.

- **Mark 4:40** And He said unto them, Why are ye so fearful? How is it that ye have no faith?
- **Isaiah 48:18a** O that thou hadst hearkened to My commandments! Then had thy peace been as a river.
- **James 1:6** But let him ask in faith, nothing wavering. For he that wavereth is like a wave of the sea driven with the wind and tossed.
- **1 John 4:18** There is no fear in love; but perfect love casteth out fear: because fear hath torment. He that feareth is not made perfect in love.

2. Nervousness may be brought on by worry, fear of man, shyness, self-consciousness, fear of failure, etc.—but fear is the root cause.

- **2 Kings 19:6b** Be not afraid of the words which thou hast heard.
- **Psalm 3:6** I will not be afraid of ten thousands of people, that have set themselves against me round about.
- **Psalm 118:6** The Lord is on my side; I will not fear: what can man do unto me?
- **Proverbs 29:25** The fear of man bringeth a snare: but whoso putteth his trust in the Lord shall be safe.
- **Jeremiah 1:8** Be not afraid of their faces: for I am with thee to deliver thee, saith the Lord.
- **Ezekiel 3:9b** Fear them not, neither be dismayed at their looks.

3. Nervousness is nearly always manifested physically; when our hearts tremble, our hands show it.

- **Job 4:14** Fear came upon me, and trembling, which made all my bones to shake.
- **Psalm 55:5** Fearfulness and trembling are come upon me, and horror hath overwhelmed me.
- **Psalm 107:26,27** They mount up to the heaven, they go down again to the depths: their soul is melted because of trouble. [27] They reel to and fro, and stagger like a drunken man, and are at their wit's end.
- **Isaiah 13:7,8a** Therefore shall all hands be faint, and every man's heart shall melt: [8a] And they shall be afraid: pangs and sorrows shall take hold of them.
- **Jeremiah 6:24** We have heard the fame thereof: our hands wax feeble: anguish hath taken hold of us, and pain, as of a woman in travail. [See also 50:43.]

4. The wicked and disobedient have a lot to be nervous about!

- **Exodus 15:15b,16a** [Moses said to the Lord:] The mighty men of Moab, trembling shall take hold upon them; all the inhabitants of Canaan shall melt away. [16] Fear and dread shall fall upon them; by the greatness of thine arm they shall be as still as a stone.
- **Leviticus 26:36** [God sent faintheartedness on the people He was about to judge, and they became ultra-nervous.] And upon them that are left alive of you I will send a faintness into their hearts in the lands of their enemies; and the sound of a shaken leaf shall chase them; and they shall flee, as fleeing from a sword; and they shall fall when none pursueth.
- **Deuteronomy 28:15,65-67** But it shall come to pass, if thou wilt not hearken unto the voice of the Lord thy God, to observe to do all His commandments and His statutes which I [Moses] command thee this day; that all these curses shall come upon thee, and overtake

thee: ... [65] And among these nations shalt thou find no ease, neither shall the sole of thy foot have rest: but the Lord shall give thee there a trembling heart, and failing of eyes, and sorrow of mind: [66] And thy life shall hang in doubt before thee; and thou shalt fear day and night, and shalt have none assurance of thy life: [67] In the morning thou shalt say, Would God it were even! And at even thou shalt say, Would God it were morning! For the fear of thine heart wherewith thou shalt fear, and for the sight of thine eyes which thou shalt see.

- **Ezekiel 7:17,18** All hands shall be feeble, and all knees shall be weak as water. [18] They shall also gird themselves with sackcloth, and horror shall cover them; and shame shall be upon all faces, and baldness upon all their heads.

- **Ezekiel 21:7** [The Lord instructed the Prophet Ezekiel how to answer the wicked when they asked about the message God gave for them:] And it shall be, when they say unto thee, Wherefore sighest thou? That thou shalt answer, For the tidings; because it cometh: and every heart shall melt, and all hands shall be feeble, and every spirit shall faint, and all knees shall be weak as water: behold, it cometh, and shall be brought to pass, saith the Lord God.

- **Nahum 2:10** [God described Nineveh, when she fearfully awaited His judgements for her rebelliousness:] She is empty, and void, and waste: and the heart melteth, and the knees smite together, and much pain is in all loins, and the faces of them all gather blackness.

- **Habakkuk 3:16a** [The Prophet Habakkuk trembled in awe of God's mighty wrath towards the wicked:] When I heard, my belly trembled; my lips quivered at the voice: rottenness entered into my bones, and I trembled in myself, that I might rest in the day of trouble.

- **Daniel 5:6** [Belshazzar, the king of Babylon, trembled in fear when he received God's message of judgement written on the wall:] Then the king's countenance was changed, and his thoughts troubled him, so that the joints of his loins were loosed, and his knees smote one against another.

- **Hebrews 10:31** [The Apostle Paul exclaimed his terror for those who utterly reject the Lord:] It is a fearful thing to fall into the hands of the living God.

5. To overcome nervousness, we must first recognize the <u>source</u>— the Devil's lies and fears—and take a stand against them in the power of the Spirit, with the promises of God's Word.

- **Job 34:29a** When He [God] giveth quietness, who then can make trouble?
- **2 Corinthians 10:4,5** (For the weapons of our warfare are not carnal, but mighty through God to the pulling down of strong holds;) [5] Casting down imaginations, and every high thing that exalteth itself against the knowledge of God, and bringing into captivity every thought to the obedience of Christ.
- **Ephesians 4:27** Neither give place to the Devil.
- **Ephesians 6:11,13b** Put on the whole armour of God, that ye may be able to stand against the wiles of the Devil. ... [13b] And having done all, to stand.
- **James 4:7** Submit yourselves therefore to God. Resist the Devil, and he will flee from you.

6. With the Lord at our side, we have nothing to be nervous or fearful about.

- **Deuteronomy 20:3b,4** Let not your hearts faint, fear not, and do not tremble, neither be ye terrified because of them; [4] For the Lord your God is He that goeth with you, to fight for you against your enemies, to save you.
- **Joshua 1:9** Have not I commanded thee? Be strong and of a good courage; be not afraid, neither be thou dismayed: for the Lord thy God is with thee whithersoever thou goest.
- **2 Kings 6:16,17** [When his servant was fearful when viewing the powerful besieging enemy troops, Elisha said:] Fear not: for they

that be with us are more than they that be with them. [17] And Elisha prayed, and said, Lord, I pray Thee, open his eyes, that he may see. And the Lord opened the eyes of the young man; and he saw: and, behold, the mountain was full of horses and chariots of fire round about Elisha.

- **Psalm 25:12,13** [Walking in the fear of God brings peace and tranquility.] What man is he that feareth the Lord? Him shall He teach in the way that He shall choose. [13] His soul shall dwell at ease; and his seed shall inherit the earth.
- **Proverbs 14:26** In the fear of the Lord is <u>strong confidence</u>: and His children shall have a place of refuge.
- **Psalm 119:165** Great peace have they which love Thy law: and nothing shall offend them.
- **Isaiah 12:2** Behold, God is my salvation; I will trust, and not be afraid: for the Lord Jehovah is my strength and my song; He also is become my salvation.
- **Isaiah 32:17,18** And the work of righteousness shall be peace; and the effect of righteousness quietness and assurance for ever. [18] And My people shall dwell in a peaceable habitation, and in sure dwellings, and in quiet resting places;
- **Zechariah 8:13b** Fear not, but let your hands be strong.
- **John 16:33a** These things I have spoken unto you, that in Me ye might have peace.
- **Romans 5:1b** We have peace with God through our Lord Jesus Christ:
- **Romans 15:13** Now the God of hope fill you with all joy and peace in believing, that ye may abound in hope, through the power of the Holy Ghost.
- **Ephesians 2:14a** For He is our peace.
- **Colossians 3:15a** And let the peace of God rule in your hearts.
- **2 Thessalonians 3:16** Now the Lord of peace Himself give you peace always by all means. The Lord be with you all.
- **1 John 4:4** Ye are of God, little children, and have overcome them: because greater is He that is in you, than he that is in the world.

7. The sure cure: Keep your heart and mind on the Lord and His Word.

- **Job 22:21a** Acquaint now thyself with Him, and be at peace.
- **Psalm 34:4** I sought the Lord, and He heard me, and delivered me from all my fears.
- **Psalm 112:7,8a** He shall not be afraid of evil tidings: his heart is fixed, trusting in the Lord. [8a] His heart is established, he shall not be afraid.
- **Psalm 119:165** Great peace have they which love Thy law: and nothing shall offend them.
- **Proverbs 3:25a,26a** Be not afraid of sudden fear. [26a] For the Lord shall be thy confidence.
- **Isaiah 26:3** Thou wilt keep him in perfect peace, whose mind is stayed on Thee: because he trusteth in Thee.
- **John 14:27** Peace I leave with you, My peace I give unto you: not as the world giveth, give I unto you. Let not your heart be troubled, neither let it be afraid.

8. Pray for a calm, trusting spirit.

- **Philippians 4:6,7** Be careful [anxious] for nothing; but in every thing by prayer and supplication with thanksgiving let your requests be made known unto God. [7] And the peace of God, which passeth all understanding, shall keep your hearts and minds through Christ Jesus.
- **2 Thessalonians 2:2a** Be not soon shaken in mind, or be troubled, neither by spirit, nor by word.
- **2 Timothy 1:7** For God hath not given us the spirit of fear; but of power, and of love, and of a sound mind.
- **Galatians 5:22** But the fruit of the Spirit is love, joy, <u>peace</u>. ...
- **Romans 15:33** Now the God of peace be with you all.

[See also Insecurity, page 223.]

NIGHTMARES AND BAD DREAMS

Definition: A frightening or terrifying dream. (The word "nightmare" comes from the Old English word "mare" (or goblin) which meant an evil spirit or demon haunting people in their sleep.)

1. We have nothing to fear because God has promised us protection against nightmares.

- **Psalm 4:8** I will both lay me down in peace, and sleep: for Thou, Lord, only makest me dwell in safety.
- **Psalm 91:5a,6a** Thou shalt not be afraid for the terror by night … 6a Nor for the pestilence that walketh in darkness.
- **Proverbs 3:24** When thou liest down, thou shalt not be afraid: yea, thou shalt lie down, and thy sleep shall be sweet.
- **2 Timothy 1:7** For God hath not given us the spirit of fear; but of power, and of love, and of a sound mind.
- **1 John 4:4** Ye are of God, little children, and have overcome them: because greater is He that is in you, than he that is in the world.
- **1 John 4:18a** There is no fear in love; but perfect love casteth out fear.

2. We shouldn't feel intimidated or condemned by nightmares, but recognize them as the spiritual attacks of the Enemy that they are, and resist and overcome them with the Lord's help.

- **1 Corinthians 10:13** There hath no temptation taken you but such as is common to man: but God is faithful, who will not suffer you to be tempted above that ye are able; but will with the temptation also make a way to escape, that ye may be able to bear it.
- **1 Peter 5:8,9a** Be sober, be vigilant; because your adversary the Devil, as a roaring lion, walketh about, seeking whom he may devour: 9a Whom resist stedfast in the faith.

3. Sometimes bad dreams can be triggered by bad experiences or sights, so avoid these, if possible.

- **Psalm 101:3a** I will set no wicked thing before mine eyes: ... it shall not cleave to me.
- **Psalm 119:37** Turn away mine eyes from beholding vanity; and quicken Thou me in Thy way.
- **Romans 12:9b** Abhor that which is evil; cleave to that which is good.
- **1 Peter 1:13a** Wherefore gird up the loins of your mind.

4. Some bad dreams result from simple, natural causes, or can be spiritually meaningless.

- **Ecclesiastes 5:3a** [Going to sleep with our minds still filled with concerns of the day:] For a dream cometh through the multitude of business.
- **Ecclesiastes 5:7** For in the multitude of dreams and many words there are also divers vanities: but fear thou God.
- **Isaiah 29:8a** [Something we ate or some unmet physical need:] It shall even be as when an hungry man dreameth, and, behold, he eateth; but he awaketh, and his soul is empty: or as when a thirsty man dreameth, and, behold, he drinketh; but he awaketh, and, behold, he is faint, and his soul hath appetite.

5. Some troublesome dreams may actually be from the Lord, but these clearly differ from nightmares in that they always have a purpose, either prophetic, or to warn, or to offer positive lessons.

- **Genesis 40:5-23** [Joseph interpreted the troubling dreams of others:] And they dreamed a dream both of them, each man his dream in one night, each man according to the interpretation of his dream, the butler and the baker of the king of Egypt, which were bound in the prison. [6] And Joseph came in unto them in the morning, and looked upon them, and, behold, they were sad. [The dreams, which were from the Lord, were fulfilled, one a dream of blessing and the other, a dream of judgment.]

- **Genesis 41:1,8,32** And it came to pass at the end of two full years, that Pharaoh dreamed: and, behold, he stood by the river. ... [8] And it came to pass in the morning that his spirit was troubled; and he sent and called for all the magicians of Egypt, and all the wise men thereof: and Pharaoh told them his dream; but there was none that could interpret them unto Pharaoh. ... [But Joseph interpreted it, saying:] [32] And for that the dream was doubled unto Pharaoh twice; it is because the thing is established by God, and God will shortly bring it to pass. [This dream helped preserve Egypt, as well as Joseph's family, in time of famine.]
- **Job 4:13-17** In thoughts from the visions of the night, when deep sleep falleth on men, [14] Fear came upon me, and trembling, which made all my bones to shake. [15] Then a spirit passed before my face; the hair of my flesh stood up: [16] It stood still, but I could not discern the form thereof: an image was before mine eyes, there was silence, and I heard a voice, saying, [17] Shall mortal man be more just than God? Shall a man be more pure than His Maker?
- **Job 7:13,14** When I say, My bed shall comfort me, my couch shall ease my complaint; [14] Then Thou scarest me with dreams, and terrifiest me through visions.
- **Isaiah 21:4** [The prophet received a frightful message of the judgment of Babylon from the Lord, which greatly disturbed his sleep:] My heart panted, fearfulness affrighted me: the night of my pleasure hath He turned into fear unto me.
- **Daniel 2:1** And in the second year of the reign of Nebuchadnezzar Nebuchadnezzar dreamed dreams, wherewith his spirit was troubled, and his sleep brake from him.
- **Matthew 27:19** When he [Pilate] was set down on the judgment seat, his wife sent unto him, saying, Have thou nothing to do with that just Man: for I have suffered many things this day in a dream because of Him.

6. Our first and surest defense against nightmares is to <u>pray</u> against them!

- **Psalm 34:4** I sought the Lord, and He heard me, and delivered me from all my fears.
- **Matthew 18:18a** Verily I say unto you, Whatsoever ye shall bind on earth shall be bound in Heaven.
- **Matthew 18:19** [Ask others to pray with you:] Again I say unto you, That if two of you shall agree on earth as touching any thing that they shall ask, it shall be done for them of My Father which is in Heaven.
- **Ephesians 6:12,13,16,18** For we wrestle not against flesh and blood, but against principalities, against powers, against the rulers of the darkness of this world, against spiritual wickedness in high places. [13] Wherefore take unto you the whole armour of God, that ye may be able to withstand in the evil day, and having done all, to stand. ... [16] Above all, taking the shield of faith, wherewith ye shall be able to quench all the fiery darts of the wicked. ... [18] Praying always with all prayer and supplication in the Spirit, and watching thereunto with all perseverance and supplication for all
- **Philippians 4:6-7** Be careful for nothing; but in every thing by prayer and supplication with thanksgiving let your requests be made known unto God. [7] And the peace of God, which passeth all understanding, shall keep your hearts and minds through Christ Jesus.

7. We should also specifically ask the Lord for positive, edifying, faith-building dreams, which God has promised to give to His children.

- **Numbers 12:6b** I the Lord will make myself known unto him in a vision, and will speak unto him in a dream.
- **Job 33:15-17** In a dream, in a vision of the night, when deep sleep falleth upon men, in slumberings upon the bed; [16] Then He openeth

the ears of men, and sealeth their instruction, [17] That He may withdraw man from his purpose, and hide pride from man.

- **Jeremiah 23:28a** The prophet that hath a dream, let him tell a dream; and he that hath My Word, let him speak My Word faithfully.
- **Joel 2:28** And it shall come to pass afterward, that I will pour out My Spirit upon all flesh; and your sons and your daughters shall prophesy, your old men shall dream dreams, your young men shall see visions.

8. We should meditate on the Lord and His Word as we go to sleep.

- **Psalm 17:4b** By the Word of Thy lips I have kept me from the paths of the Destroyer.
- **Psalm 43:2b,3** Why go I mourning because of the oppression of the enemy? [3] O send out Thy light and Thy truth: let them lead me; let them bring me unto Thy holy hill, and to Thy tabernacles.
- **Psalm 63:6,7** When I remember Thee upon my bed, and meditate on Thee in the night watches. [7] Because Thou hast been my help, therefore in the shadow of Thy wings will I rejoice.
- **Psalm 94:19** In the multitude of my thoughts within me Thy comforts delight my soul.
- **Psalm 104:34** My meditation of Him shall be sweet: I will be glad in the Lord.
- **Proverbs 6:22** When thou goest, it [the Word] shall lead thee; when thou <u>sleepest</u>, it shall <u>keep</u> thee; and when thou awakest, it shall talk with thee.
- **Isaiah 26:3** Thou wilt keep him in perfect peace, whose mind is stayed on Thee: because he trusteth in Thee.

9. We must not dwell on nightmares we may have had.

- **Psalm 119:37** Turn away mine eyes from beholding vanity; and quicken Thou me in Thy way.
- **Ephesians 4:27** Neither give place to the Devil.

- **Philippians 4:8** Finally, brethren, whatsoever things are true, whatsoever things are honest, whatsoever things are just, whatsoever things are pure, whatsoever things are lovely, whatsoever things are of good report; if there be any virtue, and if there be any praise, think on these things.
- **Philippians 1:28a** And in nothing terrified by your adversaries.

10. Here are a few more of the Lord's precious promises to claim for sweet dreams:

- **Deuteronomy 33:12a** The beloved of the Lord shall dwell in safety by Him.
- **1 Kings 8:56a** Blessed be the Lord, that hath given rest unto His people.
- **Job 11:18,19a** And thou shalt be secure, because there is hope; yea, thou shalt dig about thee, and thou shalt take thy rest in safety. [19] Also thou shalt lie down, and none shall make thee afraid.
- **Psalm 4:8** I will both lay me down in peace, and sleep: for Thou, Lord, only makest me dwell in safety.
- **Psalm 16:7** I will bless the Lord, who hath given me counsel: my reins [heart] also instruct me in the night seasons.
- **Psalm 29:11** The Lord will give strength unto His people; the Lord will bless His people with peace.
- **Psalm 34:7** The angel of the Lord encampeth round about them that fear Him, and delivereth them.
- **Psalm 42:8** Yet the Lord will command His lovingkindness in the daytime, and in the night His song shall be with me, and my prayer unto the God of my life.
- **Psalm 55:18** He hath delivered my soul in peace from the battle that was against me: for there were many with me.
- **Psalm 139:2-3,18b** Thou knowest my downsitting and mine uprising, Thou understandest my thought afar off. Thou compassest my path and my lying down, and art acquainted with all my ways. … [18b] When I awake, I am still with Thee.

- **Ecclesiastes 5:12a** The sleep of a labouring man is sweet, whether he eat little or much.
- **John 14:27** Peace I leave with you, My peace I give unto you: not as the world giveth, give I unto you. Let not your heart be troubled, neither let it be afraid.
- **2 Peter 2:9a** The Lord knoweth how to deliver the godly out of temptations.
- **Hebrews 4:9** There remaineth therefore a rest to the people of God.

PEER PRESSURE

Definition: Peers are people of equal standing with one another, in age, rank or status. Age is often a determining factor in establishing what is commonly known as "peer groups." Peer pressure, therefore is the demand to conform to the prevailing positive or negative attitudes or actions of one's peer group.

1. The Bible cautions us not to yield to negative peer pressure.

- **Exodus 23:2** Thou shalt not follow a multitude to do evil; neither shalt thou speak in a cause to decline after many [go with the crowd] to wrest [pervert] judgment.
- **Proverbs 1:10** My son, if sinners entice thee, consent thou not.
- **Proverbs 22:24,25** Make no friendship with an angry man; and with a furious man thou shalt not go: [25] Lest thou learn his ways, and get a snare to thy soul.
- **2 Corinthians 6:14,17** Be ye not unequally yoked together with unbelievers: for what fellowship hath righteousness with unrighteousness? And what communion hath light with darkness? ... [17] Wherefore come out from among them, and be ye separate, saith the Lord, and touch not the unclean thing; and I will receive you.
- **2 Peter 3:17** Ye therefore, beloved, seeing ye know these things before, beware lest ye also, being led away with the error of the wicked, fall from your own stedfastness.

2. Just because everybody else is doing it doesn't necessarily make it right.

- **Genesis 6:12; 1 Peter 3:20b** [In Noah's day, the majority were dead wrong, so Noah had to buck the tide in order to survive.] And God looked upon the earth, and, behold, it was corrupt; for all flesh had corrupted his way upon the earth. ... [1 Peter 3:20b] Once the longsuffering of God waited in the days of Noah, while the ark was a preparing, wherein few, that is, eight souls were saved by water.

- **Isaiah 1:9** [Often the true believers are a small minority.] Except the Lord of hosts had left unto us a very small remnant, we should have been as Sodom, and we should have been like unto Gomorrah. [Sodom and Gomorrah were two wicked cities which God destroyed because of sodomy and wickedness.]
- **Matthew 7:13,14** Enter ye in at the strait gate: for wide is the gate, and broad is the way, that leadeth to destruction, and many there be which go in thereat: [14] Because strait is the gate, and narrow is the way, which leadeth unto life, and few there be that find it.
- **Matthew 22:14** For many are called, but few are chosen.
- **Philippians 2:15** That ye may be blameless and harmless, the sons of God, without rebuke, in the midst of a crooked and perverse nation, among whom ye shine as lights in the world.
- **1 John 5:19** And we know that we are of God, and the whole world lieth in wickedness.
- **Revelation 13:7,8** [In the Time of the End, the Antichrist will end up ruling over most of the world, making war against all true believers.] And it was given unto him to make war with the saints, and to overcome them: and power was given him over all kindreds, and tongues, and nations. [8] And all that dwell upon the earth shall worship him, whose names are not written in the Book of Life of the Lamb slain from the foundation of the world.

3. When pressured by your peers, remember your first loyalty is to the Lord and His standard.

- **Micah 7:5-7** [Watch out if friendships or relationships cause you to stray from the Lord's standard.] Trust ye not in a friend, put ye not confidence in a guide: keep the doors of thy mouth from her that lieth in thy bosom. [6] For the son dishonoureth the father, the daughter riseth up against her mother, the daughter in law against her mother in law; a man's enemies are the men of his own house. [7] Therefore I will look unto the Lord; I will wait for the God of my salvation: my God will hear me. [See also Matthew 10:21; Luke 21:16; Jeremiah 9:4,5.]

- **Romans 12:2** And be not conformed to this world: but be ye transformed by the renewing of your mind, that ye may prove what is that good, and acceptable, and perfect, will of God.
- **Galatians 1:6-11** [Paul warned about negative influences in the Church, who sought to draw people after their own causes.] I marvel that ye are so soon removed from him that called you into the grace of Christ unto another gospel: [7] Which is not another; but there be some that trouble you, and would pervert the Gospel of Christ. [8] But though we, or an angel from Heaven, preach any other gospel unto you than that which we have preached unto you, let him be accursed. [9] As we said before, so say I now again, If any man preach any other gospel unto you than that ye have received, let him be accursed. [10] For do I now persuade men, or God? Or do I seek to please men? For if I yet pleased men, I should not be the servant of Christ. [11] But I certify you, brethren, that the Gospel which was preached of me is not after man.
- **Galatians 4:17** They zealously affect you, but not well; yea, they would exclude you [alienate you], that ye might affect [be zealous for] them.
- **Galatians 6:14** But God forbid that I should glory, save in the cross of our Lord Jesus Christ, by whom the world is crucified unto me, and I unto the world.

4. True satisfaction comes only from following and pleasing the Lord.

- **Psalm 73:25,26** Whom have I in Heaven but Thee? And there is none upon earth that I desire beside [more than] Thee. [26] My flesh and my heart faileth: but God is the strength of my heart, and my portion for ever.

- **Psalm 84:10** For a day in Thy courts is better than a thousand. I had rather be a doorkeeper in the house of my God, than to dwell in the tents of wickedness.
- **John 6:66-68** From that time many of His disciples went back, and walked no more with Him. [67] Then said Jesus unto the twelve, Will ye also go away? [68] Then Simon Peter answered Him, Lord, to whom shall we go? Thou hast the words of eternal life.

5. Being swayed by the opinions of the crowd can lead to compromise and grave mistakes.

- **2 Kings 17:15** [We, as God's children, must guard against being overly influenced by worldly trends, fads, or practices.] And they rejected His statutes, and His covenant that He made with their fathers, and His testimonies which He testified against them; and they followed vanity, and became vain, and went after the heathen that were round about them, concerning whom the Lord had charged them, that they should not do like them.
- **Proverbs 12:26** The righteous is more excellent than his neighbour: but the way of the wicked seduceth them.
- **Proverbs 16:29** A violent man enticeth his neighbour, and leadeth him into the way that is not good.
- **Matthew 5:13** Ye are the salt of the earth: but if the salt have lost his savour, wherewith shall it be salted? It is thenceforth good for nothing, but to be cast out, and to be trodden under foot of men.
- **John 12:42,43** [Today, negative peer pressure often causes people to fail to confess Jesus, just as it did in His own day.] Nevertheless among the chief rulers also many believed on Him; but because of the Pharisees they did not confess Him, lest they should be put out of the synagogue: [43] For they loved the praise of men more than the praise of God.
- **Galatians 3:1a** [Paul had real troubles with the influence of negative peer pressure in the newly formed Galatian Church:] O foolish

Galatians, who hath bewitched you, that ye should not obey the truth?
- **Galatians 5:7-9** Ye did run well; who did hinder you that ye should not obey the truth? [8] This persuasion cometh not of Him that calleth you. [9] A little leaven leaveneth the whole lump.

6. If you're faithfully following the Lord, don't expect to "fit in" with those who aren't.

- **Luke 6:22,23** Blessed are ye, when men shall hate you, and when they shall separate you from their company, and shall reproach you, and cast out your name as evil, for the Son of Man's sake. [23] Rejoice ye in that day, and leap for joy: for, behold, your reward is great in Heaven: for in the like manner did their fathers unto the prophets.
- **John 15:19** If ye were of the world, the world would love his own: but because ye are not of the world, but I have chosen you out of the world, therefore the world hateth you.
- **John 17:14-17** [It is the Word that both separates us from the world and gives us conviction to resist the negative worldly influences which surround us.] I have given them Thy Word; and the world hath hated them, because they are not of the world, even as I am not of the world. [15] I pray not that Thou shouldest take them out of the world, but that Thou shouldest keep them from the evil. [16] They are not of the world, even as I am not of the world. [17] Sanctify them through Thy truth: Thy Word is truth.
- **1 Peter 4:2-4** That he no longer should live the rest of his time in the flesh to the lusts of men, but to the will of God. [3] For the time past of our life may suffice us to have wrought the will of the Gentiles, when we walked in lasciviousness, lusts, excess of wine, revellings, banquetings, and abominable idolatries: [4] Wherein they think it strange that ye run not with them to the same excess of riot, speaking evil of you.

7. Wisely choose who you associate with and follow.

- **Psalm 119:63** I am a companion of all them that fear Thee, and of them that keep Thy precepts.
- **Proverbs 2:20** That thou mayest walk in the way of good men, and keep the paths of the righteous.
- **Proverbs 13:20** He that walketh with wise men shall be wise: but a companion of fools shall be destroyed.
- **Romans 16:17,18** Now I beseech you, brethren, mark them which cause divisions and offences contrary to the doctrine which ye have learned; and avoid them. [18] For they that are such serve not our Lord Jesus Christ, but their own belly; and by good words and fair speeches deceive the hearts of the simple.
- **Philippians 3:17** Brethren, be followers together of me, and mark them which walk so as ye have us for an ensample. [See also 1 Thessalonians 1:6.]
- **2 Thessalonians 3:7** For yourselves know how ye ought to follow us: for we behaved not ourselves disorderly among you.
- **2 Thessalonians 3:14** And if any man obey not our word by this Epistle, note that man, and have no company with him, that he may be ashamed.
- **1 John 1:7** But if we walk in the light, as He is in the light, we have fellowship one with another, and the blood of Jesus Christ His Son cleanseth us from all sin.

8. When deciding whether or not to follow along with others, first consider their sample, their attitudes and the kind of fruit they bear.

- **Matthew 7:20** Wherefore by their fruits ye shall know them.
- **Proverbs 6:27** Can a man take fire in his bosom, and his clothes not be burned?
- **Proverbs 22:3** A prudent man foreseeth the evil, and hideth himself: but the simple pass on, and are punished.

- **Matthew 12:30** He that is not with Me is against Me; and he that gathereth not with Me scattereth abroad.
- **Galatians 6:7,8** Be not deceived; God is not mocked: for whatsoever a man soweth, that shall he also reap. [8] For he that soweth to his flesh shall of the flesh reap corruption; but he that soweth to the Spirit shall of the Spirit reap life everlasting.
- **1 Peter 2:21** [The best role model to follow, of course, is Jesus.] For even hereunto were ye called: because Christ also suffered for us, leaving us an example, that ye should follow His steps. [See also Hebrews 12:2,3; 1 John 2:6.]
- **2 Peter 2:10** But chiefly them that walk after the flesh in the lust of uncleanness, and despise government. Presumptuous are they, selfwilled, they are not afraid to speak evil of dignities.
- **3 John 1:11** Beloved, follow not that which is evil, but that which is good. He that doeth good is of God: but he that doeth evil hath not seen God.

9. Combat negative peer pressure by establishing a positive peer group.

- **Philippians 1:27b** Stand fast in one spirit, with one mind striving together for the faith of the Gospel.
- **1 Thessalonians 1:5-8** [Paul and his co-workers understood that positive peer pressure among their converts must begin with their own personal examples. Once they helped to set the standard, it caught on and spread:] For our Gospel came not unto you in word only, but also in power, and in the Holy Ghost, and in much assurance; as ye know what manner of men we were among you for your sake. [6] And ye became followers of us, and of the Lord, having received the Word in much affliction, with joy of the Holy Ghost: [7] So that ye were ensamples to all that believe in Macedonia and Achaia. [8] For from you sounded out the Word of the Lord not only in Macedonia and Achaia, but also in every place your faith to God-ward is spread abroad; so that we need not to speak any thing.

- **1 Timothy 4:12** Let no man despise thy youth; but be thou an example of the believers, in word, in conversation [behavior or manner of life], in charity, in spirit, in faith, in purity.
- **2 Timothy 2:2** And the things that thou hast heard of me among many witnesses, the same commit thou to faithful men, who shall be able to teach others also.
- **Titus 2:7,8** In all things shewing thyself a pattern of good works: in doctrine shewing uncorruptness, gravity, sincerity, [8] Sound speech, that cannot be condemned; that he that is of the contrary part may be ashamed, having no evil thing to say of you.
- **1 Peter 3:15,16** But sanctify the Lord God in your hearts: and be ready always to give an answer to every man that asketh you a reason of the hope that is in you with meekness and fear: [16] Having a good conscience; that, whereas they speak evil of you, as of evildoers, they may be ashamed that falsely accuse your good conversation in Christ.

POSITIVENESS/NEGATIVE THINKING

Definition: Negative thinking is very akin to pessimism, which is the tendency to take the most unfavorable view of situations, or to expect the worst outcome in any circumstances; the practice of looking on the gloomy and dark side of things. Positiveness is optimism; the tendency or habit of seeing and expecting the good in things; looking on the bright side; anticipating favorable results; hopefulness.

1. Giving place to negative thinking only bears bad fruit.

- **Proverbs 23:7a** [If you give place to negative thoughts, you will become a negative person.] For as he <u>thinketh</u> in his heart, so <u>is</u> he.
- **Proverbs 15:13b** [Sad and negative thoughts weaken our spirits and lead to discouragement.] By sorrow of the heart, the spirit is broken.
- **Luke 6:45** [Those whose hearts and minds are filled with negative thoughts usually spread them by voicing them.] A good man out of the good treasure of his heart bringeth forth that which is good: and an evil man out of the evil treasure of his heart bringeth forth that which is evil: for out of the abundance of the heart his mouth speaketh.
- **Romans 8:6,7** [Negative thinking is not walking in "newness of life," but in the old carnal nature which is against God.] For to be carnally minded is death; but to be spiritually minded is life and peace. [7] Because the carnal mind is enmity [hostile] against God: for it is not subject to the law of God, neither indeed can be. [See also Eph.4:17.]
- **1 Corinthians 13:5** [If we're walking in love, we don't think negatively towards others.] [Love] doth not behave itself unseemly, seeketh not her own, is not easily provoked, <u>thinketh no evil</u>.
- **Hebrews 12:15** [Harboring negative, critical thoughts can lead to bitterness.] Looking diligently lest any man fail of the grace of God, lest any root of bitterness springing up trouble you, and thereby many be defiled.

2. We need to ask the Lord to "wash" our hearts and "renew" our minds so that we will think only His positive, good thoughts.

- **Psalm 51:2,7,10** Wash me throughly from mine iniquity, and cleanse me from my sin. ... [7] Purge me with hyssop, and I shall be clean: wash me, and I shall be whiter than snow. ... [10] Create in me a clean heart, O God; and renew a right spirit within me.
- **Romans 12:2** And be not conformed to this world: but be ye transformed by the renewing of your mind, that ye may prove what is that good, and acceptable, and perfect, will of God.
- **1 Corinthians 6:11b** But ye are washed, but ye are sanctified, but ye are justified in the name of the Lord Jesus, and by the Spirit of our God.
- **Ephesians 4:22-24** That ye put off concerning the former conversation the old man, which is corrupt according to the deceitful lusts; [23] And be <u>renewed</u> in the spirit of your <u>mind</u>; [24] And that ye put on the new man, which after God is created in righteousness and true holiness.
- **Titus 3:5** Not by works of righteousness which we have done, but according to His mercy He saved us, by the washing of regeneration, and renewing of the Holy Ghost.
- **Hebrews 10:22** Let us draw near with a true heart in full assurance of faith, having our hearts sprinkled from an evil conscience, and our bodies washed with pure water.

3. Ask the Lord to help you learn to recognize the Enemy's negative thoughts so you can resist them!

- **1 Thessalonians 5:21** Prove [test or try] all things; hold fast that which is good.
- **Matthew 7:16-20** [What kind of fruit do these thoughts bear?] Ye shall know them by their fruits. ... [17] Even so every good tree bringeth forth good fruit; but a corrupt tree bringeth forth evil fruit. [18] A good tree cannot bring forth evil fruit, neither can a corrupt tree

bring forth good fruit. [19] Every tree that bringeth not forth good fruit is hewn down, and cast into the fire. [20] Wherefore by their fruits ye shall know them.

- **2 Corinthians 2:11** Lest Satan should get an advantage of us: for we are not ignorant of his devices.
- **Hebrews 3:12,13** Take heed, brethren, lest there be in any of you an evil heart of unbelief, in departing from the living God. [13] But exhort one another daily, while it is called To day; lest any of you be hardened through the deceitfulness of sin.
- **Hebrews 4:12** [Measure your thoughts with the Word.] For the Word of God is quick [alive], and powerful, and sharper than any twoedged sword, piercing even to the dividing asunder of soul and spirit, and of the joints and marrow, and is a discerner of the thoughts and intents of the heart. [See also Acts 17:11.]
- **1 John 4:1a** Beloved, believe not every spirit, but try [test] the spirits whether they are of God.

4. Stop yourself at the first negative thought.

- **Psalm 119:59** I thought on my ways, and turned my feet unto Thy testimonies.
- **Psalm 119:113** I hate vain thoughts: but Thy law do I love.
- **Proverbs 4:23** Keep thy heart with all diligence; for out of it are the issues of life.
- **2 Corinthians 10:3-5** For though we walk in the flesh, we do not war after the flesh: [4] (For the weapons of our warfare are not carnal but mighty through God to the pulling down of strong holds;) [5] Casting down imaginations, and every high thing that exalteth itself against the knowledge of God, and bringing into captivity every thought to the obedience of Christ.
- **Ephesians 4:27** Neither give place to the Devil.
- **James 4:7** Resist the Devil and he will flee from you!

5. Think on the good things!

- **1 Samuel 30:6b** And David was greatly distressed … but David encouraged himself in the Lord his God.
- **Psalm 27:13** I had fainted, unless I had believed to see the goodness of the Lord in the land of the living.
- **Psalm 94:19** In the multitude of my thoughts within me Thy comforts delight my soul.
- **Proverbs 16:20b** Whoso trusteth in the Lord, happy is he. [See also Psalm 146:5.]
- **Proverbs 23:7a** For as he thinketh in his heart, so is he.
- **Isaiah 26:3** Thou wilt keep him in perfect peace, whose mind is stayed on Thee: because he trusteth in Thee.
- **1 Corinthians 2:2** [Dwell on others' good qualities; see Jesus in them!] For I determined not to know any thing among you, save Jesus Christ, and Him crucified.
- **Ephesians 4:32** [Remembering how much we appreciate love and understanding helps us avoid being critical of others.] And be ye kind one to another, tenderhearted, forgiving one another, even as God for Christ's sake hath forgiven you.
- **Philippians. 4:8** Finally, brethren, whatsoever things are true, whatsoever things are honest, whatsoever things are just, whatsoever things are pure, whatsoever things are lovely, whatsoever things are of good report; if there be any virtue, and if there be any praise, think on these things.
- **1 Peter 1:8** Whom having not seen, ye love; in whom, though now ye see Him not, yet believing, ye rejoice with joy unspeakable and full of glory.

6. Take a positive stand against the Devil and his negativeness.

- **2 Corinthians 10:3-5** For though we walk in the flesh, we do not war after the flesh: ⁴(For the weapons of our warfare are not carnal, but mighty through God to the pulling down of strong holds;) ⁵Casting down imaginations, and every high thing that exalteth itself against the knowledge of God, and bringing into captivity every thought to the obedience of Christ.

- **Ephesians 6:10,11,16,17** Finally, my brethren, be strong in the Lord, and in the power of His might. [11] Put on the whole armour of God, that ye may be able to stand against the wiles of the Devil. [16] Above all, taking the shield of faith, wherewith ye shall be able to quench all the fiery darts of the wicked. [17] And take the helmet of salvation, and the sword of the Spirit, which is the Word of God.

- **1 Timothy 6:12** Fight the good fight of faith, lay hold on eternal life whereunto thou art also called, and hast professed a good profession before many witnesses.

- **James 4:7** Submit yourselves therefore to God. Resist the Devil, and he will flee from you.

7. Keep your heart and mind filled with God's Word.

- **Joshua 1:8** This Book of the Law shall not depart out of thy mouth; but thou shalt meditate therein day and night, that thou mayest observe to do according to all that is written therein: for then thou shalt make thy way prosperous, and then thou shalt have good success.

- **Psalm 1:2** His delight is in the law of the Lord; and in His law doth he meditate day and night.

- **Psalm 37:31** The law of his God is in his heart; none of his steps shall slide.

- **Psalm 119:11** Thy Word have I hid in mine heart, that I might not sin against Thee.

- **Psalm 119:148** Mine eyes prevent the night watches, that I might meditate in Thy Word.

- **Psalm 119:162** I rejoice at Thy Word, as one that findeth great spoil.

- **1 Timothy 4:13-16** Give attendance to reading, to exhortation, to doctrine. [14] Neglect not the gift that is in thee, which was given thee by prophecy, with the laying on of the hands of the presbytery.

[15] Meditate upon these things; give thyself wholly to them; that thy profiting may appear to all. [16] Take heed unto thyself, and unto the doctrine; continue in them: for in doing this thou shalt both save thyself, and them that hear thee.

B. Think about Jesus!

* **Matthew 22:37** Thou shalt love the Lord thy God with all thy heart, and with all thy soul, and with all thy <u>mind</u>.
* **Psalm 63:5,6** My soul shall be satisfied as with marrow and fatness; and my mouth shall praise Thee with joyful lips: [6] When I remember Thee upon my bed, and meditate on Thee in the night watches.
* **Psalm 104:34** My meditation of Him shall be sweet: I will be glad in the Lord.
* **Hebrews 12:2,3** Looking unto Jesus the author and finisher of our faith; who for the joy that was set before Him endured the cross, despising the shame, and is set down at the right hand of the throne of God. [3] For consider Him that endured such contradiction of sinners against Himself, lest ye be wearied and faint in your minds.

C. God not only knows our thoughts, He can help us to have positive ones.

1 Chronicles 28:9 [King David said:] And thou, Solomon my son, know thou the God of thy father, and serve Him with a perfect heart and with a willing mind: for the Lord searcheth all hearts, and understandeth all the imaginations of the thoughts: if thou seek Him, He will be found of thee. ...

Psalm 94:19 In the multitude of my thoughts within me Thy comforts delight my soul.

- **Jeremiah 29:11** For I [the Lord] know the thoughts that I think toward you, saith the Lord, thoughts of peace, and not of evil, to give you an expected end.
- **Psalm 139:17** How precious also are Thy thoughts unto me, O God! How great is the sum of them!

10. You're going to be either positive or negative, one or the other. You can't be just a little of both!

- **Matthew 6:22,23** The light of the body is the eye: if therefore thine eye be single, thy whole body shall be full of light. [23] But if thine eye be evil, thy whole body shall be full of darkness. If therefore the light that is in thee be darkness, how great is that darkness!
- **Matthew 7:18** A good tree cannot bring forth evil fruit, neither can a corrupt tree bring forth good fruit.
- **James 3:11** Doth a fountain send forth at the same place sweet water and bitter?
- **Revelation 3:15b,16** I [Jesus] would thou wert cold or hot. [16] So then because thou art lukewarm, and neither cold nor hot, I will spue thee out of my mouth.

11. Count your blessings, recounting all the wonderful things the Lord has done for you.

- **Psalm 40:5** Many, O Lord My God, are Thy wonderful works which Thou hast done, and Thy thoughts which are to us-ward: they cannot be reckoned up in order unto Thee: if I would declare and speak of them, they are more than can be numbered.
- **Psalm 68:19** Blessed be the Lord, who daily loadeth us with benefits, even the God of our salvation. Selah.
- **Psalm 103:2** Bless the Lord, O my soul, and forget not all His benefits.
- **Psalm 126:3** The Lord hath done great things for us; whereof we are glad.

- **Proverbs 10:22** The blessing of the Lord, it maketh rich, and He addeth no sorrow with it.
- **Luke 1:46b,47,49** My soul doth magnify the Lord, [47] And my spirit hath rejoiced in God my Saviour. [49] For He that is mighty hath done to me great things; and holy is His name.
- **Ephesians 5:20** Giving thanks always for all things unto God and the Father in the name of our Lord Jesus Christ.
- **1 Thessalonians 5:18** In every thing give thanks: for this is the will of God in Christ Jesus concerning you.

12. Take a positive approach to tests and trials by seeing the Lord's hand in all He sends your way.

- **Psalm 119:71** It is good for me that I have been afflicted; that I might learn Thy statutes.
- **Habakkuk 3:17,18** Although the fig tree shall not blossom, neither shall fruit be in the vines; the labour of the olive shall fail, and the fields shall yield no meat; the flock shall be cut off from the fold, and there shall be no herd in the stalls: [18] Yet I will rejoice in the Lord, I will joy in the God of my salvation.
- **Romans 8:28** And we know that all things work together for good to them that love God, to them who are the called according to His purpose.
- **1 Thessalonians 5:18** In every thing give thanks: for this is the will of God in Christ Jesus concerning you. [See also Philippians 4:4.]
- **James 1:2-4** My brethren, count it all joy when ye fall into divers temptations; [3] Knowing this, that the trying of your faith worketh patience. [4] But let patience have her perfect work, that ye may be perfect and entire, wanting nothing.
- **1 Peter 4:12,13** Beloved, think it not strange concerning the fiery trial which is to try you, as though some strange thing happened unto you: [13] But rejoice, inasmuch as ye are partakers of Christ's sufferings; that, when His glory shall be revealed, ye may be glad also with exceeding joy. [See also 1 Peter 1:6.]

13. Positive speech has a good effect on everyone, both those who voice it and those who hear it.

- **Psalm 35:28** And my tongue shall speak of Thy righteousness and of Thy praise all the day long.
- **Psalm 66:16** Come and hear, all ye that fear God, and I will declare what He hath done for my soul.
- **Psalm 100:4** Enter into His gates with thanksgiving, and into His courts with praise: be thankful unto Him, and bless His name.
- **Psalm 145:4,7** One generation shall praise Thy works to another, and shall declare Thy mighty acts. [7] They shall abundantly utter the memory of Thy great goodness, and shall sing of Thy righteousness.
- **Luke 6:45** A good man out of the good treasure of his heart bringeth forth that which is good; and an evil man out of the evil treasure of his heart bringeth forth that which is evil: for out of the abundance of the heart his mouth speaketh.

14. Taking positive action is a declaration of your faith: It pleases God and works miracles!

- **Joshua 3:15,16,17** [The children of Israel started crossing the Jordan by faith, even though the waters had not yet parted:] And as they that bare the ark were come unto Jordan, and the feet of the priests that bare the ark were dipped in the brim of the water (for Jordan overfloweth all his banks all the time of harvest). [16] That the waters which came down from above and rose up upon an heap very far from the city Adam, that is beside Zaretan: and those that came down toward the sea of the plain, even the salt sea, failed, and were cut off: and the people passed over right against Jericho. [17] And the priests that bare the ark of the covenant of the Lord stood firm on dry ground in the midst of Jordan, and all the Israelites passed over on dry ground, until all the people were passed clean over Jordan.

Matthew 9:20-22 [Reach out to Jesus with faith.] And, behold, a woman, which was diseased with an issue of blood twelve years, came behind Him, and touched the hem of His garment: [21] For she said within herself, If I may but touch His garment, I shall be whole. [22] But Jesus turned Him about, and when He saw her, He said, Daughter, be of good comfort; thy faith hath made thee whole. And the woman was made whole from that hour.

Mark 10:47-52 [Call on Jesus.] And when he heard that it was Jesus of Nazareth, he began to cry out, and say, Jesus, Thou Son of David, have mercy on me. [48] And many charged him that he should hold his peace: but he cried the more a great deal, Thou Son of David, have mercy on me. [49] And Jesus stood still, and commanded him to be called. And they call the blind man, saying unto him, Be of good comfort, rise; He calleth thee. [50] And he, casting away his garment, rose, and came to Jesus. [51] And Jesus answered and said unto him, what wilt thou that I should do unto thee? The blind man said unto Him, Lord, that I might receive my sight. [52] And Jesus said unto him, Go thy way; thy faith hath made thee whole. And immediately he received his sight, and followed Jesus in the way.

Luke 5:4-7 Now when He had left speaking, He said unto Simon, Launch out into the deep, and let down your nets for a draught. And Simon answering said unto Him, Master, we have toiled all the night, and have taken nothing: nevertheless at Thy word I will let down the net. [6] And when they had thus done, they inclosed a great multitude of fishes: and their net brake. [7] And they beckoned unto their partners, which were in the other ship, that they should come and help them. And they came, and filled both the ships, so that they began to sink.

Luke 17:14 And when He saw them [the ten lepers], He said unto them, Go shew yourselves unto the priests. And it came to pass, that, as they went, they were cleansed.

Philippians 4:13 I can do all things through Christ which strengtheneth me.

15. Keep positive by helping someone else with their problems instead of thinking about your own.

- **Proverbs 27:17** Iron sharpeneth iron; so a man sharpeneth the countenance of his friend.
- **Romans 15:1** We then that are strong ought to bear the infirmities of the weak, and not to please ourselves.
- **1 Corinthians 15:58** Therefore, my beloved brethren, be ye steadfast, unmovable, <u>always abounding in the work of the Lord</u>, forasmuch as ye know that your labour is not in vain in the Lord.
- **Galatians 4:18a** But it is good to be <u>zealously affected always</u> in a good thing.
- **Galatians 6:2** Bear ye one another's burdens, and so fulfil the law c Christ.

16. Cultivate positive attitudes towards others.

- **Romans 12:10** Be kindly affectioned one to another with brotherly love; in honour preferring one another.
- **1 Corinthians 2:2** For I determined not to know any thing among you, save Jesus Christ, and Him crucified.
- **Ephesians 4:32** And be ye kind one to another, tenderhearted, forgiving one another, even as God for Christ's sake hath forgiven you.
- **Colossians 3:12** Put on therefore, as the elect of God, holy and beloved, bowels of mercies, kindness, humbleness of mind, meekness, longsuffering.
- **1 Peter 4:8** And above all things have fervent charity [love] among yourselves: for charity shall cover the multitude of sins.

17. Positive people are the kind others like to be around.

- **Psalm 34:2** My soul shall make her boast in the Lord: the humble shall hear thereof, and be glad.

- **Psalm 119:74** They that fear Thee will be glad when they see me; because I have hoped in Thy Word.
- **Proverbs 22:11** He that loveth pureness of heart, for the grace of his lips the king shall be his friend.
- **Mark 3:8** And from Jerusalem, and from Idumaea, and from beyond Jordan; and they about Tyre and Sidon, a great multitude, when they had heard what great things He did, came unto Him.

18. Manifesting a positive, full-of-faith spirit brings more victories and more to be positive about!

- **Proverbs 11:25** The liberal soul shall be made fat: and he that watereth shall be watered also himself.
- **Isaiah 58:10,11** And if thou draw out thy soul to the hungry, and satisfy the afflicted soul; then shall thy light rise in obscurity, and thy darkness be as the noonday; [11] And the Lord shall guide thee continually, and satisfy thy soul in drought, and make fat thy bones: and thou shalt be like a watered garden, and like a spring of water, whose waters fail not.
- **Matthew 25:29** For unto every one that hath shall be given, and he shall have abundance: but from him that hath not shall be taken away even that which he hath.
- **Luke 6:38** Give, and it shall be given unto you; good measure, pressed down, and shaken together, and running over, shall men give into your bosom. For with the same measure that ye mete withal it shall be measured to you again.
- **Luke 6:45** A good man out of the good treasure of his heart bringeth forth that which is good; and an evil man out of the evil treasure of his heart bringeth forth that which is evil: for of the abundance of the heart his mouth speaketh.
- **Galatians 6:7b** Whatsoever a man soweth, that shall he also reap.

19. Some good promises and prayers to help overcome negative thinking.

- **Isaiah 55:7** Let the wicked forsake his way, and the unrighteous man his <u>thoughts</u>: and let him return unto the Lord, and He will have mercy upon him; and to our God, for He will abundantly pardon.
- **Psalm 19:14** And let the words of my mouth and the meditation of my heart, be acceptable in <u>Thy</u> sight, O Lord, my strength, and my Redeemer.
- **Psalm 139:23,24** Search me, O God, and know my heart: try me, and know my thoughts: [24] And see if there be any wicked way in me, and lead me in the way everlasting.
- **Proverbs 16:3** Commit thy works unto the Lord, and thy <u>thoughts</u> shall be established.

PROMISES, KEEPING

Definition: Making a pledge or a vow to perform or grant a specific thing.

1. By example of His own faithfulness, Jesus taught us that we, too, should keep our promises.

- **1 Kings 8:56b** There hath not failed one word of all His good promise, which He promised by the hand of Moses His servant. [See also 2 Kings 10:10.]
- **Acts 13:32,33a** And we declare unto you glad tidings, how that the promise which was made unto the fathers, [33a] God hath fulfilled the same unto us their children.
- **2 Corinthians 1:20a** For all the promises of God in Him are Yea, and in Him Amen.
- **2 Peter 3:9a** The Lord is not slack concerning His promise, as some men count slackness; but is longsuffering to us-ward.

2. As the Lord is true to His promises to us, so He expects us to be true to our word with Him.

- **Numbers 30:2** If a man vow a vow unto the Lord, or swear an oath to bind his soul with a bond; he shall not break his word, he shall do according to all that proceedeth out of his mouth.
- **Deuteronomy 23:21** When thou shalt vow a vow unto the Lord thy God, thou shalt not slack to pay it: for the Lord thy God will surely require it of thee; and it would be sin in thee. ... [23] That which is gone out of thy lips thou shalt keep and perform ... according as thou hast vowed unto the Lord thy God, which thou hast promised with thy mouth.
- **Ecclesiastes 5:4,5** When thou vowest a vow unto God, defer not to pay it; for He hath no pleasure in fools: pay that which thou hast vowed. [5] Better is it that thou shouldest not vow, than that thou shouldest vow and not pay.

3. Failure to keep promises to others is actually failing the Lord.

- **Matthew 25:45b** Inasmuch as ye did it not to one of the least of these [My brethren], ye did it not to Me.
- **Ephesians 6:5-7** Servants, be obedient to them that are your masters according to the flesh, with fear and trembling, in singleness of your heart, as unto Christ; [6] Not with eyeservice, as menpleasers; but as the servants of Christ, doing the will of God from the heart; [7] With good will doing service, as to the Lord, and not to men. [See also Colossians 3:22b.]

4. Faithfulness in keeping promises is a reflection of our character.

- **Proverbs 22:1** A good name is rather to be chosen than great riches, and loving favour rather than silver and gold.
- **Luke 16:10** He that is faithful in that which is least is faithful also in much: and he that is unjust in the least is unjust also in much.
- **Acts 6:3** Wherefore, brethren, look ye out among you seven men of honest report, full of the Holy Ghost and wisdom, whom we may appoint over this business.
- **Romans 12:17b** Provide things honest in the sight of all men.

5. Once we have made a promise, we should keep it, even if it hurts or costs us more than we anticipated.

- **1 Samuel 1:11,27,28a** And she [Hannah] vowed a vow, and said, O Lord of hosts, if Thou wilt indeed look on the affliction of thine handmaid, and remember me, and not forget thine handmaid, but wilt give unto thine handmaid a man child, then I will give him unto the Lord all the days of his life, and there shall no rasor come upon his head. … [27] For this child I prayed; and the Lord hath given me my petition which I asked of Him: [28a] Therefore also I have lent him to the Lord; as long as he liveth he shall be lent to the Lord.

- **Psalm 15:1,4b** Lord, who shall abide in Thy tabernacle? Who shall dwell in Thy holy hill? … [4b] He that sweareth to his own hurt [keeps his oath, even if it hurts], and changeth not.
- **Proverbs 20:25** It is a snare to the man who devoureth [to speak rashly] that which is holy, and after vows to make inquiry [question his decision].
- **Ecclesiastes 5:5,6a** Better is it that thou shouldest not vow, than that thou shouldest vow and not pay. … [6a] Suffer not thy mouth to cause thy flesh to sin; neither say thou before the angel, that it was an error.
- **Jonah 2:9a** But I will sacrifice unto Thee with the voice of thanksgiving; I will pay that that I have vowed.

6. Keeping our promises is part of love.

- **Zechariah 8:16,17** These are the things that ye shall do; Speak ye every man the truth to his neighbour; execute the judgment of truth and peace in your gates: [17] And let none of you imagine evil in your hearts against his neighbour; and <u>love no false oath</u>: for all these are things that I hate, saith the Lord.
- **Matthew 7:12** Therefore all things whatsoever ye would that men should do to you, do ye even so to them: for this is the law and the prophets.
- **Romans 13:8-10** Owe no man any thing, but to love one another: for he that loveth another hath fulfilled the law. … [10] Love worketh no ill to his neighbour: therefore love is the fulfilling of the law.

7. We must be careful what we promise, lest we not be able to fulfill our vow.

- **Matthew 5:33,36,37** Again, ye have heard that it hath been said by them of old time, Thou shalt not forswear thyself, but shalt perform unto the Lord thine oaths. … [36] Neither shalt thou swear by thy head, because thou canst not make one hair white or black. [37] But let your communication be, Yea, Yea; Nay, Nay: for whatsoever is more than these cometh of evil.

- **James 4:14,15** Whereas ye know not what shall be on the morrow For what is your life? It is even a vapour, that appeareth for a little time, and then vanisheth away. [15] For that ye ought to say, If the Lord will, we shall live, and do this, or that.
- **James 5:12** But above all things, my brethren, swear not, neither by Heaven, neither by the earth, neither by any other oath: but let your Yea be Yea; and your Nay, Nay; lest ye fall into condemnation

8. The Bible offers several sobering examples of hasty, unprayerful promises which were later regretted.

- **Genesis 25:30-34** And Esau said to Jacob, Feed me, I pray thee, with that same red pottage; for I am faint: therefore was his name called Edom. [31] And Jacob said, Sell me this day thy birthright. [32] And Esau said, Behold, I am at the point to die: and what profit shall this birthright do to me? [33] And Jacob said, Swear to me this day; and he sware unto him: and he sold his birthright unto Jacob. [34] Then Jacob gave Esau bread and pottage of lentiles; and he did eat and drink, and rose up, and went his way: thus Esau despised his birthright.
- **Judges 11:30,31,34,35** And Jephthah vowed a vow unto the Lord, and said, If Thou shalt without fail deliver the children of Ammon into mine hands, [31] Then it shall be, that whatsoever cometh forth o the doors of my house to meet me, when I return in peace from the children of Ammon, shall surely be the Lord's, and I will offer it up for a burnt offering. … [34] And Jephthah came to Mizpeh unto his house, and, behold, his daughter came out to meet him with timbrels and with dances: and she was his only child; beside her he had neither son nor daughter. [35] And it came to pass, when he saw her, that he rent his clothes, and said, Alas, my daughter! Thou hast brought me very low, and thou art one of them that trouble me: for I have opened my mouth unto the Lord, and I cannot go back. [The text seems to indicate that Jephthah followed through on his vow,

although some scholars believe the verse means she was kept as an unmarried virgin, dedicated to special service to the Lord for the rest of her life.]

- **Matthew 14:6-9** But when Herod's birthday was kept, the daughter of Herodias danced before them, and pleased Herod. [7] Whereupon he promised with an oath to give her whatsoever she would ask. [8] And she, being before instructed of her mother, said, Give me here John Baptist's head in a charger. [9] And the king was sorry: nevertheless for the oath's sake, and them which sat with him at meat, he commanded it to be given her.

- **Acts 21:23-27** [Paul compromised with the concision by going to the temple to perform some Jewish ritual vows:] Do therefore this that we [the concision] say to thee: We have four men which have a vow on them; [24] Them take, and purify thyself with them, and be at charges with them, that they may shave their heads: and all may know that those things, whereof they were informed concerning thee, are nothing; but that thou thyself also walkest orderly, and keepest the law. [26] Then Paul took the men, and the next day purifying himself with them entered into the temple, to signify the accomplishment of the days of purification, until that an offering should be offered for every one of them. [27] And when the seven days were almost ended, the Jews which were of Asia, when they saw him in the temple, stirred up all the people, and laid hands on him.

9. We shouldn't be stubborn and self-righteously cling to our vow if God tells us to do something different.

- **Genesis 22:2-18** [Although Abraham agreed to offer up his son, and showed his willingness to do so in obedience to God, he hearkened to the angel who told him that he didn't have to go through with it:] And he [God] said, Take now thy son, thine only son Isaac, whom thou lovest, and get thee into the land of Moriah; and offer him there for a burnt offering upon one of the mountains which I will tell thee of. ... ⁹ And they came to the place which God had told him of; and Abraham built an altar there, and laid the wood in order, and bound Isaac his son, and laid him on the altar upon the wood. ¹⁰ And Abraham stretched forth his hand, and took the knife to slay his son. ¹¹ And the angel of the Lord called unto him out of Heaven, and said, Abraham, Abraham: and he said, Here am I. ¹² And he said, Lay not thine hand upon the lad, neither do thou any thing unto him: for now I know that thou fearest God, seeing thou hast not withheld thy son, thine only son from me. ¹³ And Abraham lifted up his eyes, and looked, and behold behind him a ram caught in a thicket by his horns: and Abraham went and took the ram, and offered him up for a burnt offering in the stead of his son.

- **1 Samuel 14:24-30,43-45** [Jonathan resisted King Saul's rash vow and spoke against it. The people stopped Saul from punishing Jonathan:] Saul had adjured the people [his soldiers who were fighting a battle], saying, Cursed be the man that eateth any food until evening, that I may be avenged on mine enemies. So none of the people tasted any food. ²⁵ ... And there was honey upon the ground. ²⁶ ... The honey dropped; but no man put his hand to his mouth: for the people feared the oath. ²⁷ But Jonathan [who had just returned from a daring raid] heard not when his father charged the people with the oath: wherefore he put forth the end of the rod that was in his hand, and dipped it in an honeycomb, and put his hand to his mouth; and his eyes were enlightened. ²⁸ Then answered one of the people, and said, Thy father straitly charged the people with an oath, saying, Cursed be the man that eateth any food this day. And the people were faint. ²⁹ Then said Jonathan, My father hath troubled the land: see, I pray you, how mine eyes have been enlightened, because I tasted a little of this honey. ³⁰ How much more, if haply the people had eaten freely to day of the spoil of their enemies which they found? For had there not been now a much greater slaughter among the Philistines? ... ⁴³ [Later, when Saul found out about Jonathan's transgression, he confronted him:]

Then Saul said to Jonathan, Tell me what thou hast done. And Jonathan told him, and said, I did but taste a little honey with the end of the rod that was in mine hand, and, lo, I must die. [44] And Saul answered, God do so and more also: for thou shalt surely die, Jonathan. [45] And the people said unto Saul, Shall Jonathan die, who hath wrought this great salvation in Israel? God forbid: as the Lord liveth, there shall not one hair of his head fall to the ground; for he hath wrought with God this day. So the people rescued Jonathan, that he died not.

- **John 13:8-9** [Peter, when corrected, took back his rash vow:] Peter saith unto Him, Thou shalt never wash my feet. Jesus answered him, If I wash thee not, thou hast no part with Me. [9] Simon Peter saith unto Him, Lord, not my feet only, but also my hands and my head.

- **Acts 20:22; 21:4,10-14** [Paul stubbornly carried out his vow to go to Jerusalem in spite of the fact that he received godly counsel and direct revelations warning him not to go. The decision resulted in his capture and eventual death in Rome:] And now, behold, I go bound in the spirit unto Jerusalem, not knowing the things that shall befall me there: [21:4] And finding disciples [at Tyre], we tarried there seven days: who said to Paul through the Spirit, that he should not go up to Jerusalem. [10] And as we tarried there [Caesarea] many days, there came down from Judaea a certain prophet, named Agabus. [11] And when he was come unto us, he took Paul's girdle, and bound his own hands and feet, and said, Thus saith the Holy Ghost, So shall the Jews at Jerusalem bind the man that owneth this girdle, and shall deliver him into the hands of the Gentiles. [12] And when we heard these things, both we, and they of that place, besought him not to go up to Jerusalem. [13] Then Paul answered, What mean ye to weep and to break mine heart? For I am ready not to be bound only, but also to die at Jerusalem for the Name of the Lord Jesus. [14] And when he would not be persuaded, we ceased, saying, The will of the Lord be done.

QUIETNESS

Definition: Quietness of spirit results from having faith and trust in God, which engenders serenity, calmness and tranquility. It is the opposite of loudness, rashness, nervous talk or activity.

1. Quietness of spirit is strength of spirit.

- **Ecclesiastes 7:8** Better is the end of a thing than the beginning thereof: and the patient in spirit is better than the proud in spirit.
- **Isaiah 30:15a** For thus saith the Lord God, the Holy One of Israel; In returning and rest shall ye be saved; in quietness and in confidence shall be your strength.
- **Luke 21:19** In your patience possess ye your souls.
- **1 Peter 3:4** But let it be the hidden man of the heart, in that which is not corruptible, even the ornament of a meek and quiet spirit, which is in the sight of God of great price.

2. Quietness, meekness of spirit and manner is something that can be learned.

- **Psalm 131:2** Surely I have behaved and quieted myself, as a child that is weaned of his mother: my soul is even as a weaned child.
- **Isaiah 7:4a** Take heed, and be quiet; fear not, neither be fainthearted.
- **Zephaniah 2:3a** Seek ye the Lord, all ye meek of the earth, which have wrought His judgment; seek righteousness, seek meekness.
- **1 Thessalonians 4:11a** Study to be quiet. [See also 1 Timothy 2:1-3.]
- **2 Thessalonians 3:11,12** For we hear that there are some which walk among you disorderly, working not at all, but are busybodies. [12] Now them that are such we command and exhort by our Lord Jesus Christ, that with quietness they work, and eat their own bread.
- **James 1:19a** Wherefore, my beloved brethren, let every man be swift to hear, slow to speak.

3. The Lord blesses an atmosphere of quiet calmness.

- **Proverbs 17:1** Better is a dry morsel, and quietness therewith, than an house full of sacrifices with strife.
- **Ecclesiastes 4:6** Better is an handful with quietness, than both the hands full with travail and vexation of spirit.
- **Ecclesiastes 9:17** The words of wise men are heard in quiet more than the cry of him that ruleth among fools.

4. Quieting our spirits before the Lord shows that we expect <u>Him</u> to work in our behalf; it's faith and trust.

- **Exodus 14:13a** And Moses said unto the people, Fear ye not, stand still, and see the salvation of the Lord, which He will shew to you to day.
- **Job 22:21** [One of Job's friends exhorts:] Acquaint now thyself with Him, and be at peace: thereby good shall come unto thee.
- **Psalm 42:5** Why art thou cast down, O my soul? And why art thou disquieted in me? Hope thou in God: for I shall yet praise Him for the help of His countenance.
- **Isaiah 40:31** But they that wait upon the Lord shall renew their strength; they shall mount up with wings as eagles; they shall run, and not be weary; and they shall walk, and not faint.
- **Lamentations 3:26** It is good that a man should both hope and quietly wait for the salvation of the Lord.
- **Acts 19:36** Seeing then that these things cannot be spoken against, ye ought to be quiet, and to do nothing rashly.
- **Philippians 4:6,7** Be careful [anxious, worried] for nothing; but in every thing by prayer and supplication with thanksgiving let your requests be made known unto God. [7] And the peace of God, which passeth all understanding, shall keep your hearts and minds through Christ Jesus.
- **Colossians 3:15a** And let the peace of God rule in your hearts.

- **Hebrews 4:9-11** There remaineth therefore a rest to the people of God. [10] For he that is entered into His rest, he also hath ceased from his own works, as God did from His. [11] Let us labour therefore to enter into that rest, lest any man fall after the same example of unbelief.

5. Fretting and operating in the energy of the flesh are futile and hinder you from doing things God's way.

- **Psalm 37:7-9** [We can either choose to wait for the Lord's leading, or fret and end up getting out of God's will.] Rest in the Lord, and wait patiently for Him: fret not thyself because of him who prospereth in his way, because of the man who bringeth wicked devices to pass. [8] Cease from anger, and forsake wrath: fret not thyself in any wise to do evil. [9] For evildoers shall be cut off: but those that wait upon the Lord, they shall inherit the earth.

- **Psalm 39:6a** Surely every man walketh in a vain shew: surely they are disquieted [uptight] in vain.

- **Psalm 127:2** It is vain for you to rise up early, to sit up late, to eat the bread of sorrows: for so He giveth His beloved sleep.

- **Luke 10:38-42** [Mary quietly learned from Jesus, while Martha grew more and more busy, until it even caused her to wrongly accuse the Lord and her sister.] Now it came to pass, as they went, that He entered into a certain village: and a certain woman named Martha received Him into her house. [39] And she had a sister called Mary, which also sat at Jesus' feet, and heard His Word. [40] But Martha was cumbered about much serving, and came to Him, and said, Lord, dost Thou not care that my sister hath left me to serve alone? Bid her therefore that she help me. [41] And Jesus answered and said unto her, Martha, Martha, thou art careful and troubled about many things: [42] But one thing is needful: and Mary hath chosen that good part, which shall not be taken away from her.

- **Luke 12:25,26** And which of you with taking thought can add to his stature one cubit? [26] If ye then be not able to do that thing which is least, why take ye thought for the rest?

6. Getting quiet before the Lord puts us in the position of being able to hear from Him and receive His instruction.

- **Numbers 9:8** And Moses said unto them, Stand still, and I will hear what the Lord will command concerning you.
- **1 Samuel 3:7-10** Now Samuel did not yet know the Lord, neither was the Word of the Lord yet revealed unto him. [8] And the Lord called Samuel again the third time. And he arose and went to Eli, and said, Here am I; for thou didst call me. And Eli perceived that the Lord had called the child. [9] Therefore Eli said unto Samuel, Go, lie down: and it shall be, if He call thee, that thou shalt say, Speak, Lord; for Thy servant heareth. So Samuel went and lay down in his place. [10] And the Lord came, and stood, and called as at other times, Samuel, Samuel. Then Samuel answered, Speak; for Thy servant heareth.
- **1 Samuel 9:27** And as they were going down to the end of the city, Samuel said to Saul, Bid the servant pass on before us, (and he passed on,) but stand thou still a while, that I may shew thee the Word of God.
- **1 Samuel 12:7** Now therefore stand still, that I may reason with you before the Lord of all the righteous acts of the Lord, which He did to you and to your fathers.
- **Job 37:14b** Stand still, and consider the wondrous works of God.
- **Psalm 4:4** Stand in awe, and sin not: commune with your own heart upon your bed, and be still.
- **Psalm 25:9** The meek will He guide in judgment: and the meek will He teach His way.
- **Psalm 46:10a** Be still, and know that I am God.
- **Habakkuk 2:20** But the Lord is in His holy temple: let all the earth keep silence before Him. [See also Zechariah 2:13.]

- **James 1:21b** Receive with meekness the engrafted Word, which is able to save your souls.

7. Quietness of spirit, like peace of mind, comes from knowing that we're doing our best to please the Lord and stay in His will.

- **2 Chronicles 20:30** So the realm of Jehoshaphat was quiet: for his God gave him rest round about.
- **Psalm 37:37** Mark the perfect man, and behold the upright: for the end of that man is peace.
- **Psalm 119:165** Great peace have they which love Thy law: and nothing shall offend them.
- **Proverbs 1:33** But whoso hearkeneth unto Me shall dwell safely, and shall be quiet from fear of evil.
- **Isaiah 32:17,18** And the work of righteousness shall be peace; and the effect of righteousness quietness and assurance for ever. [18] And My people shall dwell in a peaceable habitation, and in sure dwellings, and in quiet resting places.
- **Romans 5:1** Therefore being justified by faith, we have peace with God through our Lord Jesus Christ.

RELAXATION AND FREETIME

Definitions: Relaxation is rest or enjoyment away from one's usual duties. It is also refreshment of body or mind by getting rid of or away from tension and stress. Freetime is personal time which is not otherwise scheduled for specific work activities or duties.

1. After creating the universe, God rested from His labour. He commands us to do likewise.

- **Genesis 2:2,3** And on the seventh day God ended His work which He had made; and He rested on the seventh day from all His work which He had made. [3]And God blessed the seventh day, and sanctified it: because that in it He had rested from all His work which God created and made.
- **Exodus 20:9,11** Six days shalt thou labour, and do all thy work: [11]For in six days the Lord made heaven and earth, the sea, and all that in them is, and rested the seventh day: wherefore the Lord blessed the sabbath day, and hallowed it.
- **Exodus 23:12** Six days thou shalt do thy work, and on the seventh day thou shalt rest: that thine ox and thine ass may rest, and the son of thy handmaid, and the stranger, may be refreshed.
- **1 Kings 8:56a** Blessed be the Lord, that hath given rest unto His people.
- **Hebrews 4:4,9,10** For He spake in a certain place of the seventh day on this wise, And God did rest the seventh day from all His works … [9]There remaineth therefore a rest to the people of God. [10]For he that is entered into His rest, he also hath ceased from his own works, as God did from His.

2. Physical renewal is one of the basic requirements for human happiness and good health.

- **Psalm 103:2,5** Bless the Lord, O my soul, and forget not all His benefits: … [5]Who satisfieth thy mouth with good things; so that thy youth is renewed like the eagle's. [See also Job 33:25.]
- **Psalm 127:2** It is vain for you to rise up early, to sit up late, to eat the bread of sorrows: for so He giveth His beloved sleep.
- **Isaiah 28:12a** To whom He said, This is the rest wherewith ye may cause the weary to rest; and this is the refreshing.
- **Isaiah 30:15a** For thus saith the Lord God, the Holy One of Israel; In returning and rest shall ye be saved; in quietness and in confidence shall be your strength.

3. God intends for life to be enjoyable, and relaxation and leisure time help make it so.

- **Psalm 16:11b** In Thy presence is fulness of joy; at Thy right hand there are pleasures for evermore.
- **Psalm 23:6** Surely goodness and mercy shall follow me all the days of my life: and I will dwell in the house of the Lord for ever.
- **Psalm 30:5b** In His favour is life.
- **Psalm 36:7,8** How excellent is Thy lovingkindness, O God! Therefore the children of men put their trust under the shadow of Thy wings. [8]They shall be abundantly satisfied with the fatness of Thy house; and thou shalt make them drink of the river of Thy pleasures.
- **Proverbs 10:22** The blessing of the Lord, it maketh rich, and He addeth no sorrow with it.
- **Ecclesiastes 3:13** And also that every man should eat and drink, and enjoy the good of all his labour, it is the gift of God.
- **Mark 2:27** And He said unto them, The sabbath was made for man, and not man for the sabbath.
- **1 Timothy 6:17b** God … giveth us richly all things to enjoy.

4. Jesus and His disciples took time to relax away from the pressures and demands of their public ministry.

- **Matthew 14:23** And when He had sent the multitudes away, He went up into a mountain apart to pray: and when the evening was come, He was there alone.
- **Matthew 15:29** And Jesus departed from thence, and came nigh unto the sea of Galilee; and went up into a mountain, and sat down there.
- **Matthew 17:1** And after six days Jesus taketh Peter, James, and John his brother, and bringeth them up into an high mountain apart.
- **Mark 6:31,32** And He said unto them, Come ye yourselves apart into a desert place, and rest a while: for there were many coming and going, and they had no leisure so much as to eat. ³² And they departed into a desert place by ship privately.
- **Luke 9:10a** And the apostles, when they were returned, told Him all that they had done. And He took them, and went aside privately into a desert place.

5. If we don't take time to renew our bodies and spirits, we'll run out of physical and spiritual strength.

- **Psalm 103:4a,5** Who redeemeth thy life from destruction … ⁵ Who satisfieth thy mouth with good things; so that thy youth is renewed like the eagle's.
- **Isaiah 40:30,31** Even the youths shall faint and be weary, and the young men shall utterly fall: ³¹ But they that wait upon the Lord shall renew their strength; they shall mount up with wings as eagles; they shall run, and not be weary; and they shall walk, and not faint.
- **Luke 10:38-42** Now it came to pass, as they went, that He entered into a certain village: and a certain woman named Martha received Him into her house. ³⁹ And she had a sister called Mary, which also sat at Jesus' feet, and heard His Word. ⁴⁰ But Martha was cumbered

about much serving, and came to Him, and said, Lord, dost Thou not care that my sister hath left me to serve alone? Bid her therefore that she help me. [41] And Jesus answered and said unto her, Martha, Martha, thou art careful and troubled about many things: [42] But one thing is needful: and Mary hath chosen that good part, which shall not be taken away from her.

- **Matthew 26:41b** The spirit indeed is willing, but the flesh is weak.
- **2 Corinthians 4:16** For which cause we faint not; but though our outward man perish, yet the inward man is renewed day by day.

6. Freetime activities should be edifying and strengthening, not time wasters.

- **Romans 14:19** Let us therefore follow after the things which make for peace, and things wherewith one may edify another.
- **1 Corinthians 10:23** All things are lawful for me, but all things are not expedient: all things are lawful for me, but all things edify not.
- **1 Corinthians 10:31** Whether therefore ye eat, or drink, or whatsoever ye do, do all to the glory of God.
- **1 Corinthians 14:26b** Let all things be done unto edifying.
- **Ephesians 3:16** That He would grant you, according to the riches of His glory, to be strengthened with might by His Spirit in the inner man.

7. Word and rest time is for communing with the Lord.

- **Exodus 33:14** And He said, My presence shall go with thee, and I will give thee rest.
- **Psalm 23:1-3a** The Lord is my shepherd; I shall not want. [2]He maketh me to lie down in green pastures: He leadeth me beside the still waters. [3a]He restoreth my soul.
- **Psalm 116:7** Return unto thy rest, O my soul; for the Lord hath dealt bountifully with thee.

- **Song of Solomon 1:7a** Tell me, O Thou whom my soul loveth, where Thou feedest, where Thou makest thy flock to rest at noon.
- **Matthew 11:28-30** Come unto Me, all ye that labour and are heavy laden, and I will give you rest. [29] Take My yoke upon you, and learn of Me; for I am meek and lowly in heart: and ye shall find rest unto your souls. [30] For My yoke is easy, and My burden is light.

    [See also Ezekiel 34:14,15.]

8. What could be more refressing or re-strengthening than the Word?

- **John 6:63** It is the spirit that quickeneth; the flesh profiteth nothing: the Words that I speak unto you, they are spirit, and they are life.
- **Job 23:12** Neither have I gone back from the commandment of His lips; I have esteemed the Words of His mouth more than my necessary food. [See also Psalm 119:111.]
- **Psalm 119:103** How sweet are Thy Words unto my taste! Yea, sweeter than honey to my mouth!
- **Jeremiah 15:16a** Thy Words were found, and I did eat them; and Thy Word was unto me the joy and rejoicing of mine heart.
- **Colossians 1:9b,11a** Be filled with the knowledge of His will in all wisdom and spiritual understanding … [11a] Strengthened with all might, according to His glorious power.
- **Acts 20:32** And now, brethren, I commend you to God, and to the Word of His grace, which is able to build you up, and to give you an inheritance among all them which are sanctified.

9. At times, the Lord may ask us to sacrifice our freetime for the sake of His Work or others.

- **Jeremiah 45:1-5** [During the time of Israel's judgement, although the Lord promised to spare Baruch's life, as he'd been faithful as Jeremiah's scribe, yet he had no rest in the land which God was preparing to destroy:] The word that Jeremiah the prophet spake unto Baruch ... [3] Thou [Baruch] didst say, Woe is me now! ... I fainted in my sighing, and I find no rest. ... [4b]The Lord saith thus; Behold, ... that which I have planted I will pluck up, even this whole land ... [5b]behold, I will bring evil upon all flesh, saith the Lord: but thy life will I give unto thee for a prey in all places whither thou goest.

- **Mark 6:31b** There were many coming and going, and they had no leisure so much as to eat.

- **Mark 7:24** [During His busy travels, Jesus tried to find rest, but sometimes couldn't:] And from thence He arose, and went into the borders of Tyre and Sidon, and entered into an house, and would have no man know it: but He could not be hid. [See also Mark 3:7; Luke 9:10,11.]

- **John 9:4** I must work the works of Him that sent me, while it is day: the night cometh, when no man can work.

- **2 Corinthians 7:5a** For, when we were come into Macedonia, our flesh had no rest, but we were troubled on every side.

REPUTATION

Definition: What is generally said, believed or judged about the character of a person or thing; notice by other people of some quality or ability.

1. A good reputation—provided it is for the right reasons—is of great value.

- **Proverbs 22:1** A good name is rather to be chosen than great riches, and loving favour rather than silver and gold.
- **Ecclesiastes 7:1a** A good name is better than precious ointment.

2. If we seek to please the Lord, a good reputation among His people will follow.

- **Proverbs 3:3,4** Let not mercy and truth forsake thee: bind them about thy neck; write them upon the table of thine heart: ⁴ So shalt thou find favour and good understanding in the sight of God and man.
- **Acts 6:3** Wherefore, brethren, look ye out among you seven men of honest report, full of the Holy Ghost and wisdom, whom we may appoint over this business.
- **Romans 1:8** First, I thank my God through Jesus Christ for you all, that your faith is spoken of throughout the whole world.
- **Romans 14:17,18** For the Kingdom of God is not meat and drink; but righteousness, and peace, and joy in the Holy Ghost. ¹⁸ For he that in these things serveth Christ is acceptable to God, and approved of men.
- **Romans 16:19a** For your obedience is come abroad unto all men.
- **1 Corinthians 8:3** If any man love God, the same is known of Him.
- **Philippians 2:29,30a** Receive him [Epaphroditus, Paul's co-worker] therefore in the Lord with all gladness; and hold such in reputation: ³⁰ᵃ Because for the work of Christ he was nigh unto death, not regarding his life.

3. The Lord may even cause us to have public favor, at least temporarily, if it serves His purpose.

- **Exodus 3:21** And I will give this people favour in the sight of the Egyptians: and it shall come to pass, that, when ye go, ye shall not go empty.
- **Exodus 11:3** And the Lord gave the people favour in the sight of the Egyptians. Moreover the man Moses was very great in the land of Egypt, in the sight of Pharaoh's servants, and in the sight of the people.
- **1 Samuel 18:30b** And it came to pass, after they went forth, that David behaved himself more wisely than all the servants of Saul; so that his name was much set by [well known].
- **Luke 2:52** And Jesus increased in wisdom and stature, and in favour with God and man. [See also 1 Samuel 2:26.]
- **Acts 2:46,47** And they, continuing daily with one accord in the temple, and breaking bread from house to house, did eat their meat with gladness and singleness of heart, [47] Praising God, and having favour with all the people. And the Lord added to the church daily such as should be saved.

4. But as Christians, we should <u>not</u> be overly concerned about our reputation in worldly society.

- **Proverbs 20:6** Most men will proclaim every one his own goodness: but a faithful man who can find?
- **Proverbs 29:25a** The fear of man bringeth a snare.
- **Matthew 23:5-7** [The Pharisees were always making an outward show of their religious righteousness, but it didn't impress Jesus, who said:] But all their works they do for to be seen of men: they make broad their phylacteries, and enlarge the borders of their garments. [6] And love the uppermost rooms at feasts, and the chief seats in the synagogues, [7] And greetings in the markets, and to be called of men, Rabbi, Rabbi.

- **Luke 6:26** Woe unto you, when all men shall speak well of you! For so did their fathers to the false prophets.
- **John 5:44** How can ye believe, which receive honour one of another, and seek not the honour that cometh from God only?
- **Galatians 1:10** [Paul wrote:] For do I now persuade men, or God? Or do I seek to please men? For if I yet pleased men, I should not be the servant of Christ.
- **1 Thessalonians 2:4** But as we were allowed of God to be put in trust with the Gospel, even so we speak; not as pleasing men, but God, which trieth our hearts.
- **James 4:4** Ye adulterers and adulteresses, know ye not that the friendship of the world is enmity with God? Whosoever therefore will be a friend of the world is the enemy of God.

5. When we live godly lives, we can expect to be rejected by the world.

- **Psalm 69:9** For the zeal of Thine house hath eaten me up; and the reproaches of them that reproached Thee are fallen upon me.
- **Psalm 119:51** The proud have had me greatly in derision: yet have I not declined from Thy law.
- **Matthew 10:22** And ye shall be hated of all men for My name's sake: but he that endureth to the end shall be saved.
- **Luke 6:22** Blessed are ye, when men shall hate you, and when they shall separate you from their company, and shall reproach you, and cast out your name as evil, for the Son of Man's sake.
- **John 15:18-20** If the world hate you, ye know that it hated Me before it hated you. [19] If ye were of the world, the world would love his own: but because ye are not of the world, but I have chosen you out of the world, therefore the world hateth you. [20] Remember the word that I said unto you, The servant is not greater than his lord. If they have persecuted Me, they will also persecute you; if they have kept My saying, they will keep yours also.

- **Acts 14:2** But the unbelieving Jews stirred up the Gentiles, and made their minds evil affected against the brethren.
- **Acts 28:22b** For as concerning this sect [the Christians], we know that every where it is spoken against.
- **1 Corinthians 4:10,13** We are fools for Christ's sake, but ye are wise in Christ; we are weak, but ye are strong; ye are honourable, but we are despised. ... [13] Being defamed, we intreat: we are made as the filth of the world, and are the offscouring of all things unto this day.
- **2 Timothy 3:12** Yea, and all that will live godly in Christ Jesus shall suffer persecution.
- **Hebrews 10:33** Partly, whilst ye were made a gazingstock both by reproaches and afflictions; and partly, whilst ye became companions of them that were so used.

6. Jesus wasn't concerned about His reputation with the ungodly.

- **Isaiah 53:3** He is despised and rejected of men; a Man of sorrows, and acquainted with grief: and we hid as it were our faces from Him; He was despised, and we esteemed Him not.
- **Mark 9:12b** It is written of the Son of Man, that He must suffer many things, and be set at nought.
- **John 5:41** I [Jesus] receive not honour from men.
- **Philippians 2:5-8** Let this mind be in you, which was also in Christ Jesus: [6] who, being in the form of God, thought it not robbery to be equal with God: [7] But made Himself of no reputation, and took upon Him the form of a servant, and was made in the likeness of men: [8] And being found in fashion as a man, He humbled Himself, and became obedient unto death, even the death of the cross.
- **Hebrews 13:12** Wherefore Jesus also, that He might sanctify the people with His own blood, suffered without the gate.

7. It's what the Lord thinks of us that really matters.

- **John 12:26** If any man serve Me, let him follow Me; and where I am, there shall also My servant be: if any man serve Me, him will My Father honour.
- **Romans 2:29** But he is a Jew, which is one inwardly; and circumcision is that of the heart, in the spirit, and not in the letter; whose praise is not of men, but of God.
- **2 Corinthians 5:9** Wherefore we labour, that, whether present or absent, we may be accepted of Him.
- **2 Corinthians 6:4,8a** [Being honored of God, we learn both to abase and to abound.] But in all things approving ourselves as the ministers of God, in much patience, in afflictions, in necessities, in distresses, … [8a] By honour and dishonour, by evil report and good report.
- **Colossians 1:10** That ye might walk worthy of the Lord unto all pleasing, being fruitful in every good work, and increasing in the knowledge of God.
- **1 John 3:22** And whatsoever we ask, we receive of Him, because we keep His commandments, and do those things that are pleasing in His sight.

8. Though we shouldn't be concerned with our own reputation in the eyes of the world, we should be good samples to them as Christians, as part of our witness.

- **2 Corinthians 6:3** Giving no offence in any thing, that the ministry be not blamed.
- **Philippians 2:15** That ye may be blameless and harmless, the sons of God, without rebuke, in the midst of a crooked and perverse nation, among whom ye shine as lights in the world.
- **1 Thessalonians 5:22** Abstain from all appearance of evil.

- **1 Timothy 4:12** Let no man despise thy youth; but be thou an example of the believers, in word, in conversation, in charity, in spirit, in faith, in purity.
- **Titus 2:7,8** In all things shewing thyself a pattern of good works: in doctrine shewing uncorruptness, gravity, sincerity, [8]Sound speech, that cannot be condemned; that he that is of the contrary part may be ashamed, having no evil thing to say of you.
- **1 Peter 3:15,16** But sanctify the Lord God in your hearts: and be ready always to give an answer to every man that asketh you a reason of the hope that is in you with meekness and fear: [16]Having a good conscience; that, whereas they speak evil of you, as of evildoers, they may be ashamed that falsely accuse your good conversation in Christ.

9. If we are willing to lose our reputation in this world for Christ's sake, we will be rewarded eternally.

- **Matthew 5:10-12** Blessed are they which are persecuted for righteousness' sake: for theirs is the Kingdom of Heaven. [11]Blessed are ye, when men shall revile you, and persecute you, and shall say all manner of evil against you falsely, for My sake. [12]Rejoice, and be exceeding glad: for great is your reward in Heaven: for so persecuted they the prophets which were before you.
- **Acts 5:41** And they departed from the presence of the council, rejoicing that they were counted worthy to suffer shame for His name.
- **1 Timothy 4:10** For therefore we both labour and suffer reproach, because we trust in the living God, who is the Saviour of all men, specially of those that believe.
- **Hebrews 11:26** Esteeming the reproach of Christ greater riches than the treasures in Egypt: for he had respect unto the recompence of the reward.
- **Hebrews 13:13** Let us go forth therefore unto Him without the camp, bearing His reproach.

• **1 Peter 4:14** If ye be reproached for the name of Christ, happy are ye; for the Spirit of glory and of God resteth upon you: on their part He is evil spoken of, but on your part He is glorified.

REVENGE, SEEKING

Definition: Desire to pay back injury for injury. Vengeance and vengefulness come from the same root word and have very similar meanings. Vengeance is defined as: "Punishment given in return for an injury or offense." Vengefulness is: "Desire for revenge." Vindictiveness means: "Prone to seek revenge."

1. Revenge is born of hate and spite.

- **1 Kings 19:1,2** And Ahab told Jezebel all that Elijah had done, and withal how he had slain all the prophets [of the false god Baal] with the sword. [2] Then Jezebel sent a messenger unto Elijah, saying, So let the gods do to me, and more also, if I make not thy life as the life of one of them by to morrow about this time.

- **2 Chronicles 16:7,9b,10** And at that time Hanani the seer came to Asa king of Judah, and said unto him, Because thou hast relied on the king of Syria, and not relied on the Lord thy God, therefore is the host of the king of Syria escaped out of thine hand. [9b] Herein thou hast done foolishly: therefore from henceforth thou shalt have wars. [10] Then Asa was wroth with the seer, and put him in a prison house; for he was in a rage with him because of this thing. And Asa oppressed some of the people the same time.

- **Esther 3:6** And he [Haman] thought scorn to lay hands on Mordecai alone; for they had shewed him the people of Mordecai: wherefore Haman sought to destroy all the Jews that were throughout the whole kingdom of Ahasuerus, even the people of Mordecai.

- **Ezekiel 25:15,16a,17** [God will rebuke the evil revengers.] Thus saith the Lord God; Because the Philistines have dealt by revenge, and have taken vengeance with a despiteful heart, to destroy it for the old hatred; [16a] Therefore thus saith the Lord God; … [17] And I will execute great vengeance upon them with furious rebukes; and they shall know that I am the Lord, when I shall lay My vengeance upon them.

- **Mark 6:17-19** For Herod himself had sent forth and laid hold upon John, and bound him in prison for Herodias' sake, his brother

Philip's wife: for he had married her. [18] For John had said unto Herod, It is not lawful for thee to have thy brother's wife. [19] Therefore Herodias had a quarrel against him [John the Baptist], and would have killed him; but she could not. [See also verses 20-25 and Matthew 14:3-8.]

- **Acts 5:33** [Peter and some other apostles preached to the high priest and his council:] When they heard that, they were cut to the heart, and took counsel to slay them.
- **Acts 23:12** And when it was day, certain of the Jews banded together, and bound themselves under a curse, saying that they would neither eat nor drink till they had killed Paul.

2. Revenge is unchristian and is expressly forbidden in God's Word.

- **Leviticus 19:18** Thou shalt not avenge, nor bear any grudge against the children of thy people, but thou shalt love thy neighbour as thyself: I am the Lord.
- **Micah 6:8** He hath shewed thee, O man, what is good; and what doth the Lord require of thee, but to do justly, and to love mercy, and to walk humbly with thy God?
- **Matthew 5:38,39** Ye have heard that it hath been said, An eye for an eye, and a tooth for a tooth: [39] But I [Jesus] say unto you, That ye resist not evil: but whosoever shall smite thee on thy right cheek, turn to him the other also.
- **Luke 9:54-56a** And when His disciples James and John saw this, they said, Lord, wilt Thou that we command fire to come down from Heaven, and consume them, even as Elias did? [55] But He turned, and rebuked them, and said, Ye know not what manner of spirit ye are of. [56a] For the Son of Man is not come to destroy men's lives, but to save them.
- **John 18:10,11** Then Simon Peter having a sword drew it, and smote the high priest's servant, and cut off his right ear. The servant's name was Malchus. [11] Then said Jesus unto Peter, Put up

thy sword into the sheath: the cup which My Father hath given Me, shall I not drink it?

- **Romans 12:17** Recompense to no man evil for evil. Provide things honest in the sight of all men.
- **James 5:9** Grudge not one against another, brethren, lest ye be condemned: behold, the judge standeth before the door.

3. Those who seek revenge bring more trouble upon themselves.

- **Proverbs 11:17** The merciful man doeth good to his own soul: but he that is cruel [unmerciful or vengeful] troubleth his own flesh.
- **Proverbs 24:17,18a** Rejoice not when thine enemy falleth, and let not thine heart be glad when he stumbleth: [18] Lest the Lord see it, and it displease Him.
- **Mark 11:26** But if ye do not forgive, neither will your Father which is in Heaven forgive your trespasses. [See also Matthew 6:15.]
- **Galatians 6:7** Be not deceived; God is not mocked: for whatsoever a man soweth, that shall he also reap.
- **James 2:13a** For he shall have judgment without mercy, that hath shewed no mercy.

4. The godly solution is to return good for evil.

- **Exodus 23:4,5** If thou meet thine enemy's ox or his ass going astray, thou shalt surely bring it back to him again. [5] If thou see the ass of him that hateth thee lying under his burden, and wouldest forbear to help him, thou shalt surely help with him.
- **2 Kings 6:21,22** And the king of Israel said unto Elisha, when he saw them, My father, shall I smite them? Shall I smite them? [22] And he answered, Thou shalt not smite them: wouldest thou smite those whom thou hast taken captive with thy sword and with thy bow? Set bread and water before them, that they may eat and drink, and go to their master.
- **Proverbs 25:21,22** If thine enemy be hungry, give him bread to eat; and if he be thirsty, give him water to drink: [22] For thou shalt heap

coals of fire upon his head, and the Lord shall reward thee. [See also Romans 12:20.]

• **Matthew 5:43-48** Ye have heard that it hath been said, Thou shalt love thy neighbour, and hate thine enemy. [44] But I [Jesus] say unto you, love your enemies, bless them that curse you, do good to them that hate you, and pray for them which despitefully use you, and persecute you; [45] That ye may be the children of your Father which is in Heaven: for He maketh His sun to rise on the evil and on the good, and sendeth rain on the just and on the unjust. [46] For if ye love them which love you, what reward have ye? Do not even the publicans the same? [47] And if ye salute your brethren only, what do ye more than others? Do not even the publicans so? [48] Be ye therefore perfect, even as your Father which is in Heaven is perfect. [See also Luke 6:27,28,32-36.]

1 Thessalonians 5:15 See that none render evil for evil unto any man; but ever follow that which is good, both among yourselves, and to all men.

1 Peter 3:9 Not rendering evil for evil, or railing for railing: but contrariwise blessing; knowing that ye are thereunto called, that ye should inherit a blessing.

1 Peter 4:8 And above all things have fervent charity [love] among yourselves: for charity shall cover the multitude of sins.

• When tempted to seek revenge, commit the situation and the wrong-doers to the Lord.

Proverbs 20:22 Say not thou, I will recompense evil; but wait on the Lord, and He shall save thee.

Hosea 12:6 Therefore turn thou to thy God: keep mercy and judgment, and wait on thy God continually.

Romans 12:19 Dearly beloved, avenge not yourselves, but rather give place unto wrath: for it is written, Vengeance is Mine; I will repay, saith the Lord.

- **1 Peter 2:19,21-23** For this is thankworthy, if a man for conscience toward God endure grief, suffering wrongfully. [21] For even hereunto were ye called: because Christ also suffered for us, leaving us an example, that ye should follow His steps: [22] Who did no sin, neither was guile found in His mouth: [23] Who, when He was reviled, reviled not again; when He suffered, He threatened not; but committed Himself to Him that judgeth righteously.

6. When we are filled with God's love, it is impossible for us to be vengeful, and vice versa.

- **Proverbs 10:12** Hatred stirreth up strifes: but love covereth all sins.
- **Matthew 6:22,23** The light of the body is the eye: if therefore thine eye be single, thy whole body shall be full of light. [23] But if thine eye be evil, thy whole body shall be full of darkness. If therefore the light that is in thee be darkness, how great is that darkness! [See also Luke 11:34.]
- **1 Corinthians 13:4a,7** Charity [love] suffereth long, and is kind; [7] Beareth all things, believeth all things, hopeth all things, endureth all things.
- **Galatians 5:22** But the fruit of the Spirit is love, joy, peace, longsuffering, gentleness, goodness, faith.
- **Ephesians 4:31,32** Let all bitterness, and wrath, and anger, and clamour, and evil speaking, be put away from you, with all malice: [32] And be ye kind one to another, tenderhearted, forgiving one another, even as God for Christ's sake hath forgiven you.
- **1 John 2:9** He that saith he is in the light, and hateth his brother, is in darkness even until now.

7. Showing forgiveness and mercy is better than revenge, because it brings on God's blessing.

- **Psalm 18:25** With the merciful Thou wilt shew Thyself merciful; with an upright man Thou wilt shew Thyself upright.

- **Proverbs 3:3,4** Let not mercy and truth forsake thee: bind them about thy neck; write them upon the table of thine heart: [4] So shalt thou find favour and good understanding in the sight of God and man.
- **Matthew 5:7** Blessed are the merciful: for they shall obtain mercy.
- **Matthew 6:12,14** And forgive us our debts, as we forgive our debtors. [14] For if ye forgive men their trespasses, your Heavenly Father will also forgive you.
- **Mark 11:25** And when ye stand praying, forgive, if ye have ought against any: that your Father also which is in Heaven may forgive you your trespasses.
- **Luke 6:37** Judge not, and ye shall not be judged: condemn not, and ye shall not be condemned: forgive, and ye shall be forgiven.

SAMPLE; EXAMPLE

Definition: A part or thing that exhibits or represents the quality or characteristics of the whole or group; an example, which is something that serves as a model or pattern to be followed.

1. The Lord likens our witness to a light shining in dark places.

- **Matthew 5:14-16** Ye are the light of the world. A city that is set on an hill cannot be hid. [15] Neither do men light a candle, and put it under a bushel, but on a candlestick; and it giveth light unto all that are in the house. [16] Let your light so shine before men, that they may see your good works, and glorify your Father which is in Heaven.
- **Judges 5:31b** Let them that love Him be as the sun when he goeth forth in his might.
- **Isaiah 60:3** And the Gentiles shall come to thy light, and kings to the brightness of thy rising.
- **Ephesians 5:8** For ye were sometimes darkness, but now are ye light in the Lord: walk as children of light.
- **Philippians 2:15,16a** That ye may be blameless and harmless, the sons of God, without rebuke, in the midst of a crooked and perverse nation, among whom ye shine as lights in the world; [16a] Holding forth the Word of life.

2. As Christians we are God's representatives, the "Gospel bound in shoe leather."

- **2 Corinthians 3:2** Ye are our epistle written in our hearts, known and read of all men.
- **Philippians 1:27** Only let your conversation be as it becometh the Gospel of Christ: that whether I come and see you, or else be absent, I may hear of your affairs, that ye stand fast in one spirit, with one mind striving together for the faith of the Gospel.

- **1 Timothy 4:12** Let no man despise thy youth; but be thou an example of the believers, in word, in conversation, in charity, in spirit, in faith, in purity.
- **Titus 2:7,8** In all things shewing thyself a pattern of good works: in doctrine shewing uncorruptness, gravity, sincerity, [8] Sound speech, that cannot be condemned; that he that is of the contrary part may be ashamed, having no evil thing to say of you.
- **1 Peter 1:15** But as He which hath called you is holy, so be ye holy in all manner of conversation.

3. Our greatest sample is <u>love</u>.

- **John 13:35** By this shall all men know that ye are My disciples, if ye have love one to another.
- **1 Corinthians 13:1-3,8a** Though I speak with the tongues of men and of angels, and have not charity [love], I am become as sounding brass, or a tinkling cymbal. [2] And though I have the gift of prophecy, and understand all mysteries, and all knowledge; and though I have all faith, so that I could remove mountains, and have not charity, I am nothing. [3] And though I bestow all my goods to feed the poor, and though I give my body to be burned, and have not charity, it profiteth me nothing. … [8a] Charity never faileth.
- **2 Timothy 1:13** Hold fast the form of sound words, which thou hast heard of me, in faith and love which is in Christ Jesus.
- **1 Peter 4:8** And above all things have fervent charity among yourselves: for charity shall cover the multitude of sins.

4. Our personal example must be consistent with our witness, lest we bring reproach to the cause of Christ.

- **Romans 2:21-24** Thou therefore which teachest another, teachest thou not thyself? Thou that preachest a man should not steal, dost thou steal? [22] Thou that sayest a man should not commit adultery, dost thou commit adultery? Thou that abhorrest idols, dost thou commit sacrilege? [23] Thou that makest thy boast of the law, through breaking the law dishonourest thou God? [24] For the name of God is blasphemed among the Gentiles through you, as it is written.

- **Romans 14:16** Let not then your good be evil spoken of.
- **1 Corinthians 8:9** But take heed lest by any means this liberty of yours become a stumblingblock to them that are weak.
- **1 Corinthians 9:27** But I keep under my body, and bring it into subjection: lest that by any means, when I have preached to others, I myself should be a castaway.
- **1 Corinthians 10:23** All things are lawful for me, but all things are not expedient: all things are lawful for me, but all things edify not.
- **2 Corinthians 6:3** Giving no offence in any thing, that the ministry be not blamed. [See also 1 Timothy 5:14b.]
- **1 Thessalonians 5:22** Abstain from all appearance of evil.
- **1 Timothy 4:16** Take heed unto thyself, and unto the doctrine; continue in them: for in doing this thou shalt both save thyself, and them that hear thee.
- **1 John 2:6** He that saith he abideth in Him ought himself also so to walk, even as He walked.

5. We should endeavor to maintain a good sample even when mistreated.

- **James 5:10** Take, my brethren, the prophets, who have spoken in the name of the Lord, for an example of suffering affliction, and of patience.
- **1 Peter 2:12,15** Having your conversation honest among the Gentiles: that, whereas they speak against you as evildoers, they may by your good works, which they shall behold, glorify God in the day of visitation. … [15] For so is the will of God, that with well doing ye may put to silence the ignorance of foolish men.
- **1 Peter 2:21-23** For even hereunto were ye called: because Christ also suffered for us, leaving us an example, that ye should follow His steps: [22] Who did no sin, neither was guile found in His mouth:

[23] Who, when He was reviled, reviled not again; when He suffered, He threatened not; but committed Himself to Him that judgeth righteously.

- **1 Peter 3:9,16** Not rendering evil for evil, or railing for railing: but contrariwise blessing; knowing that ye are thereunto called, that ye should inherit a blessing. ... [16] Having a good conscience; that, whereas they speak evil of you, as of evildoers, they may be ashamed that falsely accuse your good conversation in Christ.

6. A sample is better than a sermon!

- **John 10:4** [Jesus taught that a good shepherd leads the sheep only where he has gone before.] And when he putteth forth his own sheep, he goeth before them, and the sheep follow him: for they know his voice.
- **John 13:15** For I have given you an example, that ye should do as I have done to you.
- **Acts 20:35** I have shewed you all things, how that so labouring ye ought to support the weak, and to remember the words of the Lord Jesus, how He said, It is more blessed to give than to receive.
- **1 Corinthians 11:1** Be ye followers of me, even as I also am of Christ.
- **Philippians 3:17-19** [Paul used his good sample to bring to light the hypocrisy of others:] Brethren, be followers together of me, and mark them which walk so as ye have us for an ensample. [18] (For many walk, of whom I have told you often, and now tell you even weeping, that they are the enemies of the cross of Christ: [19] Whose end is destruction, whose God is their belly, and whose glory is in their shame, who mind earthly things.)
- **Philippians 4:9** Those things, which ye have both learned, and received, and heard, and seen in me, do: and the God of peace shall be with you.
- **2 Thessalonians 3:7-9** For yourselves know how ye ought to follow us: for we behaved not ourselves disorderly among you; [8] Neither

did we eat any man's bread for nought; but wrought with labour and travail night and day, that we might not be chargeable to any of you: [9] Not because we have not power, but to make ourselves an ensample unto you to follow us.

- **Hebrew 13:7** Remember them which have the rule over you, who have spoken unto you the Word of God: whose faith follow, considering the end of their conversation.

SECRETS: WHEN TO KEEP, AND WHEN NOT TO

Definition: Something kept from the knowledge or view of others, or shared only privately with a few.

1. Keeping secrets is related to faithfulness and loyalty.

- **Joshua 2:1,4,14** [Rahab the harlot, knew that the Lord was going to give the land to the children of Israel, so she secretly harbored and hid the two spies.] And Joshua the son of Nun sent out of Shittim two men to spy secretly, saying, Go view the land, even Jericho. And they went, and came into an harlot's house, named Rahab, and lodged there. ... ⁴ And the woman took the two men, and hid them, and said thus [to the soldiers of Jericho who searched for the men], There came men unto me, but I wist not whence they were. ... ¹⁴ And the men [whom Rahab had hidden] answered her [after the soldiers had gone], Our life for yours, if ye utter not this our business. And it shall be, when the Lord hath given us the land, that we will deal kindly and truly with thee. [For the whole story, see verses 1-21 and chapter 6:17-25, as well as Hebrews 11:31, where Rahab, an ancestor of David and of Jesus, was named as a heroine of the faith.]
- **Proverbs 11:13** A talebearer [gossip] revealeth secrets: but he that is of a faithful spirit concealeth the matter. [See also 20:19.]

2. Keeping secrets can be a matter of the protection of the Lord's work.

- **Judges 16:4-6,15-21** [When Samson was enticed by Delilah to reveal the secret of his strength, it caused him to lose his strength, and then to be captured and blinded by his enemies.] And the lords of the Philistines came up unto [Delilah], and said unto her, Entice him, and see wherein his great strength lieth, and by what means we may prevail against him, that we may bind him to afflict him: and we will give thee every one of us eleven hundred pieces of silver. [6] And Delilah said to Samson, Tell me, I pray thee, wherein thy great strength lieth, and wherewith thou mightest be bound to afflict thee. ... [16] And it came to pass, when she pressed him daily with her words, and urged him, so that his soul was vexed unto death; [17] That he told her all his heart, and said unto her, There hath not come a rasor upon mine head; for I have been a Nazarite unto God from my mother's womb: if I be shaven, then my strength will go from me, and I shall become weak, and be like any other man. [18] And when Delilah saw that he had told her all his heart, she sent and called for the lords of the Philistines. ... [19] And she made him sleep upon her knees; and she called for a man, and she caused him to shave off the seven locks of his head; and she began to afflict him, and his strength went from him. ... [21] But the Philistines took him, and put out his eyes, and brought him down to Gaza, and bound him with fetters of brass; and he did grind in the prison house. [Samson had fought mightily against the enemies of Israel, but this mistake cost him his freedom, his eyesight and eventually his life. Nevertheless, the Lord got a victory from seeming defeat when the Philistines made a spectacle of a now-repentant Samson in their pagan temple, and he literally brought down the house, earning him a place in God's Hall of Fame. See Judges 6:28-31 and Hebrews 11:32.]

- **1 Samuel 19:2** But Jonathan Saul's son delighted much in David: and Jonathan told David, saying, Saul my father seeketh to kill thee: now therefore, I pray thee, take heed to thyself until the morning, and abide in a secret place, and hide thyself. [See also 1 Samuel 20:19.]
- **Proverbs 13:3** He that keepeth his mouth keepeth his life: but he that openeth wide his lips shall have destruction.
- **Jeremiah 36:19** [After Baruch the scribe read Jeremiah's prophecy against Jerusalem to the princes, they needed to make a report of this to the king. Since they assumed that he would not receive the message very well, the princes thoughtfully advised Baruch:] Go, hide thee, thou and Jeremiah; and let no man know where ye be.

- **Daniel 12:4a** [After giving Daniel a very specific endtime prophecy from the Lord, the angel told him:] But thou, O Daniel, shut up the words, and seal the book, even to the time of the End. [See also Revelation 10:4 and 5:1-5.]
- **Matthew 12:14-16** Then the Pharisees went out, and held a council against Him, how they might destroy Him. [15] But when Jesus knew it, He withdrew Himself from thence: and great multitudes followed Him, and He healed them all; [16] And charged them that they should not make Him known.
- **Luke 20:2-8,20** [Jesus wisely answered a question with a question:] And spake unto Him, saying, Tell us [the chief priest, scribes and elders], by what authority doest Thou these things? Or who is he that gave Thee this authority? [3] And He answered and said unto them, I will also ask you one thing; and answer Me: [4] The baptism of John, was it from Heaven, or of men? [5] And they reasoned with themselves, saying, If we shall say, From Heaven; He will say, Why then believed ye Him not? [6] But and if we say, Of men; all the people will stone us: for they be persuaded that John was a prophet. [7] And they answered, that they could not tell whence it was. [8] And Jesus said unto them, Neither tell I you by what authority I do these things. ... [20] And they watched Him, and sent forth spies, which should feign themselves just men, that they might take hold of His words, that so they might deliver Him unto the power and authority of the governor. [See also Mark 12:13.]
- **John 2:24,25** But Jesus did not commit [entrust] Himself unto them [the masses who followed Him after seeing the miracles He did], because He knew all men, [25] And needed not that any should testify of man: for He knew what was in man.
- **John 7:1-11** After these things Jesus walked in Galilee: for He would not walk in Jewry, because the Jews sought to kill Him. [2] Now the Jews' feast of tabernacles was at hand. [3] His brethren therefore said unto Him, Depart hence, and go into Judaea, that Thy disciples also may see the works that Thou doest. [4] For there is no man that doeth any thing in secret, and he himself seeketh to be known

openly. If thou do these things, shew thyself to the world. ... [6] Then Jesus said unto them, My time is not yet come: but your time is alway ready. [7] The world cannot hate you; but Me it hateth, because I testify of it, that the works thereof are evil. [8] Go ye up unto this feast: I go not up yet unto this feast; for My time is not yet full come. [9] When He had said these words unto them, He abode still in Galilee. [10] But when His brethren were gone up, then went He also up unto the feast, not openly, but as it were in secret. [11] Then the Jews sought Him at the feast, and said, Where is He? [12] And there was much murmuring among the people concerning Him: for some said, He is a good Man: others said, Nay; but He deceiveth the people. [13] Howbeit no man spake openly of Him for fear of the Jews.

- **Acts 23:21b,22** [When a plot to assassinate Paul arose, Paul's nephew heard about it and told the chief captain of the governing Romans:] There lie in wait for him of them more than forty men, which have bound themselves with an oath, that they will neither eat nor drink till they have killed him: and now are they ready, looking for a promise from thee. [22] So the chief captain then let the young man depart, and charged him, See thou tell no man that thou hast shewed these things to me.

- **Acts 26:26** [Paul acknowledged that King Agrippa was aware of his activities:] For the king knoweth of these things [Paul had been preaching about Jesus], before whom also I speak freely: for I am persuaded that none of these things are hidden from him; for this thing was not done in a corner.

3. Jesus at times revealed certain matters only to His disciples, and asked them to keep it a secret.

- **Matthew 9:30** [Upon healing the two blind men:] And their eyes were opened; and Jesus straitly charged them, saying, See that no man know it.

- **Matthew 13:10-17** And the disciples came, and said unto Him, Why speakest Thou unto them in parables? [11] He answered and

said unto them, Because it is given unto you to know the mysteries of the Kingdom of Heaven, but to them it is not given. ...
[13] Therefore speak I to them in parables: because they seeing see not; and hearing they hear not, neither do they understand. [14] And in them is fulfilled the prophecy of Esaias, which saith, By hearing ye shall hear, and shall not understand; and seeing ye shall see, and shall not perceive: [15] For this people's heart is waxed gross, and their ears are dull of hearing, and their eyes they have closed; lest at any time they should see with their eyes, and hear with their ears, and should understand with their heart, and should be converted, and I should heal them. [16] But blessed are your eyes, for they see: and your ears, for they hear. [17] For verily I say unto you, That many prophets and righteous men have desired to see those things which ye see, and have not seen them; and to hear those things which ye hear, and have not heard them. [See also Mark 4:10-12.]

- **Matthew 13:34,35; Mark 4:34** All these things spake Jesus unto the multitude in parables; and without a parable spake He not unto them: [35] That it might be fulfilled which was spoken by the prophet, saying, I will open My mouth in parables; I will utter things which have been kept secret from the foundation of the world. [Mark 4:34] But without a parable spake He not unto them: and when they were alone, He expounded all things to His disciples.
- **Mark 1:43-45** [Jesus healed a leper:] And He straitly charged him, and forthwith sent him away; [44] And saith unto him, See thou say nothing to any man: but go thy way, shew thyself to the priest, and offer for thy cleansing those things which Moses commanded, for a testimony unto them. [45] But he went out, and began to publish it much, and to blaze abroad the matter, insomuch that Jesus could no more openly enter into the city, but was without in desert places: and they came to Him from every quarter.
- **Mark 9:9** [After the transfiguration, when Moses and Elijah appeared to Jesus to speak about His death:] And as they came down from the mountain, He charged them [Peter, James and John]

that they should tell no man what things they had seen, till the Son of Man were risen from the dead.

- **Luke 8:56** [Jesus raised Jairus' daughter from the dead:] And her parents were astonished: but He charged them that they should tell no man what was done.

- **Luke 9:20,21** He said unto them [His disciples], But whom say ye that I am? Peter answering said, The Christ of God. [21] And He straitly charged them, and commanded them to tell no man that thing.

4. Keeping secrets should <u>not</u> be to cover up sin or wrongdoing.

- **Deuteronomy 13:6,8** [God commanded His people not to cover up the sins of their own families or friends:] If thy brother, the son of thy mother, or thy son, or thy daughter, or the wife of thy bosom, or thy friend, which is as thine own soul, entice thee secretly, saying, Let us go and serve other gods, which thou hast not known, thou, nor thy fathers; [8] Thou shalt not consent unto him, nor hearken unto him; neither shall thine eye pity him, neither shalt thou spare, neither shalt thou conceal him.

- **Joshua 7:1,11,19,20** [Achan hid a forbidden treasure under his tent, and caused Israel to lose the blessing of God:] But the children of Israel committed a trespass in the accursed thing: for Achan ... took of the accursed thing: and the anger of the Lord was kindled against the children of Israel. ... [And the Lord said:] [11] Israel hath sinned, and they have also transgressed My covenant which I commanded them: for they have even taken of the accursed thing, and have also stolen, and dissembled [deceived] also, and they have put it even among their own stuff. ... [19] And Joshua said unto Achan, My son, give, I pray thee, glory to the Lord God of Israel, and make confession unto Him; and tell me now what thou hast done; hide it not from me. [20] And Achan answered Joshua, and said, Indeed I have sinned against the Lord God of Israel, and thus and thus have I done. [For the whole story, see all of chapter 7.]

- **Proverbs 1:10** My son, if sinners entice thee, consent thou not.

- **Proverbs 28:13** He that covereth his sins shall not prosper: but whoso confesseth and forsaketh them shall have mercy.
- **Isaiah 29:15** Woe unto them that seek deep to hide their counsel from the Lord, and their works are in the dark, and they say, Who seeth us? And who knoweth us?
- **Jeremiah 23:24** Can any hide himself in secret places that I shall not see him? Saith the Lord. Do not I fill Heaven and earth? Saith the Lord.
- **1 Timothy 5:22b** Neither be partaker of other men's sins.
- **James 4:17** Therefore to him that knoweth to do good, and doeth it not, to him it is sin.
- **2 Peter 3:17b** Beware lest ye also, being led away with the error of the wicked, fall from your own stedfastness.

5. Keeping secrets should not mean being dishonest.

- **2 Corinthians 4:2** But have renounced the hidden things of dishonesty, not walking in craftiness, nor handling the Word of God deceitfully; but by manifestation of the truth commending ourselves to every man's conscience in the sight of God.
- **2 Corinthians 8:21** Providing for honest things, not only in the sight of the Lord, but also in the sight of men. [See also Romans 12:17b.]
- **Hebrews 13:18** Pray for us: for we trust we have a good conscience, in all things willing to live honestly.
- **1 Peter 2:12-15** Having your conversation honest among the Gentiles: that, whereas they speak against you as evildoers, they may by your good works, which they shall behold, glorify God in the day of visitation. [13] Submit yourselves to every ordinance of man for the Lord's sake: whether it be to the king, as supreme; [14] Or unto governors, as unto them that are sent by him for the punishment of evildoers, and for the praise of them that do well. [15] For so is the will of God, that with well doing ye may put to silence the ignorance of foolish men.

6. One of the best ways to avoid revealing secrets is to avoid idle talk.

- **Psalm 39:1a** I said, I will take heed to my ways, that I sin not with my tongue: I will keep my mouth with a bridle.
- **Psalm 141:3** Set a watch, O Lord, before my mouth; keep the door of my lips.
- **Proverbs 10:19** In the multitude of words there wanteth not sin: but he that refraineth his lips is wise.
- **Proverbs 17:27** He that hath knowledge spareth his words: and a man of understanding is of an excellent spirit.
- **Proverbs 21:23** Whoso keepeth his mouth and his tongue keepeth his soul from troubles.
- **Proverbs 29:11** A fool uttereth all his mind: but a wise man keepeth it in till afterwards.
- **Ecclesiastes 10:20** Curse not the king, no not in thy thought; and curse not the rich in thy bedchamber: for a bird of the air shall carry the voice, and that which hath wings shall tell the matter.
- **1 Thessalonians 4:11a** Study to be quiet, and to do [mind] your own business.

7. Disclosing secrets causes loss of confidence and friendship.

- **Proverbs 16:28b** A whisperer separateth chief friends.
- **Proverbs 18:8** [Betraying the confidence of others can cause deep wounds.] The words of a talebearer are as wounds, and they go down into the innermost parts of the belly.
- **Proverbs 25:9b,10a** Discover [reveal] not a secret to another: [10a] Lest he that heareth it put thee to shame.

8. Disclosing secrets is often a matter of gossiping.

- **Leviticus 19:16a** Thou shalt not go up and down as a talebearer among thy people.

- **Proverbs 20:3** It is an honour for a man to cease from strife: but every fool will be meddling.
- **Proverbs 20:19** He that goeth about as a talebearer revealeth secrets: therefore meddle not with him that flattereth with his lips.
- **1 Thessalonians 4:11a** Study to be quiet, and to do [mind] your own business.
- **1 Timothy 5:13** And withal they [the younger widows] learn to be idle, wandering about from house to house; and not only idle, but tattlers also and busybodies, speaking things which they ought not.

9. There are no secrets kept from an all-seeing God or those to whom He reveals them.

- **1 Chronicles 28:9** And thou, Solomon my son, know thou the God of thy father, and serve Him with a perfect heart and with a willing mind: for the Lord searcheth all hearts, and understandeth all the imaginations of the thoughts: if Thou seek Him, He will be found of thee; but if thou forsake Him, He will cast thee off for ever.
- **2 Kings 6:8-12** [The king of Syria was frustrated by God's intelligence service.—Elisha the prophet knew his every top secret strategic move, and notified the king of Israel.] Then the king of Syria warred against Israel, and took counsel with his servants, saying, In such and such a place shall be my camp. [9] And the man of God sent unto the king of Israel, saying, Beware that thou pass not such a place; for thither the Syrians are come down. [10] And the king of Israel sent to the place which the man of God told him and warned him of, and saved himself there, not once nor twice.
[11] Therefore the heart of the king of Syria was sore troubled for this thing; and he called his servants, and said unto them, Will ye not shew me which of us is for the king of Israel? [12] And one of his servants said, None, my lord, O king: but Elisha, the prophet that is in Israel, telleth the king of Israel the words that thou speakest in thy bedchamber.

- **Psalm 44:21** Shall not God search this out? For He knoweth the secrets of the heart.
- **Psalm 139:1-24** [David knew that the Lord knew everything about him, inside and out.] O Lord, Thou hast searched me, and known me. [2] Thou knowest my downsitting and mine uprising, thou understandest my thought afar off. [3] Thou compassest my path and my lying down, and art acquainted with all my ways. [4] For there is not a word in my tongue, but, lo, O Lord, Thou knowest it altogether. ... [23] Search me, O God, and know my heart: try me, and know my thoughts: [24] And see if there be any wicked way in me, and lead me in the way everlasting.
- **Proverbs 15:3** The eyes of the Lord are in every place, beholding the evil and the good.
- **Ecclesiastes 12:14** For God shall bring every work into judgment, with every secret thing, whether it be good, or whether it be evil.
- **Jeremiah 17:9-10** The heart is deceitful above all things, and desperately wicked: who can know it? [10] I the Lord search the heart, I try the reins, even to give every man according to his ways, and according to the fruit of his doings.
- **Daniel 2:20-23,27-30,47** [King Nebuchadnezzar wanted the wise men of his kingdom to tell him what dream he dreamt, as well as what it meant—otherwise they would be put to death. The Lord revealed both the dream and the interpretation to Daniel:] Daniel answered and said, Blessed be the name of God for ever and ever: for wisdom and might are His: [21] And He changeth the times and the seasons: He removeth kings, and setteth up kings: He giveth wisdom unto the wise, and knowledge to them that know understanding: [22] He revealeth the deep and secret things: He knoweth what is in the darkness, and the light dwelleth with Him. [23] I thank Thee, and praise Thee, O Thou God of my fathers, who hast given me wisdom and might, and hast made known unto me now what we desired of Thee: for Thou hast now made known unto us the king's matter. ... [27] Daniel answered in the presence of the king, and said, The secret which the king hath demanded

cannot the wise men, the astrologers, the magicians, the soothsayers, shew unto the king; [28] But there is a God in Heaven that revealeth secrets, and maketh known to the king Nebuchadnezzar what shall be in the Latter Days. Thy dream, and the visions of thy head upon thy bed, are these; [29] As for thee, O king, thy thoughts came into thy mind upon thy bed, what should come to pass hereafter: and He that revealeth secrets maketh known to thee what shall come to pass. [30] But as for me, this secret is not revealed to me for any wisdom that I have more than any living, but for their sakes that shall make known the interpretation to the king, and that thou mightest know the thoughts of thy heart. ... [After Daniel described the king's dream and the interpretation:] [47] The king answered unto Daniel, and said, Of a truth it is, that your God is a God of gods, and a Lord of kings, and a revealer of secrets, seeing thou couldest reveal this secret.

- **Daniel 8:23-25** [The Lord will defeat the Antichrist's secret strategies.] And in the latter time of their kingdom, when the transgressors are come to the full, a king of fierce countenance, and understanding dark sentences [secret strategies], shall stand up [the Antichrist]. [24] And his power shall be mighty, but not by his own power [but by the Devil's]: and he shall destroy wonderfully, and shall prosper, and practise, and shall destroy the mighty and the holy people. [25] And through his policy also he shall cause craft [deceit and deception] to prosper in his hand; and he shall magnify himself in his heart, and by peace shall destroy many: he shall also stand up against the Prince of princes [Jesus]; but he shall be broken without hand.

- **Amos 3:7** Surely the Lord God will do nothing, but He revealeth His secret unto His servants the prophets.

- **Matthew 10:26b** There is nothing covered, that shall not be revealed; and hid, that shall not be known.

- **Mark 4:21,22** And He [Jesus] said unto them, Is a candle brought to be put under a bushel, or under a bed? And not to be set on a candlestick? [22] For there is nothing hid, which shall not be manifested; neither was any thing kept secret, but that it should come abroad.

- **Mark 13:23** But take ye heed: behold, I [Jesus] have foretold you all things [about the Endtime]. [See also Isaiah 44:7.]
- **Luke 12:2,3** For there is nothing covered, that shall not be revealed; neither hid, that shall not be known. ³ Therefore whatsoever ye have spoken in darkness shall be heard in the light; and that which ye have spoken in the ear in closets shall be proclaimed upon the housetops.
- **John 15:15** Henceforth I call you not servants; for the servant knoweth not what his lord doeth: but I have called you friends; for all things that I have heard of My Father I have made known unto you.
- **John 16:12** [However, Jesus also said:] I have yet many things to say unto you, but ye cannot bear them now. [See also Ecclesiastes 8:5b and 1 Corinthians 3:1-2.]
- **John 16:25,29** [Jesus said:] These things have I spoken unto you [His disciples] in proverbs: but the time cometh, when I shall no more speak unto you in proverbs, but I shall shew you plainly of the Father. ... ²⁹ His disciples said unto Him, Lo, now speakest Thou plainly, and speakest no proverb.
- **Romans 2:16** In the day when God shall judge the secrets of men by Jesus Christ according to my gospel.
- **Romans 8:26,27** [The Spirit knows secret things we don't even know we need to pray for, and makes intercession for us.] Likewise the Spirit also helpeth our infirmities: for we know not what we should pray for as we ought: but the Spirit Itself maketh intercession for us with groanings which cannot be uttered. ²⁷ And He that searcheth the hearts knoweth what is the mind of the Spirit, because He maketh intercession for the saints according to the will of God.
- **1 Corinthians 3:13** Every man's work shall be made manifest: for the day shall declare it, because it shall be revealed by fire; and the fire shall try every man's work of what sort it is.

- **1 Corinthians 4:5** Therefore judge nothing before the time, until the Lord come, who both will bring to light the hidden things of darkness, and will make manifest the counsels of the hearts: and then shall every man have praise of God.
- **Hebrews 4:12,13** For the Word of God ... is a discerner of the thoughts and intents of the heart. [13] Neither is there any creature that is not manifest in His sight: but all things are naked and opened unto the eyes of Him with whom we have to do.

SELFISHNESS AND SELF-CENTEREDNESS

Definition: Being concerned chiefly or only with one's self, without thinking of others.

1. Selfishness is a lack of love and consideration for the needs of others.

- **Genesis 4:9** And the Lord said unto Cain, Where is Abel thy brother? And he said, I know not: Am I my brother's keeper?
- **Proverbs 18:17** He that is first in his <u>own</u> cause seemeth just; but his neighbour cometh and searcheth him.
- **Proverbs 24:11,12** If thou forbear to deliver them that are drawn unto death, and those that are ready to be slain; [12] If thou sayest, Behold, we knew it not; doth not He that pondereth the heart consider it? And He that keepeth thy soul, doth not He know it? And shall not He render to every man according to his works?
- **Ezekiel 34:8b,10,18,23,24** [God spoke against selfish shepherds, and He promised to raise up a David of the Last Days, who will unselfishly feed the sheep:] Neither did My shepherds search for My flock, but the shepherds fed themselves, and fed not My flock. ... [10] Thus saith the Lord God; Behold, I am against the shepherds; and I will require My flock at their hand, and cause them to cease from feeding the flock; neither shall the shepherds feed themselves any more; for I will deliver My flock from their mouth, that they may not be meat for them. ... [18] Seemeth it a small thing unto you to have eaten up the good pasture, but ye must tread down with your feet the residue of your pastures? And to have drunk of the deep waters, but ye must foul the residue with your feet? ... [23] And I will set up one shepherd over them, and he shall feed them, even My servant David; he shall feed them, and he shall be their shepherd. [24] And I the Lord will be their God, and My servant David a prince among them; I the Lord have spoken it.
- **Zechariah 7:6** And when ye did eat, and when ye did drink, did not ye eat for yourselves, and drink for yourselves?

- **Matthew 25:42-45** For I was an hungred, and ye gave Me no meat: I was thirsty, and ye gave Me no drink: [43] I was a stranger, and ye took Me not in: naked, and ye clothed Me not: sick , and in prison and ye visited Me not. [44] Then shall they also answer, saying, Lord, when saw we Thee an hungred, or athirst, or a stranger, or naked, or sick, or in prison, and did not minister unto Thee? [45] Then shall He answer them, saying, Verily I say unto you, Inasmuch as ye did it <u>not</u> to one of the least of these, ye did it not to <u>Me</u>.
- **Philippians 2:21** [Selfishness causes the Lord's work to suffer:] For all seek their own, not the things which are Jesus Christ's.
- **2 Timothy 3:1,2a** [As the world enters the Time of the End, selfishness becomes more pronounced:] This know also, that in the Last Days perilous times shall come. [2a] For men shall be lovers of their own selves, covetous. [See also Matthew 24:12.]
- **James 2:15,16** If a brother or sister be naked, and destitute of daily food, [16] And one of you say unto them, Depart in peace, be ye warmed and filled; notwithstanding ye give them not those things which are needful to the body; what doth it profit?
- **James 4:17** Therefore to him that knoweth to do good, and doeth it not, to him it is sin.
- **1 John 3:17** But whoso hath this world's good, and seeth his brother have need, and shutteth up his bowels of compassion from him, how dwelleth the love of God in him?

2. Selfishness hoards itself poor.

- **Proverbs 11:24b** There is that withholdeth more than is meet, but it tendeth to poverty.
- **Proverbs 13:7a** There is that maketh himself rich, yet hath nothing.
- **Proverbs 15:27a** He that is greedy of gain troubleth his own house.
- **Proverbs 28:27b** He that hideth his eyes [from the needs of others] shall have many a curse.
- **Ecclesiastes 5:13** There is a sore evil which I have seen under the sun, namely, riches kept for the owners thereof to their hurt.

- **Haggai 1:6,9,10** Ye have sown much, and bring in little; ye eat, but ye have not enough; ye drink, but ye are not filled with drink; ye clothe you, but there is none warm; and he that earneth wages earneth wages to put it into a bag with holes. [9] Ye looked for much, and, lo, it came to little; and when ye brought it home, I did blow upon it. Why? Saith the Lord of hosts. Because of Mine house that is waste, and ye run every man unto his own house. [10] Therefore the heaven over you is stayed from dew, and the earth is stayed from her fruit.

- **Mark 10:21,22** Then Jesus beholding him loved him, and said unto him, One thing thou lackest: go thy way, sell whatsoever thou hast, and give to the poor, and thou shalt have treasure in Heaven: and come, take up the cross, and follow Me. [22] And he was sad at that saying, and went away grieved: for he had great possessions.

- **Luke 12:15** And [Jesus] said unto them, Take heed, and beware of covetousness: for a man's life consisteth not in the abundance of the things which he possesseth.

- **2 Corinthians 9:6a** But this I say, He which soweth sparingly shall reap also sparingly.

- **Galatians 6:7** Be not deceived; God is not mocked: for whatsoever a man soweth, that shall he also reap. [See Genesis 31:5-9,41,42 for the story of how God helped Jacob collect his due from his selfish father-in-law, Laban.]

- **James 5:1-5** Go to now, ye rich men, weep and howl for your miseries that shall come upon you. [2] Your riches are corrupted, and your garments are motheaten. [3] Your gold and silver is cankered; and the rust of them shall be a witness against you, and shall eat your flesh as it were fire. Ye have heaped treasure together for the Last Days. [4] Behold, the hire of the labourers who have reaped down your fields, which is of you kept back by fraud, crieth: and the cries of them which have reaped are entered into the ears of the Lord of sabaoth. [5] Ye have lived in pleasure on the earth, and been wanton; ye have nourished your hearts, as in a day of slaughter.

3. Selfishness is the cause of many of the world's evils, including war, suffering and misery.

• **Jeremiah 5:26-28** For among My people are found wicked men: they lay wait, as he that setteth snares; they set a trap, they catch men. [27] As a cage is full of birds, so are their houses full of deceit: therefore they are become great, and waxen rich. [28] They are waxen fat, they shine: yea, they overpass the deeds of the wicked: they judge not the cause, the cause of the fatherless, yet they prosper; and the right of the needy do they not judge.

• **Hosea 12:7** He is a merchant, the balances of deceit are in his hand: he loveth to oppress.

• **Micah 6:12** For the rich men thereof are full of violence, and the inhabitants thereof have spoken lies, and their tongue is deceitful in their mouth.

• **1 Timothy 6:9,10** But they that will be rich fall into temptation and a snare, and into many foolish and hurtful lusts, which drown men in destruction and perdition. [10] For the love of money is the root of all evil: which while some coveted after, they have erred from the faith, and pierced themselves through with many sorrows.

• **James 4:1,2a** From whence come wars and fightings among you? Come they not hence, even of your lusts that war in your members? [2a] Ye lust, and have not: ye kill, and desire to have, and cannot obtain: ye fight and war, yet ye have not.

4. Self-centeredness and trying to get your own way yields bad fruit.

• **1 Samuel 2:22-25a and 3:13** [Eli, the priest was judged by God for letting his sons have their own way:] Now Eli was very old, and heard all that his sons did unto all Israel; and how they lay with the women that assembled at the door of the tabernacle of the congregation. [23] And he said unto them, Why do ye such things? For I hear of your evil dealings by all this people. [24] Nay, my sons; for it is no good report that I hear: ye make the Lord's people to transgress. [25a] If one man sin against another, the judge shall judge him: but if a man sin against the Lord, who shall intreat for him? Notwithstanding they hearkened not unto the voice of their father. [3:13] For I have told him that I will judge his house for ever for the iniquity which he knoweth; because his sons made themselves vile, and he restrained them not.

- **1 Kings 1:1a,5,6a** [The bad fruit of King David spoiling his son:] Now King David was old and stricken in years; [5] Then Adonijah the son of Haggith exalted himself, saying, I will be king: and he prepared him chariots and horsemen, and fifty men to run before him. [6a] And his father had not displeased him at any time in saying, Why hast thou done so? [See verses 16-21.]

- **Proverbs 1:30-32** They would none of My counsel: they despised all My reproof. [31] Therefore shall they eat of the fruit of their own way, and be filled with their own devices. [32] For the turning away of the simple shall slay them, and the prosperity of fools shall destroy them.

- **Proverbs 14:14a** The backslider in heart shall be filled with his own ways.

- **Isaiah 65:2** I have spread out My hands all the day unto a rebellious people, which walketh in a way that was not good, after their own thoughts.

- **Jeremiah 7:24** But they hearkened not, nor inclined their ear, but walked in the counsels and in the imagination of their evil heart, and went backward, and not forward.

- **Luke 15:12,13** [The story of the Prodigal Son:] And the younger of them said to his father, Father, give me the portion of goods that falleth to me. And he divided unto them his living. [13] And not many days after the younger son gathered all together, and took his journey into a far country, and there wasted his substance with riotous living.

5. Pursuing our own desires and self-interests won't bring satisfaction.

- **Job 9:4b** Who hath hardened himself against Him, and hath prospered?
- **Job 27:8** For what is the hope of the hypocrite, though he hath gained, when God taketh away his soul?
- **Psalm 106:15** And He gave them their request; but sent leanness into their soul.
- **Proverbs 27:20** Hell and destruction are never full; so the eyes of man are never satisfied.
- **Ecclesiastes 1:8** All things are full of labour; man cannot utter it: the eye is not satisfied with seeing, nor the ear filled with hearing.
- **Ecclesiastes 2:10,11** [A self-indulgent King Solomon said:] And whatsoever mine eyes desired I kept not from them, I withheld not my heart from any joy; for my heart rejoiced in all my labour: and this was my portion of all my labour. [11] Then I looked on all the works that my hands had wrought, and on the labour that I had laboured to do: and, behold, all was vanity and vexation of spirit, and there was no profit under the sun.

6. The true Christian life is one of self-denial—just the opposite of self-centeredness.

- **Luke 9:23** And He said to them all, If any man will come after Me, let him <u>deny</u> himself, and take up his cross daily, and follow Me. [See Titus 2:12.]
- **Luke 14:26,27** If any man come to Me, and hate not his father, and mother, and wife, and children, and brethren, and sisters, yea, and <u>his own life also</u>, he cannot be My disciple. [27] And whosoever doth not bear his cross, and come after Me, cannot be My disciple.
- **Acts 20:24** But none of these things move me, neither count I my life dear unto myself, so that I might finish my course with joy, and

the ministry, which I have received of the Lord Jesus, to testify the gospel of the grace of God.

- **Revelation 12:11** And they overcame him [the Devil] by the blood of the Lamb, and by the word of their testimony; and they loved not their lives unto the death.
- **2 Corinthians 5:15** He died for all, that they which live should <u>not</u> henceforth live unto <u>themselves</u>, but unto Him which died for them, and rose again.
- **Galatians 5:24** And they that are Christ's have crucified the flesh with the affections and lusts.

7. When we put the Lord and others before ourselves, the Lord usually grants us our personal desires.

- **Psalm 34:9,10** O fear the Lord, ye His saints: for there is no want to them that fear Him. [10] The young lions do lack, and suffer hunger: but they that seek the Lord shall not want any good thing.
- **Psalm 37:4** Delight thyself also in the Lord; and He shall give thee the desires of thine heart. [See Psalm 21:2; 145:19.]
- **Psalm 84:11b** No good thing will He withhold from them that walk uprightly.
- **Matthew 6:33** But seek ye first the Kingdom of God, and His righteousness; and all these things shall be added unto you.
- **1 Timothy 6:17** Charge them that are rich in this world, that they be not highminded, nor trust in uncertain riches, but in the living God, who giveth us richly all things to enjoy.

8. The Word warns against using personal charm, motivated by pride, to draw others to yourself or to get your own way. We should rather draw people to the Lord.

- **Proverbs 25:27** It is not good to eat much honey: so for men to search their own glory is not glory.

- **John 5:44** How can ye believe, which receive honour one of another, and seek not the honour that cometh from God only?
- **John 7:18a** He that speaketh of himself seeketh his own glory.
- **1 Corinthians 5:6** Your glorying is not good. Know ye not that a little leaven leaveneth the whole lump?
- **1 Corinthians 6:20** For ye are bought with a price: therefore glorify God in your body, and in your spirit, which are God's.
- **1 Corinthians 10:31,33** Whether therefore ye eat, or drink, or whatsoever ye do, do all to the glory of God. ... [33] Even as I please all men in all things, not seeking mine own profit, but the profit of many, that they may be saved.
- **2 Corinthians 4:5** For we preach not ourselves, but Christ Jesus the Lord; and ourselves your servants for Jesus' sake.
- **1 Thessalonians 2:3-6** For our exhortation was not of deceit, nor of uncleanness, nor in guile: [4] But as we were allowed of God to be put in trust with the Gospel, even so we speak; not as pleasing men, but God, which trieth our hearts. [5] For neither at any time used we flattering words, as ye know, nor a cloke of covetousness; God is witness: [6] Nor of men sought we glory, neither of you, nor yet of others, when we might have been burdensome, as the apostles of Christ.
- **Philippians 2:21** For all seek their own, not the things which are Jesus Christ's.

9. God always blesses unselfishness.

- **Deuteronomy 15:10** Thou shalt surely give him [the poor], and thine heart shall not be grieved when thou givest unto him: because that for this thing the Lord thy God shall bless thee in all thy works, and in all that thou puttest thine hand unto.
- **Proverbs 11:24a-26** There is that scattereth, and yet increaseth. [25] The liberal soul shall be made fat: and he that watereth shall be watered also himself. [26] He that withholdeth corn, the people shall curse him: but blessing shall be upon the head of him that selleth it.

- **Proverbs 13:7b** There is that maketh himself poor, yet hath great riches.
- **Proverbs 14:21b** He that hath mercy on the poor, happy is he.
- **Isaiah 58:10,11** And if thou draw out thy soul to the hungry, and satisfy the afflicted soul; then shall thy light rise in obscurity, and thy darkness be as the noonday: [11] And the Lord shall guide thee continually, and satisfy thy soul in drought, and make fat thy bones: and thou shalt be like a watered garden, and like a spring of water, whose waters fail not.
- **Matthew 6:3,4** But when thou doest alms [give to the needy], let not thy left hand know what thy right hand doeth: [4] That thine alms [giving] may be in secret: and thy Father which seeth in secret Himself shall reward thee openly.
- **Luke 6:38** Give, and it shall be given unto you; good measure, pressed down, and shaken together, and running over, shall men give into your bosom. For with the same measure that ye mete withal it shall be measured to you again.
- **John 12:24,25** Verily, verily, I say unto you, Except a corn of wheat fall into the ground and die, it abideth alone: but if it die, it bringeth forth much fruit. [25] He that loveth his life shall lose it; and he that hateth his life in this world shall keep it unto life eternal.
- **Acts 20:35** I have shewed you all things, how that so labouring ye ought to support the weak, and to remember the words of the Lord Jesus, how He said, It is more blessed to give than to receive.

10. Unselfishness is a cornerstone of Christianity.

- **Romans 15:1-3a** We then that are strong ought to bear the infirmities of the weak, and not to please ourselves. [2] Let every one of us please his neighbour for his good to edification. [3a] For even Christ pleased not Himself.
- **1 Corinthians 10:24** Let no man seek his own, but every man another's wealth.
- **1 Corinthians 13:5b** Charity [love] seeketh not her own.

- **2 Corinthians 5:14a,15** For the love of Christ constraineth us. [15] And that He died for all, that they which live should not henceforth live unto themselves, but unto Him which died for them, and rose again.
- **2 Corinthians 9:7** Every man according as he purposeth in his heart, so let him give; not grudgingly, or of necessity: for God loveth a cheerful giver.
- **Galatians 6:2** Bear ye one another's burdens, and so fulfil the law of Christ.
- **Galatians 6:10** As we have therefore opportunity, let us do good unto all men, especially unto them who are of the household of faith.
- **Philippians 2:4** Look not every man on his own things, but every man also on the things of others.
- **James 2:8** If ye fulfil the royal law according to the Scripture, Thou shalt love thy neighbour as thyself, ye do well.
- **1 John 3:16** Hereby perceive we the love of God, because He laid down His life for us: and we ought to lay down our lives for the brethren.

11. Jesus taught unselfishness by His own loving sample.

- **Mark 10:45** For even the Son of Man came not to be ministered unto, but to minister, and to give His life a ransom for many. [See also Isaiah 53:12; 1 Timothy 2:6a.]
- **John 15:12,13** This is My commandment, That ye love one another, as I have loved you. [13] Greater love hath no man than this, that a man lay down his life for his friends.
- **2 Corinthians 8:9** For ye know the grace of our Lord Jesus Christ, that, though He was rich, yet for your sakes He became poor, that ye through His poverty might be rich.
- **1 John 3:16** Hereby perceive we the love of God, because he laid down his life for us: and we ought to lay down our lives for the brethren.

12. In the Lord's work, commitment and unselfishness go hand-in-hand.

- **Matthew 26:39** And He went a little further, and fell on His face, and prayed, saying, O My Father, if it be possible, let this cup pass from Me: nevertheless not as I will, but as Thou wilt.
- **Jeremiah 42:6** Whether it be good, or whether it be evil [difficult or sacrificial], we will obey the voice of the Lord our God, to whom we send thee; that it may be well with us, when we obey the voice of the Lord our God.
- **Luke 17:10** So likewise ye, when ye shall have done all those things which are commanded you, say, We are unprofitable servants: we have done that which was our duty to do.
- **1 Corinthians 10:33** Even as I please all men in all things, not seeking mine own profit, but the profit of many, that they may be saved.

   [See also 2 Corinthians 5:15; Philippians 3:8; Hebrews 11:24-26.]

13. True Christianity gives sacrificially and calls nothing its own.

- **Matthew 5:42** Give to him that asketh thee, and from him that would borrow of thee turn not thou away.
- **Luke 3:11** He answereth and saith unto them, He that hath two coats, let him impart to him that hath none; and he that hath meat, let him do likewise.
- **Luke 6:30** Give to every man that asketh of thee; and of him that taketh away thy goods ask them not again.
- **Acts 2:44,45** And all that believed were together, and had all things common; [45] And sold their possessions and goods, and parted them to all men, as every man had need.
- **Acts 4:32** And the multitude of them that believed were of one heart and of one soul: neither said any of them that ought of the things which he possessed was his own; but they had all things common.

14. Unselfishness was characterized by many of God's "greats."

• **Genesis 13:9** [When strife arose between the herdsmen of his nephew, Lot, and his own, Abraham wisely offered to divide up their land, giving Lot first choice of the best land:] Is not the whole land before thee? Separate thyself, I pray thee, from me: if thou wilt take the left hand, then I will go to the right; or if thou depart to the right hand, then I will go to the left.

• **Genesis 50:21** [Joseph showed extraordinary kindness to his brothers, who previously had sold him, tried to kill him, and then sold him to Egyptian traders as a slave:] Now therefore fear ye not: I will nourish you, and your little ones. And he comforted them, and spake kindly unto them.

• **1 Samuel 18:4** [Jonathan, the son of King Saul, befriended David and gave his belongings to him:] And Jonathan stripped himself of the robe that was upon him, and gave it to David, and his garments, even to his sword, and to his bow, and to his girdle.

• **1 Kings 17:8-16** [The poor widow of Zarephath shared what was left of her food with Elijah, and was blessed during the drought:] And the Word of the Lord came unto [Elijah], saying, [9] Arise, get thee to Zarephath, ... and dwell there: behold, I have commanded a widow woman there to sustain thee. [10] So he arose and went to Zarephath. And when he came to the gate of the city, behold, the widow woman was there gathering of sticks: and he called to her, and said, Fetch me, I pray thee, a little water in a vessel, that I may drink. [11] And as she was going to fetch it, he called to her, and said, Bring me, I pray thee, a morsel of bread in thine hand. [12] And she said, As the Lord thy God liveth, I have not a cake, but an handful of meal in a barrel, and a little oil in a cruse: and, behold, I am gathering two sticks, that I may go in and dress it for me and my son, that we may eat it, and die. [13] And Elijah said unto her, Fear not; go and do as thou hast said: but make me thereof a little cake <u>first</u>, and bring it unto me, and <u>after</u> make for thee and for thy son. [14] For thus saith the Lord God of Israel, The barrel of meal shall not waste, neither shall the cruse of oil fail, until the day that the Lord sendeth rain upon the earth. [15] And she went and did according to the saying of Elijah: and she, and he, and her house, did eat many days. [16] And the barrel of meal wasted not, neither did the cruse of oil fail, according to the Word of the Lord, which He spake by Elijah.

- **Mark 12:41-44** [The poor widow shared with God unselfishly from her heart all that she had:] And Jesus sat over against the treasury, and beheld how the people cast money into the treasury: and many that were rich cast in much. [42] And there came a certain poor widow, and she threw in two mites, which make a farthing. [43] And He called unto Him His disciples, and saith unto them, Verily I say unto you, That this poor widow hath cast more in, than all they which have cast into the treasury: [44] For all they did cast in of their abundance; but she of her want did cast in all that she had, even all her living.

- **Mark 14:3-9** [The woman who anointed Jesus with an expensive ointment is to be honored:] And being in Bethany in the house of Simon the leper, as He sat at meat, there came a woman having an alabaster box of ointment of spikenard very precious; and she brake the box, and poured it on His head. [4] And there were some that had indignation within themselves, and said, Why was this waste of the ointment made? [5] For it might have been sold for more than three hundred pence, and have been given to the poor. And they murmured against her. [6] And Jesus said, Let her alone; why trouble ye her? She hath wrought a good work on Me. [7] For ye have the poor with you always, and whensoever ye will ye may do them good: but Me ye have not always. [8] She hath done what she could: she is come aforehand to anoint My body to the burying. [9] Verily I say unto you, Wheresoever this Gospel shall be preached throughout the whole world, this also that she hath done shall be spoken of for a memorial

- **Luke 10:29-37** [The Good Samaritan is an example to us all of unselfish kindness shown to a stranger:] But he [a religious lawyer], willing to justify himself, said unto Jesus, And who is my neighbour

[30] And Jesus answering said, A certain man went down from Jerusalem to Jericho, and fell among thieves, which stripped him of his raiment, and wounded him, and departed, leaving him half dead. [31] And by chance there came down a certain priest that way: and when he saw him, he passed by on the other side. [32] And likewise a Levite, when he was at the place, came and looked on him, and passed by on the other side. [33] But a certain Samaritan, as he journeyed, came where he was: and when he saw him, he had compassion on him, [34] And went to him, and bound up his wounds, pouring in oil and wine, and set him on his own beast, and brought him to an inn, and took care of him. [35] And on the morrow when he departed, he took out two pence, and gave them to the host, and said unto him, Take care of him; and whatsoever thou spendest more, when I come again, I will repay thee. [36] Which now of these three, thinkest thou, was neighbour unto him that fell among the thieves? [37] And he said, He that shewed mercy on him. Then said Jesus unto him, Go, and do thou likewise.

- **Romans 16:4** [Paul said of Priscilla and Aquila:] Who have for my life laid down their own necks: unto whom not only I give thanks, but also all the churches of the Gentiles.

- **Philippians 2:30** [Epaphroditus:] Because for the work of Christ he was nigh unto death, not regarding his life, to supply your lack of service toward me.

SHYNESS AND TIMIDITY

Definition: Shyness and timidity are the tendency to be self-conscious or uneasy when in the company of others; bashfulness.

1. Some causes of shyness:

- **Genesis 3:10,11** [Fear of exposure of wrongdoing:] And he [Adam] said, I heard Thy voice [God's] in the garden, and I was afraid, because I was naked; and I hid myself. [11] And He said, Who told thee that thou wast naked? Hast thou eaten of the tree, whereof I commanded thee that thou shouldest not eat?
- **Ezra 9:6** [Shame and guilt for our sins:] And said, O my God, I am ashamed and blush to lift up my face to Thee, my God: for our iniquities are increased over our head, and our trespass is grown up unto the heavens.
- **Job 23:15,16** [Being in awe of God:] Therefore am I troubled at His presence: when I consider, I am afraid of Him. [16] For God maketh my heart soft, and the Almighty troubleth me.
- **Proverbs 29:25a** [Fear of man:] The fear of man bringeth a snare. [See also Isaiah 51:12.]
- **Ezekiel 2:6** [Negative peer pressure:] And thou, son of man, be not afraid of them, neither be afraid of their words, though briers and thorns be with thee, and thou dost dwell among scorpions: be not afraid of their words, nor be dismayed at their looks, though they be a rebellious house.
- **Matthew 25:24,25** [Lack of faith:] Then he which had received the one talent came and said, Lord, I knew Thee that Thou art an hard man, reaping where Thou hast not sown, and gathering where Thou hast not strawed: [25] And I was afraid, and went and hid Thy talent in the earth: lo, there Thou hast that is Thine.
- **2 Corinthians 10:1** [The difficulty of public speaking as opposed to writing:] Now I Paul myself beseech you by the meekness and gentleness of Christ, who in presence am base [timid] among you, but being absent am bold toward you.

- **2 Timothy 1:7,8a** [Spirit of fear:] For God hath not given us the spirit of fear; but of power, and of love, and of a sound mind. [8a] Be not thou therefore ashamed of the testimony of our Lord, nor of me His prisoner.
- **1 John 4:18** [Lack of unselfish love for others, which causes self-consciousness:] There is no fear in love; but perfect love casteth out fear: because fear hath torment. He that feareth is not made perfect in love.

2. Since shyness often comes from <u>fear</u>, faith is the cure, which comes through reading God's Word and being filled with His Spirit.

- **John 6:63** It is the Spirit that quickeneth; the flesh profiteth nothing: the Words that I speak unto you, they are spirit, and they are life.
- **John 7:38,39a** He that believeth on Me, as the Scripture hath said, out of his belly shall flow rivers of living water. [39a] (But this spake He of the Spirit, which they that believe on Him should receive.)
- **Acts 4:13** Now when they [the religious leaders] saw the boldness of Peter and John, and perceived that they were unlearned and ignorant men, they marvelled; and they took knowledge of them, that they had been with Jesus.
- **Romans 10:17** So then faith cometh by hearing, and hearing by the Word of God.
- **Ephesians 5:18-20** [Just get full of Jesus and He will help you to forget yourself:] And be not drunk with wine, wherein is excess; but be filled with the Spirit. [19] Speaking to yourselves in psalms and hymns and spiritual songs, singing and making melody in your heart to the Lord; [20] Giving thanks always for all things unto God and the Father in the name of our Lord Jesus Christ.

3. Don't be self-conscious, be Christ-conscious!

- **Isaiah 26:3** Thou wilt keep him in perfect peace, whose mind is stayed on Thee: because he trusteth in Thee.

- **Romans 7:18a,24,25a** For I know that in me (that is, in my flesh,) dwelleth no good thing. ... [24] O wretched man that I am! Who shall deliver me from the body of this death? [25a] I thank God through Jesus Christ our Lord. So then with the mind I myself serve the law of God.
- **Romans 8:15** For ye have not received the spirit of bondage again to fear; but ye have received the Spirit of adoption, whereby we cry, Abba, Father.
- **1 Corinthians 2:2** For I determined not to know any thing among you, save Jesus Christ, and Him crucified.
- **1 Corinthians 2:16** For who hath known the mind of the Lord, that he may instruct Him? But we have the mind of Christ.
- **Galatians 2:20** I am crucified with Christ: nevertheless I live; yet not I, but Christ liveth in me: and the life which I now live in the flesh I live by the faith of the Son of God, who loved me, and gave Himself for me.
- **Philippians 2:5** Let this mind be in you, which was also in Christ Jesus.
- **Philippians 3:8-10** Yea doubtless, and I count all things but loss for the excellency of the knowledge of Christ Jesus my Lord: for whom I have suffered the loss of all things, and do count them but dung, that I may win Christ, [9] And be found in Him, not having mine own righteousness, which is of the law, but that which is through the faith of Christ, the righteousness which is of God by faith: [10] That I may know Him, and the power of His resurrection, and the fellowship of His sufferings, being made conformable unto His death.

4. If we are walking in love and seeking to please Jesus, then we shouldn't worry about what others think or say about us.

- **Romans 1:16a** For I am not ashamed of the Gospel of Christ: for it is the power of God unto salvation to every one that believeth.

- **Galatians 1:10** For do I now persuade men, or God? Or do I seek to please men? for if I yet pleased men, I should not be the servant of Christ.
- **Ephesians 6:6** Not with eyeservice, as menpleasers; but as the servants of Christ, doing the will of God from the heart.
- **1 Thessalonians 2:2,4** But even after that we had suffered before, and were shamefully entreated, as ye know, at Philippi, we were bold in our God to speak unto you the Gospel of God with much contention. … [4] But as we were allowed of God to be put in trust with the Gospel, even so we speak; not as pleasing men, but God, which trieth our hearts.
- **Hebrews 13:6** So that we may boldly say, The Lord is my Helper, and I will not fear what man shall do unto me.

5. Get busy sharing the Lord and His love with others and you will soon find that He has delivered you from shyness!

- **Psalm 119:46** I will speak of Thy testimonies also before kings, and will not be ashamed.
- **Matthew 5:14-16** Ye are the light of the world. A city that is set on an hill cannot be hid. [15] Neither do men light a candle, and put it under a bushel, but on a candlestick; and it giveth light unto all that are in the house. [16] Let your light so shine before men, that they may see your good works, and glorify your Father which is in Heaven.
- **Ephesians 6:19,20** And for me, that utterance may be given unto me, that I may open my mouth boldly, to make known the mystery of the Gospel, [20] For which I am an ambassador in bonds: that therein I may speak boldly, as I ought to speak.

6. The Bible gives us thrilling examples of men, women and even children whom the Lord helped overcome their shyness so they could go on to do great things for Him.

- **Exodus 4:10-12** [If Moses hadn't yielded his shyness to the Lord, he never would have been able to lead the Exodus:] And Moses said unto the Lord, O my Lord, I am not eloquent, neither heretofore, nor since Thou hast spoken unto Thy servant: but I am slow of speech, and of a slow tongue. [11] And the Lord said unto him, Who hath made man's mouth? Or who maketh the dumb, or deaf, or the seeing, or the blind? Have not I the Lord? [12] Now therefore go, and I will be with thy mouth, and teach thee what thou shalt say.

- **Ruth 3:3-5** [If Ruth had been too shy to act upon Naomi's counsel to present herself to Boaz, how could she have become a forebear of David and Jesus?] Wash thyself therefore, and anoint thee, and put thy raiment upon thee, and get thee down to the [threshing] floor: but make not thyself known unto the man, until he shall have done eating and drinking. [4] And it shall be, when he lieth down, that thou shalt mark the place where he shall lie, and thou shalt go in, and uncover his feet, and lay thee down; and he will tell thee what thou shalt do. [5] And she said unto her, All that thou sayest unto me I will do.

- **1 Samuel 10:21b,22** [Though young Saul was head and shoulders above all others, he was so shy that when Samuel sought him to anoint him king over Israel, Saul hid among the baggage:] And Saul the son of Kish was taken: and when they sought him, he could not be found. [22] Therefore they enquired of the Lord further, if the man should yet come thither. And the Lord answered, Behold, he hath hid himself among the stuff. [See also 1 Samuel 15:17.]

- **1 King 3:7-12** [King Solomon:] And now, O Lord my God, Thou hast made Thy servant king instead of David my father: and I am but a little child: I know not how to go out or come in. [8] And Thy servant is in the midst of Thy people which Thou hast chosen, a great people, that cannot be numbered nor counted for multitude. [9] Give therefore Thy servant an understanding heart to judge Thy people, that I may discern between good and bad: for who is able to judge this Thy so great a people? [10] And the speech pleased the Lord, that Solomon had asked this thing. [11] And God said unto him, Because thou hast asked this thing, and hast not asked for thyself long life; neither hast asked riches for thyself, nor hast asked the life of thine enemies; but hast asked for thyself understanding to discern judgment; [12] Behold, I have done according to thy words: lo, I have given thee a wise and an understanding heart; so that there was none like thee before thee, neither after thee shall any arise like unto thee.

- **2 Kings 5:1-3** [One little Hebrew maid wasn't too shy to speak up for the Lord, and as a result the commander of the Syrian army, Naaman, got healed, and God was glorified:] Now Naaman, captain of the host of the king of Syria, was a great man with his master, and honourable, because by him the Lord had given deliverance unto Syria: he was also a mighty man in valour, but he was a leper. [2] And the Syrians had gone out by companies, and had brought away captive out of the land of Israel a little maid; and she waited on Naaman's wife. [3] And she said unto her mistress, Would God my lord were with the prophet that is in Samaria! For he would recover him of his leprosy.

- **Jeremiah 1:6-9** [Young Jeremiah forsook his shyness, and God used him mightily to boldly warn the wicked nation:] Then said I, Ah, Lord God! Behold, I cannot speak: for I am a child. [7] But the Lord said unto me, Say not, I am a child: for thou shalt go to all that I shall send thee, and whatsoever I command thee thou shalt speak. [8] Be not afraid of their faces: for I am with thee to deliver thee, saith the Lord. [9] Then the Lord put forth His hand, and touched my mouth. And the Lord said unto me, Behold, I have put My words in thy mouth.

- **John 6:5-11** [If the little lad had been too shy to approach the disciples with his humble offering, the Lord may have never had the opportunity to do the miracle:] When Jesus then lifted up His eyes, and saw a great company come unto Him, He saith unto Philip, Whence shall we buy bread, that these may eat? [6] And this He said to prove him: for He Himself knew what He would do. [7] Philip answered Him, Two hundred pennyworth of bread is not sufficient for them, that every one of them may take a little. [8] One of His disciples, Andrew, Simon Peter's brother, saith unto Him, [9] There is a lad here, which hath five barley loaves, and two small fishes: but what are they among so many? [10] And Jesus said, Make the men sit down. Now there was much grass in the place. So the men sat down, in number about five thousand. [11] And Jesus took the loaves; and when He had given thanks, He distributed to the disciples, and the disciples to them that were set down; and likewise of the fishes as much as they would.

7. Boldness is a gift of God, so ask for it and by faith you can receive it!

- **Acts 1:8** But ye shall receive power, after that the Holy Ghost is come upon you: and ye shall be witnesses unto Me both in Jerusalem, and in all Judaea, and in Samaria, and unto the uttermost part of the earth.
- **Acts 4:29-31** [The apostles prayed for boldness and the Lord miraculously answered:] And now, Lord, behold their threatenings: and grant unto Thy servants, that with all boldness they may speak Thy Word, [30] By stretching forth Thine hand to heal; and that signs and wonders may be done by the name of Thy Holy Child Jesus. [31] And when they had prayed, the place was shaken where they were assembled together; and they were all filled with the Holy Ghost, and they spake the Word of God with boldness.
- **2 Corinthians 3:12** Seeing then that we have such hope, we use great plainness [boldness] of speech.
- **Ephesians 3:12** In whom [Jesus] we have boldness and access with confidence by the faith of Him.

• **Hebrews 4:15,16** [Boldly ask for boldness!] For we have not an High Priest which cannot be touched with the feeling of our infirmities; but was in all points tempted like as we are, yet without sin. [16] Let us therefore come boldly unto the throne of grace, that we may obtain mercy, and find grace to help in time of need.

SORROW

Definition: Sadness felt after a loss (as of something loved), often accompanied by feelings of guilt and regret; mental distress caused by loss or disappointment; the opposite of joy.

1. No matter what loss we may suffer, we'll <u>always</u> have Jesus!

- **Deuteronomy 33:27a** The eternal God is thy refuge, and underneath are the everlasting arms.
- **Psalm 27:10** When my father and my mother forsake me, then the Lord will take me up.
- **Psalm 34:22** The Lord redeemeth the soul of His servants: and none of them that trust in Him shall be desolate.
- **Psalm 142:4,5** I looked on my right hand, and beheld, but there was no man that would know me: refuge failed me; no man cared for my soul. ⁵ I cried unto Thee, O Lord: I said, Thou art my refuge and my portion in the land of the living.
- **Isaiah 54:5,6** For thy Maker is thine husband; the Lord of hosts is His name; and thy Redeemer the Holy One of Israel; The God of the whole earth shall He be called. ⁶ For the Lord hath called thee as a woman forsaken and grieved in spirit, and a wife of youth, when thou wast refused, saith thy God.
- **Isaiah 54:10** For the mountains shall depart, and the hills be removed; but My kindness shall not depart from thee, neither shall the covenant of My peace be removed, saith the Lord that hath mercy on thee.
- **Matthew 28:20b** Lo, I [Jesus] am with you alway, even unto the end of the world. Amen.
- **John 14:18** I [Jesus] will not leave you comfortless: I will come to you.
- **2 Timothy 4:16a,17a** At my first answer no man stood with me, but all men forsook me: ... ¹⁷ᵃ Notwithstanding the Lord stood with me, and strengthened me.
- **Hebrews 13:5b** I [Jesus] will never leave thee, nor forsake thee.

2. God understands exactly what you're going through.

- **Exodus 3:7** And the Lord said, I have surely seen the affliction of My people which are in Egypt, and have heard their cry by reason of their taskmasters; for I know their sorrows.
- **Psalm 103:13,14** Like as a father pitieth his children, so the Lord pitieth them that fear Him. [14] For He knoweth our frame; He remembereth that we are dust.
- **Isaiah 53:3a,4a** He is despised and rejected of men; a man of sorrows, and acquainted with grief: … [4a] Surely He hath borne our griefs, and carried our sorrows.
- **Isaiah 63:9** In all their affliction He was afflicted, and the angel of His presence saved them: in His love and in His pity He redeemed them; and He bare them, and carried them all the days of old.
- **Hebrews 4:15** For we have not an High Priest which cannot be touched with the feeling of our infirmities; but He [Jesus] was in all points tempted like as we are, yet without sin. [See also Hebrews 2:18.]

3. The Lord knows every tear you've shed.

- **2 Kings 20:5b** I [God] have heard thy prayer, I have seen thy tears: behold, I will heal thee.
- **Psalm 6:6,9** I am weary with my groaning; all the night make I my bed to swim; I water my couch with my tears. … [9] The Lord hath heard my supplication; the Lord will receive my prayer.
- **Psalm 39:12a** Hear my prayer, O Lord, and give ear unto my cry; hold not Thy peace at my tears.
- **Psalm 56:8b** Put Thou my tears into Thy bottle: are they not in Thy Book?
- **Psalm 66:16,17,19** Come and hear, all ye that fear God, and I will declare what He hath done for my soul. [17] I cried unto Him with my mouth, and He was extolled with my tongue. … [19] But verily God hath heard me; He hath attended to the voice of my prayer.

4. Unhappiness can be the fruit of getting out of touch with the Lord.

- **Genesis 3:16,17** [Sorrow was part of God's punishment for the original sins of Adam and Eve:] Unto the woman He said, I will greatly multiply thy sorrow and thy conception; in sorrow thou shalt bring forth children; and thy desire shall be to thy husband, and he shall rule over thee. [17] And unto Adam He said, Because thou hast hearkened unto the voice of thy wife, and hast eaten of the tree, of which I commanded thee, saying, Thou shalt not eat of it: cursed is the ground for thy sake; in sorrow shalt thou eat of it all the days of thy life.

- **Leviticus 26:14-16a** [Sorrow was part of God's punishment on the disobedient. The Lord told His people:] But if ye will not hearken unto Me, and will not do all these commandments; [15] And if ye shall despise My statutes, or if your soul abhor My judgments, so that ye will not do all My commandments, but that ye break My covenant: [16a] I also will do this unto you; I will even appoint over you terror, consumption [wasting disease], and the burning ague [fever], that shall consume the eyes, and cause sorrow of heart. [See also Deuteronomy 28:65.]

- **Psalm 16:4a** Their sorrows shall be multiplied that hasten after another god.

- **Psalm 32:10** Many sorrows shall be to the wicked: but he that trusteth in the Lord, mercy shall compass him about.

- **Proverbs 23:29,30** [Alcohol abuse can bring much sorrow:] Who hath woe? Who hath sorrow? Who hath contentions? Who hath babbling? Who hath wounds without cause? Who hath redness of eyes? [30] They that tarry long at the wine; they that go to seek mixed wine [strong drink].

- **Proverbs 29:18** Where there is no vision, the people perish: but he that keepeth the law, happy is he.

• **Jeremiah 30:15** Why criest thou for thine affliction? Thy sorrow is incurable for the multitude of thine iniquity: because thy sins were increased, I [the Lord] have done these things unto thee.

5. The sorrow of the world [sorrow without hope] is death!

• **Proverbs 12:25** Heaviness in the heart of man maketh it stoop: but a good word maketh it glad.
• **Proverbs 15:13** A merry heart maketh a cheerful countenance: but by sorrow of the heart the spirit is broken.
• **Proverbs 17:22** A merry heart doeth good like a medicine: but a broken spirit drieth the bones.
• **Proverbs 18:14** The spirit of a man will sustain his infirmity; but a wounded spirit who can bear?
• **2 Corinthians 2:7** [Paul encouraged the brethren to forgive a man who'd repented of a serious sin, so that he wouldn't be overcome by sorrow:] So that contrariwise ye ought rather to forgive him, and comfort him, lest perhaps such a one should be swallowed up with overmuch sorrow.
• **2 Corinthians 7:10** [Godly sorrow bears good fruit, but worldly sorrow doesn't.] For godly sorrow worketh repentance to salvation not to be repented of [regretted]: but the sorrow of the world worketh death.
• **1 Thessalonians 4:13** [Paul wrote:] But I would ... that ye sorrow not, even as others which have no hope.

6. Examples of sorrow as a result of sin:

• **Genesis 4:13** [After Cain killed his brother Abel, he murmured against God's punishment.] And Cain said unto the Lord, My punishment is greater than I can bear.
• **1 Kings 21:4** [When Naboth refused to sell his family's land to selfish King Ahab:] Ahab came into his house heavy and displeased because of the word which Naboth the Jezreelite had spoken to him: for he had said, I will not give thee the inheritance of my

fathers. And he laid him down upon his bed, and turned away his face, and would eat no bread.

- **Matthew 27:3-5** Then Judas, which had betrayed Him, when he saw that He was condemned, repented himself, and brought again the thirty pieces of silver to the chief priests and elders, [4] Saying, I have sinned in that I have betrayed the innocent blood. And they said, What is that to us? See thou to that. [5] And he cast down the pieces of silver in the temple, and departed, and went and hanged himself.

- **Luke 18:22-24** [When Jesus told the rich young ruler to forsake his riches to the poor, he refused and went away sorrowful:] Now when Jesus heard these things, He said unto him, Yet lackest thou one thing: sell all that thou hast, and distribute unto the poor, and thou shalt have treasure in Heaven: and come, follow Me. [23] And when he heard this, he was very sorrowful: for he was very rich. [24] And when Jesus saw that he was very sorrowful, He said, How hardly shall they that have riches enter into the Kingdom of God! [For the whole story see verses 18-25.]

- **1 Timothy 6:10** [Pursuit of worldly wealth brings sorrow.] For the love of money is the root of all evil: which while some coveted after, they have erred from the faith, and pierced themselves through with many sorrows.

7. God sometimes allows sorrow in our lives for a reason.

- **Ecclesiastes 3:1,4** To every thing there is a season, and a time to every purpose under the heaven: [4] A time to weep, and a time to laugh; a time to mourn, and a time to dance.

- **Ecclesiastes 7:3,4** [To make us wiser:] Sorrow is better than laughter: for by the sadness of the countenance the heart is made better. [4] The heart of the wise is in the house of mourning; but the heart of fools is in the house of mirth.

- **Romans 8:28** [To somehow bring us good:] And we know that all things work together for good to them that love God, to them who are the called according to His purpose.
- **Psalm 119:50,67** [To drive us to His Word:] This is my comfort in my affliction: for Thy Word hath quickened me. [67] Before I was afflicted I went astray: but now have I kept Thy Word.
- **2 Corinthians 1:4** [To teach us compassion and make us a greater blessing to others:] Who [God] comforteth us in all our tribulation, that we may be able to comfort them which are in any trouble, by the comfort wherewith we ourselves are comforted of God.
- **2 Corinthians 7:9-11** [To bring us to repentance:] Now I rejoice, not that ye were made sorry, but that ye sorrowed to repentance: for ye were made sorry after a godly manner, that ye might receive damage by us in nothing. [10] For godly sorrow worketh repentance to salvation not to be repented of: but the sorrow of the world worketh death. [11] For behold this selfsame thing, that ye sorrowed after a godly sort, what carefulness it wrought in you, yea, what clearing of yourselves, yea, what indignation, yea, what fear, yea, what vehement desire, yea, what zeal, yea, what revenge! In all things ye have approved yourselves to be clear in this matter. [See also James 4:8-10.]
- **2 Timothy 2:12a** [To prepare us for greater service:] If we suffer, we shall also reign with Him.
- **James 1:2-4** [To teach us patience:] My brethren, count it all joy when ye fall into divers temptations; [3] Knowing this, that the trying of your faith worketh patience. [4] But let patience have her perfect work, that ye may be perfect and entire, wanting [lacking] nothing.
- **1 Peter 1:6-8** [To try us, and to draw us closer to Jesus:] Wherein ye greatly rejoice, though now for a season, if need be, ye are in heaviness through manifold temptations: [7] That the trial of your faith, being much more precious than of gold that perisheth, though it be tried with fire, might be found unto praise and honour and glory at the appearing of Jesus Christ: [8] Whom having not seen, ye

love; in whom, though now ye see Him not, yet believing, ye rejoice with joy unspeakable and full of glory.

- **1 Peter 5:10** [To strengthen us:] But the God of all grace, who hath called us unto His eternal glory by Christ Jesus, after that ye have suffered a while, make you perfect, stablish, strengthen, settle you.

8. Trust God through your sorrow; example of King David.

- **1 Samuel 30:6** [When King David and his men were away, his town was pillaged and their wives and children were kidnapped. When he returned his people had turned against him.] And David was greatly distressed; for the people spake of stoning him, because the soul of all the people was grieved, every man for his sons and for his daughters: but David encouraged himself in the Lord his God. [And God blessed David and helped him retrieve all that had been taken. See the whole chapter for the full story.]
- **Psalm 13:2,5** How long shall I take counsel in my soul, having sorrow in my heart daily? How long shall mine enemy be exalted over me? ^{5} But I have trusted in Thy mercy; my heart shall rejoice in Thy salvation.
- **Psalm 38:6,9,15,17,18,21,22** I am troubled; I am bowed down greatly; I go mourning all the day long. ^{9} Lord, all my desire is before Thee; and my groaning is not hid from Thee. ^{15} For in Thee, O Lord, do I hope: Thou wilt hear, O Lord my God. ^{17} For I am ready to halt, and my sorrow is continually before me. ^{18} For I will declare mine iniquity; I will be sorry for my sin. ^{21} Forsake me not, O Lord: O my God, be not far from me. ^{22} Make haste to help me, O Lord my salvation.
- **Psalm 42:9,11** I will say unto God my Rock, Why hast thou forgotten me? Why go I mourning because of the oppression of the enemy? ^{11} Why art thou cast down, O my soul? And why art thou disquieted within me? Hope thou in God: for I shall yet praise Him, who is the health of my countenance, and my God.

- **Psalm 55:2,4,6,7,8,22** Attend unto me, and hear me: I mourn in my complaint, and make a noise. [4] My heart is sore pained within me: and the terrors of death are fallen upon me. [6] And I said, Oh that I had wings like a dove! For then would I fly away, and be at rest. [7] Lo, then would I wander far off, and remain in the wilderness. Selah. [8] I would hasten my escape from the windy storm and tempest. [22] Cast thy burden upon the Lord, and He shall sustain thee: He shall never suffer the righteous to be moved.
- **Psalm 69:29-31** But I am poor and sorrowful: let Thy salvation, O God, set me up on high. [30] I will praise the name of God with a song, and will magnify Him with thanksgiving. [31] This also shall please the Lord better than an ox or bullock [given in sacrifice] that hath horns and hoofs.

9. The Lord promises special care for the brokenhearted.

- **Psalm 51:17** The sacrifices of God are a broken spirit: a broken and a contrite heart, O God, Thou wilt not despise.
- **Psalm 71:20,21** Thou, which hast shewed me great and sore troubles, shalt quicken me again, and shalt bring me up again from the depths of the earth. [21] Thou shalt increase my greatness, and comfort me on every side.
- **Psalm 147:3** He healeth the broken in heart, and bindeth up their wounds.
- **Isaiah 30:19** For the people shall dwell in Zion at Jerusalem: thou shalt weep no more: He will be very gracious unto thee at the voice of thy cry; when He shall hear it, He will answer thee.
- **Isaiah 57:15** For thus saith the High and Lofty One that inhabiteth eternity, whose name is Holy; I dwell in the high and holy place, with him also that is of a contrite and humble spirit, to revive the spirit of the humble, and to revive the heart of the contrite ones.
- **Isaiah 61:1-3** The Spirit of the Lord God is upon Me; because the Lord hath anointed Me to preach good tidings unto the meek; He hath sent Me to bind up the brokenhearted, to proclaim liberty to

the captives, and the opening of the prison to them that are bound; [2] To proclaim the acceptable year of the Lord, and the day of vengeance of our God; to comfort all that mourn; [3] To appoint unto them that mourn in Zion, to give unto them beauty for ashes, the oil of joy for mourning, the garment of praise for the spirit of heaviness; that they might be called trees of righteousness, the planting of the Lord, that He might be glorified.

- **Ezekiel 34:16a** I will seek that which was lost, and bring again that which was driven away, and will bind up that which was broken, and will strengthen that which was sick.
- **Jeremiah 31:12** Therefore they shall come and sing in the height of Zion, and shall flow together to the goodness of the Lord, for wheat, and for wine, and for oil, and for the young of the flock and of the herd: and their soul shall be as a watered garden; and they shall not sorrow any more at all.
- **Matthew 5:4** Blessed are they that mourn: for they shall be comforted. [See also Luke 6:21.]

10. Sorrow will give way to joy.

- **Job 11:16** Thou shalt forget thy misery, and remember it as waters that pass away.
- **Psalm 30:5,11** For His anger endureth but a moment; in His favour is life: weeping may endure for a night, but joy cometh in the morning. [11] Thou hast turned for me my mourning into dancing: Thou hast put off my sackcloth, and girded me with gladness.
- **Psalm 126:5,6** They that sow in tears shall reap in joy. [6] He that goeth forth and weepeth, bearing precious seed, shall doubtless come again with rejoicing, bringing his sheaves with him.
- **Psalm 127:2** It is vain for you to rise up early, to sit up late, to eat the bread of sorrows: for so He giveth His beloved sleep.
- **Isaiah 49:13** Sing, O Heavens; and be joyful, O earth; and break forth into singing, O mountains: for the Lord hath comforted His people, and will have mercy upon His afflicted.

- **Isaiah 54:11** O thou afflicted, tossed with tempest, and not comforted, behold, I will lay thy stones with fair colours, and lay thy foundations with sapphires.
- **Luke 6:21b** Blessed are ye that weep now: for ye shall laugh.
- **John 16:20b** Ye shall be sorrowful, but your sorrow shall be turned into joy.

11. Earth has no sorrow that Heaven cannot heal!

- **Isaiah 14:3a** And it shall come to pass in the day that the Lord shall give thee rest from thy sorrow, and from thy fear.
- **Isaiah 25:8a** He will swallow up death in victory; and the Lord God will wipe away tears from off all faces.
- **Isaiah 35:10** And the ransomed of the Lord shall return, and come to Zion with songs and everlasting joy upon their heads: they shall obtain joy and gladness, and sorrow and sighing shall flee away. [See also 51:11.]
- **Isaiah 60:20** Thy sun shall no more go down; neither shall thy moon withdraw itself: for the Lord shall be thine everlasting light, and the days of thy mourning shall be ended.
- **Luke 12:32** Fear not, little flock; for it is your Father's good pleasure to give you the Kingdom.
- **Luke 16:19-22a,25** There was a certain rich man, which was clothed in purple and fine linen, and fared sumptuously every day: [20] And there was a certain beggar named Lazarus, which was laid at his gate, full of sores, [21] And desiring to be fed with the crumbs which fell from the rich man's table: moreover the dogs came and licked his sores. ... [22a] And it came to pass, that the beggar died, and was carried by the angels into Abraham's bosom. ... [25] But Abraham said [to the selfish rich man who was in Hell], Son, remember that thou in thy lifetime receivedst thy good things, and likewise Lazarus evil things: but now he is comforted, and thou art tormented.
- **John 16:21,22** A woman when she is in travail hath sorrow, because her hour is come: but as soon as she is delivered of the

child, she remembereth no more the anguish, for joy that a man is born into the world. [22] And ye now therefore have sorrow: but I will see you again, and your heart shall rejoice, and your joy no man taketh from you.

- **Romans 8:18** For I reckon that the sufferings of this present time are not worthy to be compared with the glory which shall be revealed in us.

- **2 Corinthians 1:7** And our hope of you is stedfast, knowing, that as ye are partakers of the sufferings, so shall ye be also of the consolation.

- **2 Corinthians 4:17** For our light affliction, which is but for a moment, worketh for us a far more exceeding and eternal weight of glory.

- **2 Timothy 2:12a** If we suffer, we shall also reign with Him.

- **Revelation 7:17** For the Lamb which is in the midst of the throne shall feed them, and shall lead them unto living fountains of waters: and God shall wipe away all tears from their eyes.

- **Revelation 21:4** And God shall wipe away all tears from their eyes; and there shall be no more death, neither sorrow, nor crying, neither shall there be any more pain: for the former things are passed away.

TOLERANCE OF OTHERS

Definition: Willingness or ability to accept the views, beliefs, practices, etc., of others that differ from one's own; freedom from bigotry (bias, discrimination) or prejudice. In the Bible, long-suffering, patience, and forbearance are all closely related to tolerance of others.

1. Being tolerant means being loving and considerate of others who differ from us.

- **Matthew 5:43-47** Ye have heard that it hath been said, Thou shalt love thy neighbour, and hate thine enemy. [44] But I say unto you, love your enemies, bless them that curse you, do good to them that hate you, and pray for them which despitefully use you, and persecute you; [45] That ye may be the children of your Father which is in Heaven: for He maketh His sun to rise on the evil and on the good, and sendeth rain on the just and on the unjust. [46] For if ye love them which love you, what reward have ye? Do not even the publicans the same? [47] And if ye salute your brethren only, what do ye more than others? Do not even the publicans so?
- **Romans 12:18** If it be possible, as much as lieth in you, live peaceably with all men. [See also Psalm 34:14.]
- **Romans 14:2-6** [Paul's teachings on tolerance:] For one believeth that he may eat all things: another, who is weak, eateth herbs. [3] Let not him that eateth despise him that eateth not; and let not him which eateth not judge him that eateth: for God hath received him. [4] Who art thou that judgest another man's servant? To his own master he standeth or falleth. Yea, he shall be holden up: for God is able to make him stand. [5] One man esteemeth one day above another: another esteemeth every day alike. Let every man be fully persuaded in his own mind. [There are times when we need to simply "agree to disagree" on smaller matters.] [6] He that regardeth the day, regardeth it unto the Lord; and he that regardeth not the day, to the Lord he doth not regard it. He that eateth, eateth to the

Lord, for he giveth God thanks; and he that eateth not, to the Lord
he eateth not, and giveth God thanks.

- **1 Corinthians 3:1-5** [Being intolerant of the differences of others
can reveal a lack of maturity.] And I, brethren, could not speak unto
you as unto spiritual, but as unto carnal, even as unto babes in
Christ. [2] I have fed you with milk, and not with meat: for hitherto ye
were not able to bear it, neither yet now are ye able. [3] For ye are yet
carnal: for whereas there is among you envying, and strife, and
divisions, are ye not carnal, and walk as men? [4] For while one saith,
I am of Paul; and another, I am of Apollos; are ye not carnal? [5] Who
then is Paul, and who is Apollos, but ministers by whom ye
believed, even as the Lord gave to every man?

- **Philippians 3:15** [With some differences of opinion, sometimes we
just need to let the Lord show others whether they are right or
wrong.] Let us therefore, as many as be perfect [mature], be thus
minded: and if in any thing ye be otherwise minded, God shall
reveal even this unto you.

- **1 Thessalonians 5:15** See that none render evil for evil unto any
man; but ever follow that which is good, both among yourselves,
and to all men.

- **Hebrews 12:14** Follow peace with all men, and holiness, without
which no man shall see the Lord.

2. Being tolerant means being patient and forgiving of others' errors.

- **Matthew 18:21,22** Then came Peter to Him, and said, Lord, how oft
shall my brother sin against me, and I forgive him? till seven times?
[22] Jesus saith unto him, I say not unto thee, Until seven times: but,
Until seventy times seven.

- **Luke 17:4** And if he trespass against thee seven times in a day, and
seven times in a day turn again to thee, saying, I repent; thou shalt
forgive him.

- **Romans 15:5** [Being mindful of God's patience with our errors and sins helps us be tolerant of others.] Now the God of patience and consolation grant you to be likeminded one toward another according to Christ Jesus.

- **1 Corinthians 13:4a,7** Charity [love] suffereth long, and is kind. … [7] Beareth all things, believeth all things, hopeth all things, endureth all things.

- **2 Corinthians 6:4,6** [Good leaders possess great patience and tolerance of others.] But in all things approving ourselves as the ministers of God, in much patience, in afflictions, in necessities, in distresses, … [6] By pureness, by knowledge, by longsuffering, by kindness, by the Holy Ghost, by love unfeigned [sincere].

- **Ephesians 4:1b,2** Walk worthy of the vocation wherewith ye are called, [2] With all lowliness and meekness, with longsuffering, forbearing one another in love.

- **Colossians 3:12,13** Put on therefore, as the elect of God, holy and beloved, bowels of mercies, kindness, humbleness of mind, meekness, longsuffering; [13] Forbearing one another, and forgiving one another, if any man have a quarrel against any: even as Christ forgave you, so also do ye.

3. Being tolerant means being understanding with those who are weaker.

- **Romans 14:1** [We are encouraged to tolerate the weaknesses of one another, except when it comes to speaking doubt and sowing discord.] Him that is weak in the faith receive ye, but not to doubtful disputations. [See also Job 4:3,4.]

- **Romans 15:1,2** We then that are strong ought to bear the infirmities of the weak, and not to please ourselves. Let every one of us please his neighbour for his good to edification.

- **Galatians 6:1** Brethren, if a man be overtaken in a fault, ye which are spiritual, restore such an one in the spirit of meekness; considering thyself, lest thou also be tempted.

- **1 Corinthians 10:23,24** All things are lawful for me, but all things are not expedient: all things are lawful for me, but all things edify not. [24] Let no man seek his own, but every man another's wealth [well-being].

4. To be winsome with others, dwell on points of agreement and things you have in common.

- **Luke 9:49,50** [Jesus emphasized the positive:] And John answered and said, Master, we saw one casting out devils in Thy name; and we forbad him, because he followeth not with us. [50] And Jesus said unto him, Forbid him not: for he that is not against us is for us.

- **Romans 14:19** Let us therefore follow after the things which make for peace, and things wherewith one may edify another.

- **1 Corinthians 9:19-22** [Paul was adaptable, relating himself to people on their level, rather than expecting them to adapt to him. In this way he was able to win many to Christ who otherwise wouldn't have listened.] For though I be free from all men, yet have I made myself servant unto all, that I might gain the more. [20] And unto the Jews I became as a Jew, that I might gain the Jews; to them that are under the law, as under the law, that I might gain them that are under the law; [21] To them that are without law, as without law, (being not without law to God, but under the law to Christ,) that I might gain them that are without law. [22] To the weak became I as weak, that I might gain the weak: I am made all things to all men, that I might by all means save some.

- **Ephesians 4:3** Endeavouring to keep the unity of the Spirit in the bond of peace.

- **Philippians 1:15-18** [Paul showed great tolerance with other Christians, some of whom even opposed him:] Some indeed preach Christ even of envy and strife; and some also of good will: [16] The one preach Christ of contention, [in selfish ambition] not sincerely, supposing to add affliction to my bonds: [17] But the other of love, knowing that I am set for the defence of the gospel. [18] What then?

Notwithstanding, every way, whether in pretence, or in truth, Christ is preached; and I therein do rejoice, yea, and will rejoice.

- **Philippians 4:8** [Looking for the good in others helps us to be tolerant of their weaknesses and faults.] Finally, brethren, whatsoever things are true, whatsoever things are honest, whatsoever things are just, whatsoever things are pure, whatsoever things are lovely, whatsoever things are of good report; if there be any virtue, and if there be any praise, think on these things.

5. The Lord expects us to be tolerant, as we appreciate the tolerance of others.

- **Leviticus 19:34a** [Tolerance comes from putting yourself in the other person's shoes.] But the stranger that dwelleth with you shall be unto you as one born among you, and thou shalt love him as thyself; for ye were strangers in the land of Egypt.
- **Matthew 7:2-5** [If we're self-righteous and intolerant of those who we feel have done wrong, in judging them we're committing an even worse sin.] For with what judgment ye judge, ye shall be judged: and with what measure ye mete, it shall be measured to you again. ³ And why beholdest thou the mote that is in thy brother's eye, but considerest not the beam that is in thine own eye? ⁴ Or how wilt thou say to thy brother, Let me pull out the mote out of thine eye; and, behold, a beam is in thine own eye? ⁵ Thou hypocrite, first cast out the beam out of thine own eye; and then shalt thou see clearly to cast out the mote out of thy brother's eye.
- **Matthew 7:12** Therefore all things whatsoever ye would that men should do to you, do ye even so to them: for this is the law and the prophets.
- **Luke 6:31-33** And as ye would that men should do to you, do ye also to them likewise. ³² For if ye love them which love you, what thank have ye? For sinners also love those that love them. ³³ And if ye do good to them which do good to you, what thank have ye? For sinners also do even the same.

6. You shouldn't be tolerant of evil or deliberate wrongdoing.

- **Genesis 6:3a** [Continual disobedience and rebellion will eventually bring on the Lord's retribution.] And the Lord said, My Spirit shall not always strive with man.

- **Nehemiah 13:28** [Nehemiah expelled from fellowship a compromising traitor who, though the son of the high priest, intermarried with the daughter of Israel's then arch-enemy, Sanballat:] And one of the sons of Joiada, the son of Eliashib the high priest, was son in law to Sanballat the Horonite: therefore I chased him from me.

- **Psalm 101:3b-5** [King David vowed to God that he won't tolerate or compromise with backslidden troublemakers:] I hate the work of them that turn aside; it shall not cleave to me. ⁴ A froward [perverse] heart shall depart from me: I will not know a wicked person.
⁵ Whoso privily slandereth his neighbour, him will I cut off: him that hath an high look and a proud heart will not I suffer.

- **Proverbs 29:1** He, that being often reproved hardeneth his neck, shall suddenly be destroyed, and that without remedy.

- **Isaiah 42:14** [God is very slow to anger, but when judgment finally comes, it is very thorough and swift.] I have long time holden My peace; I have been still, and refrained Myself: now will I cry like a travailing woman; I will destroy and devour at once.

- **Isaiah 63:9,10** [The Lord first shows compassion and great understanding, but if we continually choose to rebel against His Spirit, we can expect to be punished.] In all their affliction He [God] was afflicted, and the angel of His presence saved them: in His love and in His pity He redeemed them; and He bare them, and carried them all the days of old. ¹⁰ But they rebelled, and vexed His Holy Spirit: therefore He was turned to be their enemy, and He fought against them.

- **Proverbs 22:10** [There comes a time when you need to rid the barrel of its rotten apples.] Cast out the scorner, and contention shall go out; yea, strife and reproach shall cease.

- **Matthew 18:15-17** [Jesus' clear-cut guideline for disciplining wrongdoing among the brethren:] Moreover if thy brother shall trespass against thee, go and tell him his fault between thee and him alone: if he shall hear thee, thou hast gained thy brother. [16] But if he will not hear thee, then take with thee one or two more, that in the mouth of two or three witnesses every word may be established. [17] And if he shall neglect to hear them, tell it unto the church: but if he neglect to hear the church, let him be unto thee as an heathen man and a publican.

- **Romans 16:17** [Paul warned not to co-exist with those who continually cause divisions among brethren.] Now I beseech you, brethren, mark them which cause divisions and offences contrary to the doctrine which ye have learned; and avoid them.

- **Matthew 4:9-11** [Don't listen to or tolerate the Devil:] And [the Devil] saith unto Him, All these things will I give Thee, if Thou wilt fall down and worship me. [10] Then saith Jesus unto him, Get thee hence, Satan: for it is written, Thou shalt worship the Lord thy God, and Him only shalt thou serve. [11] Then the Devil leaveth Him.

- **Ephesians 4:27** Neither give place to the Devil.

- **2 Thessalonians 3:6,14,15** [Serious problems warrant excommunication, but such cases should still be treated with brotherly love.] Now we command you, brethren, in the name of our Lord Jesus Christ, that ye withdraw yourselves from every brother that walketh disorderly, and not after the tradition which he received of us. … And if any man obey not our word by this Epistle, note that man, and have no company with him, that he may be ashamed. [15] Yet count him not as an enemy, but admonish him as a brother. [See also 1 Corinthians 5:11-13; 1 Timothy 6:5.]

- **Revelation 2:21,22** And I [Jesus] gave her [the errant church of Thyatira] space to repent of her fornication; and she repented not. [22] Behold, I will cast her into a bed, and them that commit [spiritual] adultery with her into great tribulation, except they repent of their deeds.

7. God shows supernatural love, patience and tolerance with us. We should do the same with others.

- **2 Chronicles 7:14** If My people, which are called by My name, shall humble themselves, and pray, and seek My face, and turn from their wicked ways; then will I hear from Heaven, and will forgive their sin, and will heal their land.
- **Psalm 86:15** But Thou, O Lord, art a God full of compassion, and gracious, longsuffering, and plenteous in mercy and truth.
- **Psalm 103:8-10** The Lord is merciful and gracious, slow to anger, and plenteous in mercy. [9] He will not always chide: neither will He keep his anger for ever. [10] He hath not dealt with us after our sins; nor rewarded us according to our iniquities.
- **Isaiah 48:9** For My name's sake will I defer mine anger, and for My praise will I refrain for thee, that I cut thee not off.
- **Acts 17:30** [God's tolerance also depends on our accountability.] And the times of this ignorance God winked at; but now commandeth all men every where to repent.
- **Romans 2:4** Or despisest thou the riches of His goodness and forbearance and longsuffering; not knowing that the goodness of God leadeth thee to repentance?
- **Romans 5:8** But God commendeth His love toward us, in that, while we were yet sinners, Christ died for us.
- **2 Peter 3:9** The Lord is not slack concerning His promise, as some men count slackness; but is longsuffering to us-ward, not willing that any should perish, but that all should come to repentance.

8. Being tolerant and striving to keep the peace brings on blessings and happiness.

- **Proverbs 12:20b** To the counsellors of peace is joy.
- **Galatians 5:22** But the fruit of the Spirit is love, joy, peace, longsuffering, gentleness, goodness, faith.

- **Colossians 1:11** [Be] strengthened with all might, according to His glorious power, unto all patience and longsuffering with joyfulness.
- **Matthew 5:9** Blessed are the peacemakers: for they shall be called the children of God.

WISDOM

Definition: The God-given ability to judge or discern correctly and to follow the best course of action, based on knowledge and understanding; learning and experience acquired over a period of time; ability to see beneath the surface of things.

1. Wisdom is an invaluable gift of God.

- **Proverbs 16:16** How much better is it to get wisdom than gold! And to get understanding rather to be chosen than silver!
- **Job 28:12-19** Where shall wisdom be found? And where is the place of understanding? [13] Man knoweth not the price thereof; neither is it found in the land of the living. [15] It cannot be gotten for gold, neither shall silver be weighed for the price thereof. [17] The gold and the crystal cannot equal it: and the exchange of it shall not be for jewels of fine gold.
- **Proverbs 3:13,14** Happy is the man that findeth wisdom, and the man that getteth understanding. [14] For the merchandise of it is better than the merchandise of silver, and the gain thereof than fine gold. [See also Proverbs 16:16.]
- **Proverbs 8:11** For wisdom is better than rubies; and all the things that may be desired are not to be compared to it.

2. Wisdom is one of the most important virtues in life.

- **Proverbs 4:7** Wisdom is the principal thing; therefore get wisdom: and with all thy getting get understanding.
- **Ecclesiastes 7:19** Wisdom strengtheneth the wise more than ten mighty men which are in the city.
- **Ecclesiastes 9:16a,18a** Then said I, Wisdom is better than strength. [18a] Wisdom is better than weapons of war.
- **Ecclesiastes 7:12b** Wisdom giveth life to them that have it.
- **Isaiah 33:6a** And wisdom and knowledge shall be the stability of thy times.

3. Wisdom—or the lack of it—can make the difference between success and failure, victory and defeat.

- **Proverbs 2:10-12** When wisdom entereth into thine heart, and knowledge is pleasant unto thy soul; [11] Discretion shall preserve thee, understanding shall keep thee: [12] To deliver thee from the way of the evil man, from the man that speaketh froward things.

- **Proverbs 3:21-23** My son, let not them depart from thine eyes: keep sound wisdom and discretion: [22] So shall they be life unto thy soul, and grace to thy neck. [23] Then shalt thou walk in thy way safely, and thy foot shall not stumble.

- **Proverbs 4:5,6** Get wisdom, get understanding: forget it not; neither decline from the words of my mouth. [6] Forsake her not, and she shall preserve thee: love her, and she shall keep thee.

- **Matthew 10:16** Behold, I send you forth as sheep in the midst of wolves: be ye therefore wise as serpents, and harmless as doves.

- **Ephesians 5:15,16** See then that ye walk circumspectly, not as fools, but as wise, [16] Redeeming the time, because the days are evil.

4. Wisdom begins with a fear (reverence, respect) of the Lord.

- **Proverbs 9:10** The fear of the Lord is the beginning of wisdom: and the knowledge of the holy is understanding. [See also Psalm 111:10a.]

- **Job 28:28** And unto man He said, Behold, the fear of the Lord, that is wisdom; and to depart from evil is understanding.

- **Proverbs 8:13,14** The fear of the Lord is to hate evil: pride, and arrogancy, and the evil way, and the froward mouth, do I hate. [14] Counsel is Mine, and sound wisdom: I am understanding; I have strength.

- **Proverbs 15:33a** The fear of the Lord is the instruction of wisdom.

5. Wisdom is the ability to see matters as the Lord sees them, in order to judge them correctly.

- **John 7:24** Judge not according to the appearance, but judge righteous judgment.
- **1 Samuel 16:7b** For the Lord seeth not as man seeth; for man looketh on the outward appearance, but the Lord looketh on the heart.
- **Proverbs 24:23** These things also belong to the wise. It is not good to have respect of persons in judgment.
- **Isaiah 55:8,9** For My thoughts are not your thoughts, neither are your ways My ways, saith the Lord. [9] For as the heavens are higher than the earth, so are My ways higher than your ways, and My thoughts than your thoughts.
- **John 5:30** I can of Mine own self do nothing: as I hear, I judge: and My judgment is just; because I seek not Mine own will, but the will of the Father which hath sent Me.
- **John 8:15,16** Ye judge after the flesh; I judge no man. [16] And yet if I judge, My judgment is true: for I am not alone, but I and the Father that sent Me.

6. Wisdom is to rightly apply and then follow the Word of God. It i built upon a knowledge and understanding of God's Word.

- **Deuteronomy 4:5,6** Behold, I have taught you statutes and judgments, even as the Lord my God commanded me, that ye should do so in the land whither ye go to possess it. [6] Keep therefore and do them; for this is your wisdom and your understanding in the sight of the nations, which shall hear all these statutes, and say, Surely this great nation is a wise and understanding people.
- **Psalm 19:7b** The testimony of the Lord is sure, making wise the simple
- **Psalm 119:98-100** Thou through Thy commandments hast made me wiser than mine enemies: for they are ever with me. [99] I have more understanding than all my teachers: for Thy testimonies are

my meditation. [100] I understand more than the ancients, because I keep Thy precepts.

- **Psalm 119:104** Through Thy precepts I get understanding: therefore I hate every false way.
- **Psalm 119:130** The entrance of Thy Words giveth light; it giveth understanding unto the simple.
- **Psalm 119:169b** Give me understanding according to Thy Word.
- **Matthew 7:24,25** Therefore whosoever heareth these sayings of Mine, and doeth them, I will liken him unto a wise man, which built his house upon a rock: [25] And the rain descended, and the floods came, and the winds blew, and beat upon that house; and it fell not: for it was founded upon a rock.
- **Colossians 3:16a** Let the Word of Christ dwell in you richly in all wisdom.
- **2 Timothy 3:15** And that from a child thou hast known the Holy Scriptures, which are able to make thee wise unto salvation through faith which is in Christ Jesus. [See also verses 16-17 and 2 Timothy 2:15.]

7. We behave wisely when we prayerfully look to the Lord for guidance.

- **Isaiah 30:21** And thine ears shall hear a word behind thee, saying, This is the way, walk ye in it, when ye turn to the right hand, and when ye turn to the left.
- **Isaiah 42:16** And I will bring the blind by a way that they knew not; I will lead them in paths that they have not known: I will make darkness light before them, and crooked things straight. These things will I do unto them, and not forsake them.
- **Isaiah 48:17** Thus saith the Lord, thy Redeemer, the Holy One of Israel; I am the Lord thy God which teacheth thee to profit, which leadeth thee by the way that thou shouldest go.
- **Jeremiah 33:3** Call unto Me, and I will answer thee, and shew thee great and mighty things, which thou knowest not.

• **Hosea 6:3a** Then shall we know, if we follow on to know the Lord.

8. Wisdom is also gained through godly counsel, correction and instruction.

• **Proverbs 1:5** A wise man will hear, and will increase learning; and a man of understanding shall attain unto wise counsels.
• **Proverbs 9:8b,9** Rebuke a wise man, and he will love thee. [9] Give instruction to a wise man, and he will be yet wiser: teach a just man, and he will increase in learning.
• **Proverbs 12:15** The way of a fool is right in his own eyes: but he that hearkeneth unto counsel is wise.
• **Proverbs 13:1** A wise son heareth his father's instruction: but a scorner heareth not rebuke.
• **Proverbs 13:10b** With the well advised is wisdom.
• **Proverbs 13:20** He that walketh with wise men shall be wise: but a companion of fools shall be destroyed.
• **Proverbs 15:31** The ear that heareth the reproof of life abideth among the wise.
• **Proverbs 19:20** Hear counsel, and receive instruction, that thou mayest be wise in thy latter end.
• **Ecclesiastes 7:5** It is better to hear the rebuke of the wise, than for a man to hear the song of fools.

9. Personal experience also teaches wisdom.

• **Deuteronomy 32:7** Remember the days of old, consider the years of many generations: ask thy father, and he will shew thee; thy elders, and they will tell thee.
• **Job 32:7** I said, Days should speak, and multitude of years should teach wisdom.
• **Job 12:12** With the ancient is wisdom; and in length of days understanding.

10. Wisdom is a gift of the Spirit, which we can receive by petitioning God.

- **1 Corinthians 12:7,8** But the manifestation of the Spirit is given to every man to profit withal. [8] For to one is given by the Spirit the word of wisdom; to another the word of knowledge by the same Spirit.
- **James 1:5** If any of you lack wisdom, let him ask of God, that giveth to all men liberally, and upbraideth not; and it shall be given him.
- **John 14:26** But the Comforter, which is the Holy Ghost, whom the Father will send in My name, He shall teach you all things, and bring all things to your remembrance, whatsoever I have said unto you. [See also John 16:13.]
- **1 Corinthians 2:9,10,12,13** But as it is written, Eye hath not seen, nor ear heard, neither have entered into the heart of man, the things which God hath prepared for them that love Him. [10] But God hath revealed them unto us by His Spirit: for the Spirit searcheth all things, yea, the deep things of God. [12] Now we have received, not the spirit of the world, but the Spirit which is of God; that we might know the things that are freely given to us of God. [13] Which things also we speak, not in the words which man's wisdom teacheth, but which the Holy Ghost teacheth; comparing spiritual things with spiritual.
- **Ephesians 1:17** That the God of our Lord Jesus Christ, the Father of glory, may give unto you the spirit of wisdom and revelation in the knowledge of Him.
- **1 John 2:20** But ye have an unction [anointing] from the Holy One, and ye know all things.

11. Though wisdom is a gift of God, we must earnestly seek it and apply ourselves to receive it.

- **Psalm 90:12** So teach us to number our days, that we may apply our hearts unto wisdom.

- **Proverbs 2:1-6,9** My son, if thou wilt receive my words, and hide my commandments with thee; [2] So that thou incline thine ear unto wisdom, and apply thine heart to understanding; [3] Yea, if thou criest after knowledge, and liftest up thy voice for understanding; [4] If thou seekest her as silver, and searchest for her as for hid treasures; [5] Then shalt thou understand the fear of the Lord, and find the knowledge of God. [6] For the Lord giveth wisdom: out of His mouth cometh knowledge and understanding. [9] Then shalt thou understand righteousness, and judgment, and equity; yea, every good path.
- **Proverbs 5:1,2** My son, attend unto My wisdom, and bow thine ear to My understanding: [2] That thou mayest regard discretion, and that thy lips may keep knowledge.
- **Proverbs 8:33,35** Hear instruction, and be wise, and refuse it not. [35] For whoso findeth Me findeth life, and shall obtain favour of the Lord.
- **Proverbs 18:15** The heart of the prudent getteth knowledge; and the ear of the wise seeketh knowledge.

12. The Lord gives His wisdom to those who do not trust in their own.

- **1 Kings 3:7-12** [Solomon's prayer, when he became king:] And now, O Lord my God, Thou hast made thy servant king instead of David my father: and I am but a little child: I know not how to go out or come in. [8] And Thy servant is in the midst of Thy people which Thou hast chosen, a great people, that cannot be numbered nor counted for multitude. [9] Give therefore Thy servant an understanding heart to judge Thy people, that I may discern between good and bad: for who is able to judge this Thy so great a people? [10] And the speech pleased the Lord, that Solomon had asked this thing. [11] And God said unto him, Because thou hast asked this thing, and hast not asked for thyself long life; neither hast asked riches for thyself, nor hast asked the life of thine enemies;

but hast asked for thyself understanding to discern judgment; [12] Behold, I have done according to thy words: lo, I have given thee a wise and an understanding heart; so that there was none like thee before thee, neither after thee shall any arise like unto thee.

- **Proverbs 3:5-7** Trust in the Lord with all thine heart; and lean not unto thine own understanding. [6] In all thy ways acknowledge Him, and He shall direct thy paths. [7] Be not wise in thine own eyes: fear the Lord, and depart from evil.
- **Proverbs 11:2b** With the lowly is wisdom.
- **Proverbs 23:4b** Cease from thine own wisdom.
- **Luke 10:21** In that hour Jesus rejoiced in Spirit, and said, I thank Thee, O Father, Lord of Heaven and earth, that Thou hast hid these things from the [worldly] wise and prudent, and hast revealed them unto babes [the unlearned]: even so, Father; for so it seemed good in Thy sight.

13. The wisdom of this world is not the wisdom of God.

- **1 Corinthians 3:18,19** Let no man deceive himself. If any man among you seemeth to be wise in this world, let him become a fool, that he may be wise. [19] For the wisdom of this world is foolishness with God. For it is written, He taketh the wise in their own craftiness.
- **Proverbs 26:12** Seest thou a man wise in his own conceit? there is more hope of a fool than of him.
- **Isaiah 5:21** Woe unto them that are wise in their own eyes, and prudent in their own sight!
- **Romans 1:22** Professing themselves to be wise, they became fools.
- **James 3:14-17** But if ye have bitter envying and strife in your hearts, glory not, and lie not against the truth. [15] This wisdom descendeth not from above, but is earthly, sensual, devilish.

14. Wisdom and obedience to God go hand in hand.

- **Psalm 111:10b** A good understanding have all they that do His commandments.

- **Psalm 119:34,35** Give me understanding, and I shall keep Thy law; yea, I shall observe it with my whole heart. [35] Make me to go in the path of Thy commandments; for therein do I delight.
- **Ecclesiastes 2:26a** For God giveth to a man that is good in His sight [obedient to Him] wisdom, and knowledge, and joy. [See also 2 Timothy 1:13,14.]

15. The common sense that the Lord gives about practical matters is also a part of His gift of wisdom.

- **Job 32:8** But there is a spirit in man: and the inspiration of the Almighty giveth them understanding.
- **Exodus 31:1-6** And the Lord spake unto Moses, saying, [2] See, I have called by name Bezaleel the son of Uri, the son of Hur, of the tribe of Judah: [3] And I have filled him with the Spirit of God, in wisdom, and in understanding, and in knowledge, and in all manner of workmanship, [4] To devise cunning works, to work in gold, and in silver, and in brass, [5] And in cutting of stones, to set them, and in carving of timber, to work in all manner of workmanship. [6] And I, behold, I have given with him Aholiab, the son of Ahisamach, of the tribe of Dan: and in the hearts of all that are wise hearted I have put wisdom, that they may make all that I have commanded thee. [See also Exodus 36:2.]

16. It's wise to be prayerful and cautious.

- **Ecclesiastes 8:5** A wise man's heart discerneth both time and judgment.
- **Proverbs 14:29** He that is slow to wrath is of great understanding: but he that is hasty of spirit exalteth folly.
- **Proverbs 19:11** The discretion of a man deferreth his anger; and it is his glory to pass over a transgression.

• **James 1:19,20** Wherefore, my beloved brethren, let every man be swift to hear, slow to speak, slow to wrath: [20] For the wrath of man worketh not the righteousness of God.

17. In conversation, the wise are sometimes silent, never hasty, always prayerful.

• **Job 13:5** O that ye would altogether hold your peace! And it should be your wisdom.

• **Job 15:2,3** Should a wise man utter vain knowledge, and fill his belly with the east wind? [3] Should he reason with unprofitable talk? Or with speeches wherewith he can do no good?

• **Proverbs 10:32** The lips of the righteous know what is acceptable: but the mouth of the wicked speaketh frowardness.

• **Proverbs 17:27** He that hath knowledge spareth his words: and a man of understanding is of an excellent spirit.

• **James 3:13** Who is a wise man and endued with knowledge among you? Let him shew out of a good conversation his works with meekness of wisdom.

18. When we are guided by the Lord's wisdom, the results are always good.

• **Proverbs 16:20** He that handleth a matter wisely shall find good: and whoso trusteth in the Lord, happy is he.

• **Proverbs 19:8** He that getteth wisdom loveth his own soul: he that keepeth understanding shall find good.

• **James 3:17,18** But the wisdom that is from above is first pure, then peaceable, gentle, and easy to be intreated, full of mercy and good fruits, without partiality, and without hypocrisy. [18]And the fruit of righteousness is sown in peace of them that make peace.

• **Proverbs 11:30** The fruit of the righteous is a tree of life; and he that winneth souls is wise.

WORRY

Definition: anxiety; fear or nervousness about what might happen; fearful concern. In the King James translation of the New Testament, the word most commonly used for worry is "care," which also means worry or anxiety.

1. Worry is a lack of faith and trust, from looking at circumstances instead of the Lord.

- **Psalm 127:2** [Just relax. Worrying surely won't help!] It is vain for you to rise up early, to sit up late, to eat the bread of sorrows: for so He giveth His beloved sleep.
- **Matthew 6:25-34** [Jesus teaches us, His servants, not to worry about the future or about His faithfulness to supply our daily needs.] Therefore I say unto you, Take no thought for your life, what ye shall eat, or what ye shall drink; nor yet for your body, what ye shall put on. Is not the life more than meat, and the body than raiment? [26] Behold the fowls of the air: for they sow not, neither do they reap, nor gather into barns; yet your Heavenly Father feedeth them. Are ye not much better than they? [27] Which of you by taking thought can add one cubit unto his stature? [28] And why take ye thought for raiment? Consider the lilies of the field, how they grow; they toil not, neither do they spin: [29] And yet I say unto you, That even Solomon in all his glory was not arrayed like one of these. [30] Wherefore, if God so clothe the grass of the field, which to day is, and to morrow is cast into the oven, shall He not much more clothe you, O ye of little faith? [31] Therefore take no thought, saying, What shall we eat? or, What shall we drink? or, Wherewithal shall we be clothed? [32] (For after all these things do the Gentiles seek:) for your Heavenly Father knoweth that ye have need of all these things. [33] But seek ye first the Kingdom of God, and His righteousness; and all these things shall be added unto you. [34] Take therefore no thought for the morrow: for the morrow shall take thought for the things of itself. Sufficient unto the day is the evil thereof.

- **Matthew 8:24-26** [Jesus can give you peace in the midst of storm.] And, behold, there arose a great tempest in the sea, insomuch that the ship was covered with the waves: but He was asleep. [25] And His disciples came to Him, and awoke Him, saying, Lord, save us: we perish. [26] And He saith unto them, Why are ye fearful, O ye of little faith? Then He arose, and rebuked the winds and the sea; and there was a great calm.

- **Matthew 14:25-31** [Look to the Lord, not to the waves!] And in the fourth watch of the night Jesus went unto them, walking on the sea. [26] And when the disciples saw Him walking on the sea, they were troubled, saying, It is a spirit; and they cried out for fear. [27] But straightway Jesus spake unto them, saying, Be of good cheer; it is I; be not afraid. [28] And Peter answered Him and said, Lord, if it be Thou, bid me come unto Thee on the water. [29] And He said, Come. And when Peter was come down out of the ship, he walked on the water, to go to Jesus. [30] But when he saw the wind boisterous, he was afraid; and beginning to sink, he cried, saying, Lord, save me. [31] And immediately Jesus stretched forth His hand, and caught him, and said unto him, O thou of little faith, wherefore didst thou doubt?

- **Luke 21:34** And take heed to yourselves, lest at any time your hearts be overcharged with … cares [anxieties] of this life, and so that Day [of Christ's coming] come upon you unawares.

2. Worry and fear can cause you to make serious mistakes, which faith and trust could have prevented.

- **Numbers 13:28-33** [The Devil uses worry and fear to exaggerate our troubles. Ten of the twelve spies sent by Moses to reconnoiter the Promised Land worried about the adversaries they would encounter there. When they returned from their forty-day mission, they reported that there were giants in the land, and when Caleb tried to speak faith, they exaggerated, saying all the inhabitants were giants, which caused the Hebrews to fear and hesitate to claim the land. They said:] Nevertheless the people be strong that dwell in the land, and the cities are walled, and very great: and moreover we saw the children of Anak [the giant] there. … [30] And Caleb stilled the people before Moses, and said, Let us go up at once, and possess it; for we are well able to overcome it. [31] But the men that went up with him said, We be not able to go up against the people; for they are stronger than we. [32] And they brought up an evil report of the land which they had searched unto the children of Israel, saying, The land, through which we have gone to search it, is a <u>land that eateth up the inhabitants thereof</u>; and <u>all</u> the people that we saw in it are men of a great stature. [33] And there we saw the giants, the sons of Anak, which come of the giants: and we were in our own sight as grasshoppers, and so we were in their sight.

- **Numbers 14:1-4,34** [Worry can be contagious. The Hebrews who heard the fearful story of the 10 spies, began to fear and then to murmur, speaking defeat, which led to panic and rebellion:] And all the congregation lifted up their voice, and cried; and the people wept that night. [2] And all the children of Israel murmured against Moses and against Aaron: and the whole congregation said unto them, Would God that we had died in the land of Egypt! Or would God we had died in this wilderness! … [3] Were it not better for us to return into Egypt? [4] And they said one to another, Let us make a captain, and let us return into Egypt. … [Because of their disobedience and rebellion, God cursed them in this way:] [34] After the number of the days in which ye searched the land, even forty days, each day for a year, shall ye bear your iniquities, even forty years, and ye shall know My breach of promise. [See also Deuteronomy 1:27.]

- **Job 3:25,26** [Job's worry seemed to demoralize him till trouble actually came:] For the thing which I greatly feared is come upon me, and that which I was afraid of is come unto me. [26] I was not in safety, neither had I rest, neither was I quiet; yet trouble came. [See also Proverbs 10:24.]

- **Isaiah 28:16b** [If you trust the Lord you won't act hastily.] He that believeth shall not make haste. [See also Proverbs 19:2b.]
- **Matthew 25:24,25** [Worry and fear caused someone to bury their talent, rather than use and invest it:] Then he which had received the one talent came and said, Lord, I knew thee that thou art an hard man, reaping where thou hast not sown, and gathering where thou hast not strawed: [25] And I was afraid, and went and hid thy talent in the earth: lo, there thou hast that is thine. [See verses 14-29 for the whole parable.]
- **Romans 8:15** [Worry and fear put us in bondage, but God has freed us from it.] For ye have not received the spirit of bondage again to fear; but ye have received the Spirit of adoption, whereby we cry, Abba, Father.

3. Unwisely comparing yourself with the ungodly can cause needless worry.

- **Psalm 37:1** Fret not thyself because of evildoers, neither be thou envious against the workers of iniquity.
- **Psalm 37:7,35,36** Rest in the Lord, and wait patiently for Him: fret not thyself because of him who prospereth in his way, because of the man who bringeth wicked devices to pass. ... [35] I have seen the wicked in great power, and spreading himself like a green bay tree. [36] Yet he passed away, and, lo, he was not: yea, I sought him, but he could not be found.
- **Proverbs 24:19** Fret not thyself because of evil men, neither be thou envious at the wicked.
- **Isaiah 8:12b,13** [Don't let the fear of others rub off on you. Fear the Lord and follow Him.] Neither fear ye their fear, nor be afraid. [13] Sanctify the Lord of hosts himself; and let Him be your fear, and let Him be your dread.

4. The Lord tells us to cast our worries and burdens on <u>Him</u>.

- **Psalm 55:22** Cast thy burden upon the Lord, and He shall sustain thee: He shall never suffer the righteous to be moved.
- **Matthew 11:28-30** Come unto Me, all ye that labour and are heavy laden, and I will give you rest. [29] Take My yoke upon you, and learn of Me; for I am meek and lowly in heart: and ye shall find rest unto your souls. [30] For My yoke is easy, and My burden is light.
- **1 Peter 5:7** Casting all your care upon Him; for He careth for you.

5. It is impossible to worry when we are meditating on the Lord and His Word.

- **Psalm 112:7,8b** He shall not be afraid of evil tidings: his heart is fixed, trusting in the Lord. [8b] His heart is established, he shall not be afraid.
- **Psalm 119:165** Great peace have they which love Thy law: and nothing shall offend them.
- **Proverbs 1:33** But whoso hearkeneth unto Me shall dwell safely, and shall be quiet from fear of evil.
- **Proverbs 3:1,2** My son, forget not My law; but let thine heart keep My commandments: [2] For length of days, and long life, and <u>peace</u>, shall they add to thee.
- **Isaiah 26:3** Thou wilt keep him in perfect peace, whose mind is stayed on Thee: because he trusteth in Thee.
- **Isaiah 48:18** O that thou hadst hearkened to My commandments! Then had thy peace been as a river, and thy righteousness as the waves of the sea.
- **Philippians 4:6,7** Be careful [worried or anxious] for nothing; but in every thing by prayer and supplication with thanksgiving let your requests be made known unto God. [7] And the peace of God, which passeth all understanding, shall keep your hearts and minds through Christ Jesus.

6. We have <u>nothing</u> to worry or fear because God is with us and will not fail!

- **Deuteronomy 1:29,30a** Then I said unto you, Dread not, neither be afraid of them. [30a] The Lord your God which goeth before you, He shall fight for you.

- **Deuteronomy 20:3,4** And shall say unto them, Hear, O Israel, ye approach this day unto battle against your enemies: let not your hearts faint, fear not, and do not tremble, neither be ye terrified because of them; [4] For the Lord your God is He that goeth with you, to fight for you against your enemies, to save you.

- **Deuteronomy 31:6** Be strong and of a good courage, fear not, nor be afraid of them: for the Lord thy God, He it is that doth go with thee; He will not fail thee, nor forsake thee.

- **Psalm 23:4** Yea, though I walk through the valley of the shadow of death, I will fear no evil: for Thou art with me; Thy rod and Thy staff they comfort me.

- **Zechariah 8:13b** So will I save you, and ye shall be a blessing: fear not, but let your hands be strong.

- **Mark 5:36b** Be not afraid, only believe.

- **John 14:1** Let not your heart be troubled: ye believe in God, believe also in Me.

- **John 14:27** Peace I leave with you, My peace I give unto you: not as the world giveth, give I unto you. Let not your heart be troubled, neither let it be afraid.

- **1 John 5:4-5** For whatsoever is born of God overcometh the world: and this is the victory that overcometh the world, even our faith. [5] Who is he that overcometh the world, but he that believeth that Jesus is the Son of God?

Also available from Aurora...

Discovering Truth—Bible Basics

This companion volume to *Keys to Happier Living* will help you quickly find what the Bible has to say on a wide range of topics related to your faith and daily life.

From Jesus, With Love

A heart-warming collection of capsules of wisdom, comfort and instruction from the greatest Teacher of all: Jesus Himself!

My King and I

Looking for ways to express your thankfulness to God? The sample praises in this book will provide you with the words to say and a springboard from which to formulate your own! Learn the art of praise today!

Dare to Be Different

A collection of inspirational and refreshingly iconoclastic essays on some of the fundamental issues of Christian life and faith. Guaranteed to challenge you to be different and make a difference!

The *Get Activated!* series

If you would like to learn more about how you can develop your personal relationship with God and receive His blessings, love, and happiness in your life, don't miss *Get Activated!*—a series of booklets covering the fundamentals of faith and how to apply them to your life today. Titles include:

Prayer Power	Love's Many Faces
Hearing from Heaven	Understanding God's Word
Obstacles Are for Overcoming	God's Gifts